This Day in *San Diego* History

This Day in
San Diego
History

LINDA H. PEQUEGNAT

Sunbelt Publications
San Diego, California

This Day in San Diego History
Sunbelt Publications, Inc.
Copyright © 2009 by Linda Pequegnat
All rights reserved. First edition 2009

Cover and book design by Will Dalrymple
Edited by Will Dalrymple
Project management by Jennifer Redmond
Printed in the United States of America

Sunbelt Publications, Inc.
P.O. Box 191126
San Diego, CA 92159-1126
(619) 258-4911, fax: (619) 258-4916
www.sunbeltbooks.com

"Adventures in the Natural History and Cultural Heritage of the Californias"
A Series Edited by Lowell Lindsay

12 11 10 09   5 4 3 2 1

Library of Congress Cataloging-in-Publication Data

Pequegnat, Linda H.
    This day in San Diego history / Linda H. Pequegnat. — 1st ed.
p. cm. — (Adventures in the natural history and cultural heritage of the Californias)
    Includes bibliographical references.
    ISBN 978-0-932653-90-1
    1. San Diego (Calif.)—History—Calendars. I. Title.
    F869.S22P48 2009
    979.4'985—dc22   2008044071

Cover photograph by Michael L. Seljos, used by permission.

CONTENTS

PREFACE

THESE TRUE STORIES about the San Diego area—one for each day of the year—were gathered from a variety of historical sources, mostly newspapers and books.

I have lived in California since the eighth grade; I missed out on the fourth-grade study of California history that is taught here in California schools. But even the fourth grade California history book does not go into San Diego's history very much—except to say that the first California mission was started in San Diego by Father Junípero Serra in 1769.

When my husband, a native Californian, took a teaching job in another state, we were sad to move away from California. I knew I would especially miss San Diego in the new inland area where we would be living—so far away from the ocean and everything I loved. That job lasted 20 years, during which time we kept in touch with San Diego by returning every summer during school vacations.

When my husband retired, we moved back to San Diego. I was happy to be back, and I felt that in order to appreciate where we lived, it was important to have an understanding of the history of the area. So I took up my research on San Diego history and decided to arrange it with an event for each day of the year.

There are many, many newcomers to the San Diego area who, like me, did not live here all their lives and did not have the opportunity to learn about California's history—or San Diego's particular history.

To pick up a history book and start in to learn about San Diego's past, at a later age in life, might not sound exactly appealing to many of us. But the interesting true stories in this book—one story for each day of the year—are an easy way to enjoy the rich heritage of San Diego's past.

Hoping you have fun—and learn something new at the same time—about San Diego's interesting past events, places, and people.

Linda H. Pequegnat, Ph.D.
La Jolla, CA

INTRODUCTION

SAN DIEGO IS A CITY OF HISTORY—the discovery of San Diego Bay by early Spanish explorers; the founding of the San Diego Mission, the first in what is now the state of California; the colorful Rancho Days, when California was a part of Mexico; the Battle of San Pasqual during the Mexican-American War, after which California became a state in the United States; the discovery of gold in the Julian–Cuyamaca area, sparking the growth of new towns and new immigration; the spectacular Panama-California Exposition, celebrating the opening of the Panama Canal and signaling a new era of trade and travel for our city.

The early Spanish influence is especially strong, as evidenced by our red-tiled roofs and Spanish-style architecture—the San Diego Mission, "Mother of the Missions," near the San Diego River; the Junípero Serra Museum on Presidio Hill, overseeing Old Town and the Harbor; the Cabrillo Monument, marking the entrance to San Diego Bay.

San Diego's early populations are part of our rich heritage—the native inhabitants, dating back over 9,000 years, who enjoyed the natural abundance of food and game, and who knew how to live in harmony with their environment; the Catholic missionaries and Spanish soldiers, who served the needs of mission and presidio; the Californios, who tamed the land on their great ranchos, when California was part of Mexico; the American settlers who arrived thereafter.

Our past is filled with courageous and far-seeing individuals—Father Junípero Serra, "Father of the Missions," who traveled hundreds of dangerous miles to found the San Diego Mission; Alonzo Horton, developer of New Town San Diego, who enticed both businesses and residents away from Old Town San Diego; John Spreckles, who owned and developed many San Diego businesses, including the *San Diego Union* newspaper and the Hotel Del Coronado; George Marston, businessman who, among other accomplishments, built the Junípero Serra Museum and Presidio Park, and donated them to the city; Ellen Browning Scripps, tireless philanthropist, whose contributions funded hospitals, schools, and countless other worthy San Diego ventures.

The big issues and challenges facing San Diego over the years have contributed to its development—the secularization of the missions, leaving the buildings in ruins and a population adrift; the efforts to procure a railroad connection to the eastern United States, hard-fought for over 30 years; the eventual success of those efforts, resulting in the big land boom and population explosion that followed.

A variety of industries have been important to San Diego—the early Chinese fishermen and railroad workers, who labored so hard for so little; the tuna fishing industry, striving to balance environmental care and profitability; the Navy and the Marines, and their important military bases here; the aircraft industry, who built Lindbergh's *Spirit of St. Louis* as well as planes for the war effort during World War II, and later rockets and boosters for the space program.

And on and on it goes. All these fascinating people, places, events and issues are described here—one story for each day of the year.

It was suggested to me that these stories would be interesting as well as educational for fourth grade teachers to read to their classes each day as part of their study of California history—with an accent on the San Diego area that is not covered in their regular textbook. The teacher may choose to read just the first paragraph or two to their students, to give them an idea of what happened on "This Day in San Diego History." Spanish names abound in San Diego. I have given the definitions of those that I thought might not be familiar, but I may have missed some. Geography is important to the understanding of some of the stories. The textbook that is used by fourth graders in the San Diego schools contains many good maps.

You will find that it's fun and instructive to wake up each day and read about what happened on "This Day in San Diego History." It's fun to read the "story for the day" to guests in your home or at a dinner party. And it's always a special treat for people to find out what happened in San Diego's past history on their birthdays!

I appreciate the many historians whose works I studied to obtain information about San Diego's history for this book. Most especially are Iris Engstrand, professor of history at the University of San Diego, and Diana Lindsay, historian and author of several books on the history of the Anza-Borrego desert area of San Diego County. Both of these gifted historians probably have no idea of the influence their well-researched books have had on me during the course of my work on this book. I owe special thanks to Jennifer Redmond at Sunbelt Publications and Will Dalrymple, for their helpful suggestions and their excellent editorial advice.

This Day in *San Diego* History

JANUARY 1, 1915

ON THIS DAY IN SAN DIEGO HISTORY the Panama-California Exposition opened in Balboa Park. This great worldwide event to celebrate the opening of the Panama Canal had been under preparation for over five years (see SEPTEMBER 3). San Diego would be the first port of call on the Pacific coast of the United States for ships after crossing the canal.

Many of the Spanish Colonial–style buildings that we see today in Balboa Park were built for this 1915 exposition (see SEPTEMBER 12). The graceful arched Cabrillo Bridge—sometimes called the Laurel Street Bridge—was built to be the main entryway to the exposition (see APRIL 12).

The opening of the Panama-California Exposition at midnight on January 1, 1915 was a grandiose event. A large crowd of people, including many San Diego dignitaries, gathered in Balboa Park that night, waiting for the midnight hour. When it struck, President Woodrow Wilson back in Washington, D.C. pressed a Western Union telegraph button, transmitting the signal to light up the exposition. Immediately, a large light attached to a balloon 1,500 feet in the air lit up a three-mile area, which was followed by all the lights in all of the buildings being illuminated.

One historian (Richard Amero) describes the opening events in his article in the *Journal of San Diego History*:

> Mortarmen about the grounds began firing missiles that spent themselves in white clouds of dropping smoke. Red carbide fire sprang from 7,000 sticks concealed in the shrubbery and around the buildings. Eight powerful searchlights from the cruiser USS *San Diego*, flagship of the Pacific fleet, anchored off the foot of Market Street, threw their beams of light on the Tower of the California Building… Bonfires on the summits of San Diego and, farther away, on summits in the Cuyamacas, the Palomars, and San Miguel burst into flames. Gatesmen threw the gates wide open as sirens wailed, steam pipes shrieked, whistles blew, cowbells rang, rattles shook, confetti streamed down, silk and straw hats went up, and cheers arose from an official turnstile count of 31,386 to an unofficial estimate of 42,486 people on the grounds.

The Panama-California Exposition ended up lasting for two years and brought national and worldwide attention to San Diego.

JANUARY 2, 1910

ON THIS DAY IN SAN DIEGO HISTORY the electric power line that brought electricity to La Jolla for the first time was completed. Before this the people had gas lights in their homes. Actually, the electric company had trouble getting the 100 customers required before they could bring in the electric line because most of the residents liked the nice white light that gas lamps provided and did not like the more yellow glow of the electric lights.

The La Jolla residents felt so strongly about it that a large group signed a petition to try to prevent the company from running the electric line to La Jolla, and when the construction crews arrived a group of angry citizens met them and tried to scare them away.

Downtown San Diego had had gas street lights since 1881 and electricity since 1887, but it took over 20 more years before the remote suburb of La Jolla (a trip of nearly four hours from San Diego by train or early car) would be supplied with electricity—on this date in 1910. San Diego had a population of 40,000 in 1910. Compare that to today's population of nearly one and a half million in the city of San Diego and just under three million in San Diego County. La Jolla's population in 1905, just five years before the electric line was completed, was only 1,300, and there were only 264 buildings in the entire town.

Electricity took a little longer to get to the backcountry town of Ramona. Electricity first reached Ramona in 1924 when a line was extended from the San Pasqual terminal for a cost of $35,000, which was assessed to the tax payers by the Ramona Lighting District.

The remote desert town of Borrego Springs didn't receive electricity until 1945. The electricity came from the Imperial Valley where the Imperial Irrigation District had a power line running westward along Highway 78 past Ocotillo Wells. The DiGiorgio Fruit Company, which had plans to grow grapes in the Borrego Valley, needed electricity to pump irrigation water from their wells, so they paid most of the $500,000 to San Diego Gas & Electric to extend the electric line to Borrego Springs. At first there were only eight customers in the sparsely populated Borrego Valley. By 1952 there were over 300.

JANUARY 3, 1543

ON THIS DAY IN SAN DIEGO HISTORY Juan Rodriguez Cabrillo died. Cabrillo was the Spanish explorer who first discovered San Diego Bay in 1542 (see SEPTEMBER 28).

Cabrillo sailed two ships from Guatemala in June of 1542. Three months later, on September 28, he discovered San Diego Bay, which he named San Miguel Arcángel. Later, in 1602, it was named San Diego de Alcalá by Sebastián Vizcaíno, who did not recognize it as the same bay that Cabrillo had named 60 years before (see NOVEMBER 10).

After leaving San Diego, Cabrillo and his two ships sailed northward to what are now Catalina Island, San Pedro, and Santa Monica. When they reached what is believed to be San Miguel Island—they called it Isla de la Posesión—Cabrillo fell and injured himself. Two months later on January 3, 1543, he died of the injury. He was buried on the island. A sad entry in the ship's log reads:

> Passing the Winter on the Island of La Posesión, on the third of the month of January, 1543, Juan Rodriguez Cabrillo departed from this life, as the result of a fall which he suffered on said island...

Many years later, in 1901, a strange gray stone was found on Santa Rosa Island, which is located next to San Miguel Island. It is about 14 inches long, 4 inches wide and 3 inches thick. On it are carved a cross, the initials JR, and a primitive stick figure. It is believed to be the gravestone for Cabrillo, who was known to his men as Juan Rodriguez and usually signed his name that way. The stone is now located in the Lowie Museum at the University of California at Berkeley. A replica of the stone is in San Diego at the Cabrillo National Monument.

It is believed that the island called La Posesión by Cabrillo was really Santa Rosa Island and not San Miguel Island—or that the stone was moved by the Indians and carried off. It is suspected that perhaps an Indian carved the primitive stick figure on the stone, which was not typical of Spanish grave markers of those times. The stone was not found attached to any grave, so the actual burial place of Cabrillo remains a mystery.

JANUARY 4, 1776

ON THIS DAY IN SAN DIEGO HISTORY Juan Bautista de Anza and his party of settlers arrived at the San Gabriel Mission for a rest after traveling across the desert in what is now eastern San Diego County. They were on their way to Monterey and San Francisco to establish Spanish settlements there.

Juan Bautista de Anza, a Spanish military officer, had led the party of settlers and soldiers from Mexico through the deserts and mountains in what is now southern Arizona and southern California. They had been traveling for three months and were ready for a rest at the San Gabriel Mission, located just east of the present-day city of Los Angeles, before continuing onward to Monterey.

Part of their trip took them through the Anza-Borrego Desert in northeast San Diego County, and they camped for several days in what is now the Borrego Springs area. Just 11 days before reaching the San Gabriel Mission, the Anza party was camping in Coyote Canyon just north of Borrego Springs. Today there is a monument in Coyote Canyon marking the location where the party camped and where a baby was born, on December 24, 1775.

The Anza party was delayed in San Gabriel for seven weeks because a few days before their arrival at the mission they received news that the San Diego Mission had been burned by the Indians, killing Padre Luis Jaime and two soldiers (see NOVEMBER 5). Anza and some of his soldiers joined a group from the San Gabriel Mission who traveled south to San Diego to help restore order at the San Diego Mission.

When they finally left San Gabriel, the Anza party would have to travel another 350 miles and two more months to reach Monterey and San Francisco, where they started a settlement, a mission, and a presidio (military base). This was in September and October of 1776—the same year that the original 13 colonies on the East Coast adopted the Declaration of Independence to separate from England and to create the United States of America. It would be another 74 years before California would become a state in the United States, in 1850.

For more about the Anza expedition, see OCTOBER 4 and DECEMBER 21.

JANUARY 5, 1916

ON THIS DAY IN SAN DIEGO HISTORY…it began to rain! The people of San Diego were very happy about the rain because they were worried about a possible water shortage. The city had been growing rapidly, and there had been several years of low rainfall. San Diego was concerned about obtaining water—from any source—and that led them to hire a "rainmaker."

Charles Mallory Hatfield—the "Rainmaker"—had quite an effect on San Diego in 1916. He had a reputation as a successful rainmaker in the Southwest and in Alaska, with many "successes" between 1903 and 1912. In fact, he was a bit of a folk hero in southern California, where he had used chemicals and evaporating tanks to make rain. He called himself the "Moisture Accelerator," but most people knew him as the Rainmaker.

In December 1915 Charley Hatfield offered his services on a "no rain, no pay" basis. He agreed to fill Morena Reservoir for free to four-fifths capacity and to charge only for the 40th to 50th inch at $1,000 per inch.

Hatfield started operations on January 1, 1916 at Morena Dam where he built a 28-foot tower and set up his tank and other paraphernalia, from which mysterious smoke and fumes were said to have emanated into the air.

On January 5 it started to rain. A heavier rain fell on January 10, and on the 14th a torrential downpour developed. The San Diego River overflowed its banks on January 17. The Tijuana River overflowed and destroyed homes and gardens on January 18. The *San Diego Union* headlines read "Is Rainmaker at Work?" making a joke out of the situation. But the rain did not stop!

See JANUARY 28 for what happened to the Rainmaker.

JANUARY 6, 1888

ON THIS DAY IN SAN DIEGO HISTORY a full-page ad appeared on the third page of the *San Diego Union*. The page was totally blank except for these three lines in the middle of the page:

Look out for La Jolla Park!
Hotel being built.
Pacific Coast Land Bureau

This ad, announcing the construction of the fancy 80-room, 3-story La Jolla Park Hotel, ran for the next 25 days on page 3 of the newspaper. This was at the same time that the Hotel del Coronado was being built. In fact, old pictures of the La Jolla Park Hotel look a lot like a smaller version of the Hotel del Coronado. It was built at the ocean end of Grand Avenue—now named Girard Avenue—on the ocean side of Prospect Street. That would be between the present-day La Valencia and Colonial hotels. The estimated cost of the La Jolla Park Hotel was $18,250.

There was a land boom going on in the 1880s, and lots were being sold in the new subdivision called La Jolla Park. It was important to have a large, first class hotel in La Jolla in order to entice potential buyers to come there and look over the place. Back then the trip from San Diego to La Jolla was by horse and buggy and took four hours, so many people preferred to spend the night in La Jolla before the long trip back to San Diego. The train from San Diego went only as far as Pacific Beach until 1894 when the train line was finally extended to La Jolla (see APRIL 25).

Financial problems prevented the La Jolla Park Hotel from opening at the scheduled time, and it sat empty for nearly four years. It was finally rescued by two gentlemen, Hamilton Johnson and C.H. Ritchie, who had owned the Royal Hawaiian Hotel in Honolulu. The La Jolla Park Hotel finally opened on January 1, 1893, with 60 guests for dinner on the opening day.

The hotel was open for only three years before closing down again in early 1896. The hotel burned to the ground in June 1896. Arson was suspected, but it was never proved. The great land boom of the 1880s in southern California had slowed down. Many unprofitable hotels burned down around this time. The La Jolla Park Hotel was insured for $10,000.

JANUARY 7, 1852

ON THIS DAY IN SAN DIEGO HISTORY a "treaty of peace and friendship" was signed between the United States and the heads of the different groups of Diegueño (Kumeyaay) Indians in San Diego County. This occurred following the Mexican-American War of 1846–48. After the war, California was no longer a part of Mexico but was a part of the United States (see FEBRUARY 2).

After the war a great number of people came from all over the United States to settle in the new state of California. This influx included the gold rush of 1849. Often the newcomers took advantage of the Indians—settling on their land without permission or tricking them into gambling away some of their possessions. So there was a need for this "treaty of peace and friendship."

One of the most prominent of the 22 heads of Diegueño (Kumeyaay) Indian groups to sign the treaty on this date was Pedro José Panto, capitán of the San Pasqual Indian pueblo.

Capitán Panto is said to have helped the Americans in the Battle of San Pasqual (see DECEMBER 6). Capitán Panto's daughter, Felicita, wrote the following account of her father's connection to the Battle of San Pasqual:

> Early one rainy morning we saw soldiers that were not Mexicans come riding down the mountain side. They looked like ghosts coming through the mist, and then the fighting began.
>
> The Indians fled in fear to the mountains on the north side of the Valley from where they looked down and watched the battle. All day long they fought. We saw some Americans killed and knew they were in a bad way.
>
> That afternoon Panto, my father, called his men together and asked them if they wished to help the Americans in their trouble. The men said they did. When darkness was near Panto sent a messenger to the Mexican chief telling him to trouble the Americans no more that night or else the Indians would help the Americans. The Mexican chief heeded the message and the Americans were left to bury their dead and to rest because of my father's message. The Americanos do not know of this but my people know of it.

9

JANUARY 8, 1876

ON THIS DAY IN SAN DIEGO HISTORY the Stonewall Gold Mine was sold at a San Diego Sheriff's auction because of unpaid debts. The Stonewall Mine was located at the base of the Cuyamaca Mountains about ten miles south of Julian on the south edge of today's Lake Cuyamaca—except Lake Cuyamaca was not there then. The Cuyamaca Dam was not built until 1889 (see FEBRUARY 22).

The Stonewall Mine was one of many gold mines in the Julian–Banner–Cuyamaca area (see JUNE 28). Gold was first discovered in San Diego County in 1870 (see FEBRUARY 15). A town called Cuyamaca City built up near the Stonewall Mine. Today there is nothing left of Cuyamaca City nor of the mine (see AUGUST 26). In the town of Julian today on Main Street there is a building called the Stonewall Stores that was built to resemble the original Stonewall Mine building with its interesting high, steep-sloped roof.

The owners of the Stonewall Mine had experienced hard times during 1875 when gold production was down and they were struggling financially. They had borrowed money using the mine as collateral and were then unable to repay the debt. The mine sold for the highest bid of $3,246 at the auction on this date in 1876. The new owners did not reopen the mine, and it sat closed for eight years between 1876 and 1884.

In 1884 the Stonewall Mine was sold for $7,500. The new owners reopened it, and it began running full-time. During a three-month period in 1885, the mine yielded between $18,000 and $20,000 in gold for the new owners.

In 1886 the mine was sold again for $150,000 to Robert W. Waterman, who would later become the governor of California. He invested heavily in a 600-foot shaft that hit a payload of gold. The mine's most productive years were 1887 through 1890.

The Stonewall Mine was overall the most productive gold mine in San Diego County, yielding a total of over $2 million between 1870 and 1891 (see JUNE 28). During these times gold sold for $20.67 per ounce. Compare that to today's high price for gold.

JANUARY 9, 1769

ON THIS DAY IN SAN DIEGO HISTORY a Spanish ship named the *San Carlos* sailed from La Paz in Baja California, Mexico. Its mission was to sail to San Diego with supplies and soldiers to meet up with the overland expeditions from Baja California.

There were two overland expeditions. The first one was led by Captain Fernando de Rivera and Father Juan Crespí. The second one was led by Gaspar de Portolá (Baja California's governor and a former military officer from Spain) and Father Junípero Serra (president of the Franciscan missions of Baja California). It was Father Serra's job to start missions in Alta California, the first of which would be at San Diego.

A second ship, the *San Antonio*, left La Paz in February 1769—also headed for San Diego with supplies. Both ships were delayed due to difficult winds, strong currents, and navigational problems. Both ships arrived by the end of April 1769 with most of each crew suffering from scurvy or some other disease (see APRIL 29). More than 60 men died in a temporary hospital set up on the beach during their first few months in San Diego. A third ship, the *San José*, disappeared at sea and never arrived.

When the first overland expedition of Captain Rivera and Father Crespí arrived in San Diego in May 1769, they were overjoyed to see the ships, the *San Carlos* and the *San Antonio*, anchored near the mouth of San Diego Bay. The Serra-Portolá expedition arrived six weeks later, on July 1, 1769. Father Serra blessed the wooden cross that was raised on Presidio Hill by the soldiers and thereby officially founded the Misión San Diego de Alcalá on July 16, 1769.

For more information on Father Serra, see SEPTEMBER 14.

JANUARY 10, 1899

ON THIS DAY IN SAN DIEGO HISTORY the train depot in La Jolla blew down in a strong windstorm. The depot had been built hastily five years before in 1894 when the railroad track was extended to the La Jolla Park Hotel and was only a shed of flimsy construction that was open on two sides. It was located in the middle of Prospect Street near Fay Avenue. It was immediately rebuilt.

Before the hasty construction in 1894 of the 1,400-foot railroad track extension and the flimsy depot, the tracks ended several blocks to the south on Prospect Street in front of the Scripps residence—now the San Diego Museum of Contemporary Art. The event was described by Ellen Mills, a newspaper writer and daughter of an early and influential La Jolla couple, Anson and Eleanor ("Nellie") Mills:

> An attractive hotel [the La Jolla Park Hotel] had been built on the ocean side of Prospect Street facing Girard. This induced the railroad company to have its terminal near the hotel. They had no franchise on Prospect Street so on Saturday after the Court House had closed, a large crew of men with every equipment for labor appeared on the scene with tools and a camping outfit, including a wagon where their food was prepared. The men were worked in relays until Monday morning, and the track was finished up to Girard, where it was operated for years.

Both of the engines for the train that ran from San Diego to La Jolla in the 1890s had come from the elevated railroad in New York City. The engines had been built for short hauls only. On some of the longer stretches between San Diego and La Jolla, the train had to stop and rest. Older residents recalled the jerk on the back of their necks when the train started up again. The train had to go backwards for one of its trips to and from La Jolla until a Y-switch and a turntable were built. The engineer of the morning train from La Jolla to San Diego would blow the whistle five minutes before the train started up so that passengers would have time for another cup of coffee before catching the train.

JANUARY 11, 1817

ON THIS DAY IN SAN DIEGO HISTORY an Indian who was later known as the capitán (Spanish for "captain") of the San Pascual Indian pueblo was baptized Pedro José Panto Escarcar at the age of 14 at the San Diego Mission with a group of Indians from a place known as Santa Isabel (Santa Ysabel).

Pedro José Panto later lived in the Indian pueblo (Spanish for "village" or "town") of San Pascual since sometime before September 1837 and was Capitán of the pueblo until his death in 1874. "San Pascual" is the Spanish spelling, and "San Pasqual" is the Americanized version. Panto played an important role in helping the Indians of the San Pasqual Valley to retain their rights to the land.

It is believed that the valley of San Pasqual was occupied by Indians for thousands of years before the first contact with Europeans. Most of the Indians living there in the late 1700s were gathered into the San Diego and San Luis Rey missions. The San Pascual Indian pueblo came into existence after the secularization (changing ownership from church land to public land) of the missions in 1834. The Indians were awarded the entire valley of San Pasqual bordering the San Bernardo Rancho on the west.

The Indians of the San Pascual pueblo had a diversity of skills, as listed in a census from 1835 describing *vaqueros* (cowboys), carpenters, blacksmiths, millers, leather workers, cheesemakers, and so on. The pueblo was described by an early historian as "composed of Indians selected from the ... missions for their intelligence, good behavior, industry, and fitness in all respects for earning their own living and managing their own affairs."

During the Mexican-American War of 1846–48, the San Pasqual Valley became famous for the Battle of San Pasqual (see DECEMBER 6).

After the war, Pedro José Panto worked hard to protect the San Pascual pueblo from encroachment by illegal squatters (see JANUARY 7). Unfortunately, after Panto's death in 1874 the San Pasqual community of Indians continued to decline at the hands of the white squatters (see APRIL 27).

JANUARY 12, 1916

ON THIS DAY IN SAN DIEGO HISTORY John Nolen, an urban planner and landscape architect, sent a design plan to George W. Marston, an influential San Diego businessman, for the creation of parks and museums at Presidio Hill and Old Town.

George Marston wanted to find a way to help preserve San Diego's historical past. Presidio Hill was where the San Diego Mission was first located by the Spanish priests and soldiers who came to San Diego in 1769 (see JULY 16).

Marston began buying lots on Presidio Hill in 1907 to preserve the historic site when he bought 14 lots above Old Town for $6,000. By 1928 he had 20 acres. He tried for many years to convince the city of San Diego to preserve and develop the site, but the city was not interested. So Marston began the work himself to create Presidio Park and to preserve the historic character of Old Town.

John Nolan, the urban planner who delivered plans to Marston on this date, suggested organizing a "permanent local society to take charge of the property." This would result later, in 1928, with the formation of the San Diego Historical Society, which today oversees the operation of the Junípero Serra Museum on top of Presidio Hill, as well as many other historical sites in San Diego, including the Marston House at the north end of Balboa Park. The San Diego Historical Society also maintains a museum in Balboa Park.

It took 13 more years for the completion of the Presidio Hill work. It was not until July 16, 1929, on the 160th anniversary of the founding of the San Diego Mission on the same spot, that the beautiful Junípero Serra Museum was dedicated. The building itself was designed by a young, popular architect, William Templeton Johnson (see FEBRUARY 10).

JANUARY 13, 1984

ON THIS DAY IN SAN DIEGO HISTORY an article appeared in the *Vista Morning Press* newspaper in which Hans Doe—also known as "Mr. Water"—explained the need for the Vista Irrigation District to join the Metropolitan Water District back in the 1950s. Vista is a community in north San Diego County located east of Oceanside and Carlsbad.

There was a severe drought in southern California from 1950 to 1951, and there were many ranchers and farmers in the Vista area who wanted the Vista Irrigation District to join up with the Metropolitan Water District in order to buy imported water.

The Metropolitan Water District, sometimes called the "Mighty Met," is the largest water agency in the country and was formed in Los Angeles in 1928 to sell water to smaller water districts who paid to join it. It serves over 127 cities in six southern California counties, including San Diego County. There was a controversy in Vista as to whether Vista should join the Mighty Met or not. Water has always been a source of concern for San Diego County—as well as the rest of southern California—because ours is an area of low rainfall, high population, and high water use. As a result, most of our water has to be imported from other areas (see SEPTEMBER 23 and DECEMBER 14).

Hans Doe, Mr. Water, made this statement in the January 13, 1984 Vista newspaper:

> There were a half dozen of us or more out our way who had more money wrapped up in land and avocados than we should have had, and it was obvious that our water supply was kind of iffy. So we took an interest in the Vista Irrigation District and wanted to annex onto the Metropolitan Water District and be entitled to buy imported water. By 1949 to 1950 Lake Henshaw was pretty near empty. It got down to less than a day's supply of water. We drilled about 50 wells near the lake with the idea that we could get maybe 100 to 300 acre feet of recoverable water in the ground water basin, and we thought that Henshaw would be able to supply us with about half the water we needed. We had to look to the Metropolitan Water District for the balance.

After much political haggling, Vista finally joined the Metropolitan Water District in 1954. Hans Doe played an important role in these efforts to obtain more water for the agricultural needs of the region.

JANUARY 14, 1930

ON THIS DAY IN SAN DIEGO HISTORY a Navy plane was flying over La Jolla at about 3 p.m., and suddenly machine gun bullets rained down over Girard Avenue. One bullet tore through the roof of the Mission Garage, and another went through the roof of Charles Mason's house. Several bullet holes were left in the pavement on the street. Fortunately, no one was injured and there was little damage done, but the event caused a great deal of excitement.

In 1930, Coronado's North Island had an Army and Navy Aviation School that had been there since 1917. This was before the North Island Naval Air Station was located there in 1935. Maybe the Navy plane that flew over La Jolla on this date in 1930 had some aviation students aboard from North Island who had not yet learned how to handle the machine guns properly?

San Diego's civic leaders and the chamber of commerce had been working hard to interest the Navy into building naval bases in San Diego since the early 1900s (see MARCH 28, APRIL 14, and OCTOBER 25).

Another military facility, the Miramar Naval Air Station (now a Marine Air Station) was located only a few miles east of La Jolla. It had started out as an army camp, Camp Kearny, but it was closed down between 1920 and 1932, and then the Navy took it over as a base for helium blimps. Large runways were not built there until 1940, so it is doubtful that the naval plane that sprayed Girard Avenue with bullets on this date in 1930 would have come from the Miramar base.

JANUARY 15, 1941

ON THIS DAY IN SAN DIEGO HISTORY an army camp called Camp Callan was opened at a location three and one-half miles north of La Jolla—where part of the University of California San Diego (UCSD) is now located. The camp was named for Major General Robert A. Callan.

World War II was being fought in Europe at this time, but the United States had not yet entered the war. This happened some 11 months later in December 1941 when the Japanese bombed U.S. military ships in Pearl Harbor, Hawaii.

World War II had a great effect on San Diego, with the town's strong Navy presence and with its many important aircraft companies that then contributed to the war effort, such as General Dynamics' Convair, Ryan Aircraft, Rohr Aircraft, and Solar Turbines. But it also had an effect on the little seaside town of La Jolla—mainly because of the nearby Camp Callan.

Soldiers started arriving at Camp Callan in March 1941, and after that La Jolla began to look like a military town. Soldiers crowded the streets of La Jolla, and soon there was a need to provide some kind of a clubhouse for them. At first a recreational center was opened up in the St. James by-the-Sea Episcopal Church in June. Then in July the first official U.S.O. (United Service Organizations) Club was established in a former store at 1015 Prospect Street—next door to where The Spot restaurant is now located. The U.S.O. was open to servicemen from 9 a.m. until 10 p.m. every day. After Pearl Harbor on December 7, as more soldiers came to Camp Callan, a much larger building was needed, so the U.S.O. Club moved to the corner of Eads and Silverado (see MARCH 8).

After the war, Camp Callan closed down, and the buildings were sold to the city of San Diego on March 22, 1946 for $200,000 to provide lumber for homes that were being built for returning servicemen.

JANUARY 16, 1877

ON THIS DAY IN SAN DIEGO HISTORY the *San Diego Union* newspaper announced that the population of El Cajon Rancho consisted of 25 families—with a total of 90 people.

Before that the rancho was owned by the Pedrorena family through a Mexican land grant. And before that it was originally a part of the San Diego Mission lands, until the secularization of the missions during the 1830s (see SEPTEMBER 30).

After the end of the Mexican-American War, when California became a part of the United States, sections of the rancho gradually came into the possession of Americans. The El Cajon Rancho was opened up for settlement in 1868, but the development was slow at first—with only 25 families living there some eight years later, on this date in 1877.

The El Cajon Rancho was the third largest rancho in San Diego County when the ranchos were first established in the 1830s and 1840s. It consisted of 48,800 acres when it was granted to María Antonia Estudillo Pedrorena in 1845 (see DECEMBER 25). Only the Rancho Santa Margarita y Las Flores, where Camp Pendleton is now located, and the Rancho de la Misión San Diego de Alcalá, the San Diego Mission lands, were larger.

After the El Cajon Rancho was opened up for settlement, much of it was subdivided. The nearby Boston Ranch, now Bostonia, was owned and developed by a group of investors from Boston and was once one of the largest muscat grape vineyards in California. The Chase Rancho occupied the entire southern end of the El Cajon Valley and was at one time planted entirely in wheat.

The former El Cajon Rancho, which was once owned by one family during the Rancho Days, is now filled with thousands of families living in the cities of El Cajon, Bostonia, Santee, Lakeside, and Flinn Springs.

JANUARY 17, 1930

ON THIS DAY IN SAN DIEGO HISTORY a freak snowstorm fell on the desert around Borrego Springs and dumped nearly four inches of snow in the center of Borrego Valley.

Borrego (spelled "Borego" back then) had opened its own post office only two years before—in 1928. Borego's mail came down from Julian by truck, two days a week at first and then three days a week. A man named Milo Porter had the job of driving up to Julian to get the mail and bringing it down to Borego. The job paid $60 a month, and he furnished his own transportation and his own gasoline.

On this day of the unusual snowstorm in the desert, Mr. Porter and Edward Butz, the 14-year-old boy who was riding with him, got stuck in the snow on their way up the Banner grade toward Julian. The *Ramona Sentinel* newspaper reported on the event:

> They were forced to abandon the car to the storm and continue the journey on foot, with the mail sacks on their backs. Through the blinding storm they trudged, the cold becoming more intense with each step, fighting the drowsy pangs of frost-bite, until Edward Butz finally became so drowsy that he declared that he could go no further, and he lay down on the doorstep of an abandoned cabin. Milo Porter continued his way through the snowdrifts until he reached the county road camp [below Julian] where he explained his dilemma…to the boys there. Hastily they got some mules together and rode back down the grade to where Edward Butz was found sleeping where Milo Porter had left him. To the nearness of the road camp and the kindness of the boys who work there, Edward Butz owes being awakened from the sleep of the frost-bitten.

Milo Porter and Edward Butz spent the night at the road camp and made it into Julian the next day.

JANUARY 18, 1886

ON THIS DAY IN SAN DIEGO HISTORY Frank T. Botsford arrived in San Diego by boat from the East Coast. He was 35 years old and had been a stockbroker in New York City. Two months later he visited La Jolla for the first time and he called it "Magnificent." Eight days later he bought the 400-acre La Jolla Park for $2,200 with the idea of subdividing it and selling off small lots. Botsford later became known as the "Father of La Jolla."

The La Jolla Park land had been owned by several different individuals before Frank Botsford purchased it in 1886, but no one had tried to develop the land or to subdivide it until Botsford came along. There had been a great land boom going on in southern California during the 1880s, and San Diego had been a part of it (see NOVEMBER 15). But La Jolla was just a bare hillside above the ocean. It was noted for its beautiful rocky coastline, the caves, and its tidepools at low tide. People would come to La Jolla on a long, dusty 14-mile mule-drawn cart ride from San Diego to picnic by the beach at low tide, but no one lived there yet in 1886.

Frank Botsford and his partner, George Heald, had a lot of work to do before selling off the lots in La Jolla Park. They had to draw up a plot map of the subdivided lots, scrape out lines for streets, plant trees, and so on. They finally made plans for a great auction to sell the lots (see APRIL 30).

One of the first houses to be built in La Jolla Park was Frank and Adelaide Botsford's house at the corner of Ivanhoe Avenue and Prospect Street. It was torn down in 1938. Another early house in La Jolla was that of Botsford's partner, George Heald, located at the corner of Silverado Street and Exchange Place. It was torn down in 1936 (see JUNE 8).

JANUARY 19, 1905

ON THIS DAY IN SAN DIEGO HISTORY the name of the post office in La Jolla was changed from Lajollie to La Jolla. The U.S. Post Office Department in Washington, D.C. had made a mistake and misread the spelling of La Jolla in the town's original application to establish its post office in 1894—just seven years after the big auction in 1887 that sold the first lots in La Jolla (see JANUARY 18 and APRIL 30).

The first post office in La Jolla was located in the La Jolla Park Hotel, until the hotel burned down in 1896 (see JUNE 14). The post office would change locations six more times after this. One night in September of 1914, when it was located on Girard Avenue, a robbery was attempted—see SEPTEMBER 19 for the full story.

The La Jolla Post Office remained at the Girard Street location—on the west side of Girard just north of Silverado Street (near the present-day Warwick's bookstore)—until March 19, 1932. On that day it was moved to 7907 Herschel Avenue at the corner of Wall Street—the present-day location of a four-story bank building. The post office only remained at the Herschel Avenue location for three and a half years before moving to its present location on Wall Street at Ivanhoe on September 13, 1935.

In 1935 to 1936 a renowned artist, Belle Baranceanu, a resident of La Jolla, painted a mural on the wall of the new post office titled *Scenic View of the Village*. She painted many Depression-era murals under the WPA (Works Progress Administration), one of which called *San Diego* is in the National Museum of Art in Washington, D.C.

When the post office was first built in 1935, it had only 14 post office employees. By 1960, there were 72 employees—so an addition was designed by the architect William Lumpkins, who had also designed the rotunda at the La Jolla Athenaeum Music & Arts Library on Wall Street down the street from the post office in 1955. The La Jolla Post Office is a historically significant building because of the Baranceanu mural and the Lumpkins-designed addition.

JANUARY 20, 1872

ON THIS DAY IN SAN DIEGO HISTORY a land grant for the Otay Rancho was issued by the U.S. Land Commission to Magdalena Estudillo, sister of José Antonio Estudillo who was famous in San Diego for building La Casa de Estudillo in Old Town in 1828.

The Estudillo family was a prominent family in early San Diego history. The family had many land holdings in southern California, including, in addition to the Otay Rancho, the Janal Rancho (adjacent to the Otay Rancho east of the present-day city of Chula Vista), the El Cajon Rancho, the San Jacinto Rancho (in present-day Riverside County), and the Temecula Rancho (also in Riverside County).

The Otay Rancho, consisting of 6,658 acres, had been granted to Magdalena Estudillo in 1829 when California was still a part of Mexico. The Estudillos then refiled for a land grant with the United States Government after it took over California following the Mexican-American War, which ended in 1848 (see DECEMBER 6).

Otay means "brushy" in the local Indian language, and it is believed that the Otay Rancho land had been an Indian *rancheria* (settlement) that had been occupied by the Kumeyaay Indians since the earliest historical times.

The Otay Rancho was located southeast of the present-day city of Chula Vista and just west of the Lower Otay Dam. To give an idea of the value of the land in 1872, the *San Diego Union* newspaper reported on June 7, 1872 that "[a]n undivided one-sixth interest in the Otay Rancho brought 35¢ an acre at public auction yesterday."

A few miles west of the rancho was the village of Otay, which developed during the land boom of 1887 to 1889. The early town was connected to San Diego by a steam railroad. The early developers promised that Otay would become a large suburban city, and it was called the "Magic City." The main industry at Otay at the time was a watch factory, said to be the first one of its kind west of the Mississippi River. In 1889 the watch factory claimed a production of 250 watches daily and stated in an advertisement that it would be employing 600 people. The 1880s' land boom collapsed, and so did the plans for the watch factory and the hopes for the development of the large Magic City of Otay.

JANUARY 21, 1836

ON THIS DAY IN SAN DIEGO HISTORY a mortgage was placed on 600 head of cattle at the Valle de San José Rancho by Silvestre de Portilla. This rancho was located in northeastern San Diego County near today's Lake Henshaw and the present-day town of Warner Springs.

Portilla had applied to the Mexican governor of California for a grant to the rancho in March of 1834, but the issuing of the formal grant was delayed until April of 1836. So Portilla had been using the land for his cattle before receiving the legal grant, as evidenced by the date of the mortgage on the cattle—January 21, 1836—some three months earlier.

The map that Portilla presented to obtain the land grant showed the rancho to include the entire San José Valley.

Four years later in 1840 a claim was made by José Antonio Pico, older brother of Pío and Andrés Pico (see AUGUST 22), for the place called Agua Caliente (Spanish for "Hot Springs"), which belonged to the Mission San Luis Rey. The map that José Antonio Pico presented showed the San José Valley divided into two parts. The northern portion, which included Aqua Caliente, consisted of some 26,689 acres, and the southern portion consisted of 17,634 acres. The Mexican governor of California at that time, Governor Alvarado, granted the northern part of the valley, including Aqua Caliente, to José Antonio Pico. This land grant was called the San José Del Valle Rancho. The southern part of the valley, called the Valle de San José Rancho, was retained by Silvestre de la Portilla. Pico was ordered to pay the Mission San Luis Rey for the granary and any other property that the mission had on the land.

There were continuing troubles with the Indians over this land, and this probably caused both Portillo and Pico to eventually abandon the land.

Later, in 1844, the entire San José Valley was granted to Juan José Warner, and the land became known as the Warner Rancho (see AUGUST 30 and NOVEMBER 28).

JANUARY 22, 1912

ON THIS DAY IN SAN DIEGO HISTORY the first motion pictures were shown in La Jolla. The movies were shown in the auditorium of the bath house at La Jolla Cove using an "Edison machine" that did not have a fire shutter. The owners used a piece of tin to shut off the light to keep the film—and the bath house auditorium—from catching on fire. Movies were shown there for only two months, after which time the movie house was closed down because of the fire hazard. This was the second bath house at La Jolla Cove. The first one had burned down in 1905 (see AUGUST 28).

After the bath house movie theater was closed down, movies were shown starting in the summer of 1912 at an outdoor theater located on the southeast corner of Silverado and Drury Lane—between Fay and Girard streets—where the La Jolla Shoe Repair shop is now located.

In January 1913 the W.C. Sheppard Building was built at Girard and Wall Street, and the Orient Theater, seating 500 people, was opened there. Its name was later changed to the Garden Theater. In 1914 a rival theater, the La Jolla Theater, opened across the street on Girard Avenue but was open only a short time before closing down.

The Sheppard Building was taken down, along with the Garden Theater, in 1924 but was replaced in March 1925 by the Granada Theater, which seated 712 people. The Granada Theater lasted for 27 years at the corner of Girard and Wall. It closed down in May 1952 when the entire building was taken over by Stevenson's Department Store and later by Walker-Scott Department Store. Today Jack's Restaurant is located where the Granada Theatre once was.

Meanwhile, a new movie theater, the Playhouse Theater, had opened up in March 1948 at 7730 Girard. The Playhouse Theater was purchased by the owners of the Granada Theater in July 1948, and its name was changed to the Cove Theater. The Cove continued to serve La Jolla's movie needs for nearly 55 years—closing down in January 2003 to the regret of many La Jolla residents—leaving La Jolla with no local downtown theater.

JANUARY 23, 1972

ON THIS DAY IN SAN DIEGO HISTORY an article appeared in the *San Diego Union* newspaper reporting on the number of Indians living on the various Indian reservations in the San Diego area:

Inaja Indian Reservation: 840 acres, located about 8 miles south of Julian, used mainly for grazing and wild game hunting, population 0 (compared to 34 in 1933).

La Jolla Reservation: 8,227 acres, located near Mount Palomar, set aside in 1892, population 23.

Mesa Grande Reservation: 120 acres, located south of Lake Henshaw and west of Santa Ysabel, population 38. (Now contains 920 acres after obtaining new land from the Bureau of Land Management.)

Pala Reservation: 1,700 acres, east of Oceanside on Highway 76, set aside in 1903 for the Indians displaced from Warner Springs, population 255. (Now contains 12,308 acres.)

Pauma Reservation: 250 acres in Pauma Valley 30 miles east of Oceanside, population 59. (Now joined with the Yuima Reservation and containing nearly 6,000 acres.)

San Pasqual (Pascual) Reservation: 1,400 acres, set aside in 1910, population 19. (Originally located east of Escondido where Lake Wohlford and the Wild Animal Park are today, now relocated to five parcels situated east of Valley Center.)

Santa Ysabel Reservation: 2,000 acres, in northeastern San Diego County near Lake Henshaw, established in 1875, population 127. (Now contains 15,527 acres.)

Viejas Reservation: 1,600 acres, 35 miles east of San Diego near Interstate 8, established in 1930 for Indians displaced by construction of El Capitan Reservoir, population 98 (compared to 80 in 1938). Viejas got its name from the valley named by the Spanish El Valle de Las Viejas (The Valley of the Old Women) because the Spaniards approaching the valley found only old Indian women there after the Indian men had run away to hide to avoid a fight with the Spanish.

JANUARY 24, 1954

ON THIS DAY IN SAN DIEGO HISTORY the Park Vista Hotel opened in La Jolla at the corner of Prospect Street and Girard Avenue. This corner lot was the first lot sold in La Jolla at the big land auction in 1887 (see APRIL 30). The Cabrillo Hotel was built on part of this lot in 1909, but the rest of the corner remained vacant for years, until 1953, when construction was begun on the Park Vista Hotel, a four-story modern building with 21 rooms and 6 kitchenette apartments.

The old Cabrillo Hotel was the first hotel to be built in La Jolla after the La Jolla Park Hotel burned down in 1896 (see JANUARY 6). It was a very successful hotel that was designed by Irving Gill (see AUGUST 29). It was a four-story, 46-room hotel done in the Mission-style architecture with a concrete exterior.

There were also several small cottage-hotels in La Jolla that were built in the early days. The first one was the Cottage Hotel built in 1887 at the corner of Prospect and Herschel streets. The Montezuma Cottage, built in 1895 two blocks away at Prospect and Jenner streets, had several successive owners, and the name was changed to Seaside Inn and later to Ocean View Hotel. It was demolished in 1931. But after the loss of the La Jolla Park Hotel in 1896, there was a need for something larger than these small cottage-hotels, so the Cabrillo Hotel filled that need.

The La Valencia Hotel was built next door to the Cabrillo Hotel in 1926 (see DECEMBER 15). The distinctive tower, where the Sky Room Restaurant is located today, was added to the La Valencia two years later in 1928. The old Cabrillo Hotel, which was known as the "Hotel of Pleasant Memories," was remodeled and incorporated into the La Valencia Hotel in 1956. It is known now as La Valencia West.

The Park Vista Hotel, which opened on this date in 1954, later changed its name to Prospect Park Inn Hotel. It is now called the La Jolla Inn and is located at 1110 Prospect Street in a small, modern brick building next door to and contrasting in style with the large, old Spanish-style La Valencia Hotel.

JANUARY 25, 1845

ON THIS DAY IN SAN DIEGO HISTORY the Cañada de San Vicente Rancho was granted to Juan Lopez by the last Mexican governor of California, Pío Pico. This was a tract of land consisting of 13,316 acres occupying the San Vicente and Padre Barona valleys south of Ramona and northeast of Lakeside.

Later, after the end of the Mexican-American War of 1846–48, California became a part of the United States, and the United States government set up a land commission to examine titles to the rancho lands—to define the rancho boundaries and to decide on the validity of claims to the lands. Many of the ranchos had very loosely described titles, which could not be validated. As a result, many of the original rancho owners lost their claims.

In 1852, after California had become a state in the United States, a claim was filed to the U.S. Land Commission for the Cañada de San Vicente Rancho by José Domingo Yorba (see OCTOBER 29).

The Barona Valley, located in the southern part of the rancho, is now the Barona Indian Reservation. The Barona Valley is named for Padre Joséf Barona, who was born in Spain, came to California, and served at the San Diego Mission for 12 years between 1798 and 1810. It was during Padre Barona's ministry at the San Diego Mission that it became the largest and most prosperous of all the California missions.

The United States government acquired the land in the Barona Valley in 1933 to provide a home for part of the Capitan Grande Indians (a branch of the Ipai and Tipai tribes—also called Kumeyaay), whose former lands were almost all covered by the waters of the El Capitan Reservoir. Today the Barona Indian Reservation operates the Barona Gambling Casino and Resort on Wildcat Canyon Road northeast of Lakeside.

The San Vicente Valley, which was a part of the Cañada de San Vicente Rancho, was the route used by the Pony Express from San Diego to Julian during San Diego County's gold rush days of the early 1870s (see FEBRUARY 15). Later, the San Vicente Dam was built in 1943 on San Vicente Creek, blocking the old Mussey Grade Road that went between San Diego and Ramona. A new road, today's Highway 67, was built west of the old Mussey Grade Road and San Vicente Lake to connect between El Cajon and Ramona (see also SEPTEMBER 25).

JANUARY 26, 1850

ON THIS DAY IN SAN DIEGO HISTORY Judge Benjamin Hayes was passing through Temecula and described in his diary the Apis Adobe—the home of Pablo Apis, a Luiseño Indian chief who had previously lived at the San Luis Rey Mission.

Judge Hayes wrote:

> A vineyard is being set out here. There is a pear and peach orchard. The bottoms of the creek occasionally spread out to the width of nearly a mile. Thirty or more thatch wigwams; the Chief [Pablo Apis] lives in an adobe house, with an adobe corral around it; his house has several rooms. There are some other adobe houses in the village.

Pablo Apis had located his adobe house where there was a nearby water supply (Temecula Creek) and where there was a view across the surrounding land. There were only two high points along the south bank of Temecula Creek in the area of the Apis Land Grant. The Indian village of Temecula already occupied one of them, so Apis built his adobe house on the other high point to the east of the Temecula Indian village. Both were located near the present-day State Highway 79 and east of the present-day Interstate 15. The present-day downtown Old Temecula is located a few miles northwest of the old Apis Adobe and the old Indian village of Temecula.

The old Gila Trail (also known as the Emigrant Trail, the Butterfield Stage Road, and the Overland Mail Road)—going from the Colorado River at Yuma to Los Angeles—went past the Apis Adobe. This had its advantages and disadvantages. Sometimes Apis sold beef and other foods to the travelers passing by. But since this was the route used by the gold seekers of the California Gold Rush, he had to worry about being robbed by some of the people passing by. So Pablo Apis used to dress in Californio clothing so that he looked like a white rancher instead of an Indian (see SEPTEMBER 17).

JANUARY 27, 1847

ON THIS DAY IN SAN DIEGO HISTORY the Mormon Battalion arrived in San Diego. This was a group of volunteers who came to help out the United States Army in its fight against Mexico in the Mexican-American War of 1846–48 (see DECEMBER 1).

The Mormon Battalion had marched from Iowa via Santa Fe, New Mexico to California. They went through the desert on a trail that is now San Diego County Highway S-2, going through Box Canyon and San Felipe Valley. However, they arrived too late to help in the war, since the Californios (Mexican Californians) had already surrendered to the United States at Cahuenga Pass near Los Angeles on January 13, 1847. The Mormon Battalion received orders to turn south to San Diego instead of continuing on to Los Angeles. They arrived in San Diego to see the American flag flying in the Old Town Plaza in place of the previous Mexican flag.

After arriving in San Diego, the Mormon Battalion volunteers hired themselves out to clean up and do repairs that were needed. They whitewashed the buildings, repaired carts, dug wells, and built a bakery.

One of the Mormon soldiers wrote in his diary describing San Diego at that time:

> There are around us extensive gardens and Vineyards; wells and cisterns more or less fallen into decay and disorder; but also Olive and picturesque Date Trees, flourishing and ornamental. There is no fuel for Miles around, and the dependence for Water is some distant Pools in the sandy San Diego River, which runs (sometimes) down to the Sea.

The wife of Captain Jesse Hunter of the Mormon Battalion gave birth to the first American child born in San Diego. The baby was named Diego in honor of the place where he was born, on April 26, 1847. The boy was cared for by local Mexican women when his mother died shortly after he was born.

Most of the soldiers of the Mormon Battalion returned to Salt Lake City, but some stayed on at San Diego, using the former San Diego Mission as their headquarters.

JANUARY 28, 1916

ON THIS DAY IN SAN DIEGO HISTORY a flood destroyed the concrete bridge over the San Diego River at Old Town. The day before, on January 27, the Lower Otay Dam washed out, flooding Otay Valley and causing damage and injury to many Japanese farmers living there. Then the Sweetwater Dam ruptured.

Some people think it all started when San Diego—with its need for more water for its growing population—hired a "rainmaker" after several years of low rainfall. The "Rainmaker," Charles Mallory Hatfield, was well-known for his many "successes" in the Southwest and in Alaska. He began his work in San Diego on January 1, 1916. On January 5 it started to rain—and it kept on raining and raining throughout the rest of January, with the San Diego and Tijuana rivers overflowing their banks and with floods isolating the backcountry. Canyons in Balboa Park were flowing with raging rivers. A Santa Fe train was marooned north of San Diego by flood waters, and the passengers had to be rescued by boats.

Hatfield later appeared at City Hall to collect the money the city had agreed to pay him if he succeeded in producing rain. Because he was blamed for the flood damage, the city did not pay him. He sued the city but finally gave up all hopes of being paid when the city attorney insisted that Hatfield was liable for all the flood damage claims against the city.

So the "successful" rainmaker left San Diego—not so successful after all. We are told that after this experience he switched careers to selling sewing machines in Glendale. Charles Mallory Hatfield's secret rainmaking formula died with him in 1958.

See also JANUARY 5.

JANUARY 29, 1927

ON THIS DAY IN SAN DIEGO HISTORY the cornerstone was laid for the construction of the La Jolla Beach & Yacht Club in La Jolla Shores. A group of La Jolla citizens organized the club with the idea of taking advantage of the natural slough, or marshy bay area, located one mile south of the Scripps Institution of Oceanography and making it into a small yacht harbor and club. They bought 14 acres of land with 1,000 feet of ocean frontage. The club opened in July of 1927, but the yacht harbor became too expensive and impractical to complete.

There was a pier on the property estimated to be 15 feet wide and over 100 feet long. The pier disappeared sometime during the 1930s. Scuba divers have recently spotted remnants of the pier underwater, offshore from the present-day La Jolla Beach & Tennis Club.

When the plans for the yacht harbor were finally abandoned, the clubhouse and surrounding property, including the beach rights, were sold in 1935 to Frederick William Kellogg, a retired newspaper publisher and longtime summer resident of La Jolla, and his wife, Florence Scripps Kellogg (see JUNE 19). Mr. Kellogg began construction of additional buildings that would later became the La Jolla Beach & Tennis Club. Today it is one of the outstanding private clubs in the country and a great asset to La Jolla.

As early as 1916 there had been a small roadside inn, the Spindrift Inn, at Long Beach (as the bare, undeveloped La Jolla Shores area was called). This was ten years before the La Jolla Shores residential development was started (see APRIL 21). The Spindrift Inn operated as a small inn and restaurant until 1935, when F.W. Kellogg bought the property. It was located next door to the La Jolla Beach & Yacht Club that Mr. Kellogg had just purchased. Later, in 1941, on the oceanfront location of the Spindrift Inn, the Marine Room restaurant would open. On opening day there, Lobster Newburg cost $1.35, Rainbow Trout Almondine was $1.25, and martinis were 35 cents! Maybe those were just the special opening-day prices to entice customers to come in?

JANUARY 30, 1931

ON THIS DAY IN SAN DIEGO HISTORY the director of the San Diego Museum of Man wrote a letter to Ellen Browning Scripps thanking her for making possible the acquisition of ancient Egyptian treasures from archeological excavations.

Museum Director Clinton G. Abbott wrote to Miss Scripps:

> I indeed wish that you might see them as displayed upon a table in my office before going into the cases on the Egyptian Balcony. However as I know that this is impossible, I can simply tell you of the enthusiasm of the whole Museum Staff and thank you most warmly for this very important donation.

Ellen Browning Scripps was 94 years old at the time and in ill health, so she was unable to come to the Museum of Man to see the new additions to the Egyptian Exhibit. She died a little over a year later at the age of 95.

Scripps had been providing funding for important archeological work in Egypt since 1911, when she became a member of the Egypt Exploration Fund. In 1916 Miss Scripps was informed that if she donated to some specific archeological excavations, some of the recovered objects could be placed in a museum of her choice. Scripps wrote back the following letter: "An association for a comprehensive art museum in San Diego is now in its formative stage; and I shall be interested in retaining such collections as may be of real value toward it."

Scripps had donated to the Egypt Exploration Society for specific excavations at a site called Tel El Amarna, which was founded in 1370 B.C. by the Pharaoh Akhenaten. His queen was Nefertiti, and they had six daughters. He had a son-in-law named Tutankhamen—the famous King Tut, whose tomb and treasures were discovered in another location in 1922. The San Diego Museum received many collections from the Tel El Amarna excavations, which can be seen today in the Museum of Man in Balboa Park.

To learn more about Ellen Browning Scripps, see OCTOBER 18.

JANUARY 31, 1888

ON THIS DAY IN SAN DIEGO HISTORY the newly reestablished San Diego Board of Health held a meeting to elect a president—Dr. Thomas C. Stockton, who was a native of New Brunswick, Canada and who had come to San Diego nine years before in 1869.

The San Diego Board of Health was first established in 1850 by the San Diego City Council, but there are no records of any regular meetings of that early board. In 1869 another board of health was established in an attempt to prevent the spread of small pox and other contagious diseases (see MARCH 6).

The newly formed 1888 board of health was criticized by the *San Diego Union* newspaper for not moving fast enough to clean up the city:

> It is time the Board of Health set about the work for which their body is supposed to be particularly created. The filthy condition of the city is not only disgraceful, but dangerous to health and even to life. It is time that the matter be taken in hand in a spirit of vigor and thoroughness. There is absolutely no excuse for the present neglect. The work to be done is so apparent, the foulness so offensive to eye and nostril that it is impossible to walk far in any direction without the shameful supineness of the Health Department being fully demonstrated. If new ordinances are needed, let them be made. The situation is too serious for trifling. Clean the city.

The county health officer was forced to resign a few months later, and a new health officer was appointed. Within a few months the newspaper editorials began to praise the health department and the new health officer for being well-organized and efficient.

San Diego's population had increased from 2,637 in 1880 to nearly 40,000 in 1887 due to the great land boom and the coming of the railroad to San Diego (see NOVEMBER 15). This rapid rise in population undoubtedly contributed to the spread of contagious diseases in those early days before the discovery of antibiotics.

See MARCH 6 for the board of health's mortality report for 1887.

FEBRUARY 1, 1926

ON THIS DAY IN SAN DIEGO HISTORY a new high-wing monoplane that was built in San Diego by Ryan Airlines was tested to fly passengers between San Diego and Los Angeles.

T. Claude Ryan had been an Army reserve pilot. He was a graduate of the cadet school at March Field in Riverside and Mather Field in Sacramento. Ryan came to San Diego in 1922 with the idea of promoting commercial aviation. He bought a war-surplus biplane for $400 and used a small dirt landing strip on the tidelands at the foot of Broadway. By 1925 he had purchased more planes and was using Dutch Flats on Point Loma, northwest of what is now the Marine Corps Recruit Depot, for an airstrip.

Ryan organized Ryan Airlines with his partner, B. Franklin Mahoney. The air service that they began between San Diego and Los Angeles was the first regularly scheduled year-round passenger airline service in the United States. Ryan was dissatisfied with the available airplanes at the time, so he proceeded to design the new M-1 high-wing monoplane that was tested on this day in 1926.

The next year, in 1927, Ryan Airlines would build the *Spirit of St. Louis*, the plane that Charles Lindbergh would fly nonstop across the Atlantic Ocean from the United States to Europe. It cost $10,000 and took 60 days to build. The *Spirit of St. Louis* is now on display in the Aerospace Museum at the Smithsonian Institution in Washington, D.C. You might be surprised to see how small this little plane looks. It makes you wonder how Charles Lindbergh could make that 33½-hour flight from New York to Paris in such a tiny plane.

San Diego has an exact replica of the *Spirit of St. Louis* that is sometimes kept in the lobby of the Aerospace Museum in Balboa Park and sometimes in a storage hangar in El Cajon. San Diego's replica is believed to be the only replica of the *Spirit of St. Louis* that can actually fly.

The success of Lindbergh's flight also brought success to the Ryan Airline Company for building a plane that could do the job. The company grew over the years to become one of our country's leading corporations in the field of aviation and aerospace technology. The company was purchased by Teledyne in 1969 for $128 million and was known as Teledyne Ryan Aeronautical until it was bought out by Northrop Grumman in 1999. The company is now known as Northrop Grumman Ryan Aeronautical.

FEBRUARY 2, 1848

ON THIS DAY IN SAN DIEGO HISTORY the Treaty of Guadalupe Hidalgo was signed, marking the end of the Mexican-American War. This was important for San Diego because San Diego, as well as the rest of California, was now a part of the United States and no longer a part of Mexico.

The treaty was signed at the little town of Guadalupe Hidalgo, located a few miles north of Mexico City. The town was named for Our Lady of Guadalupe, the patron saint of the Mexican Indians, and for Miguel Hidalgo y Costilla, who, carrying the banner of Our Lady of Guadalupe, had begun the war for Mexican independence from Spain at this spot in Mexico in 1810.

The Treaty of Guadalupe Hidalgo and the takeover of California by the United States would also have other effects on San Diego. For one thing, the discovery of gold near Sacramento at about this time brought a lot of gold seekers through San Diego on their way north to the mining areas. Many stopped in San Diego and opened up businesses. More houses were built in San Diego as the population increased from 150 in 1840 to 650 by 1850.

According to the Treaty of Guadalupe Hidalgo, the United States was pledged to protect the Californios (Mexican Californians) who lived here "in the free enjoyment of their liberty, property, and religion" and to honor the Spanish and Mexican land grants that had been made to them in the form of ranchos. The United States government opened up a land commission in 1851 to examine land titles, define boundaries, and decide on the validity of land claims.

Nevertheless, this was the beginning of the end of the old, leisurely life of the Rancho Days in California. Over time most of the 30 original San Diego County ranchos, totaling hundreds of thousands of acres of nearly barren cattle ranges, have, with the addition of water and other improvements, turned into cities and towns, resorts and recreation centers, citrus and avocado groves, and country estates. Only a few of the original ranchos located in more remote areas, such as the Warner Ranch located near Lake Henshaw in northeastern San Diego County, remain much as they were in past times.

FEBRUARY 3, 1914

ON THIS DAY IN SAN DIEGO HISTORY a consulting architect, Arthur B. Benton, studying the possibility of restoring the San Diego Mission, wrote a letter to George W. Marston about the status of the mission ruins. Marston was a prominent San Diego businessman and president of the Land Marks Club's Mission Restoration Committee.

The architect reported that there had been no further deterioration of the mission ruins during the past 14 years since their reinforcement and capping over in 1900. Built in 1813—the fourth mission on that site (see DECEMBER 8)—all that was left in 1900 was the south wall of the church and a few remains of adobe walls on some of the outbuildings. The five-bell campanile had collapsed, leaving only the base. One delay after another prevented the restoration of the mission (see JULY 2).

Benton recommended that the church building—the main architectural feature on the site—be the first building to be restored—and that the restoration should preserve the original architectural character of the building. He stated that, if the restoration could be intelligently accomplished, San Diego would be noted, not only for being the site of the first Spanish mission in California, but would also be able to claim the honor of pioneering the proper restoration of historic Spanish Colonial structures.

Father Antonio Ubach, San Diego's Catholic pastor for 41 years—from 1866 until 1907—had been promoting the restoration of the deteriorating mission throughout the length of his tenure, but there had never been enough funds. In the late 1880s Father Ubach relocated his school for Indian children from Old Town to a location adjacent to the crumbling mission, where it operated for over 20 years until his death in 1907.

Restoration of the San Diego Mission finally began, after many delays, in 1930 (see JULY 13). During the restoration, the original wood-carved stations of the cross, which had been brought over from Spain by Father Ubach, were hung on the walls of the nave.

FEBRUARY 4, 1870

ON THIS DAY IN SAN DIEGO HISTORY the California State Legislature approved the transfer of 1,400 acres of pueblo land in San Diego for a public park. The park was first called City Park. The name was changed to Balboa Park in 1910 in preparation for the Panama-California Exposition of 1915 that was to take place there (see JANUARY 1 and SEPTEMBER 3).

Alonzo Horton, the "Father of New San Diego" (see OCTOBER 24), had suggested a public park for San Diego three years before—in 1867. At first the board of trustees of the San Diego Chamber of Commerce suggested 320 acres for a park. Most people thought that 320 acres was more than enough for a park for a town of 2,310 people. But trustee Ephraim Morse suggested that, since the city had over 40,000 acres of city-owned land available, perhaps the city should reserve nine tracts, or 1,400 acres, for the park. Morse suggested the area bordered by 6th, 28th, Ash, and Upas streets. The state legislature approved, thus preventing the city from selling the land for private development.

The park remained a wilderness area for some time, covered by chaparral and sagebrush. Today we know the park as a great recreational and educational area with many museums, display areas, and the world-famous San Diego Zoo. Balboa Park today is a far cry from the barren wilderness area that it once was, what with the beautiful buildings and lushly landscaped grounds planted with exotic plants from all over the world—thanks to San Diego horticulturist Kate Sessions (see MARCH 24).

Sessions especially liked palm trees, and she planted more than 50 species of palms in Balboa Park's Palm Canyon, many of which came from Baja California. While preparing Balboa Park for the 1915 Panama-California Exposition, she worked closely with a New York landscape designer, Samuel Parsons Jr., who had designed New York's Central Park. The two landscape artists both disagreed with people who were pushing for lakes and dams in Balboa Park's canyons and succeeded in preventing that from happening. They also both agreed that the park should be kept simple for the 1915 exposition, but they failed to prevent the ornate Spanish Mediterranean–style buildings that caught on with the public and have made Balboa Park the uniquely attractive place that it is.

FEBRUARY 5, 1774

ON THIS DAY IN SAN DIEGO HISTORY Juan Bautista de Anza was approaching the junction of the Gila River and the Colorado River near the present-day city of Yuma, Arizona. The expedition would cross the Colorado River into California, travel across the desert, and go through the Borrego Valley—camping near the present-day town of Borrego Springs in the northeastern part of what is now San Diego County. Then they would head up Coyote Canyon on their way to the San Gabriel Mission near Los Angeles. They would stop and rest at the San Gabriel Mission before continuing on the long journey to Monterey and San Francisco.

This was a preliminary expedition to find a land route from Mexico to San Francisco in preparation for Anza's second expedition of 1775 where he would bring settlers and soldiers to settle at Monterey and San Francisco (see OCTOBER 4).

At the location where the Gila and Colorado Rivers join, Anza met with the chief of the Yuma Indians who lived there. The chief's Indian name was Olleyquotequiebe. Since Anza and the other Spaniards had trouble saying that name, Anza renamed him Salvador Palma. They became friends, and Palma offered the help of some of the Yuma Indians—to help guide Anza through the desert on Indian trails and to help him find springs and water holes.

Anza also had the help of his own Indian aide named Sebastian Tarabal, who was familiar with the Indian trails in the desert and mountains of the area and who had recently walked from the San Gabriel Mission near Los Angeles to Sonora, Mexico. Also accompanying Anza were two Franciscan padres (Catholic priests), Francisco Garcés and Juan Marcelo Díaz. Both were from Spain and were sent to Mexico to help establish missions in the New World.

In addition, Anza brought along 21 soldiers, 5 mule packers, an interpreter, and a carpenter. He also brought 140 saddle horses, 65 beef cattle, and, according to Don Garate in his 1994 summary of Anza's expeditions, "enough mules to carry thirty-five loads of provisions, munitions of war, tobacco, baggage, and other supplies necessary for unknown lands."

FEBRUARY 6, 1940

ON THIS DAY IN SAN DIEGO HISTORY the first of a series of articles called "Desert Diary" appeared in the February issue of the *Desert Magazine*. The article was written by Marshal South about living in the desert with his wife and three children at their hand-built house on Ghost Mountain. Ghost Mountain is now a part of the Anza-Borrego Desert State Park in northeast San Diego County. They lived there for 17 years—from 1930 until 1947.

They called their home on Ghost Mountain "Yaquitepec" (from Yaqui, a freedom-loving Sonoran Indian tribe, and *tepec*, the Aztec word for hill). Marshal South wrote this about his love of the desert: "The Desert! Either you will love it or you will hate it. If you hate it you will fly from it and never wish to see its face again. If you love it, it will hold you and draw you as will no other land on earth."

There is no doubt that South loved the desert. A question frequently asked of him was "Don't you get lonely, away up here on the mountain?" South, who had a definite gift for writing, answered the question in his article "Desert Diary 1" in the February 1940 issue of the *Desert Magazine*:

> Lonely! How is it possible to be lonely in the desert? There are no two days the same. Always, on the mighty canvass of the sky and the stretching leagues of the wasteland, the Great Spirit is painting new pictures... Coyotes range their beats with nightly regularity... And sometimes grey foxes wander in on friendly calls... Owls come and sit on the corner of our ramada at night and regale us with woeful discourse.

Marshal South continued to write his articles for the *Desert Magazine* for eight years—from 1940 until his death in 1948. Sunbelt Publications' book *Marshal South and the Ghost Mountain Chronicles: An Experiment in Primitive Living*, edited by Diana Lindsay, contains the complete collection of South's articles about his Ghost Mountain experiences. It also tells some interesting facts about his unusual life and has an introduction by his son and daughter-in-law, Rider South and Lucile South (see also APRIL 22).

FEBRUARY 7, 1881

ON THIS DAY IN SAN DIEGO HISTORY an article in the *San Diego Union* newspaper stated that the owner of the Rancho Santa Margarita y Las Flores, Juan Forster, had obtained a loan on the rancho for $207,000 from Charles Crocker of San Francisco.

The rancho contained 133,441 acres and was the largest rancho in San Diego County. It was located in the northwestern corner of the county—extending from Oceanside to Orange County and eastward to Fallbrook, where the U.S. Marine Base at Camp Pendleton is now located.

Juan Forster was the brother-in-law of the Pico brothers, Andrés and Pío, who were the original owners of the rancho, beginning in 1841. They transferred ownership to Forster in 1864. (For more on the Pico brothers, see AUGUST 22.)

Forster also owned the Rancho de la Nación, where National City and Chula Vista are located today, and the San Felipe Rancho, in northeast San Diego County between the present-day towns of Julian and Borrego Springs. He also owned land in what is now Orange County in the San Juan Capistrano district.

So Juan Forster was a very wealthy man who lived a fancy life entertaining at his ranchos. But when he died in 1882, only one year after taking out the $207,000 loan on the Rancho Santa Margarita y Las Flores, practically none of his fortune was left.

FEBRUARY 8, 1897

ON THIS DAY IN SAN DIEGO HISTORY Miss Ellen Browning Scripps began the construction of her home on Prospect Street in La Jolla on an ocean-view lot that sloped down to the sea. At the time, La Jolla had a population of about 100 people. She named her home South Moulton Villa—after the street on which she was born in London in 1836, South Moulton Street.

Miss Scripps also built two cottages on her Prospect Street property. One was for her library and the other for visitors. Later, in 1904, she built another guest cottage down the street for her half-sister, Eliza Virginia Scripps, that was called Wisteria Cottage. That cottage housed John Cole's Book Store for nearly 40 years. It is now the home of the La Jolla Historical Society.

South Moulton Villa was a wood-frame house that burned down in a dramatic fire in 1915 (see AUGUST 7). Miss Scripps hired Irving Gill, a San Diego architect, to build her a new house (see APRIL 26 and AUGUST 29). Gill had recently designed the La Jolla Women's Club across the street from her property. The new South Moulton was built of concrete and stucco, which was very modern for 1916. It was also fireproof. The house was large—two stories as seen from the front on Prospect Street and three stories as seen from the sloping grounds in the back.

This lovely building has been remodeled and now houses the Museum of Contemporary Art in La Jolla. The 500-seat Sherwood Auditorium, where musical and stage productions are now held, was added in 1960.

For more information on Ellen Browning Scripps, see OCTOBER 18.

FEBRUARY 9, 1857

ON THIS DAY IN SAN DIEGO HISTORY Sam Warnock filed a claim for 160 acres in the northern part of Ballena Valley. Ballena Valley is located east of the present-day town of Ramona, about halfway between Ramona and Santa Ysabel. But in those days Ramona did not exist. It wouldn't be settled until the 1880s (see SEPTEMBER 7). In fact, a town named Ballena was to become one of San Diego County's largest backcountry settlements in the 1860s and 1870s (see SEPTEMBER 5).

Sam Warnock grew grain on his ranch in the Ballena Valley in 1857. The 1858 tax assessment showed that he had 125 head of cattle and 60 wild horses.

Warnock was one of the first white, non-Mexican, settlers in the area. He had served in the army at Fort Yuma, a military fort on the Colorado River that was established to protect immigrants and gold seekers from hostile Indians on their way to California.

After being discharged from the Army, Sam Warnock and his friend Joe Swycaffer started a business carrying Army mail between Fort Yuma and San Diego, something they did from 1854 to 1856. They each rode a mule, leading a pack mule over an old trail that had been used for centuries by the Indians. Their mail line was called the Jackass Mail because only mules could negotiate over the rugged Cuyamaca Mountains (see also JULY 9).

Warnock and Swycaffer did some scouting in San Diego's backcountry and were impressed with the Ballena Valley because of its springs and good grazing lands. So Sam Warnock filed a claim on this date in 1857 and became one of the first settlers in the Ballena Valley to raise grain and cattle.

Later, during the Civil War in 1861, Warnock sold grain to the Union Army at Camp Wright in Oak Grove, north of Warner Springs. In 1870 he opened up a store and post office in Ballena near a spring where the main gate of the Golden Eagle Horse Ranch is now located on State Highway 78. The Ballena store and post office are long gone, having closed down in 1902.

FEBRUARY 10, 1929

ON THIS DAY IN SAN DIEGO HISTORY construction was underway on a new museum, the Serra Museum in Presidio Park at the top of Presidio Hill. This is the location Father Junípero Serra blessed for the founding of the San Diego Mission in 1769—the first Spanish Mission in Alta California (see JULY 16).

The new museum and park on Presidio Hill were made possible through the efforts of George W. Marston, an influential San Diego businessman (see JANUARY 12 and OCTOBER 22).

The *San Diego Union* described the Serra Museum as "a glorious link with San Diego's glamorous past" and called Presidio Hill the "Plymouth Rock of the West." The building was designed by William Templeton Johnson, a well-known architect of the time who designed many attractive buildings in the San Diego area (see JUNE 26 and MAY 8).

Designed in the Spanish Mission Revival style, the Serra Museum was considered to be one of Johnson's greatest Spanish Colonial designs. Johnson, aware of the historical significance of the Presidio Hill location, described the building he designed for the site like this: "Almost as soon as a ship enters the harbor, the passengers can sight this imposing memorial to the vision of our early Spanish Californians."

Many visitors and newcomers to San Diego, when they see the impressive Serra Museum with its mission-like tower looming up above their heads on Presidio Hill, mistakenly think that this building is the original San Diego Mission. Even though it is built on the original site of the mission founded by Father Serra in 1769, that mission was moved six miles inland in 1774 where the permanent mission was built and where it is still located today, after having been restored in 1930 (see OCTOBER 17).

FEBRUARY 11, 1888

ON THIS DAY IN SAN DIEGO HISTORY Louis Rose died. He was the first Jewish settler in San Diego. Rose was born in Germany in 1807. He came to the United States in his mid-30s and settled in New Orleans, where he became an American citizen in 1846. He came to San Diego in 1850.

Louis Rose was involved in many business ventures in the San Diego area, including having a general store and small hotel in Old Town and buying 325 acres on Point Loma—southwest of Old Town on San Diego Bay—for a development he named Roseville. The property was located between today's Liberty Station (formerly the Naval Training Center) and today's Shelter Island Drive. Shelter Island did not exist until the early 1900s.

Rose also bought 650 acres in a canyon east of Mount Soledad in 1854 that he named Rose Canyon, where he operated a tannery and a brickyard on the part of the property near Mission Bay.

Rose invested with some success in silver and copper mines in San Diego's east county. One of his worst investments was his mattress business, where he manufactured mattresses filled with dried seaweed. It sounds like a clever idea, what with seaweed available on the San Diego coast, but the product never became popular or profitable.

Rose became stressed financially after overspending on Roseville, which never reached the kind of development that he had hoped it would. He died, almost penniless, on this day in 1888. He was buried in a small Jewish cemetery that he had established near Roseville. In 1939 the bodies in the Jewish cemetery were moved to make room for a government housing project. Today Sharp Cabrillo Hospital is located there.

Later, in the 1960s, historians began to question where Rose's grave was located. A Masonic lodge member remembered the area in Mount Hope Cemetery where Rose's body had been moved to, and the Masonic lodge, which Rose had helped to found, paid for a new headstone for his grave in 1969.

A monument was also dedicated to Rose in 1934 and installed on Old Highway 101, just north of Rose Canyon (see MAY 30).

FEBRUARY 12, 1978

ON THIS DAY IN SAN DIEGO HISTORY work was underway for the reconstruction of the Electric Building on the Prado at Balboa Park. The last of 200 unique molds had been removed from the facade of the old building to be duplicated on the new, reconstructed building. That new building is now the Casa de Balboa, which today houses the San Diego History Museum, the Museum of Photographic Arts, and the Model Railroad Museum. The old Electric Building, also known as the Canadian Building and the Palace of Electricity, housed the San Diego Aerospace Museum and Hall of Fame.

Then, just ten days after the molds had been removed, a fire broke out in the middle of the night, burning the old building to the ground. Most of the treasures of the Aerospace Museum were destroyed, including the only replica of Charles Lindbergh's plane, the *Spirit of St. Louis* (see SEPTEMBER 21). Other planes were also lost in the fire, as well as many priceless aviation items, including an important aviation library and archive.

Almost immediately the San Diego Chamber of Commerce started a fundraising campaign, which brought in $110,000 to rebuild the *Spirit of St. Louis* replica—which, rebuilt, still flies today on special occasions. Additional fundraising replaced many of the other items that had been lost or damaged. A few of the things that were retrieved from the ashes of the fire were a moon rock, some wrought-iron balcony railings, and the contents of the Hall of Fame office.

Two years later, in 1980, the aerospace exhibits were moved into a remodeled structure built for the 1935 California Pacific International Exposition (see MAY 29) called the Ford Building. The San Diego Aerospace Museum, with over 65 historical planes on exhibit, is still located in the remodeled Ford Building at the south end of Balboa Park near the Starlight Bowl.

Just two weeks after the Aerospace Museum fire, the Old Globe Shakespearean Theatre in Balboa Park was also destroyed by fire. The theater was built in 1935 for the California Pacific International Exposition as a replica of Shakespeare's original Globe Theatre from sixteenth-century England. In the effort to raise funds for rebuilding the popular and beloved theater, over $6 million was received from both private and public sources in slightly over a year. The 550-seat Old Globe was rebuilt in 1981 and reopened in January 1982, along with the new 750-seat outdoor Festival Stage Theatre.

FEBRUARY 13, 1871

ON THIS DAY IN SAN DIEGO HISTORY George V. King discovered one of the richest veins of gold in the Banner–Julian area. His find was the beginning of the Golden Chariot Mine.

King had hiked up a wooded canyon past two established gold mines near the town of Banner, the Redmond Mine and the Ready Relief Mine (see FEBRUARY 20). When he reached the scrub oak and manzanita-covered mountainside above, he discovered a large quartz boulder containing gold. He named it the Golden Chariot Mine. Chariot Canyon and Chariot Mountain took their names from the mine. The mine was one of the richest in southern California and eventually realized about $700,000 worth of gold.

At first, King and his partners hiked up the steep canyon from Banner each day to break off enough ore from the surface vein to give them up to five dollars worth of gold, after pounding the ore in hand mortars. Later they began to use burros to transport sacks of the best ore down a steep trail that dropped 3,000 feet to the mill at Banner. Their first five tons of ore yielded $6,000—a lot of money for those times.

George King sold out his share of the Golden Chariot Mine two years later to his partners for $25,000. At the end of 1873, investors from San Francisco bought the mine for $90,000. The new owners had a road built by local Indians from the mine to the Banner mill. Later the new owners built a ten-stamp mill and steam plant for extracting gold at the mine site.

The Golden Chariot Mine tapped into a complex quartz vein requiring digging four deep mine shafts, the deepest of which was 350 feet. In 1874 the mine employed over 50 miners.

The site of the Golden Chariot Mine can be visited today in a high-clearance vehicle via a steep, rough road, Chariot Canyon Road, that takes off from Highway 78 across from the Banner Store. According to Leland Fetzer in his book *A Good Camp: Gold Mines of Julian and the Cuyamacas*, the mine site "consists of a cluster of new, well-maintained buildings prominently marked with no trespassing signs."

For more about gold mining in the Banner area, see NOVEMBER 27.

FEBRUARY 14, 1888

ON THIS DAY IN SAN DIEGO HISTORY—Valentine's Day in 1888—the Hotel Del Coronado had its grand opening. It was a magnificent hotel of the time with 399 rooms, most of which contained a fireplace and a wall safe.

The hotel was built during the great San Diego land boom of the 1880s by Elisha S. Babcock and H.L. Story. They had bought the entire Coronado Peninsula in 1885 (see NOVEMBER 13).

Babcock and Story promised to build the largest hotel in the world—one that would be "too gorgeous to be true." In January 1887 Coronado had 30 homes, and the construction of the Hotel Del Coronado was started in March. The workmen were mostly Chinese from San Francisco. The hotel staff came from Boston. The grounds of the hotel were landscaped by Kate Sessions, a well-known horticulturist who also landscaped most of Balboa Park (see DECEMBER 2).

At the grand opening, the people were especially impressed with the spectacular circular dining room and the equally impressive Grand Ballroom—as people still are today.

In 1887 John D. Spreckels, an important San Diego businessman, acquired an interest in the Coronado Beach Company, and in 1903 he became the sole owner. (For more about Spreckels, see JULY 26.)

Coronado later became an incorporated city, and the majestic Hotel Del Coronado, the pride of Coronado, is still today the San Diego area's grandest and most historically significant hotel.

Coronado means "Crowned" in Spanish, and the hotel is indeed the crown of Coronado. The town and the hotel were named for the Mexican islands offshore nearby, the Islas de los Coronados. This magnificent old hotel, beloved by so many San Diegans, is often referred to simply and affectionately as the "Hotel Del."

FEBRUARY 15, 1870

ON THIS DAY IN SAN DIEGO HISTORY prospectors looking for gold in the Julian area, about 55 miles northeast of San Diego, organized the Julian Mining District. Placer gold had been discovered a few weeks before in a creek bed northwest of Julian by A.H. "Fred" Coleman. But the first gold-bearing quartz sources in the area had not been found yet. Then just five days after the Julian Mining District was formed, the first gold-bearing quartz ledge was discovered by Drury Bailey (see FEBRUARY 20). Other gold-bearing quartz veins were found later in the Banner area down the mountain east of Julian—which became the Redmond Mine (see NOVEMBER 27) and the Golden Chariot Mine (see FEBRUARY 13).

The Julian Mining District that was formed on this date in 1870 was defined as a rectangle of land measuring 5 miles by 4 miles. It was specified that a recorder would record all mining claims in the district, and they elected Mike Julian, for whom the town of Julian was named, as the first recorder (see JULY 30). It was also specified that each claim would have to be registered within 15 days or it would be forfeited, and that each miner could take two claims. Any disputes over a claim would be resolved by an arbitration board.

When word got out in San Diego that gold had been discovered in the Julian area, the *San Diego Union* wrote this report:

> Of course, the arrival of a large quantity of rich gold bearing quartz created intense excitement in town. A stampede immediately ensued, and the road has now for several days been lined with teams of every description, and men mounted on foot, en route to the mines. From persons who returned yesterday we learn that there are now on the ground not less than six hundred persons, and the number is daily increasing.

It sounds something like the crowds going to Julian today when San Diegans hear that snow has fallen in the mountains.

See JUNE 28 for more on other gold mines that were established in the Julian–Banner–Cuyamaca region of San Diego County.

FEBRUARY 16, 1842

ON THIS DAY IN SAN DIEGO HISTORY a land grant for the San Bernardo Rancho was granted to Captain Joseph Snook, an English seaman who had come to California in 1830. The grant was approved by Governor Juan Bautista Alvarado, the Mexican governor of California at the time.

During the days of the missions, from the late 1700s until 1834—before their secularization (see SEPTEMBER 30)—the lands of the San Bernardo Rancho were used as ranch lands under control of the San Diego Mission. A map made in 1800 shows an Indian *rancheria* (settlement) on the lands along the San Dieguito River.

Captain Snook was married in San Diego in 1837 to María Antonia Alvarado—daughter of the cousin of Governor Juan Bautista Alvarado. In order to ask for a land grant, Snook had to become a Catholic and a Mexican citizen, so he applied for citizenship, was baptized, and changed his name to José Francisco. He left his seafaring activities and petitioned for the 8,882 acres of the San Bernardo Rancho.

The rancho just to the north of San Bernardo Rancho, El Rincón del Diablo Rancho—the location of the present-day city of Escondido—was granted the following year, in 1843, to Captain Snook's wife's father, Juan Bautista Alvarado (a cousin of the Governor of Mexican California with the same name).

Later, Captain Snook applied for an additional land grant to add another 8,800 acres to the San Bernardo Rancho (see MAY 26).

The former rancho has been turned into the attractively planned community of Rancho Bernardo, which was developed in the late 1960s and now forms an important residential community 23 miles north of the center of San Diego.

FEBRUARY 17, 1927

ON THIS DAY IN SAN DIEGO HISTORY the *San Diego Union* wrote that after the flood of 1927 in Mission Valley—even though it was the most damaging flood since the flood of 1916 (see JANUARY 5 and JANUARY 28)—the storm had filled the county reservoirs and "a 10-year period of prosperity was assured for the city."

San Diego has a long history of alternating periods of droughts and floods, and the task of supplying enough water for its growing population has long been a problem—especially during the drought periods (see SEPTEMBER 23 and DECEMBER 14).

Mission Valley flooded in 1921, 1927, 1933, 1937, 1938, 1965, 1978, and 1980. None of these floods approached the magnitude of the 1916 floods. In the moderate flood that occurred in 1921, it was estimated that 4 billion gallons of water rushed through Mission Gorge. The *San Diego Union* urged that a dam should be built there. It was not until 1932–1935 that the El Capitan Dam was built upstream on the San Diego River and 1941–1942 that the San Vicente Dam was constructed on a tributary of the San Diego River.

A dirt road ran through Mission Valley until the early 1930s, when it was replaced by a two-lane paved road and later expanded into the multi-lane Interstate 8 freeway.

In the 1940s there were 20 dairies in Mission Valley, and vegetable gardening was the second most important industry there. In the mid-50s a mobile home park was started in Mission Valley. It was later turned into a residential housing development. The Town & Country Hotel was built in 1953.

During the 1960s Mission Valley took a different direction, into the commercial development that we see today. The May Company would be the first department store in Mission Valley—built on the location of a former ranch. After the flood of 1965, they made an engineering study of the flood problem at their proposed location and made adjustments to their construction plans, including putting the parking on the lower level and the shops on the upper levels.

In 1988 the multi-million dollar San Diego River Improvement Project was started in Mission Valley between Stadium Way and Highway 163 (see MARCH 11 and MAY 21).

FEBRUARY 18, 1850

ON THIS DAY IN SAN DIEGO HISTORY an act was passed by the newly-formed state of California to divide California into 28 counties. San Diego was the first of the counties to be established. The original San Diego County was much larger than it is today. It included all of today's Imperial County and much of Riverside and San Bernardino counties.

Even though the California Constitution was signed in October 1849, it took nearly another year—until September 9, 1850—for the United States to accept California as a state of the United States.

Before this, California was a part of Mexico, until the Mexican-American War was won by the United States in 1848. (See DECEMBER 6 to learn about Battle of San Pasqual and FEBRUARY 2 to learn about the Treaty of Guadalupe Hidalgo.)

San Diego County, as it was established on this date in 1850, was reduced in size when Riverside County was established in 1893 from a large part of the northeastern section of the county.

In 1907 the size of San Diego County was reduced further when 4,089 square miles of the eastern part of the county was taken to form Imperial County.

Even with these reductions in size, San Diego still remains a very large county geographically—and very environmentally diverse—with coastal, inland valley, rolling foothill, mountain, and desert areas all within its boundaries.

FEBRUARY 19, 1894

ON THIS DAY IN SAN DIEGO HISTORY the Ramona Town Hall and Library was dedicated—except the town was named Nuevo then and did not become Ramona until over a year later—in June of 1895 (see JUNE 18).

The Barnett family, Augustus and Martha, donated the building to the town to serve as a permanent library and meeting place. They hired William Hebbard, a prominent San Diego architect, to design the building. The town hall was built of 16-inch thick adobe blocks. The walls measured 22 inches after the brick veneers were added. The building cost the Barnetts $10,000 to build. That doesn't sound like very much today, but in 1894 it was a large amount of money.

Augustus Barnett was born in New York state in 1817 and came to California at the age of 52, shortly after the transcontinental railroad was completed, from the east to San Francisco, in 1869. He settled first in San José but moved to San Diego five years later looking for a better climate. After living in San Diego for two years, he filed for a homestead in 1880 for land located between the San Vicente and Santa Maria valleys—near the present-day town of Ramona. He later added more land to his homestead until his El Rancherea contained 1,300 acres plus a large adobe ranch house. He made most of his money in the field of finance but became respected in the area as a farmer and for his generosity in donating the town hall to the community.

The Ramona Town Hall has served many purposes in the over 100 years that it has been there. In addition to the library, it housed the first high school in Ramona (see SEPTEMBER 2). It has also housed a real estate office, Ramona's state bank, the municipal court and jail, and the chamber of commerce. During the depression of the 1930s, it was the headquarters for the local activities of the Civilian Conservation Corps (CCC).

The attractive and restored Ramona Town Hall still stands elegantly today in downtown Ramona on the north side of Main Street.

FEBRUARY 20, 1870

ON THIS DAY IN SAN DIEGO HISTORY Drury Bailey, the "Father of Julian," discovered the first gold-bearing quartz ledge that was one of the sources of the gold discovered about the same time by A.H. "Fred" Coleman in the nearby Coleman Creek as placer gold. Placer gold is the gold that is washed down from the quartz source into the streambeds where it can be collected by panning. Drury Bailey had worked his way up the mountainside looking for the gold-bearing quartz source. He named his mine the Warrior's Rest. Two days later, on George Washington's birthday, the rich quartz ledge that became the Washington Mine was discovered nearby by three other prospectors.

Later, Bailey prospected down the mountain to the Banner area and found an even richer gold-bearing quartz ledge—located across the creek from the Redman Mine (see NOVEMBER 27). Drury named it the Ready Relief Mine. The story goes that he found the mine when his finances were almost gone, and he wrote to his brother, James, saying, "Come at once. I have *ready relief.*"

The Ready Relief stamp mill mine yielded high values of gold—$300–$500 per ton, with one sample making mining history with a yield of $250,000 per ton.

Later, some San Diego investors bought out Drury Bailey's interests in the Ready Relief Mine, and the mine continued to be profitable. He repurchased the mine in 1881 after one of the partners died, and it continued to be a consistent producer for him. It was said that "it was the only mine in the district which kept a pick going" during the slump of the 1890s. After working the Ready Relief mine for 30 years, the Bailey brothers finally sold their mine to a group of Boston investors for $300,000. Drury Bailey died in 1921.

Drury Bailey was the man who developed the town of Julian City, which he named after his cousin, Mike Julian (see JULY 30).

FEBRUARY 21, 1926

ON THIS DAY IN SAN DIEGO HISTORY the La Jolla Shores residential development celebrated its opening day. It was a well-advertised affair with the promise that movie stars, directors, and producers would be there.

The *La Jolla Journal* newspaper wrote:

> If Evans-Lee Corporation, owners of scenic and beautiful "La Jolla Shores," were not satisfied with their opening day February 21—they were hard to please...
>
> All through the day, buses and electric cars were taxed to bring the crowd, and a double line of autos streamed through La Jolla proper, heading for the red & white flags that marked the tract. Planes charged over Mt. Soledad and performed aerial gymnastics...
>
> A house built on the tract must cost at least $5,000 and all plans and designs must be submitted to an art jury composed of two members of the Company and an architect chosen by them. Thus it is planned to keep the development of La Jolla Shores along artistic and harmonious lines.

Approximately 9,000 to 10,000 people came to the grand opening of La Jolla Shores, and approximately 120 lots were sold totaling $240,000—or about $2,000 per lot.

The La Jolla Beach & Yacht Club (known today as the La Jolla Beach & Tennis Club) was organized shortly afterwards (see JANUARY 29).

Today the La Jolla Shores beach is one of the most popular beaches in the San Diego area, and the Shores is a highly sought-after community to live in. The price today for a La Jolla Shores lot would be something like 300 to 1,000 times more than in 1926 (see also JUNE 19).

FEBRUARY 22, 1889

ON THIS DAY IN SAN DIEGO HISTORY there was a giant celebration for the opening of the Flume. The story of the Flume is one of the more colorful events in San Diego's continuing saga of obtaining sufficient water for its needs.

With a population of 30,000 in 1886—compared to only 3,000 in 1870—there was not enough water for a growing San Diego. So a group of concerned citizens joined together to form the San Diego Flume Company with the intent of importing water from the "wet" backcountry.

In 1888 Cuyamaca Dam was built at the headwaters of Boulder Creek, a tributary of the San Diego River, creating the Cuyamaca Reservoir. The Flume was to carry water from the reservoir for 35 miles to San Diego. It was the talk of the town when it was completed in 1889 "in all its wooden majesty," according to the *San Diego Union*.

Here are some of the staggering details: the Flume was six feet wide, 16 inches deep, and lined with redwood. It was laid out along a rock and dirt path carved into the backcountry mountains. 315 trestles had to be built to cross hills and canyons. There were five tunnels, the longest of which was 1,850 feet. Nine million feet of lumber had to be transported to the site using more than 100 wagons, 800 horses and mules, and several hundred men. Remember, there were no gas automobiles or trucks in 1888.

The giant celebration for the opening of the Flume coincided with George Washington's birthday. There were ten scheduled speakers and a giant parade. One of the big events of the celebration was to float some dignitaries, including California governor Robert Waterman, down a portion of the Flume in boats.

The grand finale and climax of the day was to be when two streams of of the new water were sprayed high into the air from fire hoses at 5th and Beech streets. The hoses spouted water on cue, over 100 feet into the air, and everybody crowded around for a cupful. People remarked how tasty the new mountain water was compared to the old San Diego water. What they didn't know was that the sprays were not mountain water at all—because the valves had not yet been installed and the Flume was air locked. Regular old San Diego water had to be substituted for the event. The new mountain water did not begin flowing through the city's water lines until three weeks later. For more about San Diego's continuing water problems, see DECEMBER 14.

FEBRUARY 23, 1848

ON THIS DAY IN SAN DIEGO HISTORY Captain Joseph Snook (also known as José Francisco de Sales) died on the San Bernardo Rancho. He was born in England and served as captain of several ships before coming to California in 1830 at the age of 32. Later he became the owner of the San Bernardo Rancho (see FEBRUARY 16 and MAY 26).

Captain Snook was buried in the nave of the Presidio Chapel on Presidio Hill—where he and his wife, María Antonia Alvarado, were married 11 years before.

In his will, Captain Snook left his wife the right to use the property at San Bernardo Rancho for the rest of her life. They also had a house in Old Town San Diego on Fitch Street, which he left to her. María Antonia continued to live in the house in Old Town until her death from smallpox in 1862. Four years after her death, the property in Old Town was sold to Sheriff James McCoy for $250. It is now the parking lot behind the visitor center in Old Town State Park

Captain Snook left his library, guns, and clothing to his brother, John Snook, as well as 100 head of cattle and the privilege of keeping them on the San Bernardo Rancho. In 1848 John Snook registered his cattle with the "CS" brand and built a house and corral on the ranch property. John Snook did not manage his ranching business very well, and when he died in 1852, "he died very poor and what property he had was not near sufficient to satisfy his creditors," according to a letter from María Antonia Snook's second husband, Henry Clayton, sent to the Snook relatives in England.

By 1887, nearly 40 years after Captain Snook had died, there was a small settlement named Bernardo on the old San Bernardo Rancho property, with a post office and "a population of 700, a public schoolhouse, fine farms, wheat and cattle ranches, and several apiaries [honey bee farms]," according to Douglas Gunn in his 1887 book, *Picturesque San Diego*.

Later, a general store was opened called the Bernardo store, and it was a popular stopping place for travelers traversing the rancho on the road between San Diego and Escondido. When the Lake Hodges Dam was built along the San Dieguito River, the lake waters covered the site of the store and small settlement.

FEBRUARY 24, 1897

ON THIS DAY IN SAN DIEGO HISTORY the cornerstone was laid on Point Loma for the construction of the first building of the School for the Revival of Lost Mysteries of Antiquity. The school was started by Katherine Tingley, a lady from Boston who was associated with a philosophical and religious movement called Theosophy.

Tingley had been told about the Point Loma area of San Diego some ten years before. Although she had never seen California or Point Loma, she was convinced that this would be the right location for her school. So she had her agents purchase the 130 acres on Point Loma, sight unseen by her.

Eventually 50 buildings were built, including the first outdoor Greek theater built in the United States. Three of the buildings were topped with exotic-looking green or purple domes. There was an impressive Egyptian arch and gateway at the entrance. Later the site grew from the original 130 acres to 500 acres. The school was known locally as "Lomaland," and after 1900 it was called the Raja Yoga (Royal Union) School. It then became the headquarters of the Theosophical Society and a commune called Point Loma Universal Brotherhood and Theosophical Society Homestead, where families came to live and to practice their ideal of Theosophy, or "divine wisdom."

Katherine Tingley became the head of the worldwide movement of Theosophy, and she described its goals by saying: "Some day our race will be one race, one Universal Brotherhood, one government, one language, and we shall enjoy eternal peace." Noble goals, indeed, but after Tingley's death in 1929 and the financial problems that followed, the Lomaland school and commune eventually closed down in 1941.

After World War II, the site became the home of California Western University and later became Point Loma College. Today it is the Point Loma Nazarene University (see also OCTOBER 28).

FEBRUARY 25, 1875

ON THIS DAY IN SAN DIEGO HISTORY a Wells Fargo stagecoach was robbed outside of Julian. The stagecoach was carrying four passengers and a treasure box containing $1,000.

In those days the Wells Fargo stagecoaches often carried gold from the gold mines in the vicinity of Julian (see NOVEMBER 27).

The robbers stopped the stage at dusk about seven miles outside of Julian as it was slowly climbing up the grade. They asked for the treasure box. The driver refused to give it to them. Then, while one robber pointed a shotgun at the stagecoach driver, the other robber climbed onto the stage and took the treasure box.

Three of the passengers had gotten off the stage at the beginning of the grade and were walking ahead on foot. The fourth passenger was ill and remained hidden in the stagecoach. The robbers ordered the stagecoach driver to drive on, then broke open the treasure box, took the $1,000 and disappeared.

When the driver reached Julian City (as Julian was called then), he reported the robbery, and a group of men set out to look for the gunmen. Wells Fargo Bank set a reward of $750 for the capture of the gunmen, but they were never found.

For a follow-up on this story, see the story for OCTOBER 1 as recorded by the *San Diego Union* newspaper some 60 years later.

FEBRUARY 26, 1943

ON THIS DAY IN SAN DIEGO HISTORY a popular resort hotel in the south section of La Jolla, the Windansea Hotel, burned down. The fire started in the kitchen at one o'clock in the morning and was discovered by the hotel managers, who risked their lives to warn the guests. All of the guests managed to escape except for one, an invalid, who apparently became confused in the excitement. The kitchen and all of the 22 rooms were destroyed. The dining room and lounge were severely damaged and had to he torn down.

The Windansea Hotel was built 34 years before, in 1909, and was located south of the center of La Jolla at the corner of Neptune Place and Playa del Sur—with a great view of the ocean. The hotel was a one-story wood building and had started out as a road house and restaurant. A contest was held at the time to give it a name. Mrs. Montgomery Brackett won the prize of six dinners at the restaurant with her name of Windansea.

The owners of the hotel estimated the fire loss to be $36,000. They said that the hotel would be rebuilt, but it never was. It is believed that the fire was caused by a gas range in the kitchen located too close to a wooden wall—which smoldered for some time before bursting into flames.

Today a very popular surfing beach—Windansea Beach—is located near the location of the old Windansea Hotel, and it probably got its name from the name of the hotel.

FEBRUARY 27, 1869

ON THIS DAY IN SAN DIEGO HISTORY two of the first pieces of land in La Jolla were sold to two brothers, Samuel Sizer and Daniel Sizer. La Joya (as it was spelled then; La Joya is Spanish for "Jewel" or "Gem") was part of the city of San Diego's pueblo lands. Before that, La Joya had existed for many years as an Indian settlement.

Pueblo lots 1259 and 1261 each contained 80 acres and were sold to the Sizer brothers for $1.25 per acre—or $100 for each 80-acre lot. The lots were adjacent to each other and were bounded by the present-day streets of La Jolla Boulevard to the west, Fay Avenue to the east, Marine Street to the north, and Palomar Avenue to the south. Today the area is primarily a residential area, situated a few blocks to the south of present-day downtown La Jolla. La Jolla High School is located today on a part of Daniel Sizer's tract (lot 1259).

A few months later, in May 1869, an article in the *San Diego Union* newspaper described the brothers' lots as: "a very promising place. They have good fresh water at a depth of 14 feet, and plenty of it. Their vineyard of 5,000 [grape] vines is doing well. The vegetable garden is fine. We expect to eat watermelons at this place on the 4th of July."

In 1870, while trying to dig another well, Daniel Sizer fell down the well to his death. His brother, Samuel, left the San Diego area shortly afterward. Their land, as well as many other acres of La Jolla land, was later acquired by a railroad company that was trying to buy land between San Diego and Los Angeles with the hope of constructing a railroad route between the two cities (see NOVEMBER 9).

The first real development of La Jolla didn't begin until some 16 years later, during the real estate boom of the 1880s (see JANUARY 18).

FEBRUARY 28, 1926

ON THIS DAY IN SAN DIEGO HISTORY the conductor of the San Diego Oratorio Society, Nino Marcelli—who would later become conductor of the San Diego Symphony—received outstanding praise from the *San Diego Union* for his musical performances with the choral group. Marcelli had founded the Oratorio Society a year before and had also conducted the San Diego High School Symphony Orchestra since 1920.

According to the *San Diego Union* article:

> What Marcelli has done since 1921 is important musical history in this city. His high school orchestra concerts are events of real significance, and can be measured by the highest musical standards... [for] there is no more strict or able judge of musicianship and interpretation than Marcelli in San Diego, or in this part of the country for that matter...

According to Melvin Goldzband in his book *San Diego Symphony from Overture to Encore*, even though some people think that the San Diego Symphony was born in 1910, Nino Marcelli would become the "Real Father of the San Diego Symphony Orchestra" when it was incorporated in 1928 as the Civic Symphony Orchestra of San Diego with him as its conductor. The name was later changed to the San Diego Symphony Orchestra.

Nina Marcelli was born in Rome in 1890 and also lived in Chile before coming to the United States during World War I, where he conducted theater orchestra in New York City. After becoming an American citizen, he enlisted in the U.S. Infantry, serving in France in the Black Hawk division and as bandmaster of the American Infantry's Paris Band. After the war he went to San Francisco and played cello with the San Francisco Symphony. He came to San Diego in 1920, where he served as conductor of the San Diego High School Symphony until 1926.

Marcelli was also a composer and received much acclaim for his musical compositions as well as for his conducting. He served as conductor of the San Diego Symphony for nine years—from 1928 until 1937. Following his departure, the San Diego Symphony's succeeding conductors were: Nicolai Sokoloff, 1939–1940; Fabien Sevitsky, 1949–1952; Robert Shaw, 1953–1958; Earl Bernard Murray, 1959–1966; Zoltan Rozsnyai, 1967–1971; Peter Eros, 1971–1980; David Atherton, 1980–1987 (see NOVEMBER 2); Yoav Talmi, 1989–1996; Jung-Ho Pak, 1998–2002; Jahja Ling, 2004–. The symphony did not perform during World War II.

FEBRUARY 29, 1930

ON THIS DAY IN SAN DIEGO HISTORY Anne Morrow Lindbergh, wife of Charles Lindbergh, launched a sailplane glider from the top of Mount Soledad in La Jolla and sailed to the flatlands below. She became the first woman in the United States to receive a first class glider license and the tenth person overall to receive the first class designation.

Her husband, Charles Lindbergh, had completed a successful 20-minute glider flight over the ridge at Point Loma to become the ninth person in the United States to receive a first class glider license, which convinced her to make the attempt.

Previously, in 1927, Charles Lindbergh was the first person in the world to fly a plane solo and non-stop across the Atlantic Ocean, from the United States to Europe. His plane, *The Spirit of St. Louis*, was built in San Diego (see SEPTEMBER 21).

After Anne Lindbergh's amazing glider flight from Mount Soledad, a group of local San Diego women formed the Anne Lindbergh Gliders Club. Later the Mount Soledad Gliders Club was formed, which included a special "women's division."

In the late 1930s, a group of students from San Diego High School began building their own gliders. They took them to Torrey Pines beach and towed them into the air behind cars. The gliders were released from the tow and soared in the updrafts caused by the winds hitting the cliffs. The local fishermen and the police were not favorably impressed by the cars driving on the beach, so a better launching location was found at the top of the cliffs, and the Torrey Pines Gliderport resulted. Today the Torrey Pines Gliderport is still used for dramatic glider plane launches.

MARCH 1, 1883

ON THIS DAY IN SAN DIEGO HISTORY the Los Vallecitos de San Marcos Rancho (Spanish for "Little Valley of St. Mark") was granted to Lorenzo Soto. The 8,877-acre rancho was located between the present-day towns of Escondido and Vista. The town of San Marcos later got its name from the rancho.

The rancho was originally granted to José María Alvarado in 1840 at a time when California was a part of Mexico. After the Mexican-American War of 1846–48, California became a part of the United States, and the U.S. Land Commission was set up in 1851 to control the land grants in California (see FEBRUARY 2).

Lorenzo Soto was born in 1821 and was the son of Francisco Soto, the first white child born in the settlement of San Francisco in 1776. Lorenzo Soto came to southern California in 1847 when he served in a military force fighting for the Californios against the United States in the Mexican-American War. After the war he settled in Old Town San Diego and lived in the old Carrillo Adobe. He later married the widow of Tomas Alvarado and lived in the Alvarado house in Old Town.

The land and climate of Los Vallecitos de San Marcos Rancho were later combined with plenty of water from Lake Hodges, which was built in 1918 to make the area a productive agricultural region. The town of San Marcos was established there on the Escondido branch of the Santa Fe railroad in 1887.

MARCH 2, 1948

ON THIS DAY IN SAN DIEGO HISTORY a new 650-seat movie theater, the Playhouse Theater, opened in La Jolla on Girard Avenue. In case you have never heard of the Playhouse Theater, that is because the name was changed to the Cove Theater four months later.

There was already a movie theater in La Jolla—the Granada Theater—located at the corner of Girard and Wall streets. The Granada Theater, which seated 712 people, was opened in 1925. The owners of the Granada Theater bought the Playhouse Theater in July 1948, four months after it was built, and changed its name to the Cove Theater shortly after.

Spencer Wilson became the manager of the Playhouse Theater when it opened and continued his tenure as manager of the Cove for many years. He had come to La Jolla in 1933 and had become manager of the Granada Theater, serving as its manager until it closed down in 1952—but he continued to manage the Cove Theater until his retirement in 1992. He served for nearly 60 years managing La Jolla's theaters. Many people who went to movies in La Jolla remember this kind gentleman fondly.

The building on Girard Avenue that the Cove Theater was leasing came up for renewal in 2003, and the new owners of the building decided not to lease the building to a theater anymore—so the last showing of a movie at the Cove was in January 2003, and the Cove Theater closed down for good—after 55 years—the end of a nostalgic era in La Jolla history.

MARCH 3, 1882

ON THIS DAY IN SAN DIEGO HISTORY Helen Hunt Jackson arrived in San Diego to gather information before writing her famous novel *Ramona*.

The author was concerned about the wrongs that had been done to the southern California Indians. She had previously been commissioned by President Chester A. Arthur to investigate for the U.S. Government the ways the Mission Indians and Mexicans were cheated out of their lands by American promoters and swindlers. One historian wrote that "Mrs. Jackson turned in an exhaustive, shocking report, but it was shelved and forgotten" after it was received in Washington.

So Jackson set out to expose the situation through her novel *Ramona*—the story about a romance between the beautiful Ramona, a half-Scottish, half-Indian adopted daughter of the owners of a southern California rancho, and Alessandro, a brave full-blooded Indian. The book was published in 1884—two years after Mrs. Jackson's visit to southern California. It was a great success and created a lot of interest in southern California.

While in the San Diego area in 1882, Jackson visited with Father Antonio Ubach, a well-loved pastor of San Diego churches, and he showed her the different San Diego Indian sites. Mrs. Jackson said that Father Ubach "was much loved by the Indians." She also visited the Temecula area and the Guajome Rancho east of the present-day town of Oceanside. It has been suggested that Mrs. Jackson fashioned the character of Father Gaspara in the novel after Father Ubach and that the locale of the story was patterned after Rancho Guajome (see JULY 19).

Helen Hunt Jackson died in 1885—only one year after *Ramona* was published—and did not live long enough to experience the amazing success of her best-selling novel.

A dramatic outdoor production of the Ramona story is performed every year in May at the Ramona Bowl in Hemet, California in Riverside County.

For more about Helen Hunt Jackson, see DECEMBER 20.

MARCH 4, 1887

ON THIS DAY IN SAN DIEGO HISTORY an advertisement in the *San Diego Union* newspaper offered lots and land for sale at Santa Maria Rancho—the area now known as Ramona.

The lots were 50' by 140' in size, costing $100 each on Main Street and $50 on other streets. There were also larger tracts of 5, 10, 20, and 40 acres for sale at $50 per acre. A total of 3,800 acres were subdivided and were for sale in the Santa Maria Valley at the time. The terms of purchase were one-third down, and the balance in one to two years at 7% interest.

The ad was placed by the "Santa Maria Land & Water Company, Milton Santee, President & Manager." Santee, a Los Angeles engineer and land promoter, would later marry the widow of George Cowles, who owned the Cowles Ranch near the present-day town of Santee. The town of Santee was later named for Milton Santee instead of George Cowles, the original settler in the area, but there is a mountain in the area named for Cowles.

The newspaper ad called the new proposed subdivision the "Gem Ranche of San Diego County—Pure Water—Pure Air—…Good Hotel—Finest Vineyard Soil in southern California, and the choicest spot for Deciduous Fruits."

The Santa Maria Rancho, originally known as Valle de Pamo (from *paamuu*, a Kumeyaay Indian word meaning "unknown"), consisting of 17,798 acres, was originally granted jointly to the Californio José Joaquin Ortega and the Englishman Edward Stokes in the early 1840s by the Mexican governor of California. Ortega and Stokes also received the grant to the 17,719-acre Santa Ysabel Rancho in 1844 (see MAY 14). Ortega and Stokes were related by the 1840 marriage of Stokes to Ortega's daughter, Refugio.

After gold was discovered in 1870 in the Julian–Banner area, a small settlement was established in the Santa Maria Valley called Nuevo (Spanish for "New")—a small stopping place on the way from San Diego to the gold mines (see SEPTEMBER 7). This later became the town of Ramona after the land sale by the Santa Maria Land & Water Company, which occurred on this day in 1887.

MARCH 5, 1900

ON THIS DAY IN SAN DIEGO HISTORY a 130-foot deep shaft was dug by the Barona Copper and Smelting Company to mine the large ledge of copper on the Daley Ranch, located in the Barona Valley a few miles south of the town of Ramona. The Daley Ranch was formerly known as the Barona Ranch before Thomas J. Daley bought it in 1885. Shortly after buying the ranch, Daley discovered a surface outcropping of copper ore on the property.

Daley sold the property to the Boston and Maine Company for $100,000. Over the years several companies worked the copper without much success. But between 1914 and 1919, when the copper mine was being worked by the San Jacinto Mining and Milling Company, the mine yielded 175,000 pounds of copper. In 1919 alone about 150,000 pounds of copper was taken from the mine at a price of 27 cents per pound—a high price at the time due to World War I and the need for metals. But compare that to the price of copper today.

In 1924 George W. Lindsay bought the 100-acre property that contained the copper mine. He leased the mine to other operators, but no one was able to make it pay off. In 1935, after a study of the mine's potential by geologists, it was determined that operating the mine would no longer be profitable. The mine has been inactive ever since.

Gold was also mined near Ramona in the San Vicente Valley between 1924 and 1930. The gold mine was located where expensive homes now stand in the Country Estates development. Water was pumped up from San Vicente Creek, where the golf course of the San Vicente Country Club is located today. Jet blasts of water were used to force the gold-bearing rock to the surface. But the mine produced only about $14,500 in gold before it closed down in 1930.

There is a creek in the area called Klondike Creek—a tributary of San Vicente Creek. It was named after the Klondike River in the Yukon Territory of northern Canada where large amounts of gold-bearing gravel were found in the late 1890s and early 1900s, causing a gold rush and yielding many millions of dollars in gold. Wishful thinking that the Klondike Creek in San Diego County would live up to the Klondike name and reputation!

MARCH 6, 1888

ON THIS DAY IN SAN DIEGO HISTORY—the *San Diego Union* newspaper published the San Diego Board of Health Report, a mortality report listing causes of deaths for the previous year of 1887:

> During the year there were 248 deaths, as follows: Cholera morbus, 1; Cholera infantum, 5; diarrhea, 2; dysentery, 1; measles, 2; diphtheria, 3; croup [labored, suffocative breathing with hoarse coughing], 2; erysipelas [an acute streptococcus skin disease], 1; fever, typhoid, 10; fever, remittent and intermittent, 9; fever, malaria, 4; hydrocephalus, 1; meningitis, 8; phthysis pulmonans [pulmonary consumption], 48; marasmus [wasting away and ematiation], 4; cancer, 1; pneumonia, 17; pleurisy, 1; bronchitis, 2; enteritis [inflammation of the intestine], 5; gastritis [inflammation of the stomach], 4; peritonitis, 3; diseases of the liver, 1; diseases of the bowels, 9; Bright's disease [kidney infection], 17; convulsions, 3; brain diseases, 8; old age, 6; stillbirths, 10; inanition [starvation], 2; uremia [toxic blood due to kidney failure], 3; tuberculosis, 5; congestion of the lungs, 3; paralysis, 6; asthma, 1; pyemia [blood poisoning], 2; railroad accidents, 3; gunshot, 4; cerebral hemorrhage, 4; other causes, 26.

The population of San Diego at the time was approximately 40,000. A total of 248 deaths equals $^6/_{10}$ of 1% of the population. As a comparison, the 2000 census shows the population of San Diego County to be approximately 3,000,000. A death rate comparable to the 1887 figure of 0.6% would be 18,000 deaths. According to the San Diego County Department of Health Services, the total number of deaths in San Diego County in 2002 was 19,356—or approximately 0.65% of the population—not too different from the death rate in 1887. But the causes for deaths in 2002 are quite different, due largely to today's availability of antibiotics and vaccinations to treat and prevent many infectious diseases.

The top ten causes of death in San Diego County in 2002 were: diseases of the heart, 5,275; malignant neoplasms (cancer), 4,584; cerebrovascular disease (strokes, etc.), 1,459; chronic lower respiratory disease, 1,006; Alzheimer's disease, 909; unintentional injuries, 790; influenza and pneumonia, 585; diabetes, 475; suicide, 308; chronic liver disease and cirrhosis, 296; all other causes, 3,669.

The top three—heart disease, cancer, and stroke—may be considered to be stress-related diseases. Even though contagious infectious diseases are reduced today, perhaps we are living under more stress than the people in 1887?

MARCH 7, 1990

ON THIS DAY IN SAN DIEGO HISTORY the ruins of the Pablo Apis adobe near Temecula were bulldozed down prior to the construction of a housing development there. One of the requirements before the construction could begin and before the historic adobe ruins could be destroyed was for an archeological study to be done around the adobe. This was completed in 1989, and the foundations of the historic adobe building were bulldozed away on this date—March 7, 1990.

Pablo Apis was a Luiseño Indian who had been educated at the San Luis Rey Mission. After the secularization of the missions in 1834 (see SEPTEMBER 30), Apis was granted 2,200 acres in the Temecula Valley. He built his adobe house sometime in the 1840s.

After the Mexican-American War of 1846–48 when California was no longer a part of Mexico but a part of the United States, the old Mexican land grants had to be re-claimed with the U.S. Land Commission. Apis filed his claim in 1852, and in 1853 it was denied by the commission because of lack of a proper map or proof of the boundaries of his claim.

Pablo Apis died sometime in late 1853 or early 1854. After his death, the rejection of the land grant was appealed in 1856, and the court ruled in favor of Apis's heirs. This provided important proof that an Indian could own land in California in the 1850s, although it was certainly not common. More often than not, the white men were able to claim the rancho lands that were supposed to go to the Indians after the secularization of the mission lands (see SEPTEMBER 17 and SEPTEMBER 30).

March 8, 1942

On this day in san diego history a dedication was held for the building that housed the U.S.O. (United Service Organization) in La Jolla. It was located at the corner of Eads and Silverado streets at 7776 Eads, where St. James Hall is now located.

The La Jolla U.S.O. was a recreational facility for U.S. servicemen who were stationed at the nearby Camp Callan, located 3.5 miles north of La Jolla where part of the University of California San Diego (UCSD) now stands. The camp was opened in 1940 after the San Diego City Council granted 710 acres of land to the Army for the price of one dollar per year. The purpose of the camp was to train military men how to fire long-range weapons in case the Japanese fleet tried to attack the West Coast during World War II. The first 269 trainees arrived in March 1941. After the Japanese attack on Pearl Harbor on December 7, 1941 and as World War II progressed, there were as many as 15,000 men in the three-week training program at Camp Callan.

There was a real fear of invasion from the Japanese during the early days of World War II. A civil defense headquarters was started up in La Jolla with 80 air raid wardens assigned emergency duties. A blackout was imposed so that lights did not show out toward the sea at night, and air raid drills were begun. There was an air raid shelter in the basement of the Art Center, and two air raid sirens were installed. Bunkers were placed on Mount Soledad, and observation posts were established all along the coastline (see August 20).

La Jollans recognized a need to provide a recreation area for the servicemen from Camp Callan, who liked to come there in their free time. The first U.S.O. was opened in a former store at 1015 Prospect Street next door to where The Spot restaurant is now located. Soon there was a need for a larger facility for the servicemen. That facility opened in January 1942 at the corner of Silverado and Eads and was dedicated on this date—March 8, 1942—complete with the Camp Callan military band playing for the event.

After World War II ended the U.S.O. building became surplus, and the city of San Diego took over the property, which was dedicated as a war memorial in 1946. In 1952 it became St. James Hall, owned by the St. James by-the-Sea Episcopal Church.

MARCH 9, 1882

On this day in San Diego history an ad appeared in the San Diego newspaper:

> la jolla for sale. This famous resort, with nearly 400 acres of land, and all the caves, is offered for sale at such a price that the buyer can realize a great profit by a little judicious outlay in such improvements that will attract the public. The owner resides East and wishes to dispose of it soon.

The owner was Charles E. Dean who had bought the 400 acres known as La Jolla Park some 11 years earlier in January 1871.

The La Jolla area was first mapped as a part of the San Diego pueblo (Spanish for "town") in an 1845 survey of San Diego County. It was located in the far northwestern corner of the pueblo and contained 60 lots. Only a portion of those lots (three) were included in the 400 acres of La Jolla Park that Charles Dean owned.

But Mr. Dean never developed La Jolla, although it is thought that he might have built a "shack" there and dug a well for water that contained only salt water.

After owning La Jolla Park for 13 years, Dean finally sold it in June 1884 to William Armstrong, who then sold it to Charles H. MacArthur in January 1886. Two months later, in March 1886, La Jolla was purchased by F.T. Botsford, later known as the "Father of La Jolla." Botsford wrote in his diary on that March 1886 day, "Bought La Jolla!"

Botsford and his partner, George Heald, subdivided the land and sold the La Jolla Park lots at a big auction in 1887 (see April 30).

MARCH 10, 1912

ON THIS DAY IN SAN DIEGO HISTORY construction began on a house of unusual design in the 3000 block of Laurel Street in the Burlingame residential tract, located east of Balboa Park and south of the North Park subdivision.

The house was built for Archibald McCorkle and was a mixture of Spanish Revival architecture and Craftsman-style architecture. It had unusual tall square columns attached to its two-story front corners and a Gatehouse-style entry porch, giving it a Spanish-fortress look.

Another house, one block away in the 3100 block of Laurel Street, was started at about the same time. It was designed by the architect William Wheeler, who worked for the developer of the Burlingame tract, the McFadden & Buxton Company. This house was built for Mary Rhinehart, a widow from Colorado, whose son worked for the McFadden & Buxton Company as superintendent of the building department. This single-story house had a feature that became popular with other houses in the community. It had a two-story tower on one side of the house with windows all around to take advantage of the 360 degree view that included the mountains to the east, the bay and Coronados Islands to the south, Point Loma and Coronado to the west, Switzer Canyon to the north, and the nearby construction of ornate buildings in Balboa Park that was underway for the Panama-California Exposition of 1915–16 (see SEPTEMBER 3).

Both of these houses are still there today, and both have been designated as San Diego Historic Landmarks—as have many other homes in the Burlingame tract that were built between 1912 and 1921.

The Burlingame residential tract was promoted by the developers, Joseph McFadden and George Buxton, as the "Tract of Character." They promised "an exclusive community of unique character for the well-to-do American family" and offered homes with an interesting diversity of architectural designs and styles. When you visit the area today, it is still a "tract of character," with impressive and unique styles of homes that have been well maintained over the years.

MARCH 11, 1973

ON THIS DAY IN SAN DIEGO HISTORY an article in the *San Diego Union* newspaper quoted a local geographer, Philip Pryde, about the possibility of flooding in Mission Valley: "There is no doubt that a very wet period climaxed by a major cyclonic storm…could produce economically disastrous flooding in Mission Valley."

Mission Valley had flooded in the past in 1916, 1921, 1927, 1933, 1937, 1938, 1978 and 1980 (see FEBRUARY 17).

Pryde later wrote:

> Floods are a natural attribute of any river. They are usually perceived as harmful and undesirable phenomena, but this is generally because development has been unwisely permitted in the river's floodplain…
>
> [W]e do know that large floods are going to occur somewhere every year, and that a few will be bigger than any previously seen on that particular stream… An important point to consider (about Mission Valley) is the limited storage capability behind our county dams. Although their reservoirs have a considerable storage capacity, the 1916 storm would fill all of the major ones (with the possible exception of Lake Henshaw) to overflowing. So the dams, even if they were empty, would not capture all floodwaters from an exceptionally large storm.

Later, in 1988, a flood improvement project was undertaken in Mission Valley from Stadium Way downstream to Highway 163 costing $29 million. It involved raising Mission Center Road and Stadium Way seven feet, constructing earthen dikes and holding basins, and installing storm-drain pumps along the river channel and at road crossings. But even after these improvements a local engineer, Nick Napier, said, "The only way to make those roads withstand a 100-year flood would be to raise them another 20 feet."

So if the past holds any lesson for the future, there *will* be wet years, storms, and, yes, floods again in Mission Valley.

MARCH 12, 1774

ON THIS DAY IN SAN DIEGO HISTORY Juan Bautista de Anza and his overland expedition, on their way from Mexico to Monterey and San Francisco, camped at San Gregorio Springs—located just outside of the present-day town of Borrego Springs in northeast San Diego County. These springs, located just east of the low-lying Borrego Sink, are the original springs that gave the town its name. There is a historical marker there today where the Anza party camped.

This 1774 trip was a preliminary expedition to test the route in preparation for the larger overland expedition that Anza would lead the next year, taking Spanish soldiers and settlers from Mexico to Monterey and San Francisco along the same route (see FEBRUARY 5 and OCTOBER 4).

On this day, Anza wrote in his diary:

> When we arrived here we discovered more than sixty heathen [what the Spaniards called the non-Christian Indians] who were hunting. I made an effort to have some of them come to where we were encamped, sending the Californian to bring them... While among them the California Indian observed that they spoke the language of San Diego.

The "California Indian" that Anza referred to was his Indian guide, Sebastian Tarabal, a Baja California Indian who had previously walked from Mission San Gabriel (near Los Angeles) to Sonora, Mexico and who was familiar with the trails through the desert. He had also accompanied the Portolá-Serra overland expedition from Baja California to San Diego to establish the San Diego Mission in 1769.

The Indians near Borrego Springs who spoke "the language of San Diego" were Kumeyaay Indians. The Kumeyaay (called "Diegueños" by the Spanish) were the Indians associated with the San Diego Mission; they also lived in eastern San Diego County—in the mountains and desert and south to Baja California.

The Kumeyaay Indians had a lifestyle that was suited to the desert. They used clay pots and woven baskets and wore scant clothing. They hunted deer, bighorn sheep, and jackrabbits, but desert plants made up most of their diet—staples such as agave cactus and mesquite beans. In the summer, when it was hot in the desert, they migrated up to the cooler mountains, where they gathered pinyon nuts and acorns.

MARCH 13, 1897

ON THIS DAY IN SAN DIEGO HISTORY the San Diego State Normal School was founded. The name of the school was changed to San Diego State Teachers College in 1921 when it was granted college status by the State of California. We know this school today as San Diego State University.

When the school was first founded, it was located on 17 acres in the suburban community of University Heights near El Cajon Boulevard and Normal Street. In 1899 a large, lovely Beaux Arts–style main building was built, designed by William S. Hebbard and Irving Gill (see APRIL 26). In 1910 a two-story Italian Renaissance–style teacher training building was added, as well as several smaller auxiliary buildings.

By 1922 the University Heights campus was becoming very over-crowded. The original buildings were designed to accommodate 600 students, but in 1922 there were approximately 1,000 students. There were also 500 children attending classes in the teacher training school building. By 1925 the school's enrollment had reached over 1,300 students. There was not enough room on campus for the new buildings that were needed, and land prices in the University Heights area were too expensive for the school to expand into the surrounding neighborhood.

Eventually, a search was initiated for a new and larger site for the college. Between 1925 and 1927 ten potential sites were evaluated by a committee, but none of the sites were found acceptable. Finally, a 125-acre tract of land along the southern rim of the Alvarado Canyon area was donated to the college by a Los Angeles investment company, which was developing the nearby residential area of Mission Palisades. The college then began plans to relocate to the present-day location of San Diego State University—on College Avenue between El Cajon Boulevard and today's Interstate 8. In 1929 construction was started at the new location (see OCTOBER 7).

The old location in the University Heights area is now occupied by the San Diego Board of Education. The original 1899 Beaux Arts–style main building no longer exists, but the 1910 two-story Italian Renaissance–style building is still there but in a sad state of disrepair.

MARCH 14, 1835

ON THIS DAY IN SAN DIEGO HISTORY Richard Henry Dana arrived in San Diego from Boston at the age of 19 aboard a hide and tallow trader ship, the *Pilgrim*.

Dana would later write in his best-selling book *Two Years Before the Mast*:

> For landing and taking on hides, San Diego is decidedly the best place in California. The harbour is small and land-locked; there is no surf; the vessels lie within a cable's length of the beach, and the beach itself is smooth and hard sand, without rocks or stones. For these reasons it is used by all vessels in the trade as a depot…[and] it would be impossible, when loading with the cured hides for the passage home, to take them on board at any of the open ports, without getting them wet in the surf, which would spoil them.

Cattle hides and tallow were about the only exports from San Diego and southern California during the Mexican period from 1822 to 1846. Ships from the East Coast brought manufactured items like clothing, shoes, jewelry, perfumes, hardware, and fireworks. Most of the customers were from the many large ranchos, who bought colorful costumes and accessories for their parties and wedding celebrations, which often lasted as long as three days.

While in San Diego, Dana visited the "old ruinous presidio," as he called it, and the small settlement below that we now know as Old Town. Dana described the settlement as containing "about forty dark-brown looking huts, or houses, and two larger ones, plastered." The two plastered houses were the adobe houses that belonged to the Bandini and Estudillo families. These houses are preserved today and can be visited in Old Town.

Dana noted that wood was scarce and that few trees grew in the area. Dana and his shipmates also rented some horses and rode inland to visit the San Diego Mission.

After *Two Years Before the Mast* was published in 1840, Americans had a better idea of California and its people and customs.

San Diego, at the time when Richard Henry Dana was there in 1835, had a population of only 432. When he returned to San Diego some 24 years later in 1859, the population had increased to over 700, but he noted few changes in the tiny town except that the hide houses were gone. He noted "the coyotes bark still in the woods."

MARCH 15, 1837

ON THIS DAY IN SAN DIEGO HISTORY Captain Francisco María Ruiz, a Spanish military officer and former *comandante* (Spanish for "commander") of the presidio (military fort), appeared before the *alcalde* (Spanish for "mayor") of San Diego. Captain Ruiz was 83 years old at the time and had been in ill health. He wanted to transfer his ownership of the Los Peñasquitos Rancho to Francisco María Alvarado "in compensation for the board and care he had given in times of failing strength and sickness." Captain Ruiz, who had never married, died two years later in 1839.

After Francisco María Alvarado inherited the rancho, he had to reapply for ownership to the U.S. Land Commission following the Mexican-American War of 1846–48 (see APRIL 13).

Captain Ruiz had owned the Los Peñasquitos Rancho (Spanish for "The Little Cliffs") for 14 years, since it was granted to him in 1823. It was the first land grant made within the present area of San Diego County. The rancho contained 8,486 acres and occupied a narrow strip of valley—from east of Torrey Pines Mesa extending northeasterly to the San Bernardo Rancho and the Poway district. Today it is the location of a large residential development that bears essentially the same name—Rancho Peñasquitos.

Ruiz also built the first house in Old Town sometime around 1812—located down the hill from the presidio. The one-story adobe house was known as the Pear Garden House because Ruiz had planted a pear garden on the lot next door. Later the house was occupied by the Carillo family, who were relatives of Ruiz, and it was known as the Casa de Carillo. In 1883 Louis Rose, the first Jewish settler in San Diego (see FEBRUARY 11), bought the Pear Garden lot, after which it was known as Rose's Garden. The old adobe house, Casa de Carillo—the oldest house in Old Town—is now the clubhouse for the Presidio Hills Golf Course, having been restored in 1931 and dedicated as the clubhouse in 1932.

MARCH 16, 1886

ON THIS DAY IN SAN DIEGO HISTORY Frank T. Botsford wrote in his diary: "Magnificent day at La Jolla." Botsford had arrived in San Diego in January, just two months earlier. He was so taken with the natural beauty of La Jolla that he bought it eight days later!

San Diego was in the midst of a great land boom due in large part to the completion of San Diego's connection to the transcontinental railroad from the East (see NOVEMBER 15).

Botsford didn't waste any time after his purchase. Four months later he took on a partner, George W. Heald, and five months after that, in December 1886, they signed an agreement with the Pacific Coast Land Bureau to develop and subdivide the land called La Jolla Park.

The 400 acres that comprised La Jolla Park had had several owners before Frank Botsford bought the property (see MARCH 9). As with the previous owners, one of the problems facing Botsford and his partner involved providing water for the new development. This manifested itself in various ways including, among other things, drilling a well that hit granite at 47 feet; and having to buy land in Rose Canyon in an attempt to locate a source of water there (see JULY 20). Botsford and Heald also began planting trees—including palm, cedar, and eucalyptus—because La Jolla's original landscape consisted of bare hills covered only with sage and chaparral.

Frank T. Botsford became known as the "Father of La Jolla" after he successfully developed La Jolla Park and sold off lots in at a great land auction (see APRIL 30).

MARCH 17, 1904

ON THIS DAY IN SAN DIEGO HISTORY it was Arbor Day—and 2,500 school-children planted 60 pine and cypress trees in Balboa Park on the west edge of Cabrillo Canyon. Balboa Park was called City Park then. It's name was changed to Balboa Park in 1910 prior to the opening of the Panama-California Exposition—a great World's Fair that was held at the park in 1915–16 (see OCTOBER 27).

The land for the park—1,400 acres—was set aside in 1870 (see FEBRUARY 4), and it took a long time for San Diego to turn the sagebrush-covered hills and canyons into the lush landscape that we see there today.

Kate Sessions, a well-known local horticulturist, had supervised the planting of many exotic plants and trees, which she brought in from all over the world in the 1890s (see DECEMBER 2). But the work was not finished. In 1902 a park improvement committee was formed to create a master plan for the park and to find the money to pay for the improvements.

At the request of Kate Sessions and others, George Marston, an important businessman in San Diego at the time, hired a landscape architect to design a plan for the park's plantings and roads. Between 1902 and 1904 Marston spent $20,000 of his own money on the landscaping of City Park (see OCTOBER 22).

Between 1904 and 1906 a total of 14,000 more trees and shrubs were planted to beautify what we know today as Balboa Park. So in addition to visiting the interesting buildings and museums in the park, we should also pay attention to all the wonderful plants and trees that have been planted over the years to replace the native sagebrush and chaparral, which have transformed the park into the lush and exotic habitat that it now is.

MARCH 18, 1986

ON THIS DAY IN SAN DIEGO HISTORY fire broke out on the second story of the Villa Montezuma. The Villa Montezuma is a Victorian-style house located at 20th and K streets in the Sherman Heights area of San Diego. It has had an interesting and mysterious history. At the present time it is a museum that has been managed and operated by the San Diego Historical Society since 1972.

The house was built in 1887—at the height of the San Diego land boom—for Jesse Shepard, a world-famous musician and mystic who had performed in Europe for royalty and other influential people. The construction of the house was paid for by a well-to-do rancher who hoped that by bringing Jesse Shepard to San Diego where he could give his piano concerts it would attract more culture and prestige to the area. And, indeed, it did. Influential people such as governors, military commanders, and famous poets and artists of the day came to the Villa Montezuma to attend the performances, which were a combination of séance and concert. Jesse Shepard claimed that the music he played was channeled through him from the spirits of dead composers.

The Villa Montezuma is an odd mix of Victorian and Queen Anne architecture, with a tall Russian-like "onion dome" on top of the tower. There are also rich wood interiors, ornate wood ceilings, stained glass windows, tiles, and fancy fireplaces.

The Villa Montezuma also has a reputation for being haunted. The onsite manager has told of smoothing out the wrinkles on Jesse Shepard's bed before retiring to his own room, only to find the next morning that the blankets had been disturbed—as if perhaps the former owner had come back to his bed. Neighbors have reported hearing strange, haunting piano music coming from the dark and vacant house. Sometimes the stairs creak inside when no one is on them. One curator from the San Diego Historical Society claims that many of the strange sounds in the building can be explained by the odd Victorian construction—lots of nooks and crannies made of different kinds of wood that creak and groan and transmit sound in odd ways. The question still remains as to whether the Villa Montezuma is haunted or not.

MARCH 19, 1770

ON THIS DAY IN SAN DIEGO HISTORY it was the Feast Day of St. Joseph. Father Junípero Serra, Captain Gaspar de Portolá, and their companions were at the site of the new San Diego Mission, which had been dedicated only eight months before on July 16, 1769, after their long 900-mile overland trip up the Baja California peninsula from Loreto (see JANUARY 9).

The overland trip had been supplemented with supplies and food by two ships. But after nearly eight months, food and supplies were growing scarce, so one of the ships, the *San Antonio*, was sent back to Mexico for supplies and reinforcements. The situation became almost desperate while Portolá and Serra waited for the ship to return. Portolá made plans to abandon the settlement at San Diego and take his soldiers back to Baja California. Father Serra convinced him to wait until the Feast Day of St. Joseph before making his final decision.

Father Serra led his companions in prayer on this date—March 19, 1770, the Feast Day of St. Joseph—while Portolá's soldiers were packing up their things. Then, while standing on the original location of the San Diego Mission atop Presidio Hill, a lookout spotted in the distance the small white sails of the *San Antonio*—just in time to halt the abandonment of the settlement. The ship arrived in the harbor three days later, thus saving San Diego and its mission.

Father Serra said high mass every year on March 19 for the rest of his life.

MARCH 20, 1871

ON THIS DAY IN SAN DIEGO HISTORY the *San Diego Union* newspaper began daily publication. For the previous three years—since it had started publishing in 1868—it had been a weekly newspaper (see OCTOBER 10). On this date in 1871 the *Union* had 400 subscribers. San Diego had a population of less than 3,000 people.

At first, when it was a weekly newspaper, the *San Diego Union* had its offices in Old Town San Diego. But in 1870, after the development of New Town San Diego by Alonzo Horton, the paper moved its offices to 4th and D Street (now 4th and Broadway) in New Town, what we now know as downtown San Diego (see OCTOBER 24).

Later, in 1890, John Spreckels purchased the *San Diego Union*, and the paper experienced successful growth for the next 36 years under his ownership. In 1901 and 1902 the *Union* bought out some of the other San Diego newspapers, the most important of which was the *San Diego Tribune*, which had been publishing since 1895. Together the combined papers moved into the Horton Bank building at 3rd and Broadway in 1901.

The *Union*, the morning paper, and the *Evening Tribune*, the evening paper, were purchased by Ira C. Copley in 1928—shortly after the death of Spreckels in 1926. The Copley Press was started in Illinois in 1905 by Ira Copley, whose parents had established residence in San Diego in 1890.

After Ira Copley's death in 1947, his son James S. Copley took over the newspapers. After James Copley died in 1973, his wife, Helen Copley took over. In 1973, the *Union* and *Tribune* moved from their downtown location to a newer and larger facility in Mission Valley.

In the early 1990s the *Union* and *Tribune* merged, so that now we have one newspaper, the *San Diego Union-Tribune*—San Diego's very successful main daily newspaper. Helen Copley died in 2004 at the age of 81, after having published the San Diego newspaper for nearly 30 years. Her son, David Copley, took over the Copley Press, which owns eight other newspapers in addition to the *San Diego Union-Tribune*.

MARCH 21, 1949

ON THIS DAY IN SAN DIEGO HISTORY the Borrego Springs Chamber of Commerce honored Alfred Armstrong ("Doc") Beaty and his wife with lifetime memberships to the chamber—as recognition for their contributions over the many years they had lived in this desert community in northeastern San Diego County. Doc Beaty died three months later at the age of 78 (see JUNE 1).

The Beatys were some of the earliest homesteaders in the Borrego Valley. When Doc Beaty arrived with his wife, Frances, and their six-year-old daughter, Fleta, in January 1913, there were only five other families living there. In a personal interview with historian Phil Brigandi, as described in his book *Borrego Beginnings*, Fleta Beaty described what it was like to see their 320-acre homestead in this remote desert area:

> I remember we came up the hill and we looked down there, and Borrego Lake [Borrego Sink] used to be as white as snow with alkali, and my dad came up to the wagon and he says, "Well, there it is." And Mama began to cry... And she said, "You told me it was farming land, what in the world can you farm on that?"

Their homestead was located just south of today's Borrego Springs Airport. Later, Doc Beaty filed a claim for 163 additional acres at the mouth of Coyote Canyon, where he devised an irrigation system from Coyote Creek for his farming of alfalfa and onions.

They obtained their supplies from Brawley, some 60 miles away in Imperial County. It took two and a half days to get there and back in a horse-drawn wagon. Their daughter boarded in Brawley during the school terms, as there were no schools in the Borrego Valley until 1928.

In 1916 there were 16 registered voters in the Borego Precinct (Borrego was spelled with one *r* at first—a misspelling of the Spanish *borrego*, meaning "young sheep" or "lamb"). In the 1920s, after World War I, there was renewed growth in Borrego, when new homestead laws made it easier for war veterans to file for land. Then, in 1922, the first automobile route to Borrego opened up, making it easier to reach the area.

Today, Borrego Springs has a population of less than 3,000—but that increases significantly when the winter part-time residents are there. The Anza-Borrego Desert State Park (see JULY 6), which surrounds the town of Borrego Springs, attracts many visitors.

MARCH 22, 1988

ON THIS DAY IN SAN DIEGO HISTORY the San Diego City Council passed a resolution designating the Chinese Mission to the local historical register with the understanding that the building would be moved from its original location to a new location in the Chinese Thematic Historic District (see AUGUST 18). Saving the old Chinese Mission from destruction occurred after much effort on the part of San Diego's Chinese community (see JUNE 16).

Chinese people first came to California during the 1849 Gold Rush, where they worked in the gold mines. Chinese also worked on the railroads that were being built in the 1870s and 1880s.

Chinese fishermen lived by the bay in San Diego as early as the 1850s. They developed commercial fishing, and by 1870 they supplied all of the fresh fish in the city. The discovery of gold in San Diego County brought more Chinese here during the 1870s. And a new wave of Chinese arrived in the 1880s when Chinese were recruited to work on the railroad construction. Chinese remained active in the San Diego fishing industry throughout the 1880s when they fished areas ranging from Cabo San Lucas, Mexico in the south to Monterey in the north. In 1882 there were 1,000 Chinese in San Diego. San Diego's *total* population in 1880 was only 2,637.

The Chinese people were not treated well in California, primarily because they worked hard for low wages, and some people thought that they took jobs away from American citizens. The Chinese were treated better in San Diego than in San Francisco or Los Angeles. This was due, in part, to intelligent and kind people like George Marston, who helped to start the Chinese Mission School. (For more on George Marston, see OCTOBER 22).

The old Chinese Mission building, now located at 3rd and J Street, has been restored and is now the Chinese Historical Museum.

MARCH 23, 1903

ON THIS DAY IN SAN DIEGO HISTORY Elisha Babcock, owner of the Hotel Del Coronado, wrote a letter to the president of the University of California to offer the use of the boathouse at the hotel as a laboratory for the newly-formed Marine Biological Association of San Diego—which would later become the Scripps Institution of Oceanography.

The zoologist and naturalist William E. Ritter was a professor at the University of California at Berkeley. He had been conducting summer field studies with students where they collected, sorted, and classified marine organisms from coastal areas of California for 11 years—from 1892 to 1903. Dr. Ritter had been hoping to find a permanent location for a marine biology field station. He went to Pacific Grove on Monterey Bay one summer, but Stanford University had already established a marine station there. He went to Avalon on Catalina Island, which was a lovely, pristine location, but it was too remote from the mainland. He worked out of San Pedro Harbor near Los Angeles, but that location was spoiled by plans to construct a large commercial harbor.

One of the first contributors to the effort for a permanent biological station for Dr. Ritter was E.W. Scripps, head of the Scripps-Howard newspaper chain who lived on his Miramar ranch. He and his half-sister, Ellen Browning Scripps, became important financial backers for what is today the Scripps Institution of Oceanography.

After two summers at the Hotel Del Coronado boathouse, the Marine Biological lab moved to the La Jolla Cove—to a small two-room building that was built in 1905 at a cost of $1,000, funded by the Scripps family. It was known as the "Little Green Lab" or the "Bug House." Later a 177-acre seaside tract was purchased at La Jolla Shores for $1,000, and the lab was moved there in 1910. This is where the Scripps Institution of Oceanography is located today.

MARCH 24, 1940

ON THIS DAY IN SAN DIEGO HISTORY Katherine Olivia Sessions died at the age of 83. She was better known as Kate Sessions and as the "Mother of Balboa Park."

Kate Sessions was a horticulturist who was trained at the University of California at Berkeley. She supervised the plantings in City Park—the original name of Balboa Park—as well as in many other areas of San Diego starting in the 1890s (see DECEMBER 2).

When Sessions first moved to San Diego from Oakland, she was a school teacher and principal—but her real love was plants, so she went into business with some friends and opened a nursery and flower shop. The business was successful, and they built a glass hot house on Coronado. She traveled on the ferry boat every day from her flower shop in San Diego to the hot house on Coronado, until she made a deal with the city to plant 100 trees per year in City Park and to donate 300 trees per year for other areas of San Diego in exchange for free rent of 30 acres in the park for her nursery business. She imported many exotic trees and plants from all over the world to plant in the park. She also supervised the landscaping of the Hotel Del Coronado.

Palm Canyon is one of the more interesting areas of Balboa Park. It includes over 50 species of palms, many of which Sessions obtained on a trip to Baja California. She also brought back many small plants and seeds.

She was a rough and ready, hands-on horticulturist. Under her long dresses—the custom in those times—she began wearing men's boots. And she sewed large pockets onto her long skirts, so she could carry her shears, gloves, and other tools. She used to say that a 50 cent tree should be planted in a five dollar hole—to allow lots of room for the roots to take hold.

Kate Sessions was one of California's first environmentalists and conservationists long before those terms became popular, and San Diego benefited greatly from her knowledge and efforts.

MARCH 25, 1910

ON THIS DAY IN SAN DIEGO HISTORY a letter was sent to the Catholic bishop Thomas J. Conaty from a member of the Land Marks Club Mission Restoration Committee about the proposed plans to restore the San Diego Mission (see also FEBRUARY 3 and OCTOBER 17).

Under the leadership of George W. Marston and John D. Spreckels, two influential San Diego businessmen working with the committee, efforts to raise money for the restoration of the very run-down mission had been under way for several years.

Spreckels, who owned the San Diego Electric Railway, promised that if the mission were restored, and there were no objections, he would extend the streetcar line from Old Town to the mission.

But there was an objection—from Bishop Conaty, who said that the Catholic Church saw no immediate practical use for the mission site and was unwilling to have it used as a tourist attraction.

In response to Conaty's objection, a letter was written on this date—March 25, 1910—by William Clayton, a member of the Mission Restoration Committee and operating manager of the San Diego Electric Railway Company. In the letter Clayton assured the bishop that the mission property would remain in the possession of the Catholic Church to be used for whatever needs the church might have.

The restoration of the San Diego Mission did not begin until 1930, due partly to the interruption of World War I (1914–19) and to financial problems connected with the stock market crash in 1929 (see also JULY 13).

MARCH 26, 1951

ON THIS DAY IN SAN DIEGO HISTORY the Thomas Wayland Vaughn Aquarium-Museum was dedicated at the Scripps Institution of Oceanography. The man it was named after, Dr. Thomas Wayland Vaughn, was the second director of the Scripps Institution and held that position from 1924 until 1936. Ritter Hall, one of the earlier buildings at the institution, honored the first director of Scripps, Dr. William E. Ritter, director from 1905 to 1923 (see MARCH 23).

It was under Dr. Vaughn's tenure that the direction of research at the Scripps Institution expanded from primarily biological studies to the inclusion of chemical, physical, and geological studies relating to the oceans. So in 1925 the name was changed from Scripps Institution for Biological Research to Scripps Institution of Oceanography—making it the first oceanographic institution in the United States.

The Scripps Institution of Oceanography (SIO) has been a part of the University of California since 1912. This means that, in addition to doing research to discover new things about the ocean, there is also an educational program where students can learn about oceanography. When they finish their studies at SIO they receive a Master of Science (M.S.) degree or Doctor of Philosophy (Ph.D.) degree from the University of California San Diego (UCSD). In order to attend school at SIO, you must first graduate from college with a major in one of the basic sciences: physics, chemistry, biology, or geology.

The Thomas Wayland Vaughn Aquarium-Museum was available for the public to view marine organisms and to learn more about oceanography through educational exhibits for over 40 years—until 1992 when a larger and more modern facility, the Birch Aquarium, was built on the hillside above, overlooking the Pacific Ocean and the Scripps Institution of Oceanography below.

MARCH 27, 1852

ON THIS DAY IN SAN DIEGO HISTORY the *San Diego Herald* newspaper published an article reporting on a meeting that was held to start the Pacific Pioneer Yacht Club.

According to the article, a gentleman named John C. Cremony offered the following resolutions which were unanimously passed by the group:

> *Resolved*, That, taking into consideration the natural advantages of the beautiful bay and harbor of San Diego, the enterprise and talent of its inhabitants, and the noble, manly, and healthful recreation of yachting, the time has arrived for the formation of a Yacht Club, which shall have for its object the health, pastime, and enjoyment of the population of San Diego and vicinity, and that said Club be now formed.

> *Resolved*, That said Club be designated and known as the "Pacific Pioneer Yacht Club."

The Pacific Pioneer Yacht Club was started in response to the first America's Cup race that was held in 1851 off the English coast and which was called the One Hundred Guinea Cup then. The second race was scheduled for August 1852. A group of sailors from the New York Yacht Club accepted the challenge, entered the race with their specially designed schooner, *America*, and upset the fleet of English yachts—surprising everyone by winning for the United States.

The Pacific Pioneer Yacht Club existed for only a short time, but yachting continued in San Diego, and the San Diego Yacht Club was started in 1886. In 1988, 102 years later, San Diego won the America's Cup in the races off Australia. In 1992 the America's Cup races were held in the waters off San Diego. San Diego has come a long way in yachting since the beginnings in 1852.

MARCH 28, 1915

ON THIS DAY IN SAN DIEGO HISTORY Franklin Roosevelt came to San Diego to visit the Panama-California Exposition, which had opened just a few months before on January 1, 1915 (see JANUARY 1 and DECEMBER 31). Roosevelt, who would later become President of the United States in 1932, was assistant secretary of the Navy in 1915.

While Roosevelt was in San Diego, the city and military leaders wanted to impress him with the growing importance of San Diego as a Pacific port. San Diego's congressman, William Kettner, and the commander of the 4th U.S. Marines Regiment, Colonel Joseph Pendleton, were both in town during Roosevelt's visit. Their purpose was to impress upon the Navy's decision-makers the advantages of moving the Navy's west coast training station from San Francisco to San Diego.

San Diego's efforts eventually paid off because a few months later the Navy purchased Dutch Flats, part of the semi-submerged tidelands halfway between the naval coal depot on Point Loma and the downtown waterfront, for a Marine base—now known as Marine Corps Recruit Depot or MCRD. The purchase occurred after the price of Dutch Flats was lowered from $400,000 to $250,000 and after the city donated 500 additional acres of adjacent tidelands to complete the deal.

The United States government began a massive dredging and filling operation to reclaim the low-lying mudflat. When that was almost completed in March 1919, groundbreaking occurred for the first permanent buildings on the base. Joseph Pendleton, now a general, was called to San Diego in October 1919 to command all Marine Corps activities in the area. Later the Naval Training Station would be built next door to the Marine base. And later still the Marine base north of Oceanside would be named for General Pendleton—Camp Pendleton.

The military presence in San Diego is still a most important asset to the city.

MARCH 29, 1769

ON THIS DAY IN SAN DIEGO HISTORY Father Juan Crespí and Captain Don Fernando de Rivera and their party of soldiers and Indians were traveling with their horses and mules up the Baja California peninsula to establish a Catholic mission in San Diego.

The Crespí–Rivera expedition was the first of two overland expeditions to arrive in San Diego. The second expedition, with Father Junípero Serra and Captain Gaspar de Portolá, arrived six weeks later. Three ships also sailed from La Paz, Baja California with supplies and soldiers to meet up with the overland parties in San Diego (see JANUARY 9 and APRIL 29).

On this date in 1769, Father Crespí wrote in his diary:

> One Indian from San Ygnacio Mission...died in the early dawn; before we set out I buried him at the spot where I said Mass yesterday, he having received the holy sacraments of penance and extreme unction, and a cross being set up over his grave. The orders are that the other very sick Indian is to be carried on a litter by those who are well...

On his trip up the length of Baja California, Father Crespí, a Franciscan priest, stopped over to rest for a day or two at each of the Baja California missions that had been established by the Jesuits. Indians that had been converted to Christianity joined his expedition at each of the missions—until there were a total of 42 Indians accompanying him.

In addition to the 42 Christianized Indians, there were 25 soldiers and three muleteers. There were also 188 horses and mules to carry the vast quantity of supplies that would be needed on the journey and at their destination. Moreover, there were over 100 cows and calves that would be used for food and to establish a cattle herd upon arriving.

The trip up the Baja peninsula was a long and rigorous one with water holes and streams very rare along the route. The expedition was happy and relieved when they first sighted San Diego with two supply ships already anchored in the harbor (see MAY 13).

MARCH 30, 1778

ON THIS DAY IN SAN DIEGO HISTORY the first recorded contact occurred between white men and the Indians who lived in the Valle de Pamo—later named the Santa Maria Valley, and which was later to become the location of the town of Ramona.

The Indians of this valley were known as the Ipai, and they spoke the same dialect of the Yuman language as the Indians at Santa Ysabel, Mesa Grande, and Capitan Grande. Since the Pamo Valley was one of the San Diego Mission *rancherias* (Indian settlements), the Spanish called these Indians Northern Diegueños. Archeologists have found remains of a major Ipai *rancheria* on the northern outskirts of the present-day town of Ramona between Pamo Road and Lilac Street north of Washington Street.

The white man's contact with the Indians of Pamo Valley on this day in 1778 was the result of a report that these Indians were getting ready to attack the Spanish. This was three years after Indians had attacked and burned the San Diego Mission, resulting in the death of the priest, Father Luis Jayme (see NOVEMBER 5). The commander of the San Diego Presidio (military fort), José Francisco Ortega, sent a warning to the Pamo *rancheria*, to which the Pamo chief responded in an aggressive manner.

Ortega responded by sending eight soldiers to enforce his warning. The soldiers burned one of the Indian huts, killing two Indians who refused to come out of the hut. The soldiers then confiscated the Indians' bows and arrows. Ortega convicted the Indian chiefs of plotting to kill Christians and sentenced them to death. But the death penalty was apparently never carried out, since Father Lasuén and Father Figuer petitioned the governor for a reprieve after the chiefs started to show signs of respect for the church.

The Ipai Indians survived by hunting and gathering. They depended on the oak and pine forests nearby. They hunted deer, antelope, mountain sheep, rabbits, woodrats, and quail. They obtained seafood and desert plants by trading with other tribes. The Pamo Valley Indians also were known to travel to the ocean in the vicinity of Torrey Pines and La Jolla to obtain seafood.

MARCH 31, 1871

ON THIS DAY IN SAN DIEGO HISTORY in the middle of the night, the county court records were secretly moved from the Whaley House in Old Town to a new location, the Express Building, at 6th and G streets in New Town.

New Town, which is the present-day downtown San Diego, was developed by Alonzo Horton in the late 1860s and early 1870s (see OCTOBER 24). As New San Diego became more popular, businesses began moving from Old Town to New Town. The Whaley House—which had been built in Old Town in 1856–57 by Thomas Whaley, an early San Diego pioneer from New York—was being used as the San Diego County Court House from 1869 until this day—March 31, 1871—when the courthouse records were moved to New San Diego. There was still a controversy at the time as to whether New Town should be accepted as the new *center* of San Diego.

The *San Diego Union* newspaper had already moved to New Town along with many other businesses. A large fire in Old Town a year later, in 1872, assured that the center of San Diego would no longer be Old Town.

The Whaley House is believed to be the oldest brick structure in southern California. Thomas Whaley had a brickyard business with a clay-bed and kiln located in Old Town a few blocks away from the Whaley House, behind the Bandini House. The Whaley House was the center of much of old San Diego's social life in the early days of the 1850s and 1860s.

The Whaley House, located at the corner of San Diego Avenue and Harney Street in Old Town, has a reputation for being haunted. It is now a historical museum, having been restored and refurnished by the Historical Shrine Foundation of San Diego County, and it is open for the public to visit.

APRIL 1, 1871

ON THIS DAY IN SAN DIEGO HISTORY an article in the *San Diego Union* newspaper stated: "The Kimball brothers, who bought for $30,000 the National Ranch, declined today to sell it for $120,000."

The National Ranch was known as Rancho de la Nación when it was granted to John Forster in 1845 and California was part of Mexico (see DECEMBER 11).

The Kimball Brothers, who bought the 26,632-acre ranch in 1868, recognized the potential of developing the land into a subdivision after observing Alonzo Horton's success in the development of New Town San Diego (see OCTOBER 24). But without a railroad connection and without a sufficient water supply, the lot sales were slow. Nevertheless, the following year the brothers did manage to sell some choice sites for $17 per acre—compared to the $1.13 per acre that they had paid.

During the development of what was to become National City, the Kimball brothers created a water company by securing rights to the Sweetwater River. The brothers then ordered seeds from San Francisco and Hawaii and planted lemons, figs, grapes, olives, and vegetables.

The brothers worked hard to obtain a railroad connection to National City from San Diego. In 1880 they offered 10,000 acres from the National Ranch as well as many of the unsold lots in National City to the Santa Fe Railroad to extend their transcontinental line. The railroad accepted, the connection to San Diego and National City was completed in 1885, and a great real estate boom followed (see NOVEMBER 15).

In 1888 the completion of the Sweetwater Dam assured enough water for the area, and in that same year the town of Chula Vista was established from the lands of the National Ranch.

The 1880s real estate boom ended with an economic depression in 1890, and the Kimball brothers, along with many other San Diego area developers, ended up broke. Only later did the economic conditions improve to result eventually in the successful communities we see there today.

APRIL 2, 1847

ON THIS DAY IN SAN DIEGO HISTORY Captain Joseph Snook wrote his will. He was the owner of the San Bernardo Rancho, consisting of nearly 17,800 acres that was granted to him in two separate Mexican land grants. The first grant was in 1842 (see FEBRUARY 16) and the second was in 1845 (see MAY 26). Captain Snook died less than a year after writing his will (see FEBRUARY 23).

Snook stocked his rancho with hundreds of cattle, horses, mules, oxen, and sheep. According to a visitor in 1852, the San Bernardo Rancho was "one of the largest stock-raising establishments in the country." Snook also built an adobe hacienda on the rancho.

According to his will, the ranch lands went to the six nieces and nephews from his side of the family, since he and his wife had no children. Because they lived in England, they decided to sell the property, doing so in 1867 for $4,020. Only two years later the rancho was sold for $36,000, or approximately two dollars per acre—quite a jump in price in a short period of time.

Later, in 1886, one of Captain Snook's brothers, Charles Snook, filed a lawsuit against the new owners to recover a portion of the rancho land for himself, claiming that Captain Snook's will was invalid because it had not been drawn up properly and had never been admitted for probate. Charles claimed that the nieces and nephews had no legal right to sell the rancho and claimed the sale to be invalid.

The case came to trial in January 1887, and everyone expected the trial to be long and complicated. But after only three days of testimony, Charles Snook's lawyer requested that the case be dismissed. According to the *San Diego Union* newspaper: "It appeared evident that the plaintiff got a large compromise." In other words, it looked like the new owners of the San Bernardo Rancho had paid off Charles Snook to drop the case.

The old San Bernardo Rancho property was later developed into what we know today as Rancho Bernardo, a fine residential development located just south of Escondido.

APRIL 3, 1904

ON THIS DAY IN SAN DIEGO HISTORY an early resident of La Jolla, Mr. Walter S. Lieber, arrived there for the first time. He described it as follows:

> I arrived in La Jolla on April 3, 1904, intending to stay a few hours between trains, and have been here ever since. The town then had about 100 cottages, inhabited mostly by old maids and widows, with men very scarce. I rented a cottage at nine dollars a month of Mrs. Mills.

Mrs. Nellie Mills was La Jolla's first real estate agent and was active in many of its community projects—see OCTOBER 11.

Lieber goes on to describe the La Jolla he saw in 1904:

> Scripps Park [the park located above the cove] was then a place of tents and tent floors and piles of manure, tins and bottles. La Jolla had cow paths in lieu of streets, deep to the ankle in summer with dust, in winter as deep in mud; oil stoves with which to cook, oil lamps by which to read…candle lanterns to lead one along the cow paths at night, no plumbing in the houses, and many other inconveniences for a comfortable existence. Armed with shovels, pails and seives we used to go over to "Long Beach" [now La Jolla Shores beach] for the tiny clams for broth. When Prospect Street was graded, metate stones [Indian grinding stones] were found, showing that Indians had lived here.

After he had been in La Jolla for a while—and after leaving behind the nine-dollar-per-month rental he had lived in at first—Mr. Lieber bought some lots and built cottages on them that he rented to vacationers. He built the first three cottages in the years from 1915 to 1919.

Mr. Lieber later led the efforts to clean up Scripps Park and turn it into a pleasant place, instead of the sloppy area he had described in 1904. He also led the efforts to plant the row of what are now very tall Washingtonia palm trees at Scripps Park that add so much to the beauty of La Jolla.

APRIL 4, 1905

ON THIS DAY IN SAN DIEGO HISTORY an election was held to elect San Diego's mayor. It was a controversial election between an establishment Republican and a political Independent.

The Independent reform candidate, Captain John L. Sehon, was a city councilman and a retired Army officer who was supported by the *San Diego Sun* newspaper owned by E.W. Scripps (see OCTOBER 18). His Republican opponent was Danville F. Jones, who was supported by the *San Diego Union* newspaper owned by John D. Spreckels (see JULY 26). The election for mayor soon became a fight between the two newspapers and their owners.

Sehon, the Independent reform candidate, supported water development in the El Cajon Valley—on land owned by Scripps, who would benefit financially from it. The *San Diego Union* opposed the El Cajon water development because Spreckels, in addition to owning the *Union*, owned many other businesses in San Diego, and he had his own plans to sell water to the city.

On election day—April 4, 1905—Sehon, the Independent reform candidate, won the election over Jones, the establishment Republican, by a vote of 2,018 to 1,376. A third candidate, a Socialist, had 438 votes. Even though the election was won by the reform candidate, the Republicans refused to concede the election. A suit was filed challenging the right of Sehon, a retired military officer, to receive both a government pension and the mayor's salary of $1,200 per year. But when the judge tried to serve the legal papers to Sehon, Sehon could not be found.

Sehon finally showed up at 2:00 a.m. on the day he was scheduled to take over as mayor. He and a group of friends stormed over to City Hall, which was located then at 5th and G streets. Using a ladder, they climbed to the mayor's second-story office, smashed a window, and claimed possession of the office.

Two days later the judge declared Sehon ineligible for public office and declared the election null and void. Sehon ignored the judge's declaration and went on to conduct the business of mayor of San Diego as if nothing had happened. But he did appeal the ruling.

In October 1905 the State District Court of Appeals reversed the San Diego judge's ruling, in favor of Sehon. After all that turmoil, Sehon went on to carry out an eventful term as mayor.

APRIL 5, 1851

ON THIS DAY IN SAN DIEGO HISTORY Isadora Bandini, daughter of Juan Bandini, a prominent San Diego merchant and land owner, was married to Colonel Cave Johnson Couts, a U.S. Army officer (see NOVEMBER 11). As a wedding gift Isadora received the Guajome Rancho—from her sister Arcadia's husband, Abel Stearns, who had purchased it from the previous owners, two Indians from the San Luis Rey Mission (see JULY 19). The wedding took place in Old Town San Diego and involved a fiesta that lasted for a week.

Couts began construction of their ranch house at the Guajome Rancho two years later. Guajome means "Home of the Frog" or "Frog Pond" in the Indian language, and there was, indeed, a large marsh on the rancho that probably contained frogs. Couts utilized the marsh for the many adobe bricks that had to be made for the construction of the ranch house. But he also needed tile and fired bricks for the roof, floors, and chimneys. These he obtained from the nearby abandoned San Luis Rey Mission in exchange for making a large donation to the Catholic Church. These tiles, bricks, and wooden beams dated back to 1800 and were some of the earliest building materials in San Diego County.

The ranch house had thick adobe walls, a red tiled roof, and 20 rooms in four long wings that surrounded and opened onto a central patio, or garden space, with a fountain in the center. According to the Spanish custom, Cave and Isadora built separate buildings for kitchens, stables, and servants' quarters. There was also an attractive little chapel where religious services were held.

The Guajome Rancho became a friendly overnight stopping place in the early days of travel between San Diego and the north. Travelers were given a warm welcome and shown true hospitality during those Rancho Days of the 1830s to the 1860s—when California was part of Mexico and the people of California were known as Californios.

The Rancho Guajome and its adobe ranch house can be visited today at Guajome Park, located at 2210 North Santa Fe Avenue—east of Oceanside off Highway 76, southeast of the San Luis Rey Mission.

APRIL 6, 1928

ON THIS DAY IN SAN DIEGO HISTORY a committee that had been studying land sites chose a site for the relocation of the San Diego State Teachers College—now known as San Diego State University. Before moving, the college was located on a 17-acre tract in the University Heights area near El Cajon Boulevard and Normal Street, but it had outgrown that location (see MARCH 13).

The new 125 acre site was chosen over other potential sites—in spite of its considerable distance from the center of town—because it was located in the middle of a large undeveloped area, so there would be plenty of room to expand in any direction in the future. It was also a fairly level site, making it easier to build new buildings and athletic fields.

Prior to the selection, a site on East Broadway in Encanto had been chosen because of its nearness to downtown San Diego. But the $400,000 bond election that was required for San Diego to pay the state of California for the purchase of the old University Heights site was defeated by San Diego voters in 1927. It was after this failed election that the search for another site began. Eventually, the 125 acres on Mission Palisades were donated by Alphonso Bell, a real estate developer from Los Angeles, who was beginning to develop 7,580 acres in the area.

In May 1928 the San Diego voters approved by a 5-to-1 vote the bond issue to purchase the University Heights site from the State of California, thereby giving the go-ahead to move the school to its new location. The state provided money for the new buildings, which were built in the Spanish Colonial Revival style that had become popular in the 1920s.

See OCTOBER 7 about the groundbreaking ceremony for the new San Diego State Teachers College.

APRIL 7, 1923

ON THIS DAY IN SAN DIEGO HISTORY the Torrey Pines Lodge was dedicated at Torrey Pines Park thanks to the efforts of San Diego's well-known philanthropist, Miss Ellen Browning Scripps (see OCTOBER 18).

The Torrey Pines Lodge was a Southwestern-style adobe building that was used as a popular roadside restaurant for many years. It is now the visitor center and ranger station for the Torrey Pines Reserve.

Torrey Pines Park was established as a 360-acre San Diego city park in 1899 (see AUGUST 10). Later, in 1959, the park was transferred to the State Department of Parks and Recreation, and the name was changed to Torrey Pines State Reserve (see MAY 7). The beach below the state reserve is also a state beach. Today the combined areas of the beach, lagoon, cliffs, and uplands cover nearly 1,750 acres, which are maintained by the state of California.

Back in the 1920s, the narrow winding road that goes past the little adobe lodge (now the park visitor center) up from Torrey Pines beach was part of the highway between San Diego and Los Angeles. In those days, there was always a bottleneck of backed-up traffic attempting to go up the twisting grade.

In 1929 a new high-speed highway seriously threatened Torrey Pines Park. Construction of the proposed road would have involved blasting away 1,700 feet of sea cliff to create a more gradual grade from the beach to the top of the mesa. One scenic canyon was to be filled in and another canyon was to have a bridge built over it. Any remaining fill dirt from the blasting was to be dumped onto the public beach. As you can imagine, there was much opposition to these plans—especially by the League to Save Torrey Pines Park, who recommended that the new road should go to the east via Sorrento Valley, bypassing the park completely.

In 1930 a compromise was made, and a grade was cut through the eastern part of the park's uplands instead of along the cliffs. That road became Highway 101. Forty years later Interstate 5 was built, which followed the more-inland eastern route that the League to Save Torrey Pines Park had originally recommended. The old Highway 101 is now North Torrey Pines Road along that stretch—the "coastal" route between La Jolla and Del Mar, which some people today prefer to drive instead of Interstate 5.

APRIL 8, 1920

ON THIS DAY IN SAN DIEGO HISTORY The *San Diego Union* newspaper reported on the visit of the prince of Wales, calling it a "gala day in San Diego." The prince of Wales was the oldest son of the king of England and was supposed to become the next king. So H.R.H. (His Royal Highness) Edward, the prince of Wales, was a well-known worldwide celebrity. The United States has always had a special interest in the English royalty.

On the day that he arrived in San Diego Harbor on his private ship—the English battleship *Renoun*—U.S. Navy vessels fired guns and cannons into the air. A large crowd, including the mayor of San Diego, the governor of California, and other dignitaries, waited to welcome him at the foot of Broadway—where the large cruise ships dock today. This was Edward's first time to visit anywhere on the west coast of the United States. He was on his way to visit Australia, and after his ship went through the Panama Canal he decided upon San Diego as a port of call.

The prince was escorted around San Diego in an open car for a tour of the city. He was taken to Balboa Park where 25,000 people were waiting to greet him at the city stadium—later known as Balboa Stadium.

At the Hotel Del Coronado the mayor hosted a formal dinner and ball for the prince. While there, the prince met an American woman, Wallis Simpson—an event that would eventually change history. In 1936, just months after being crowned king of England, Edward proposed marriage to Simpson. However, because Simpson had been divorced, Edward could not marry her and remain king. So Edward abdicated the throne in order to marry, as he put it, "the woman I love."

APRIL 9, 1968

ON THIS DAY IN SAN DIEGO HISTORY the Borrego Mountain earthquake—measuring 6.5 on the Richter scale—rocked 31 miles of the Coyote Creek fault in the Anza-Borrego Desert State Park near the towns of Borrego Springs and Ocotillo Wells.

The Coyote Creek fault is a part of the San Jacinto fault zone, which in recent times has been more active than the southernmost end of the more famous San Andreas fault—which lies far east of San Diego on the eastern side of the Salton Sea in Imperial County.

The earthquake shook down rocks and boulders in Split Mountain Gorge, rolling one giant boulder right up to the edge of a car that was exploring there. Anza-Borrego State Park rangers had to rescue people and cars at Split Mountain and at other locations in the park. At Font's Point, a popular lookout spot, six feet of rock holding up the tip of the point collapsed and fell to the canyon below.

A 6.5 magnitude earthquake is fairly strong. Fortunately, the Anza-Borrego Desert is not a heavily-populated or built-up area. In 1987 two earthquakes occurred on two successive days along the San Jacinto fault zone, measuring 6.2 and 6.6 in magnitude (see NOVEMBER 23).

The Long Beach earthquake of 1933, which did damage in the Long Beach and Inglewood areas of the southern Los Angeles region, had a magnitude of 6.3. The famous San Francisco earthquake of 1906 that did so much damage had a magnitude of 8.3. The strongest earthquake ever recorded in North America was the Alaska earthquake in 1964—a 9.2 magnitude quake—nearly 100 times stronger than the San Francisco earthquake! (Each one-point increase on the Richter scale is 100 times stronger.)

Although there are many small faults throughout the city of San Diego, the city does not sit directly on any of the larger or more active fault zones, like the San Andreas, San Jacinto, or Elsinore fault zones. These zone all lie considerably east or north of San Diego and most of its immediate suburbs.

APRIL 10, 1852

ON THIS DAY IN SAN DIEGO HISTORY the first annual regatta of the Pacific Pioneer Yacht Club was held at San Diego Bay. The club was started only two weeks before (see MARCH 27).

The *San Diego Herald* newspaper reported on the weather on the day of the race:

> The morning was ushered in by dense fogs and small streaks of Old Sol, which seemed as if a desperate strife was going on between them for the unrestrained rule of the skies—at one moment the bright rays of the sun appeared to shine a delightful array, and then thick mists closed in…

The newspaper went on to describe the people who came to watch the regatta:

> [I]t seemed to us as though the whole country was aroused…for such a collection of natives has never been witnessed in our city. The roads [from] the neighboring inland villages were crowded with carriages of all descriptions…whilst here and there could be seen the native California Ranchero, in full costume, dashing along in all the pride of horsemanship, and riding as no other people in the world can ride. By 10 o'clock the city was alive with ladies and gentlemen anxious to participate in the amusements of the day.

People were also on boats in the bay to observe the regatta. As the *San Diego Herald* described it:

> The steamer *Sea Bird*, her decks crowded with guests and many a dashing craft of smaller size careening over the surface of the bay in gala dress, furnished ample evidence that our citizens were determined to make this day worthy of the remembrance of all who take an interest in the manly sport of yachting, for which our noble harbor is so admirably adapted.

The race was won by the *Lavinia*. Some of the other boats in the race were named the *Fanny*, the *Plutus*, the *Josephine*, the *General Hitchcock*, and the *Major Allen*. The *Fanny* was ahead for most of the race, but when the *Lavinia* surged ahead at the end, the newspaper reported: "Persons who had bet on the *Fanny* were observed to turn pale and one poor hombre who had put up every cent he was worth in the world, on her, actually fainted and was carried off the wharf."

APRIL 11, 1871

ON THIS DAY IN SAN DIEGO HISTORY the Jamacha Rancho land grant was confirmed by the U.S. Land Commission to Doña Apolinaria Lorenzana, who had received it originally in 1840 as a Mexican land grant. The rancho was located east of the National Rancho along 8 miles of the Sweetwater River and contained 8,881 acres. The Jamacha Rancho was originally an Indian *rancheria*. (Jamacha is an Indian word meaning "wild squash vine or gourd.")

The southwestern section of the rancho is now covered by Sweetwater Lake, an important source of water for the communities of National City and Chula Vista and for the agricultural lands in that area.

On the lands of the Jamacha Rancho near the foot of San Miguel Mountain are some mineral springs whose waters were said to have curative powers. The waters were called "Isham's California Waters of Life," the "Original California Waters," and "Minwell." They were supposed to prevent or cure a wide variety of diseases or to grow beautiful thick hair on bald heads. It is said that over a million dollars was once offered to buy the springs!

The springs were first recognized in 1887 when the steamship *Challenger* docked in San Diego Harbor with most of the crew suffering from scurvy. A local San Diego doctor, Dr. P.C. Remondino, recommended a healthful outdoor life and drinking plenty of fresh spring water. The captain of the ship, Captain Charles Fitzallen, left the ship in the hands of his second officer, became a sheepherder at the Jamacha Rancho, and quickly recovered—prompting an analysis of the spring water. Recognizing the potential, a traveling salesman, Alfred Huntington Isham, acquired the rights to sell the water. He bottled it and hauled it to the railroad, where it was shipped to other parts of the United States. Eventually, it was sold in Europe and other parts of the world.

Ultimately, the business failed in the wake of a national economic depression, as well as by a derogatory article, "The Great American Fraud," published in *Collier's Weekly*. Nevertheless, belief in the curative powers of the spring water from the Jamacha Rancho continued for a long time afterward.

APRIL 12, 1914

ON THIS DAY IN SAN DIEGO HISTORY the first car drove across the just-completed Cabrillo Bridge. In the car were the mayor of San Diego (Charles F. O'Neall), the secretary of the Navy (C. Aubrey Davidson), and the assistant secretary of the Navy (Franklin D. Roosevelt—who was later to become President of the United States in 1932).

The bridge was designed by Frank P. Allen Jr. as an extension of Laurel Street to provide access from the west to Balboa Park and the Panama-California Exposition, which was to open on January 1, 1915 (see JANUARY 1). The bridge spanned Cabrillo Canyon, where Highway 163—the Cabrillo Freeway—now runs. Another architect, Bertram Goodhue, had designed a bridge with three gigantic arches similar to the Alcantara Bridge in Toledo, Spain. But the exposition directors thought Goodhue's bridge would be too expensive, so they chose instead Allen's Roman-aqueduct-style bridge with seven arches.

The bridge took one year and seven months to build—with work starting in September 1912 and completed on this day in history—April 12, 1914. The bridge was 40 feet wide, 450 feet long, and 120 feet high at its highest point. It was supported by steel T-frames and reinforced concrete piers. In all, 7,700 cubic yards of concrete and 450 tons of steel were used, significantly contributing to the bridge's final cost of $225,155—$75,155 over Allen's original estimate.

The Cabrillo Bridge, with ivy gracefully draping its tall pillars, is still today one of San Diego's most artistic structures.

April 13, 1876

ON THIS DAY IN SAN DIEGO HISTORY a patent was issued by the United States Land Commission to Francisco María Alvarado for the 8,486-acre Los Peñasquitos Rancho. Alvarado had previously inherited the rancho in 1839 upon the death of the original owner, Captain Francisco María Ruiz (see MARCH 15). At that time San Diego and California were a part of Mexico. But after the Mexican-American War of 1846–48, California was a part of the United States, and the former Mexican land grants had to be renegotiated and reapplied for through the U.S. Land Commission (see FEBRUARY 2).

Francisco María Alvarado was active in the political affairs of San Diego, both before and after the Mexican-American War. He was city treasurer in 1840 and 1841 and served as justice of the peace in 1845. His daughter, Tomassa, married Captain George A. Johnson, a native of New York who came to San Diego in 1850. After marrying Alvarado's daughter, Johnson engaged in large-scale cattle raising and eventually took over the Los Peñasquitos Rancho. They renovated and enlarged the adobe house that was located in the bottom of the canyon, and they raised cattle and race horses. In 1863 Johnson also represented San Diego in the California State Legislature. A later owner of the rancho, Jacob Shell Taylor, who founded the city of Del Mar, turned the old adobe house into a hotel and resort.

On March 4, 1881 the *San Diego Union* newspaper announced the sale of Los Peñasquitos Rancho to A.N. Lancaster for $35,000. Today the large residential development of Rancho Peñasquitos, which began in the 1970s, is worth considerably more than the $35,000 it sold for in 1881.

Between 1910 and 1962 the old rancho lands were mainly used for cattle raising. In 1974 the county and city of San Diego took over 1,800 acres for the Peñasquitos Canyon Preserve that now contains 3,500 acres on Black Mountain Road.

APRIL 14, 1908

ON THIS DAY IN SAN DIEGO HISTORY the U.S. Navy's Great White Fleet arrived in San Diego. The fleet consisted of 16 battleships, 7 destroyers, and 4 auxiliary ships. It stayed four days, and 16,000 sailors visited the city while it was here.

When San Diego's city leaders learned about the world tour of the Navy's Great White Fleet, the chamber of commerce went to great lengths to get the fleet to stop over. A fleet welcoming committee was created that raised $20,000 in donations to help in the effort to attract it.

Meanwhile in Los Angeles, the civic leaders there thought that Los Angeles should be the first port of call for the Great White Fleet. When the San Diego committee heard about Los Angeles' efforts, they chartered a fishing boat to carry the San Diego mayor and a group of chamber of commerce directors to intercept the fleet 600 miles south of San Diego off the coast of Mexico. The San Diegans boarded one of the battleships and tried to convince the admirals of the benefits of stopping in San Diego first. The admirals agreed, and the committee was assured that the fleet would come to San Diego first, but the fleet commander pointed out that the San Diego Harbor was too shallow, too narrow, and too dangerous for such large ships. When the fleet did finally arrive in San Diego, it had to anchor outside the bay off Coronado. The city leaders then took the opportunity to lobby the admirals and Navy officials for a dredging project to deepen San Diego Harbor.

When the Great White Fleet arrived, over 75,000 people were there to greet the nearly two-mile procession. This was especially impressive in view of the fact that the city population at the time was less than 40,000. The entire county of San Diego had a population of less than 60,000. Many distinguished national guests as well as the governor of California came to the welcoming ceremony on Coronado Island. The *San Diego Union* newspaper reported: "Cheering Thousands Greet the Greatest Naval Parade on Record... [T]he enthusiasm was so great that the very hillsides echoed and reechoed with the mighty sounds of cheering."

APRIL 15, 1847

ON THIS DAY IN SAN DIEGO HISTORY General Andrés Pico, commander of the Californio troops in the Mexican-American War, wrote these comments about the Battle of San Pasqual, which had taken place in San Diego four months earlier: "[T]he morale of the people had fallen, due to the lack of resources… [T]ogether with my compatriots we made the last efforts, not withstanding the extreme lack of powder, arms, men, and all kinds of supplies."

The Californios (Mexican Californians), under Pico, fought against the United States Army, led by General Stephen Kearny, at the Battle of San Pasqual (see DECEMBER 6). General Pico knew that his Californios could not fight the war in a traditional way, because of a lack of military training, firearms, and supplies. And in fact they did mostly use guerilla tactics. But in spite of their many shortcomings as a military force, the Californios were willing to risk their lives to defend their homeland against the American attacks.

During the Mexican-American War, the California Indians accounted for the majority of the population in southern California, and they were mostly neutral. They did not have a strong loyalty to the Mexican government, because of having lost most of the mission lands and because of injustices done to them by the Californios. To read about how a San Pasqual Indian leader contributed to the Battle of San Pasqual, see JANUARY 7.

APRIL 16, 1888

ON THIS DAY IN SAN DIEGO HISTORY the Ocean Beach Railroad opened. But, alas, it was to be short-lived due to the economic decline of the late 1880s, which also affected the land boom that had been going on in southern California.

William H. Carlson was the owner of the Ocean Beach Railroad and also owner of the Cliff House, a resort hotel in Ocean Beach. He and his partner, Frank J. Higgins, had developed Ocean Beach in 1887 and were now promoting that development. They changed the name from Mussel Beach (named because of the mussel collecting done there for Sunday picnics) to Ocean Beach—and called it the greatest seaside resort in southern California. Carlson would later serve as mayor of San Diego from 1893 to 1896.

To get to Ocean Beach, passengers could take the ferry from San Diego to Roseville on Point Loma and then ride the train to the Cliff House. But when Carlson failed to pay a bill he owed to the Pacific Coast Steam Company, the company seized the rails, and that was the end of the Ocean Beach Railroad. It lasted only three months. The Cliff House Resort Hotel burned down six years later in 1894.

Nevertheless, Ocean Beach continued to thrive, if sporadically. In 1915 a railway company built a wooden bridge over Mission Bay connecting Ocean Beach to Mission Beach. The bridge was 1,500 feet long and 50 feet wide. It lasted a long time and became a popular place from which to fish, until it was torn down in 1951.

Ocean Beach had an amusement park called Wonderland between 1913 and 1916. It claimed to have the largest roller coaster on the West Coast. It also had a dance pavilion, roller skating rink, a large fun zone, and a children's playground. It was destroyed in 1916 by high tides.

Ocean Beach has had several other names in the past. Besides Mussel Beach, it has been known as Mussel Beds, Médanos (Spanish for "Sand Dunes"), Palmer's Place, Palmer's Ranch, and Palmiro's—the last three named for the now forgotten Mr. Palmer.

APRIL 17, 1911

ON THIS DAY IN SAN DIEGO HISTORY the California China Products Company was formed in National City to manufacture high quality porcelain. It would also manufacture earthenware and ceramic tile. It was the first porcelain factory west of Columbus, Ohio and was the only porcelain factory in the United States to use clays from its own deposits.

In 1906 John H. McKnight was a prospecting mineralogist who discovered a seam of porcelain-grade kaolin on the western side of El Cajon Mountain. McKnight took the clay to his laboratory in Los Angeles and spent four years testing and developing it into fine porcelain products. Among other things, he produced a translucent eggshell porcelain. He took on two partners, Walter and Charles B. Nordhoff, and opened the California China Products Company on this date in 1911. They sold their porcelain ware under the brand name of Kaospar—a contraction of kaolin and feldspar.

The company used clay deposits from other areas of San Diego and from Baja California for their earthenware bowls and ceramic tiles. They built a factory on a five-acre site in National City, located two blocks east of San Diego Bay and fronting on 12th Street. The first tile order for the California China Products Company was to provide over 10,000 brightly-colored Spanish-Moorish ceramic tiles for the buildings that were being constructed in Balboa Park for the Panama-California Exposition, which would open in 1915 (see JANUARY 1 and SEPTEMBER 12). You can see those tiles today on the California Building and Tower in Balboa Park, now occupied by the Museum of Man.

The second tile order was for the Santa Fe Railroad Depot built in 1914 and located in downtown San Diego at Broadway and Pacific Coast Highway. The tiles were used in the towers of the attractive Spanish Colonial Revival–style building as well as in the passenger waiting areas.

The California China Products Company closed down in 1917 due to problems with supply and labor, not lasting long enough to reap the benefits of tile's later popularity in the 1920s and afterward. However, the company had a great influence on subsequent tile makers in California.

APRIL 18, 1871

ON THIS DAY IN SAN DIEGO HISTORY a United States government patent to the 8,825-acre San Dieguito Rancho was awarded to the heirs of Juan María Osuna, who had occupied it since 1836. It is now known as Rancho Santa Fe—located about 20 miles north of San Diego and about three miles inland from Solana Beach.

San Dieguito is Spanish for "James the Lesser" and was probably named for St. James of La Marca, Ancona, Italy—a Franciscan monk who died in 1476.

As early as 1833 Governor Figueroa, governor of Mexican California, established an Indian pueblo at San Dieguito. These Indians were from the San Diego Mission and consisted of about 15 families. Six years later, in 1839, the Indians complained that Juan María Osuna had taken the best part of their land, fenced it off for growing grain, and left them with only the salt marsh land. Nevertheless, Osuna was given a provisional Mexican land grant to the rancho in 1841, which was finalized in 1845. This is another case of the Indians being defrauded from possession of their lands after the secularization of the missions (see SEPTEMBER 30).

Osuna was important politically in San Diego. He was the first *alcalde* (Spanish for "mayor") when the pueblo of San Diego was established in December 1834, and in 1839 he was justice of the peace. From 1840 to 1843 he was *majordomo* (Spanish for "manager") and administrator of the San Diego Mission. He was in a position of influence that enabled him to benefit from the land grants that were being awarded in the 1830s and 1840s.

Long after Juan María Osuna's death and after his heirs inherited the rancho, the San Dieguito Rancho was sold to the Santa Fe Railroad in 1906 for $100,000, and they changed the name to Rancho Santa Fe. They planted large numbers of eucalyptus trees on the property to use for railroad ties, but, unfortunately, the eucalyptus wood was not useful to the railroad since it would not hold the spikes necessary for attaching the rails. Meanwhile, the eucalyptus trees have grown and flourished, adding to the beauty of the upscale residential community that is in Rancho Santa Fe today.

APRIL 19, 1936

ON THIS DAY IN SAN DIEGO HISTORY the Crystal Pier in Pacific Beach was reopened after being rebuilt, lengthened by 500 feet, and widened to make room for cottages known as the Crystal Cottages.

Crystal Pier was first built ten years before, in 1926, and had a ballroom at its end that opened in 1927. The ballroom was constructed of stucco and wood and had walls covered with murals. It had a cork-lined dance floor, colored lights, and a glittering crystal ball hanging from the ceiling. The original pier had concessions all along its length out to the ballroom. Unfortunately, the ballroom only lasted three months because the pilings weakened due to an infestation of marine borers.

In the late 1920s when the Crystal Pier was first built, Pacific Beach was mostly scattered farms and pastures. Garnet Street was a dirt road that led to the pier. Little had changed since the subdivision's development had started in 1887, during the great land boom of the 1880s. A new educational institution, the San Diego College of Letters, had opened in 1888 at Garnet and Lamont with a faculty of 14, but it never quite succeeded, closing down at the end of the land boom. In 1891 its two buildings were sold, later becoming the Hotel Balboa. Like its college, the Pacific Beach development in the 1880s never quite got off the ground, and the area for a time became a center for lemon groves.

Pacific Beach's Crystal Pier still stands today, at the foot of a much more developed Garnet Street. It is the only pier on the West Coast that provides lodging over the ocean—at the Crystal Pier Hotel and Cottages.

April 20, 1822

ON THIS DAY IN SAN DIEGO HISTORY the Mexican flag was raised over the presidio (military fort) in San Diego, replacing the Spanish flag that had flown there before. Revolutionary troops in Mexico had overthrown the Spanish in September 1821 and, when the news reached San Diego on this day—April 20, 1822—San Diego realized that it no longer belonged to Spain.

Celebrations were held as San Diego, as well as the rest of California, recognized the end of the war for Mexican independence from Spain and pledged allegiance to Mexico. The only sadness came from the soldiers who had to cut off their long braids, symbols of the old Spanish regime.

The new Mexican government took control of all the mission lands and of local lands held by the Indians. The former commander of the presidio, Captain Francisco María Ruiz, led the development of San Diego to the flatlands west of Presidio Hill, helping to develop the town of San Diego—now known as Old Town.

Before this, the families of the soldiers lived at the presidio, on the hill above where Old Town would later develop. It would be nearly 50 years before Alonzo Horton would start the development called Horton's Addition, or New San Diego—today's downtown San Diego (see AUGUST 12).

After the Mexican independence from Spain, a new era was to begin in California—the Rancho Days—when large land grants were made to the Mexican California citizens, also known as Californios. There would be a total of 30 ranchos in what is now San Diego County (see SEPTEMBER 30).

APRIL 21, 1986

ON THIS DAY IN SAN DIEGO HISTORY the Chinese Mission Building received a low rating in a report authorized by the Center City Development Corporation (CCDC) to determine the historic significance of certain buildings in the Gaslamp area of San Diego. The report was an attempt to evaluate and rate buildings that would be important to retain in the redevelopment of the area.

The report, produced by Ray Brandes, a history professor at the University of San Diego and an authority on San Diego history, found few buildings worth saving and gave only faint support for the idea of a Chinese or Asian historic district. The Brandes report stated:

> The [Chinese] Mission was closed some years ago and when no longer used was sold, and rehabbed. The current condition is not good; it does not fit within that architectural category of an Oriental structure, and the building is not in proximity to the Chinese District.

The Chinese community and historic preservation groups in San Diego protested the Brandes report, and many letters were sent to the CCDC. The CCDC called a meeting to receive public input on the Brandes report. At least 50 Chinese Americans attended the meeting to voice their disagreement with the assessment of the buildings and the area's potential as a historical district (see JUNE 16).

The Chinese American citizens of San Diego continued to write letters and submitted a petition to the CCDC with 524 signatures requesting that the city preserve and restore the Chinese Mission and other significant buildings.

Eventually, in 1987, the city council did approve a Chinese/Asian Thematic Historic District in the Gaslamp area, and the Chinese Mission was finally designated a historic building in 1988 (see MARCH 22). The building was moved to its present location at 3rd and J streets. It now houses the Chinese Historical Museum (see AUGUST 18).

APRIL 22, 1940

ON THIS DAY IN SAN DIEGO HISTORY people in San Diego and southern California were reading an article in the April issue of the *Desert Magazine* called "Desert Diary" written by Marshal South, in which he describes springtime at his retreat in San Diego County's Anza-Borrego Desert.

This was the third article by Marshal South in the magazine—to be followed by a long series of articles describing the South family's "experiment in primitive living," as described by Sunbelt Publications' 2005 book edited by Diana Lindsay, *Marshal South and the Ghost Mountain Chronicles: An Experiment in Primitive Living.*

The South family lived on a remote desert hilltop called Ghost Mountain in what is now the Anza-Borrego Desert State Park. They called their home Yaquitepec—from Yaqui, a freedom-loving Sonoran Indian tribe, and *tepec*, the Aztec word for "hill."

South wrote this in the April 1940 *Desert Magazine*:

> Our personal Herald of spring has already made his call at Yaquitepec... [O]ur announcer is a Western Robin. He comes every year. We like to think that it is the same bird—and probably it is, for we have never seen more than the one each year. Oddly he seems out of place here in the desert among the frowning rocks and the cholla... The earliest of the Spring flowers are out... The roadrunner, who is one of the cheery company of feathered and furred friends who share Ghost Mountain with us, sat out on a big boulder the other day and for a long time voiced his opinions of things in general. A cheerful rascal...

He ended his article with a bit of his personal philosophy: "Somewhere, away off in a world that calls itself 'civilized,' cannon foundries are roaring and men who preach 'brotherhood' are dropping bombs upon the homes of little children. Here, in the 'savage wilderness' of the 'merciless desert' there is peace."

Marshal South went on to write his articles for the *Desert Magazine* for a total of eight years—from 1940 until his death in 1948.

The editor of the *Desert Magazine*, Randall Henderson, wrote this about Marshal South: "You may not agree with Marshal's philosophy of life in every detail—but you must respect them as honest opinions from a man who lives what he believes. This world would be a dull place if we all had the same ideas."

See also FEBRUARY 6.

APRIL 23, 1949

ON THIS DAY IN SAN DIEGO HISTORY the last streetcar of the San Diego Streetcar Company (also called the Electric Railway or Trolley) was retired from service. This was an early trolley system in San Diego that started in 1886 with a horse-drawn trolley on Broadway and 5th Avenue in downtown San Diego.

In 1892 when John Spreckels arrived in San Diego, he bought the streetcar company and eventually expanded it to Coronado, Kensington, South Bay, and La Jolla. The electric trolley was extended from San Diego to La Jolla in 1924 and ran for 16 years until it closed down in 1940 (see SEPTEMBER 15).

The demise of the San Diego Electric Railway was precipitated by the popularity of the automobile and by expansion of the bus lines, which started in 1922 between National City and Chula Vista. People either preferred to drive their own cars or to use the bus lines, which were more flexible than trolley lines limited to traveling on tracks. San Diego was the first major city in California to eliminate streetcars.

The first bus lines in San Diego were run by Western Transit Company, a privately owned company that bought John Spreckels' San Diego Electric Railway for $5.5 million in 1948 and converted it to a bus transportation company. But by 1960 the Western Transit Company was having trouble making a profit. In 1966 the voters of San Diego voted to approve the takeover of the bus company by the city for a price of $2 million, and it became the San Diego Transit.

The early San Diego Electric Railway had been closed down for over 30 years before the present-day trolley system started up with the Tijuana Trolley in 1980. That trolley went from downtown San Diego to San Ysidro, just across the border from Tijuana, making 11 stops along the way. Later, the new trolley system was expanded to other areas of San Diego by the Metropolitan Transit System (MTS). So today when the freeways and streets are clogged with extra-heavy automobile traffic, the trolley system has returned to became an alternative means of transportation in ever-growing and ever-changing San Diego.

APRIL 24, 1855

ON THIS DAY IN SAN DIEGO HISTORY the district court confirmed the land grant of Rancho Santa Margarita y Las Flores to the brothers Pío and Andrés Pico. The original grant, known as Rancho San Onofre y Santa Margarita, consisted of 89,742 acres and was granted to the brothers in 1841 by Mexican California Governor Juan Bautista Alvarado. The rancho is in the northwestern corner of San Diego County where Camp Pendleton is presently located.

The rancho was expanded in 1844 when the Picos obtained the Las Flores property from the Indians, making the rancho the largest in the county at 133,441 acres.

The Pico Brothers were successful at running the rancho. When the California government changed from Mexican to American in 1848, it is estimated that the rancho had 10,000 cattle, 2,000 horses, and 15,000 sheep.

In 1864 the Picos transferred ownership of the rancho to their brother-in-law, Juan Forster of San Juan Capistrano, in exchange for paying off Pío's gambling debts. As the last governor of Mexican California in 1845–46, Pico had also granted the Rancho de la Nación (National Ranch) to Forster (see DECEMBER 11).

Later, in 1873 Pío Pico sued his brother-in-law for title to the Rancho Santa Margarita y Las Flores, claiming fraud by him in obtaining it. The jury ruled against Pico. He died in 1894 at the age of 93, penniless from gambling debts.

For more about the Pico brothers, see AUGUST 22.

APRIL 25, 1894

ON THIS DAY IN SAN DIEGO HISTORY the *San Diego Union* newspaper reported: "Nearly two miles of rails have been laid for the La Jolla extension of the Pacific Beach railroad. Trains may run to La Jolla by May 10."

People liked to go to La Jolla on weekends to picnic and enjoy the beaches. But one of the greatest hindrances to La Jolla's development, in addition to the scarcity of drinking water, was the lack of transportation. Remember, there were no automobiles in the 1890s, so the extension of the San Diego, Old Town & Pacific Beach Railway to La Jolla was welcomed by many people.

Work on what would later be called the San Diego, Pacific Beach & La Jolla Railway started on March 14, 1894. Ten carloads of steel were received from Belleville, Illinois on April 12, and two weeks later on this date—April 25, 1894—two miles of tracks had been laid.

By May 13 the extension from Pacific Beach to La Jolla was completed, and the first train from San Diego to La Jolla—sometimes called the Abalone Express—left at 10:30 on that Sunday morning. (See MAY 15 to learn about the formal opening and celebration held in La Jolla for the new extension.) In the days to follow, the railway hosted many interesting events to entice people to take the train, including picnics, games, races, sports events, and the building of a dance pavilion.

The railroad to La Jolla survived for 25 years—until 1919 when it closed down and the tracks were torn out because gasoline cars were becoming more popular than trains (see NOVEMBER 17).

APRIL 26, 1870

ON THIS DAY IN SAN DIEGO HISTORY one of the most prominent architects in San Diego, Irving Gill, was born in Tully, New York. He was the son of a farmer, but he started studying architecture at the age of 19 in Syracuse. One year later he moved to Chicago to work for an architectural firm there. It was San Diego's luck that Gill moved here in 1893 for the good climate to cure a health condition. He recovered quickly and stayed.

In Chicago Gill had worked for the firm of Adler & Sullivan, who also employed the later-to-become-famous architect, Frank Lloyd Wright. Louis Sullivan promoted the abandonment of European Revival styles in favor of developing an American style of architecture, and Gill followed this concept also. Gill's architectural style has been called Early Modernist.

Irving Gill formed a partnership in 1896 with architect William Sterling Hebbard. Together they designed many residential and nonresidential buildings in San Diego. One of their most important commercial designs won a design competition in 1898 for a $100,000 building for the San Diego State Normal School (see MARCH 13).

The Hebbard & Gill plans were selected over seven other architectural firms from San Diego, Los Angeles, and Texas. The State Normal School's attractive Beaux Arts–style building in the University Heights area near El Cajon Boulevard and Normal Street was one of the largest and most impressive buildings in the area and brought a great deal of attention to the architects. The San Diego Board of Education and San Diego Unified School District central offices now occupy the site of the old Normal School, but the impressive original Beaux Arts–style main building no longer exists.

One of Gill & Hebbard's most famous designs was the Marston House, completed in 1905 for George Marston, a prominent San Diego businessman (see OCTOBER 22 and DECEMBER 13). The Marston House, located at the north end of Balboa Park at 7th Avenue and Upas Street, is now a museum operated by the San Diego Historical Society.

For more information on buildings in the San Diego area designed by Irving Gill, see AUGUST 29.

April 27, 1874

On this day in san diego history Pedro José Panto, the Indian leader of the San Pascual Indian Pueblo died. The Indians had been living in the San Pasqual Valley for thousands of years before white men came to California. Panto became an important influence in helping the Indians keep the lands that had been given to them.

In 1845 a Mexican citizen of San Diego petitioned Pío Pico, the governor of California, to grant him the lands in the San Pasqual Valley, claiming that the Indians there were "disreputable and had allowed the pueblo to go into decay." The governor sent someone to investigate, and the findings were reported to the governor: "This settlement comprises 61 Christian souls, and 44 unconverted Indians, with dwellings after their manner, huts of tule forming a kind of irregular Plazuela [small square]..."

The investigator went on to describe the good condition of the lands, which were being used for agriculture and grazing of livestock. He also noted the goodwill that existed between their leader, Panto, and his Californio neighbors, which included cooperative stock-raising agreements (see January 11).

Panto met with U.S. Army Captain H.S. Burton in 1856 about the white squatters on the San Pasqual pueblo land. Captain Burton reported:

> Panto is urgent in his wishes for protection against some five or six squatters, who are taking possession of the best lands granted to his people. It appears to me, that this is a very just and proper occasion for the personal interference of the superintendent of Indian Affairs. The Indians of San Pascual are friendly and are anxious to remain so...

After Panto's death, the Indians of San Pasqual were forced off their land by a deputy sheriff from San Diego in 1878 and scattered to the hills or to other Indian *rancherias* such as Mesa Grande (see August 27).

The obituary for Pedro José Panto reads as follows: "On Monday last, at San Pascual, Panto, the venerable chief of that village, was thrown from a horse and died instantly. The old settlers of southern California will remember him for his polite manners and good character."

See also January 7.

APRIL 28, 1921

ON THIS DAY IN SAN DIEGO HISTORY Miss Eliza Virginia Scripps died in London at the age of 68. "Miss Virginia" or "Miss Jenny," as she was known around La Jolla, came to La Jolla in 1901 at the age of 49 to live with her half-sister, Ellen Browning Scripps (see OCTOBER 18).

Miss Virginia was known as a character around La Jolla, in contrast to her more sedate and reserved half-sister, Ellen. In his book *La Jolla Year by Year*, Howard S.F. Randolph describes her this way:

> Virginia was one of those inexplicable people who live from time to time, constituting a law unto themselves—treasured in memory by many who knew her personally for her many kindnesses and open-hearted generosity… But she is today remembered chiefly for her eccentricities. She had the interest of the community much at heart, but her expression of this love was often shown in a strange manner. She loved neatness and order, and woe betide the luckless person who tore up a letter on leaving the post office scattering the fragments to the wind. If Virginia saw it she would compel the criminal to pick up all the pieces and deposit them in a proper container… [S]he had no hesitancy in sweeping up a gutter or in sweeping out a grocery store if she thought it necessary. And she delighted to mow the church lawn.

Eliza Virginia Scripps, like her half-sister, also donated to the welfare of her beloved La Jolla in many ways (see OCTOBER 5). But Miss Virginia's eccentricities continue to live on. There is the story told in the book *La Jolla, A Celebration of Its Past* by Patricia Daly-Lipe and Barbara Dawson, published by Sunbelt Publications, about a tea being held at The Bishops School:

> One time a Bishop's student accidentally spilled hot tea on Miss Jenny's purple satin dress. The terrified student braced herself for the inevitable outburst. But it did not happen. Instead, Miss Jenny offered profuse assurances not to worry, the dress was old and only needed to be hung to dry. Then to the shock of all ladies present in the parlor, Miss Jenny removed her gown and proceeded to sip her tea wearing undergarments only.

In spite of her eccentricities, Miss Eliza Virginia Scripps left a significant mark on La Jolla with her many generous gifts to the community that she loved.

APRIL 29, 1769

ON THIS DAY IN SAN DIEGO HISTORY the Spanish ship *San Carlos* arrived in San Diego Harbor, having left La Paz, Baja California over three months earlier. The *San Carlos* was one of three ships sailing from Mexico carrying supplies to San Diego in conjunction with two overland expeditions traveling up the Baja California peninsula with the purpose of founding a mission at San Diego. Father Junípero Serra was the priest on one of the overland expeditions.

The first of the three ships, the *San Antonio*, arrived in San Diego nearly three weeks before the *San Carlos*—even though it had left La Paz a month and a half later. The *San Carlos* had lost its way, run into bad weather, and ended up taking 110 days for the trip—compared to only 59 days for the *San Antonio*.

Now both ships were anchored in San Diego Harbor, waiting for the arrival of the third ship and the overland expeditions. The third ship, the *San José*, never arrived, having apparently been lost at sea. The crew of the *San Carlos* and the *San Antonio* were suffering from scurvy, a disease caused by a lack of fresh fruit and vegetables containing vitamin C. Two of the crew had died before reaching San Diego, and more died after reaching the harbor. The sick men were taken ashore and a search was made for green plants to eat to combat the scurvy, but it was too late for many of them.

The first overland expedition, led by Captain Don Fernando de Rivera and Father Juan Crespí, arrived in San Diego two weeks later in mid-May (see MARCH 29). They were happy to see the two ships anchored in San Diego Bay. According to Father Crespí's diary:

> As soon as our people saw the harbor and the camp not far away, they fired off a salvo (a round of gunshots) in salute, and the camp and ships at once answered back with their own armaments…a day of great merriment and rejoicing for everyone; though to our sorrow we found the camp turned into a hospital, with nearly all of the soldiers and sailors…perishing from scurvy…

The second expedition, led by Captain Gaspar de Portolá and Father Junípero Serra, arrived on July 1, 1769. Two weeks later, on July 16, 1769, Father Serra blessed a wooden cross that was raised on Presidio Hill and officially founded the Misión San Diego de Alcalá.

APRIL 30, 1887

ON THIS DAY IN SAN DIEGO HISTORY a great land auction was held in La Jolla. The owners of La Jolla Park, Frank T. Botsford, and George W. Heald, hired the Pacific Coast Land Bureau to survey the 300 acres, to create roads and streets, to draw up a map of the subdivided lots, and to conduct an auction for lot sales.

There were great festivities on the day of the auction. Lunch was served outdoors across from what is now Scripps Park to prospective buyers. As described by Patricia Schaelchlin in her book, *La Jolla: The Story of a Community, 1887–1987*:

> Three hundred people, each paying $1.00, came in "almost every wagon, and omnibus and carriage that could be raked up in the whole county"… At least six salesmen were present to take orders. Most of the buyers were real estate dealers from San Diego and Los Angeles and "almost everyone bought a lot."

The president of the Pacific Coast Land Bureau spoke from an auctioneer's stand with the Pacific Ocean gleaming in the background. Many interesting promises were made in his speech:

> We have developed a magnificent supply of spring water, and the reservoir for the storage is in full view on the hill back of us. Water mains are on all avenues, and every lot has water piped to it. The railroad is only one and a half miles from us… Telephone connection with the city [of San Diego] is being completed.

The "magnificent supply of spring water" turned out to be not so plentiful. The railroad, instead of being one and a half miles away, was actually four miles away, and the telephone service did not become available until some 12 years later—in 1899! (See OCTOBER 11.) Nevertheless, the auction was a great success. Lots were 25 feet by 140 feet and sold for between $125 (south of Pearl Street) and $3,000 (near the cove)—for a total of $61,835 in sales that day, and later sales of an additional $65,000. The owners had paid only $2,200 for the land the year before (see JANUARY 18).

MAY 1, 1769

ON THIS DAY IN SAN DIEGO HISTORY the officers and some of the crew of the Spanish ship *San Carlos* went ashore searching for a supply of water. The ship had sailed from La Paz, Baja California and had arrived at San Diego Harbor two days before.

The *San Carlos* was one of three ships that set out for San Diego from La Paz with supplies for two overland expeditions that were traveling up the entire length of Baja California to San Diego to establish a mission and a military base for Spain. Father Junípero Serra was the Catholic priest in charge of one of the overland expeditions (see JANUARY 9).

One of the passengers on the *San Carlos* wrote an account of what happened when the officers and 21 men went ashore at San Diego looking for fresh water:

> Following the west shore of the port [the shore along the Point Loma side of the bay], they discovered a short distance away a group of Indians armed with bows and arrows, to whom they made signs with white cloths calling them to a parley [a meeting]. But they kept their distance, moving away as our men moved toward them...
>
> At last it was contrived to attract them by sending forward one soldier. When he deposited his arms [weapons] on the earth, and used gestures and signs of peace, they consented to let him near. He distributed some gifts to them...ribbons, glass beads, and baubles. They were asked by signs where the watering-place was, and the natives pointed toward a grove...in the distance to the northeast, and gave us to understand that within it ran some river or arroyo, and to follow, that they would take us to it.
>
> They walked [together] some three leagues until they arrived on the banks of a river hemmed in on either bank by a hedge of leafy willows and cottonwoods. Its channel must be twenty yards wide... The country was of joyous appearance, and the lands contiguous to the river appeared eminently tillable and capable of producing every species of fruits.

This was the San Diego River, which at that time emptied into San Diego Bay before its course was changed in the 1870s and a channel constructed for it to empty into Mission Bay. Today it empties into the open ocean just south of Mission Bay at Ocean Beach.

MAY 2, 1931

ON THIS DAY IN SAN DIEGO HISTORY a three-day ceremony began, honoring the dedication of the new San Diego State College campus with its new buildings and new location at Montezuma Mesa. The college had outgrown its old location in the University Heights area of San Diego near El Cajon Boulevard and Normal Street (see MARCH 13 and APRIL 6).

The new San Diego State College campus was ten miles east of downtown, and its new Spanish-style buildings accommodated the 200 courses that were offered and the 2,000 students that were enrolled there. The tall Moorish tower, which is the dominant feature of the campus, was built at this time in 1931 on what was then the library building. The tower has a carillon chime system. In 1975 it was named the Hardy Memorial Tower in memory of Dr. Edward L. Hardy, who was the second president of San Diego State College, from 1910 to 1935.

Also in 1931, a large 100-by-400-foot letter *S* was painted on the southwest side of Cowles Mountain that could be seen from the college and for miles around. The mountain was locally called "S Mountain" or "State College Mountain." Every year, incoming freshman had the job of spreading lime on the letter to keep it white. It was obliterated in the early 1940s during World War II for security reasons, but the tradition was reinstated after the war until 1971. Remains of the letter can still barely be seen.

In 1938 an athletic stadium was built at the college. In 1952 the college had an enrollment of over 4,000 students. In 1972 the college was elevated to a university, which offered graduate degrees beyond the four years of undergraduate schooling. Now known as San Diego State University, the campus—much expanded but still located on the same site that was dedicated on this date, May 2, 1931—has a student enrollment of over 35,000.

MAY 3, 1964

ON THIS DAY IN SAN DIEGO HISTORY the last patient left the Scripps Memorial Hospital located on Prospect Street in La Jolla. A new hospital had been built on what is now Genesee Avenue, located some distance east of La Jolla.

The Prospect Street location was first used as a six-bed hospital in 1916 when Ada Gillespie, a nurse and the wife of one of La Jolla's two doctors, established the La Jolla Sanitarium. It was located on the 400 block of Prospect Street in the Kline house—built in 1904 and one of the largest homes in La Jolla at the time.

In 1918 Ellen Browning Scripps agreed to finance a new hospital building on the site, and the Kline house was sold back to Mrs. Theresa Kline and moved to another location. The new hospital, with eight patient rooms, was also called La Jolla Sanitarium and was completed in 1920.

However, in 1922 when Miss Scripps fell and broke her hip and was taken to the small La Jolla Sanitarium (also called the Gillespie Sanitarium by La Jolla locals) she realized that La Jolla needed a larger and more modern hospital. In September 1924 the new 57-bed Scripps Memorial Hospital opened on Prospect Street.

By 1946 La Jolla had a population of 10,000 compared to 2,000 in 1924, and the 57-bed hospital was inadequate for a town of that size. So in 1950 a 107-bed wing was added to the hospital.

By 1960 the population of La Jolla was over 22,000, and the hospital situation was in a crisis. There was no place to expand around the Prospect Street location, so a new location was recommended in Kearny Mesa at a 40-acre site on what is now Genesee Avenue—a controversial suggestion to most La Jollans. In 1963 a "Save Our Hospital" committee was formed which claimed that, according to the terms of the Scripps Charitable Trust, the hospital must remain in the La Jolla area and that "the abandonment of the present facility [was] contrary to the intent of the donor."

Nevertheless, the hospital decided to leave the Village, as locals called the central La Jolla area, and move to the "wilds," the undeveloped region east of the new I-5 freeway. The area on Genesee Avenue had to be incorporated into the 92037 La Jolla zip code to legally adhere to the terms of Miss Scripps' bequest.

MAY 4, 1883

ON THIS DAY IN SAN DIEGO HISTORY Helen Hunt Jackson, author of the novel *Ramona*, wrote in a letter to her friend Thomas Bailey Aldrich: "If I could write a story that would do for the Indian a thousandth part what *Uncle Tom's Cabin* did for the Negro, I would be thankful for the rest of my life."

Jackson had been promoting the cause of the Indians in the United States for several years, and she was particularly interested in the treatment of Indians at Warner's Ranch in the northeastern part of San Diego County. In 1882 Jackson was appointed to the commission to investigate the condition of the Mission Indians by the U.S. commissioner of Indian affairs. Jackson was aware that the Warner Ranch, owned by Jonathan Trumbull Warner (Juan José Warner), had been sold to John G. Downey in 1880 after its designation as an Indian reservation was terminated and was afraid that Downey would eject the Indians from his land. Jackson wrote a heated letter to the editor of *Century Magazine* stating:

> There is not in all the Century of Dishonor, so black a chapter, as the history of these Mission Indians—peaceable farmers for a hundred years—driven off their lands like foxes and wolves…driven out of good adobe houses and the white men who had driven them out, settling down calm and comfortable in the houses!—What do you think of that?

Jackson also advised that the treaties governing the rights of the Mission Indians to their lands be honored and suggested that the U.S. Bureau of Indian Affairs ask "what the Indians own feelings are about going on reservations." (For more about Indians being forced off their lands in San Diego County, see APRIL 27 and AUGUST 27.)

Jackson's recommendations in her report on the Mission Indians and her book *A Century of Dishonor* were not acted upon by the United States Congress or government officials. She then proceeded to write her romantic novel *Ramona* that was published in 1884, hoping to influence people who read it about the plight of the Indian in southern California. *Ramona* was a great success and went a long way to influence public opinion about unfairness to the Indians (see MARCH 3 and DECEMBER 20).

MAY 5, 1602

ON THIS DAY IN SAN DIEGO HISTORY Sebastián Vizcaíno, a Spanish explorer, left from Acapulco, Mexico with three ships to explore the Pacific coast of Baja California and Alta California. He was looking for good harbors for Spanish trading vessels so that Spain could maintain control of the Pacific Ocean off the west coast of North America. The presence of English and Dutch ships off the coast of California was threatening Spain's dominance.

It took five months for Vizcaíno's ships to reach San Diego Bay, where they arrived on November 10, 1602. He did not recognize it as the same place that Juan Rodriguez Cabrillo had named San Miguel 60 years before. So Vizcaíno gave it the name of San Diego in honor of the Spanish saint San Diego de Alcalá, whose feast day they were celebrating (see NOVEMBER 10, NOVEMBER 12, and NOVEMBER 20).

After leaving San Diego, Vizcaíno continued up the California coast making detailed maps, including naming and mapping Monterey Bay.

Vizcaíno and the priest accompanying his expedition, Father Antonio de la Ascensión, were both impressed with San Diego Harbor. The priest described it in his journal as "a port which must be the best to be found in all the South Sea...being protected on all sides and having good anchorage. It has very good wood and water and many fish of all kinds. On the land there is much game."

San Diego was not visited again by Europeans until 167 years after Vizcaíno's visit. It was 1769 when Spain sent three ships from La Paz, Baja California and two overland expeditions from Loreto to start the missions in California. The Misión San Diego de Alcalá started by Father Junípero Serra in July 1769 was the first of these missions (see JULY 1 and JULY 16).

MAY 6, 1949

ON THIS DAY IN SAN DIEGO HISTORY San Diego's own airline, Pacific Southwest Airlines (PSA), began its first scheduled flight with 21 passengers—heading from Lindbergh Field to the Los Angeles–Burbank airport, then continuing on to Oakland. PSA was started by Kenny and Jeanne Friedkin with a leased DC-3 plane, not much money, and a lot of hope.

PSA was a pioneer of the low-fare airline and had a reputation throughout most of California for its low prices and good, professional service. It was called "the low fare—but we do care" airline. In its early years, PSA flew many military people between the large naval bases in San Diego and Oakland and was called the "Poor Sailor's Airline."

PSA expanded during the 1950s and soon undertook the competitive Los Angeles–San Francisco market. Service was then added to the other California cities of San José, Oakland, Ontario, and Sacramento. By the end of the 1960s, PSA had become the world's largest intrastate airline and was flying more than 60% of all the air traffic in California. The airline's fares were one-half the fares being charged in other states. They accomplished this by going without first class sections, galleys, or food service.

In 1978 PSA extended service outside of California to Las Vegas, Reno, Phoenix, and Salt Lake City. (Also in 1978, a PSA 727 jetliner was involved in a frightful mid-air collision with a small single-engine Cessna resulting in a deadly crash in the North Park area of San Diego (see SEPTEMBER 25).)

By 1979 PSA was the country's 12th largest airline, flying nearly nine million passengers between 15 cities. In 1988 when PSA was bought by US Airways, it had a fleet of 55 aircraft and a lot of passenger goodwill built up from the years of its operations out of San Diego. It had come a long way since its beginning in 1949 with only one small leased airplane.

The Aerospace Museum at Balboa Park has a display on Pacific Southwest Airlines in its History of Aviation section, including replicas of the company's first ticket booth and the colorful fuchsia, orange, and red stripes that decorated the PSA planes.

MAY 7, 1959

ON THIS DAY IN SAN DIEGO HISTORY the Torrey Pines Park was transferred from the city of San Diego to the state of California, and the name changed to Torrey Pines State Reserve. This meant that the 1,000 acres of park land and the rare Torrey Pine trees would be protected as a scientific reserve operated by the California State Department of Parks and Recreation.

Prior to this transfer, the city of San Diego had been in charge of the park since 1899, when 369 acres were set aside by the city as a "free and public park" (see AUGUST 10). More acreage was added to the park over the years, primarily by donations from Ellen Browning Scripps (see OCTOBER 18).

During the 1940s there was much concern over the condition of the park and the trees. According to Bill Evarts in his beautiful book of photographs and text *Torrey Pines: Landscape and Legacy*:

> The negative impact that a relatively small number of visitors inflicted upon the Park's sensitive habitat was alarming. People still foraged for firewood among the groves. Hikers climbed the high points, eroding sandy soils and exposing vulnerable pine roots. Careless tourists left a growing accumulation of trash and litter. Many residents felt that the city had been lax in its administration of the Park.

The trustees of the Ellen Browning Scripps Foundation, which was formed after her death in 1931, expressed their concern: "The Park has been neglected since the city received this remarkable gift of Torrey Pines Point from Miss Scripps, and no provision has been made for guarding and preserving this precious heritage."

Guy Fleming, manager of the park, who had lived there in a home built for him by Ellen Browning Scripps and who later became a superintendent for the California Division of Parks, began to work at finding public or private support for the park. Thanks to the efforts of Fleming and others, it was taken over by the state of California on this date in 1959. Today there is a hiking trail named for him there, the Guy Fleming Trail (see also APRIL 7).

MAY 8, 1929

ON THIS DAY IN SAN DIEGO HISTORY George Marston wrote a letter to John Nolan describing the work being done on Presidio Hill to turn it into a park and a museum. He wrote: "We are making splendid progress on the park and on the building, and everything is coming out beautifully. The people of the city are very enthusiastic over the building. It looms up tremendously and is considered a perfect success."

John Nolan was an urban planner and landscape architect who prepared the plans for the development of Presidio Park and Old Town. George Marston, a San Diego businessman, bought the land at Presidio Hill above Old Town to preserve San Diego's historical past. He hired John Nolan to draw up plans for the project to create a park and museum (see JANUARY 12).

William Templeton Johnson, a popular architect at the time, was chosen to design the Junípero Serra Museum building. Johnson had spent some time in Europe studying architecture and had just finished designing three buildings for the United States government at the Iberian-American Exposition in Seville, Spain. So he had developed a sense of the Spanish Mediterranean style of architecture that fits in so well with the southern California environment. Johnson describes his Serra Museum as similar to the California missions in its "rugged simplicity with thick walls and simple masses, and a sturdiness and frankness in design which gave them much charm."

Johnson is said to have had more influence on the look of San Diego than any other architect. Kevin Starr in his book *Material Dreams: southern California Through the 1920s* states that "the mission-style design with its clean and simple lines, arches, and deep-set window openings that Johnson and others practiced until the late 1940s changed the look not only of San Diego but all of southern California" (see also FEBRUARY 10 and JUNE 26).

Presidio Park and the Serra Museum were dedicated in a day-long ceremony on July 16, 1929—on the 160th anniversary of the founding of the San Diego Mission at this location in 1769 by Father Junípero Serra.

MAY 9, 1922

ON THIS DAY IN SAN DIEGO HISTORY Girard Avenue in La Jolla was paved for the first time.

The first street to be paved in La Jolla was the Torrey Pines Grade in 1915. After that, in 1916 when it was proposed to pave Prospect Street, residents protested because of the expense to the property owners living on the street, who were to be assessed a fee to help pay for it. In spite of the protests, Prospect Street was paved in 1918. Even then, the street was not paved from curb to curb but only a wide strip down the middle.

Previously, La Jollans complained when the first sidewalks were put in, and a few residents refused to walk on them because the hard surface made their feet sore. They claimed the sidewalks would ruin the town.

But progress came to La Jolla in spite of the complaints, with more streets being paved one by one. The popularity of the automobile required better roads. La Jolla Boulevard was paved all the way to Pacific Beach in 1919. The paved road from San Diego to La Jolla was opened in 1920. Before the automobile, the only way to get from San Diego to La Jolla was by horse and carriage or, after 1894, by train (see APRIL 25, 1894).

After the paving of Girard Avenue in 1922, other streets were paved, one at a time, during the 1920s until all of the main streets of the village of La Jolla were finally paved.

MAY 10, 1920

ON THIS DAY IN SAN DIEGO HISTORY there was an avalanche of rock and dirt in the Carrizo Gorge in the mountains east of San Diego. It blocked one of the many tunnels along the route of the San Diego & Arizona Eastern Railway, causing the railroad to close down only six months after it opened.

The construction of the railroad took 12 years, starting in 1907 and finishing in 1919, encountering many delays along the way between San Diego and Yuma, Arizona, and was accomplished due to the financial investment and perseverance of John D. Spreckels.

The railroad was called the "Impossible Railroad" because it had to be constructed through very rugged terrain in the mountains east of San Diego—mountains that had to be crossed before reaching the desert. The 147 miles of track required 21 tunnels that were dug through solid rock, 2.5 miles of bridges and trestles, and curves over 58% of the route. The Carrizo Gorge was an especially rugged area for the tracks to cross over or to tunnel into.

In November 1919 with over 300 freight cars, 40 passenger cars, and more than 500 employees, the railroad began running trains. But after the first year of operation, its expenses were greater than its income, due partly to the closure caused by the avalanche that blocked Tunnel No. 7 on this date in 1920. Flash floods also wiped out parts of the track in 1926, 1927, and 1929.

The railroad traversed 44 miles through Baja California in order to avoid construction in the rugged Laguna Mountains of San Diego County. In 1929 Mexico cancelled its permission for the trains to run through the Baja California portion at night. Nighttime was when the trains carried freight, and the loss in freight revenue caused even more financial problems for the railroad. Added to that were tunnel closures caused by fires and heavy rains in 1932. Bypasses had to be built around some of the tunnels, and a great wooden trestle 186 feet high and 633 feet long was built crossing over Goat Canyon, a tributary of Carrizo Creek, to bypass the blocked Tunnel No. 15. The trestle was considered to be an engineering marvel.

The San Diego & Arizona Eastern Railway was a financial loss to the Spreckels family, and they sold it to the Southern Pacific Railway in 1933, which continued to operate it until 1951.

For more about the San Diego & Arizona Eastern Railway, see SEPTEMBER 9.

MAY 11, 1867

ON THIS DAY IN SAN DIEGO HISTORY Alonzo Horton received the deed to the 960 acres he had bought that fronted on San Diego Bay where downtown San Diego is now located. He paid $265 for the 960 acres—or 27½ cents per acre.

Alonzo Horton had had vision when he stepped off the boat at San Diego Harbor on a trip from his home in San Francisco. He recognized that this location was a much better location for a city than what was then the center of San Diego at Old Town. He proceeded to purchase, develop, and subdivide the land and to sell lots in what he called "Horton's Addition," which was to eventually become New San Diego and the center of San Diego business interests (see AUGUST 12 and OCTOBER 24).

But Alonzo Horton was not the first person to see the value of this location as a potential center for San Diego. William Heath Davis first came to San Diego in 1833 and was very impressed. In 1850 he joined in with several other investors and bought 160 acres along the edge of the bay. Davis laid out a 32-square block area between the present-day Broadway and Market streets, calling it "New San Diego" or "New Town." He brought in building materials for construction of new houses, but no one wanted to settle there at that time. A few stores opened up around a plaza, and Davis spent $60,000 to build a wharf and a warehouse. He also constructed a residence for himself on State Street. But still the new site failed to develop and became known as "Davis' Folly." Apparently he had the right idea, but the timing was wrong. Some 17 years later, Alonzo Horton had great success in developing his bayfront Horton's Addition into New San Diego and in enticing people and businesses away from Old Town.

Alonzo Horton would be impressed if he could come back now and see his old Horton's Addition—transformed into the impressive skyline of high-rise buildings, luxury hotels, and lavish condominiums, not to mention the ballpark, the sprawling convention center, the arching Coronado Bridge spanning the harbor, giant cruise ships, striking aircraft carriers, and beautiful historic vessels docked along the harbor.

MAY 12, 1888

ON THIS DAY IN SAN DIEGO HISTORY construction was begun on Oceanside's first pier, which was made entirely of wood. It was located at what is today's Wisconsin Avenue. But the pier lasted only three years before it was destroyed by a storm in 1891. The owner of Oceanside's South Pacific Hotel collected the lumber and pilings from the destroyed pier and stored them at his hotel until the city approved construction of a new pier two years later.

All in all there were five more piers built or reconstructed over the years, the last reconstruction being in 1987. The Oceanside Pier is now located several blocks north of where the first pier was built at Wisconsin Avenue. It is now at the end of Pier View Way, one block north of Mission Avenue, and contains a restaurant, snack bar, and bait shop. The pier is 1,942 feet long—the longest wooden pier on the West Coast.

The Oceanside area of San Diego County started out in 1870 as a township called San Luis Rey, located west of the Mission San Luis Rey that was founded in 1798 (see JUNE 13). Later, in 1883 Andrew Jackson Meyers applied for a homestead grant of 160 acres on the Oceanside Mesa. Meyers, known as the founder of Oceanside, arranged for the site to be surveyed and for J. Chauncey Hayes, a real estate agent, justice of the peace, and publisher of the *South Oceanside Diamond* newspaper, to sell the lots. Hayes was the person who petitioned for the first post office, which was called Ocean Side—with the name later changed to the one-word Oceanside.

Oceanside was incorporated as a city in 1888 when the population was approximately 1,000. This was during the 1880s land boom when the entire San Diego area enjoyed a prosperous time as new communities developed. The California Southern Railroad, completed in 1885, which connected San Diego to the Santa Fe transcontinental railroad line to the east, went through Oceanside and was important to Oceanside's development—as it was to San Diego's. Later the Surf Line was built by the Santa Fe Railroad, linking Oceanside to Orange County. The paved highway from San Diego to Los Angeles that went through Oceanside was completed by 1920.

Oceanside's population today is over 173,000, making it the third largest city in San Diego County.

MAY 13, 1769

ON THIS DAY IN SAN DIEGO HISTORY one of the two overland expeditions traveling northward from southern Baja California to establish a Spanish mission in San Diego got its first view of the San Diego area. The people on this expedition had traveled inland to the hills east of the present-day Tijuana from where they could see their first view of San Diego—the Silver Strand, the South Bay area, Point Loma, and the masts of the two Spanish ships that had already arrived at San Diego Harbor with necessary supplies (see APRIL 29).

The expedition was led by Captain Don Fernando de Rivera and the Catholic priest Father Juan Crespí. The other overland expedition, which would not arrive in San Diego until July, was led by Captain Gaspar de Portolá and the Catholic priest Father Junípero Serra. Father Crespí wrote in his diary on this day:

> We set out in the morning, course due northward... [W]e commenced climbing up over a large pass...and there for a vast distance along, was revealed to us the plain that we were to follow along the shore, with everything well grass-grown with green grass. We descried, from a small height upon the plain here, the sea reaching far inland, and there we caught sight of the ships' mainmasts, hardly discernible because of the distance they were at. I cannot tell the happiness and joy we felt upon seeing the hour arrive of our reaching our so long wished-for San Diego Harbor, with His Majesty's two packet boats, *San Carlos* and [...] [*San Antonio*] lying there.

On the next day, Father Crespí wrote in his diary: "In addition to its having rained a lot last night and gotten us all wet, at dawn today it was heavily overcast and, after the dawning, it at once turned to raining hard on us again."

This was the weather that was described in the San Diego area in May of 1769. We still get weather like that in May—and today San Diegans call it "May gray."

MAY 14, 1872

ON THIS DAY IN SAN DIEGO HISTORY ownership of the Santa Ysabel Rancho was granted to José Joaquin Ortega and his son-in-law, Edward Stokes, by the United States Land Commission. Ortega and Stokes had owned the Santa Ysabel Rancho since 1844 under a Mexican land grant—when California was a part of Mexico. After the Mexican-American War of 1846–48, California became a part of the United States, and applications for land grants had to be resubmitted to the Commission for approval.

The 17,719-acre Santa Ysabel Rancho was located seven miles southwest of Julian and 52 miles northeast of San Diego. Originally there was a large population of Indians living in the area. Then the Santa Ysabel area became an *asistencia,* or sub-mission, to the San Diego Mission. As early as 1822 there was a small chapel at Santa Ysabel and a granary, several houses, and a cemetery. At that time there were 450 Indians connected with the Santa Ysabel Mission.

One hundred years later in 1924 a new chapel was built at Santa Ysabel adjacent to the location of the original chapel. It is the same chapel that we see today, with its cemetery on the east side of Highway 79 between the Highway 78/79 junction (near Dudley's Bakery) and Lake Henshaw.

There is an interesting story about the disappearance of the mission bells from Santa Ysabel in the summer of 1926. The bells had been moved from the old decaying original adobe chapel and hung near a roadside arbor on the property near the new chapel. The bells are believed to be the oldest of all the bells brought to California in the early days. One of the bells was originally from the Baja California mission at Loreto and had on it the inscription "N.S. de Loreto, 1723" (short for Nuestra Senora de Loreto, or "Our Lady of Loreto"). The other bell was dedicated to San Pedro (St. Peter) in 1767.

Then the bells disappeared. The Indians believed that they were stolen by the non-Indian white people, but some people in the area believe that the bells were hidden away by the older Indians who are waiting for some special occasion to re-hang them at the chapel. The bells are still missing after all these years, and what happened to them still remains a mystery.

See also DECEMBER 3.

MAY 15, 1894

ON THIS DAY IN SAN DIEGO HISTORY the formal opening of the extension to La Jolla of the San Diego, Old Town & Pacific Beach Railway occurred—with a golden spike being driven into the tracks on Prospect Street at the corner of Draper Street. It was followed by a great celebration. Later the railroad would be known as the San Diego, Pacific Beach & La Jolla Railway (see APRIL 25).

The *San Diego Union* newspaper reported on the event:

> Upon arriving at the end of the railroad at La Jolla, within a few hundred yards of the [La Jolla Park] Hotel, the party grouped around the last spike, which lay glittering like pure gold on the last tie, with a silver sledge near by. Music was rendered by the City Guard band, and a photographer took several views of the scene to perpetuate it… The first stroke in driving the golden spike was made by Esteemed Knight Joseph S. Bachman [of the Elks Lodge]. He was then commanded to stay his hand, and the sledge was given to a lady, in honor of womankind generally… Mrs. Emma Harris, a guest of the La Jolla hotel, was thus honored, and she took the sledge. There was a holding of breath when she raised it to make the first blow, but contrary to tradition she did not miss the mark. With great vigor she drove the spike to its last resting place, while the assembly cheered and the band played.

Apparently the railroad did not end close enough to the La Jolla Park Hotel, which stood some three blocks away at the corner of Prospect and Girard avenues. Work soon began to extend the railroad 1,400 feet farther along Prospect Street in order to make it more convenient for passengers to reach the hotel. This article in the *San Diego Union* newspaper at the time explains:

> The extension of the La Jolla Park railroad was finished Sunday night with a rush. The company received information that an injunction would be asked for to restrain the company from building the road. To prevent delay Superintendent Boyd put an extra force at work and stayed up all night himself, the track being laid in very short order. A small depot was hastily erected, and yesterday morning saw the company ready for anybody who cared to apply for an injunction. The extension is 1,400 feet in length and runs along Prospect Street, almost to the door of the hotel.

MAY 16, 1949

ON THIS DAY IN SAN DIEGO HISTORY there was a lot of excitement surrounding San Diego's first TV broadcast by KFMB-TV, Channel 8. Even the mayor of San Diego at the time, Harley E. Knox, was there. Not everyone had a television set in their home then, so crowds of people gathered at appliance stores, where 9-inch black-and-white sets were for sale, and watched the first broadcast from a San Diego station. By 1950 there were 25,000 TVs in San Diego County.

A television transmitter was located on the top of Mount Soledad above La Jolla, where it still is today. One of Channel 8's earliest broadcasts was a baseball game between San Diego and Los Angeles. KFMB-TV, Channel 8, grew out of the KFMB radio station, started in 1943 and still serving San Diego today at 760 on the AM radio dial.

Four years after Channel 8's television debut, Channel 10 broadcast its first TV program in 1953 (see SEPTEMBER 13).

At first Channel 8 was affiliated with all three major television networks, CBS, NBC, and ABC—until NBC joined up with the new Channel 10 in 1953, and ABC affiliated with Channel 6, XETV, in 1955. Channel 8 remained affiliated with CBS, as it still is today. It is the only major TV station in the country that has remained with its original network affiliation.

Old-timers in San Diego will remember Harold Keen and Ray Wilson doing the news on Channel 8 in earlier times. A local La Jolla girl, Raquel Tejada (later known as the movie actress Raquel Welsh) was a weather girl there.

Channel 8 is still going strong as one of several local San Diego television stations.

MAY 17, 1897

ON THIS DAY IN SAN DIEGO HISTORY a stage production of *Around the World in Eighty Days* was playing at the Fisher Opera House on 4th Street in San Diego. A young black businessman, Edward W. Anderson, bought tickets for himself and his wife to attend the performance.

When the Andersons arrived at the opera house, the doorman allowed them into the foyer but refused to seat them in their orchestra circle seats. He claimed that there had been a mix-up, that duplicate tickets had been mistakenly sold, and the seats were already occupied.

The owner of the theater, John C. Fisher, stepped up and showed the Andersons a statement on the back of the tickets which stated: "The right reserved to refuse admission to holder of this ticket by return of money." Whereupon Mr. Fisher told the Andersons that he was exercising his right to refuse admission to them. Then he added, "[F]urthermore I do not allow colored people on that floor." The Andersons refused Fisher's offer to let them stand at the rear of the balcony, took their refund, and left the theater.

Edward and Mary Anderson decided to sue for damages. A California civil rights act had been passed just a few weeks previously that prohibited public houses from discriminating on the basis of race or color. However, John C. Fisher was a very popular and powerful businessman in San Diego and would be hard to defeat in court.

Nevertheless, the judge ruled in favor of the Andersons and awarded them $150 in damages. Mr. Fisher immediately appealed to the Superior Court, and the judge ruled that the Andersons had not been damaged enough to warrant the $150 in damages and ordered the case dismissed. The Andersons appealed for another hearing, which was dismissed again after John Fisher argued that his theater was not a public entertainment house but a "private enterprise" and was not liable under the civil rights act. The Andersons were ordered to pay for the cost of the suit.

The California Supreme Court refused to hear a final appeal by the Andersons in 1899, thus exhausting all of their legal avenues. Historians believe that a case of outright racial discrimination had been upheld in the California courts.

MAY 18, 1852

ON THIS DAY IN SAN DIEGO HISTORY an advertisement announcing the Stage Line, between San Diego and Los Angeles stated:

> Leaves the Franklin House in San Diego, every Monday, Wednesday, and Friday at 5 o'clock A.M., arriving at San Juan Capistrano at 7 o'clock P.M., and remaining there over night, and reaching Los Angeles the following day at 4 o'clock P.M…
>
> Stage Office—At the Franklin Hotel, San Diego.
> Seeley & Wright, Proprietors.

Since automobiles did not appear on San Diego County roads until after 1900, horse-drawn coaches were the only method of travel before train service began in the 1880s (see NOVEMBER 9).

Stagecoach travel was not easy on the bumpy roads. One of the stagecoach passengers is quoted as saying: "Our stages were the Concord type, miserable things to ride in. The motion made the passengers sea-sick, and the dust was terrible."

Although the trip from San Diego to Los Angeles normally took two days, some stage drivers claimed faster times. Don Luis Serrano, a veteran stage driver of the coastal route, recalls driving from San Diego to Los Angeles:

> Frank Shaw and I were the drivers for Seeley's stages. We left at seven a.m., one from here and the other from Los Angeles; the distance was 145 miles. We drove four-horse Concord stages… The trip took 12 hours. The horses were tough mustangs, about half-broken, and as soon as they were hitched we were off on a run. Shaw and I would meet at San Luis Rey, and always saluted each other with a vigorous crack of our whips. I drove two years without an accident, due no doubt to the efficacy of prayer.

Several stage lines served north San Diego County until about 1912. The San Diego–Escondido route was well-traveled and took eight hours. Today this route sometimes seems like eight hours to commuters on Interstate 15 when the freeway slows down during rush hours.

MAY 19, 1907

ON THIS DAY IN SAN DIEGO HISTORY late on a Sunday night, Philip S. Sparkman, a storekeeper, was shot and killed at the age of 50 in the yard in front of his store in the small community of Rincon—at the foot of Palomar Mountain in north San Diego County. The light was found on in his store, but nothing was missing. The newspapers speculated that he was shot by Indians, but no arrests were made. A few days later the coroner's jury closed the case, ruling that Sparkman had died from wounds inflicted by "parties unknown." But when the rest of the story is told, you will see it is quite unlikely that Philip Sparkman would have been harmed by Indians.

Philip Stedman Sparkman was born in England. At the age of 19 he sailed from Liverpool to the United States. He headed west to Albuquerque, New Mexico and then to California, settling in the small ranching and Indian community of Rincon, where he opened a store. He was well-respected and well-liked by the community for his honest business habits and his well-stocked store.

Sparkman was intrigued by the local Indians. He began to learn all he could about the culture and language of the Luiseño Indians (so named by the Spaniards because of their connection to the San Luis Rey Mission). He was helped in his studies by many of the local Indians who also told him stories of Indian customs and rituals.

It was not until after Philip Sparkman died that it was discovered that he had written two extensive works on the Luiseño Indians: *Grammar and Dictionary of the Luiseño Language* and *Culture of the Luiseño Indians*, which were published by the University of California Press a year after his death.

A friend of Sparkman's, Edward A. Davis of Mesa Grande, reported in a *San Diego Union* newspaper article: "His monumental work on their language is of the highest and most scientific order of any that has ever been written in this country."

And so the quiet, reserved, and simple English storekeeper in the rural community of Rincon surprised everyone with his scholarly studies of the Luiseño Indian language and culture.

Today the Indians at Rincon have a large hotel and gambling casino on their property, which is no longer a quiet rural community.

MAY 20, 1904

ON THIS DAY IN SAN DIEGO HISTORY an item appeared in Ramona's local newspaper, the *Ramona Sentinel*: "Mr. Barger went down to Foster Monday morning to continue the double metallic circuit on the telephone line from San Diego to Ramona. Clarence Telford, Arthur Stockton, Mr. Baxey and others from Ramona are assisting."

Foster was located between El Cajon and Ramona on the present-day Highway 67 near Slaughterhouse Canyon Road. (See story for OCTOBER 8 about travel between Ramona and San Diego—by stagecoach to Foster and by train from Foster to San Diego.)

It is difficult for us today to imagine that there were no telephones in Ramona before 1904. Information traveled more slowly in those days—by mail—carried mainly by horse and buggy, such as the San Antonio & San Diego Mail Line (see JULY 9) and the Butterfield Stage Line (see SEPTEMBER 16). Mail and passengers were carried by train to and from farther distances within the United States, and by boat to other parts of the world. Automobiles were only just first being developed in the early 1900s.

La Jolla had its first telephones in 1899, some five years before Ramona, but La Jolla was much closer to San Diego than Ramona (see OCTOBER 11). Wireless telephones, such as cell phones—totally unimagined in earlier times—did not appear in common usage until almost 100 years later, near the end of the twentieth century.

MAY 21, 1989

ON THIS DAY IN SAN DIEGO HISTORY San Diego residents and city leaders were talking about the First San Diego River Improvement Project that was underway to help prevent flooding in Mission Valley. The project, costing $24.5 million in assessments from Mission Valley property owners, was to raise Mission Center Road and Stadium Way by 7 feet, to install earthen dikes and holding basins, and to install storm drain pumps along the river channel and near road crossings.

On this day, May 21, 1989, an article in the *San Diego Union* newspaper quoted a local geographer, Philip Pryde, who said:

> You don't control rivers. The [San Diego River Improvement] project will keep the valley from flooding up to the capacity of that channel. We don't know what a "100-year flood" really is. But it will be bigger than the valley can handle—and there is even the small possibility that it could happen next year. When it happens, there will be an awful lot of unhappy people.

Professor Patrick Abbott, a geologist at San Diego State University, claims that, in spite of the river improvement project, which was carried out along a short portion of Mission Valley in the area of the Mission Center shopping malls:

> [t]here has never been a coordinated plan for flood control in Mission Valley. Looking at the entire length of the valley, we find four distinct areas. The first is from the ocean to near Morena Boulevard, where there is a broad, deep channel that could handle virtually any size flood.
>
> The second area, from east of Morena Boulevard to Highway 163, has little or no flood-control planning. In the third area, from Highway 163 to I-805 we see...a compromise attempt at handling floods. This area could handle medium-sized floods, but not the historically large ones. Finally, from I-805 to the east end of Mission Valley, there is little or no flood control.

MAY 22, 1900

ON THIS DAY IN SAN DIEGO HISTORY a sweeping change was made in the street names of La Jolla. Most of the original streets were named by the original developers of La Jolla—Frank T. Botsford and George W. Heald—in the 1880s. The Botsfords had lived in New York City, and so they had named some of the La Jolla streets after streets in New York. These streets have retained their original names: Wall Street, Exchange Place, Park Place, and Pearl Street.

When the city fathers decided to change the names of so many of the other La Jolla streets, they followed the same alphabetical pattern that had been used in other parts of San Diego, such as alphabetical names of gemstones in Pacific Beach, alphabetical names of trees going north from downtown San Diego, alphabetical names of birds in Mission Hills, and alphabetical names of authors and poets in Point Loma. In La Jolla, they decided to give streets the names, in alphabetical order, of famous scientists. The following street names were changed on this date—May 22, 1900:

Agassiz Avenue (now Olivetas) was formerly Vine Street and was named for the famous Swiss naturalist and teacher, Louis Agassiz (1807–73).

Bordon Avenue (now La Jolla Boulevard) was formerly Olive Avenue and was named for the American civil engineer, Simeon Bordon (1798–1856).

Cuvier Street, formerly Palm, was named after Baron George Leopold Cuvier (1769–1832), French naturalist who was the founder of the science of comparative anatomy.

Draper Avenue, formerly Orange, was named after John William Draper (1811–82), the American chemist and physiologist.

Eads Avenue, formerly Washington, was named for James Buchanan Eads (1820–87), American engineer who built the bridge over the Mississippi River in St. Louis.

Fay Avenue, formerly New York Avenue, was named for Theodore Sedgwick Fay, 1807–98, American author.

Girard Avenue, formerly Grand, was named for Charles Frederic Girard, 1822–95, American naturalist and zoologist.

Herschel Avenue, formerly Lincoln, was named for Sir William Herschel (1738–1822), German astronomer who lived in England and who discovered the planet, Uranus.

MAY 23, 1862

ON THIS DAY IN SAN DIEGO HISTORY President Abraham Lincoln signed a decree that returned ownership to the Catholic Church of 22 acres of the Rancho de la Misión San Diego de Alcalá, which included the old mission buildings and cemetery.

After the secularization of the missions in 1834 (see SEPTEMBER 30), the rancho contained nearly 59,000 acres and was the second largest rancho in what is now San Diego County. It was placed in the charge of several *majordomos* (Spanish for "managers") and administrators, but the diminished religious authority and discipline caused the Indians to drift away to their former lifestyle, leaving the mission rancho in a declining state.

In the earlier and more prosperous days of the San Diego Mission, before 1834, there were thousands of Indians connected with it. By 1842 there were only 500 Indians there. Two years later there were only 100 Indians left, and the once abundant livestock on the mission lands were reduced to four cows, five calves, and one bull. There was not enough money to pay the *majordomo*. So in 1846 the Mexican California governor, Pío Pico, gave permission for the mission rancho to be sold to Santiago Arguello. Arguello was required to pay off the debts of the mission, support the priests, and allow religious services to be held there.

During the Mexican-American War of 1846–48, the Mormon Battalion, fighting for the United States against Mexico, was stationed at the old mission for a short time. They reported the buildings to be in a dilapidated condition and occupied by only a few Indians. After the war, when California became a part of the United States, military troops occupied the mission from 1849 until 1859. Then on this date—May 23, 1862—President Lincoln returned the old mission buildings and cemetery to the church with 22 acres.

The descendents of Santiago Arguello were given the rights to the remaining lands of the old mission property in 1876. In 1885 the lands were opened up for settlement, but the old mission buildings continued to crumble and decay. They were finally restored in the 1930s (see OCTOBER 17).

MAY 24, 1915

ON THIS DAY IN SAN DIEGO HISTORY a contract was signed between Ellen Browning Scripps (see OCTOBER 18) and the Mercereau Bridge & Construction Company for the construction of a 1,000 foot pier to be built at the Scripps Institution for Biological Research—now known as the Scripps Institution of Oceanography. The cost for the pier was $26,184.

The contract that was signed on this date also included provisions for the construction of a sea water pumping station, sea water reservoir, and sea wall—at a cost of $7,048.50.

The 1,000-foot pier was used for over 70 years by Scripps scientists and students for studies of temperature, salinity, and biology of the ocean water. Small boats were launched from the pier for scientific studies of the nearby ocean areas. Despite its length, the pier was not suitable for docking or launching the large Scripps oceanographic research vessels, since the depth of water at the end of the pier is only about 25 to 30 feet. The vessels are docked instead at Point Loma. The old pier was replaced in 1988 with an all-concrete structure and was named the Ellen Browning Scripps Memorial Pier.

The Scripps institution has been located at its present La Jolla Shores site since 1910 (see JULY 12). It started out in 1903 as a small laboratory for the Marine Biological Association of San Diego located in the boathouse of the Hotel del Coronado (see MARCH 23). It then moved to a small building at the La Jolla Cove in 1905 where it remained until moving to its present location in La Jolla Shores in 1910—thanks to help from the Scripps family, E.W. Scripps and his half-sister Ellen Browning Scripps.

Scripps Institution of Oceanography is the oldest and largest oceanographic institution in the United States and was the first to grant doctorate degrees in oceanography in 1930.

See also MARCH 26 and OCTOBER 14.

May 25, 1917

ON THIS DAY IN SAN DIEGO HISTORY San Diego's growing electric railway system expanded further with the opening of the new Park Line—a 1½ mile line that extended the route from downtown San Diego through Balboa Park to connect with streetcar lines on University Avenue.

The short extension required three new steel bridges over the canyons north of Laurel Street at a cost of $60,000. The rails and overhead wires and poles cost another $30,000. When it was completed, people said it looked like the roadbed and track of a transcontinental railroad instead of a streetcar line. San Diego's complex topography of canyons and hills in the area of Balboa Park caused complications during construction, and the project went over the budget estimates. The short extension ended up costing over $125,000—a large amount for those times.

Another larger extension of the electric railway system occurred when streetcar tracks were extended to Ocean Beach, Mission Beach, Pacific Beach, and La Jolla. Later, as automobiles became more popular and as bus lines expanded, the electric railway system began to decline, going out of business in the 1940s (see APRIL 23 and SEPTEMBER 15).

However, as they say, "What comes around, goes around" and "History repeats itself"—for in 1980 the San Diego Trolley system started up again with the Tijuana Trolley, which goes from downtown San Diego via National City and Chula Vista to the Mexian border at Tijuana, making it easier for poeple to visit Tijuana without having to wait in the long lines of border traffic. Operated by the Metropolitan Transit Development Board, the trolley system continues to expand into new areas of the San Diego region.

At its peak, the old San Diego Electric Railway operated 110 rail miles costing $8.6 million over a period of 39 years of construction. By comparison, as of January 2002 the new San Diego Trolley system was operating on 46.8 rail miles, built over 22 years costing over $752 million.

MAY 26, 1845

ON THIS DAY IN SAN DIEGO HISTORY the San Bernardo Rancho was granted to Captain Joseph F. Snook by the Mexican California governor, Pío Pico. Captain Snook was an English mariner who sailed English and Mexican ships off the coast of Mexico as early as 1824. He came to California in 1830 and became a California citizen in 1833, at which time he changed his name to José Francisco.

Captain Snook had previously been granted a portion of the San Bernardo Rancho three years earlier in 1842 (see FEBRUARY 16). The total acreage of both grants amounted to 17,763 acres. The rancho extended south from what is now Escondido, across what is now Lake Hodges, to the northern boundary of Los Peñasquitos Rancho.

After receiving the second grant, Snook moved to the rancho with his family, and he later died there (see FEBRUARY 23). His widow, the former María Antonia Alvarado, married Henry Clayton, who came to San Diego with the Mexican boundary survey and was the first county surveyor. They lived part of the time in the hacienda at the San Bernardo Rancho and part of the time at María Antonia's house in Old Town. It was to San Bernardo Rancho that General Kearney's battered troops fled and waited for help from San Diego after their defeat at the Battle of San Pasqual in 1846 (see DECEMBER 6) during the Mexican-American War.

In 1867 the rancho was sold to James McCoy, former sheriff and state senator from San Diego. McCoy raised sheep on the rancho and claimed that he had the finest sheep in the county. In 1869 the San Bernardo Rancho sold for $36,000. Today the rancho lands are occupied by the residential community of Rancho Bernardo. Lake Hodges is also located on the former rancho land.

MAY 27, 1862

ON THIS DAY IN SAN DIEGO HISTORY an earthquake cracked the tower of the Point Loma lighthouse, damaged the Whaley's house in Old Town, and caused flooding in Old Town. The *Los Angeles Star* newspaper called it San Diego's "Day of Terror."

In a letter to Thomas Whaley from Augustus S. Ensworth, who was living in the Whaley house after the Whaleys had moved to San Francisco, Ensworth described the earthquake:

> I've not much of any news, with the exception, that on the 27th [of May]…at a few moments past twelve o'clock we had two shocks of an earthquake, within 2 or 3 minutes of one another, the second the most severe. Many houses in town became cracked, altho no serious damage was done. I inclose you a picture of your house, showing the cracks, but it looks worse on paper than it is… But in order to crack solid brick, I think, in many places where there are cracks, the walls must have opened considerable for the moment. I was in the yard at the time and the noise of the vibration of the windows and doors could have heard at the graveyard. It was awful! For days afterward it could be seen in the bed of the river where the earth had opened and closed, leaving the marks of long rents… [F]rom the 27th [of May]…the earth has not been at rest, nearly every 24 hrs. bring forth little young earthquakes—on yesterday 2 sometimes 3 or 4 in 24 hours. As for myself, for more than 10 days I slept in the corral, others imitated me in town.

Augustus Ensworth came to San Diego in the early 1850s. After serving as justice of the peace, he studied law on his own and collected an extensive library of law books. His letters from the 1860s are preserved in the collections of the Whaley House Museum in Old Town (see also MARCH 31).

MAY 28, 1919

ON THIS DAY IN SAN DIEGO HISTORY a Hollywood movie was being filmed in Balboa Park: *Soldiers of Fortune*, starring Wallace Berry. The film's producer, Allan Dwan, put an advertisement in the *San Diego Union* newspaper on this date to attract extras to come to see the movie being filmed:

FREE SPECTACULAR SHOW. Exposition Grounds,
Balboa Park
Come Early in Your Autos. Bring Your Lunch.

Free parking space to see Marvelous Film in the making. Have your TOPS DOWN so you can remain in your car and see the show. Work begins promptly at 10 o'clock.

NO DULL MOMENTS, Band Concert, and Spanish Dancers…will Dance for Your Entertainment When the Picture Is Not Being Made.

The producer of the film, Allan Dwan, was later quoted as saying:

I went down and used the fairgrounds [at Balboa Park] in San Diego which were perfect for a small Latin republic. They were kind of magnificent too—all in plaster. And I got practically all the people in San Diego working in the picture. There were no unions in those days, so I put an ad in the paper inviting the populace to bring their lunches and come out to Balboa Park to see a picture being made. And they came in droves. I put straw hats on them, and when I brought my actors by, I said, "Wave those straw hats," and they all waved them. Thousands of people in the picture, all having a good time, eating their lunch and waving straw hats and getting no money, being allowed to see a picture being made.

Balboa Park was becoming a popular place as a background for filming movies, ever since the Panama-California Exposition of 1915–16 (see JANUARY 1 and DECEMBER 31).

Location filming in Balboa Park and other city parks became so popular that the San Diego park commissioners had to incorporate a formal procedure and schedule for managing park sites and facilities to accommodate the filming schedules (see also JUNE 20).

MAY 29, 1935

ON THIS DAY IN SAN DIEGO HISTORY the California Pacific International Exposition opened in Balboa Park. This was San Diego's first World's Fair and second major exposition. The first one was the Panama-California Exposition of 1915–16, also held at Balboa Park (see JANUARY 1).

This 1935 exposition was especially important because it was held in the middle of the great economic depression of the 1930s, and it offered hope to San Diegans and to the rest of America that the country would soon be able to overcome its problems.

At the official opening of the exposition at 11 a.m., a U.S. Marine color guard led a parade across Cabrillo Bridge into Balboa Park. That night at 8 p.m., President Franklin Roosevelt telephoned a signal for the lights to go on and sent congratulations to the people of San Diego for their courage and confidence in putting on the fair. Sixty thousand people attended the fair on the first day. Later, in October, President Roosevelt himself came to San Diego and personally visited the exposition.

New structures built at Balboa Park for the 1935 California Pacific International Exposition included the Spanish Village, the Old Globe Shakespearean Theater, and what we now know as the Starlight Bowl. It was called the Ford Bowl in 1935 because the Ford Motor Company financed the concerts that were performed there. The name was changed to Balboa Park Bowl in 1948 and finally to Starlight Bowl in 1977 (see also OCTOBER 30).

In 1978 the Old Globe Theater would be destroyed by fire. It was rebuilt in 1981 and reopened in January 1982.

MAY 30, 1934

ON THIS DAY IN SAN DIEGO HISTORY the mayor of San Diego helped to dedicate a monument to San Diego's early pioneer Louis Rose. The inscription read: "Louis Rose, 1807–1888, Founder of Roseville, Pioneer of Rose Canyon, Brickmaker, Tanner, Outstanding Citizen." Rose was San Diego's first Jewish settler, arriving in San Diego in 1850.

The monument—a large boulder that was quarried during construction of the El Capitan Dam, with a bronze plaque on it—was located just north of the old La Jolla Junction on the median between the north- and south-bound lanes of old Highway 101—the Pacific Coast Highway. The monument is still there, but that location is now part of the University of California at San Diego (UCSD) campus on a grassy field of John Muir College. Highway 101 was eventually replaced by Interstate 5 to the east.

In 1969 the bronze plaque on the monument was stolen—probably a student prank? A replica of the plaque was reproduced from a photo of the old plaque and replaced on the monument. The Masonic Lodge, which Rose had helped to start in San Diego, paid for the new plaque.

Originally from Germany, Rose came to San Diego in 1850—the same year that California became a state. He soon opened up a general store and a small hotel in Old Town. Then he bought 325 acres on Point Loma for $82. In 1854 he bought 650 acres in and around a canyon located east of La Jolla and east of Mount Soledad. He named the canyon Rose Canyon (see also JULY 14).

Rose agreed with Alonzo Horton that Old Town was not the best location for the future development of San Diego but rather that the city should be located on the bay. Rose had hopes of developing his land in the Loma Portal area of Point Loma into the new San Diego. He laid out a townsite he called Roseville, built the Roseville Hotel, and constructed a wharf. But Rose was not as successful with his plans as was Alonzo Horton, whose Horton's Addition became San Diego's New Town (see MAY 11).

During his time in San Diego, Louis Rose served as the San Diego city treasurer, was elected a county supervisor for two terms, and worked for ten years as the city's postmaster in Old Town. Rose died in 1888 (see FEBRUARY 11).

MAY 31, 1931

ON THIS DAY IN SAN DIEGO HISTORY the Children's Pool was dedicated at La Jolla. The Children's Pool was a gift from Miss Ellen Browning Scripps and was created by the construction of a great curving breakwater to provide a safe swimming area for children. Ellen Browning Scripps was a much loved benefactress who donated to many projects in La Jolla and San Diego (see OCTOBER 18).

As early as 1921, Miss Scripps had consulted with the city engineer about how to "work out the issue with old ocean." But it took until 1931 for the project to be completed. In 1920 a near-drowning had occurred, resulting in a warning about swimming in the area.

The breakwater was built to protect a little cove across the street from Casa de Mañana, which was a hotel at the time and is now a retirement community. The cost of the project increased during the construction of the breakwater, so that it ended up costing Miss Scripps much more than originally estimated.

Miss Scripps had a special interest in the welfare of children. In her own words: "[T]he Mother Heart is strong within me... I have always had innate interest in children, particularly those handicapped in life's game."

At the dedication ceremony, the Children's Pool was presented to the city in Miss Scripps' name, and this statement was made about the gift: "[This is] the most valuable of all Miss Scripps' benefits to La Jolla, measured in terms of good to the greatest number... [and] investments in human happiness designed for the little ones."

Dr. Jacob C. Harper, who represented Miss Scripps at the dedication, added: "Adults must recognize that here at the Pool, the children have a primary claim."

In recent years a colony of seals have seen fit to occupy the Children's Pool and beach. There has been much controversy over whether to force the seals out and restore the use of the pool to children or to protect the seals and prevent people from using the Children's Pool.

JUNE 1, 1949

ON THIS DAY IN SAN DIEGO HISTORY Alfred Armstrong "Doc" Beaty died in Borrego Springs, where he had lived since 1913. Originally from Texas, "Doc" Beaty was one of the earliest homesteaders in the Borrego Valley, located in the desert area of northeast San Diego County.

Beaty was the first person to introduce commercial agriculture to Borrego Valley by growing alfalfa and onions on his irrigated 20 acres at the mouth of Coyote Canyon. He constructed ditches and a reservoir for the irrigation of his crops in this dry, desert area where rain seldom falls. He also raised mules, horses, and donkeys on his ranch, which he used in his work as a guide for hunting parties in the local mountains. He planted the first date palms in Borrego Valley in 1926 but never developed them into a successful commercial business.

"Doc" Beaty was a great promoter of the valley and helped to form the Borrego Valley Chamber of Commerce in 1929. He was also involved in forming the Borrego Valley School District in 1926, and in constructing the first road into Borrego which could be driven by an automobile, the Old Borrego Valley Road. He used his mule team and "Fresno scraper" to build the road from San Felipe Wash at the Narrows (on today's Highway 78 east of Yaqui Pass Road) up over a mesa and down into Borrego Valley. The "Fresno scraper" was an earth-moving machine invented in 1883 and used by farmers in Fresno, California to dig irrigation ditches on their farms.

He was also involved in the construction of the Truckhaven Trail from Borrego to Highway 86 near the Salton Sea in 1929 to 1930, and Yaqui Pass Road (present-day County Highway S-3) coming into Borrego from the south in 1934.

"Doc" Beaty was not a doctor, even though people called him "Doc." He was however, the unofficial veterinarian for local animals. In March 1949 "Doc" and Mrs. Beaty were recognized by the Borrego Springs Chamber of Commerce for their contributions to the community over the years (see MARCH 21). "Doc" Beaty died three months later on this date—June 1, 1949. His ashes were spread over the Santa Rosa Mountains, in view of which he had lived for 36 years and where he had led many hunting parties.

JUNE 2, 1869

ON THIS DAY IN SAN DIEGO HISTORY a stage line started up between San Diego and Yuma, Arizona. The San Diego & Fort Yuma Stage Line advertised in San Diego's new newspaper, the *San Diego Union*, which had just started up the year before in 1868 (see OCTOBER 10).

The ad for the new stage line stated:

> A weekly line of four-horse coaches will commence running between San Diego and Fort Yuma on and after Wednesday next, connecting with each steamer from San Francisco. Persons wishing to go to Arizona will find this the quickest and cheapest route. First Class Coaches and the finest horses in the country will run over this road.
>
> —John G. Capron, Proprietor

Twelve years earlier in 1857 the first stagecoach to San Diego from the East was started. It was the San Antonio & San Diego Mail Line, which brought passengers as well as mail from San Antonio, Texas to San Diego—a distance of 1,476 miles—on a trip that took 38 days (see AUGUST 31). Today that trip can be driven by car in 2 to 3 days.

There was another stage line to San Diego that started even earlier, in 1852, running between San Diego and Los Angeles (see MAY 18).

Stagecoaches driven by teams of horses were the main form of transportation in San Diego County in these early days before there were any trains or automobiles. San Diego's first train connection to and from the eastern United States was not established until 1885 (see NOVEMBER 9 and NOVEMBER 15). Automobiles were not developed until the early 1900s.

JUNE 3, 1918

ON THIS DAY IN SAN DIEGO HISTORY a contract was given to the Scofield Engineering Company out of Philadelphia to build eight concrete cargo-carrier ships. This would also involve building a shipyard as well as a channel leading to the deeper waters of San Diego Bay. Tidelands were leased at the foot of 32nd Street for the shipbuilding—22 acres of land and 77 acres of water surface.

World War I had been raging in Europe since 1914, and the United States had joined England, France, and other European countries in the war against Germany and Austria in April 1917. During the war years many Allied ships were destroyed by German submarines. President Woodrow Wilson authorized the United States Shipping Board and the Emergency Fleet Corporation to build the concrete ships because of a serious shortage of seasoned wood that was required for wooden ships. Concrete ships had been around since France and the Netherlands had built the first small concrete boats and barges, in 1849 and 1859, respectively.

In San Diego the Pacific Marine Construction Yard was managed by Philadelphia's Scofield Engineering Company, who constructed the shipyard buildings, machine and foundry shops, offices, and other facilities that would be needed to build the eight ships. San Diego had never seen such a large and grandiose engineering project, and it provided great job opportunities and economic benefits for the city.

The first two concrete ships, the *Cuyamaca* and the *San Pasqual,* were launched two years later in June 1920. By then World War I had ended, and the Concrete Ship Program was cancelled. In 1921 the shipyard and its buildings were transferred to the Navy and became the Fleet Destroyer Repair Base.

JUNE 4, 1834

ON THIS DAY IN SAN DIEGO HISTORY San Diego officially became a pueblo (Spanish for "town") and was no longer just a military post. Juan María Osuna was elected the first *alcalde* (Spanish for "mayor"). The two city councilmen were Juan Bautista Alvarado and Juan María Marrón. The city attorney was Henry Fitch.

Only 13 votes were cast in this first election, even though the town had a population of about 500. Four years later in 1838 San Diego's population had decreased to the extent that the pueblo designation was taken away, and San Diego became a department of the pueblo of Los Angeles. By 1840 San Diego had a population of only 140. This was during the time when California was a part of Mexico.

After the Mexican-American War of 1846–48, and after California became a part of the United States, San Diego was incorporated as a town again in March 1850. In the election that followed in June, Joshua Bean—who had been the last *alcalde* of the Mexican pueblo of San Diego and who was also brother of the infamous Judge Roy Bean of Texas—was elected mayor of the American town of San Diego (see also NOVEMBER 8).

In 1850 the city of San Diego's population totaled 650—and 798 in the entire county. By 1860 there were 731 people in the city and 4,324 in the county (1,249 white, 8 black, and 3,067 Indian). By 1880 San Diego's city population had jumped to 2,300 and the county's to 4,951.

The population increased rapidly in the late 1880s once San Diego had a railroad connection to the East, starting a land boom. By 1890 San Diego's population had increased to 16,159 and the county's to 34,987.

Today San Diego has a population of over 1.3 million, and the county has over 3 million.

JUNE 5, 1845

ON THIS DAY IN SAN DIEGO HISTORY a petition for the Cuyamaca Rancho was made by Augustín Olvera to California Governor Pío Pico, the last governor of Mexican California. California later became the 31st state of the United States in 1850, after the Mexican-American War of 1846–48.

Olvera was born in Mexico City in 1818 and came to California in 1834 at the age of 16. He lived in Los Angeles and became active in political affairs there. Later, the street where he lived and practiced law, Olvera Street, was named for him. It is now a well-known tourist attraction. Olvera went on to fight with the Californios against the Americans led by General Fremont in the Mexican-American War. He was one of the commission of three who negotiated peace with the Americans at Cahuenga at the end of the war. He went on to become the first county judge of Los Angeles.

At the time Olvera petitioned for the Cuyamaca Rancho—on this date in 1845—he had already been granted the Rancho Mission Vieja south of San Juan Capistrano in what is today Orange County. He petitioned for the Cuyamaca Rancho sight-unseen, as he had never been there. He saw it as an opportunity to obtain some grazing and timber land. Unfortunately, he did not submit the proper *diseño* (Spanish for "map") outlining the boundaries of the rancho. Much controversy erupted later over those boundaries—especially after gold was discovered in the area in 1870. Lawsuits ensued until an official land description of the rancho was finally drawn up in 1874 (see NOVEMBER 14 and NOVEMBER 25).

The Cuyamaca Rancho contained 35,501 acres and was located approximately 55 miles northeast of San Diego. It extended northward from Descanso to Pine Hills—just south of Julian. It was adjacent to the Santa Ysabel Rancho. Within the boundaries of the old Cuyamaca Rancho are Cuyamaca State Park, Cuyamaca Lake, and the 6,515-foot Cuyamaca Peak.

JUNE 6, 1914

ON THIS DAY IN SAN DIEGO HISTORY the Van Camp family started to pack tuna into cans in San Pedro, California on the coast near Los Angeles. The company later opened two plants in San Diego for canning tuna that was called Chicken of the Sea®.

Between 1930 and the late 1970s, San Diego was considered the "tuna capital of the world," and thousands of people in San Diego were employed by the industry. In addition to the Van Camp Sea Foods Company, several other large corporations processed their tuna in San Diego. These included StarKist® Foods, Bumble Bee® Seafood, Westgate California, and Pan Pacific.

Many of the tuna fishermen that worked out of San Diego were from Portuguese and Italian families. They would often be out to sea for two or three months at a time, fishing in the eastern tropical Pacific Ocean where yellowfin tuna were most abundant—bringing their catch back to San Diego to be processed and canned by the many canneries located here. They used enormous nets, called purse seines, that were up to a mile long and 400 feet deep.

Unfortunately, in the 1970s—after more strict environmental legislation was passed to protect marine mammals from being accidentally caught in the nets—the tuna industry in San Diego began to decline. By the 1990s there were only eight tuna boats operating out of San Diego, compared to 110 in 1980. The decline of the tuna industry was a great loss to San Diego's economy (see also OCTOBER 21).

JUNE 7, 1890

ON THIS DAY IN SAN DIEGO HISTORY San Diego's first cable car line opened—the San Diego Cable Railway Company. It was a 4.7-mile line that ran from downtown at 6th and L streets to Park and Adams Avenue. From its start at 6th and L, the line proceeded down 6th Avenue to 6th and C where it jogged left to 4th Street, went up 4th to University, east on University to Normal Street, then north to Park Avenue and east to Adams.

A power plant was installed at 4th and Spruce streets to keep the 51,000 feet of cable moving. Power was generated by two coal-fired steam engines. The average speed of the cable cars was 8 miles per hour. Spruce Street had a turntable, as did each terminal, for turning the cable cars back in the other direction.

Unfortunately, only 13 months after starting service, the company folded. Competition from other rail lines that used regular trains, a declining economy, and the failure of California National Bank, the company's backer, all contributed.

Then John D. Spreckels came on the scene. He was a wealthy San Francisco businessman who started investing in San Diego during the economic boom of the 1880s. John Spreckels and his brother Adolph began bailing out distressed businesses in San Diego during the economic decline—including the San Diego Electric Railway Company, which they bought in January 1892. (For more on John Spreckels, see JULY 26.)

Spreckels went on to make a success of the San Diego Electric Railway by expanding it and improving it until San Diego had one of the best streetcar systems in the United States.

See also APRIL 23 and MAY 25.

JUNE 8, 1887

ON THIS DAY IN SAN DIEGO HISTORY construction was started on one of the first houses to be built in La Jolla. It was the home of George W. Heald, one of the codevelopers of La Jolla Park. The grand auction and sale of lots in La Jolla had occurred only a little over a month before (see APRIL 30).

The Heald house was located on the corner of Silverado and Exchange Place. Shortly after this, Heald's partner, Frank T. Botsford—later known as the "Father of La Jolla"—built his home at the corner of Prospect and Ivanhoe.

George Heald later built a two-story building at the corner of Wall and Herschel streets that became the Heald store. Today a four-story bank building is at that location. In 1896 La Jolla's first school met on the second floor of the vacant store, until a proper school building was built in 1899 on the west side of Herschel Street just south of Wall Street. Previously, La Jolla children had attended school in Pacific Beach. The Heald store was later moved to a new location at the corner of Prospect and Girard and became the new Chase & Ludington store, until it was torn down in 1917.

When his wife died in 1891—just four years after the Heald house was built—George Heald left La Jolla and moved to San Diego. Several families lived in the Heald house over the years, until it was torn down in 1936. If you go to the corner of Silverado and Exchange Place today, you might wonder why George Heald built his house there, because you cannot see the ocean. But in those early days La Jolla was not built-up as it is today. There were no trees and no other structures, so the Heald house had a full view of the ocean.

JUNE 9, 1870

ON THIS DAY IN SAN DIEGO HISTORY the Bank of San Diego, San Diego's first bank, was officially formed. Before this, San Diego residents with extra money had to buy a safe to keep it in—or otherwise hide it or ship it to a bank in San Francisco for safe-keeping.

The Bank of San Diego was formed with an initial capitalization of $100,000. Alonzo Horton, the "Father of New San Diego" and an important San Diego businessman, was president of the new bank. (For more on Alonzo Horton, see OCTOBER 24.)

The bank later merged with Commercial Bank to become the Consolidated Bank of San Diego. Then in 1885 it joined with the Bank of Southern California to become the First National Bank, which later, in 1975, became California First Bank. It is now known as Union Bank of California.

For 90 years, from 1885 until 1975, the First National Bank was a very successful bank. Around 1900 the bank's deposits were nearly $1 million, and it became the first bank in San Diego to finance automobile purchases. In 1917 John D. Spreckels, an important San Diego businessman, purchased the bank. Spreckels owned valuable land and many businesses in San Diego and Coronado. (For more information on Spreckels, see JULY 26.)

In 1921 First National Bank was the country's first bank to have neighborhood branch offices. During the Great Depression and the financial panic of the 1930s when so many banks went out of business, First National Bank continued to thrive. In 1936 it became the first bank in San Diego County to finance private airplane ownership. By 1942 the bank's deposits totaled nearly $56 million.

The bank we knew as California First Bank from 1975 until near the end of the 1980s, and the bank we know today as Union Bank of California, grew out of the heritage of San Diego's first bank, the Bank of San Diego, which was started on this date—June 9, 1870.

JUNE 10, 1851

ON THIS DAY IN SAN DIEGO HISTORY the *San Diego Herald* newspaper reported on the Indians at Jacumba: "The Indians here are spread over the valley and seemed to be in considerable numbers; they were kindly disposed; cultivate the earth to some extent; many have been into the settlements and talked a little Spanish."

Jacumba is an Indian place-name that is believed to mean "Hut by the Water." It is located in the southeastern part of San Diego County very close to the Mexican border and is one of the oldest inhabited sites in the county. The first white family to come to Jacumba was the McClain family from Texas, who homesteaded there before the Civil War—that is, before 1861.

Later, in 1918, during the construction for the San Diego & Arizona Eastern Railway, track was laid through Jacumba. (For more information on this railroad, see SEPTEMBER 9.)

During World War II in the early 1940s, Camp Lockett, an Army cavalry training camp, operated about 30 miles west of Jacumba. An unfortunate incident occurred during the war when a small restaurant in Jacumba refused service to the African-American soldiers because of their color—until their sergeant explained who the soldiers were and requested service for them. Discrimination against black people in the United States was widespread before 1964, when the national Civil Rights Act was passed by Congress.

JUNE 11, 1869

ON THIS DAY IN SAN DIEGO HISTORY the Peninsula de San Diego Rancho was purchased for $3,000. The rancho contained over 4,000 acres and is now occupied by Coronado and North Island.

The original land grant for this rancho was given to Pedro C. Carillo in 1846 when San Diego was a part of Mexico. Carillo had served as *alcalde* (Spanish for "mayor") of San Diego and also as collector of customs. Carillo was married to Jesefa Bandini, daughter of Juan Bandini, a prominent San Diego businessman.

Later, in 1885, a group headed by Elisha Babcock purchased the peninsula property for $110,000. They subdivided the land into residential lots in a town they named Coronado. By 1887 Coronado had 30 homes, and construction was started on the grandiose Hotel del Coronado (see FEBRUARY 14).

The flat area of North Island was a sagebrush-covered wilderness until 1893 when the United States government built the Zuninga Shoal jetty. In 1901 the government obtained an additional 38 acres for military use. In 1912 a school for Army fliers was established. After much difficulty, the government finally bought the North Island property in 1922 for over $6 million. For a time the western portion of the island was set aside for Rockwell Field, an Army aviator training base, and the eastern part of the island was used for naval aviation. Since 1935 the entirety of North Island has been used as a naval air station, which has become one of the largest naval air bases in the United States.

JUNE 12, 1876

ON THIS DAY IN SAN DIEGO HISTORY the first regular meeting of the San Diego Board of Health was held. The *San Diego Union* newspaper reported that the first public health issue to be discussed was the "unhealthy condition of the water that was being delivered to the citizens of this city by the San Diego Water Company."

Some 26 years before, in 1850, San Diego's first board of health was established. There is no record of any regular meetings of that board. In 1869 another board of health was established "to prevent the spread of Small Pox and other contagious diseases in the city of San Diego." No records of meetings of this board were reported until seven years later—on this date, June 12, 1876, when they addressed the unhealthy quality of San Diego's drinking water.

During the 1800s when horses were the major source of transportation, most cities had filthy streets, with horse urine and manure littering them, as well as dead animals, spoiled food, and human waste. The major problems for cities during the last half of the nineteenth century were providing a clean water supply, proper treatment of sewage, and waste disposal. But compared to the older and larger cities in the East, San Diego was fortunate. It never became as crowded or unsanitary as they did.

Nevertheless, San Diego's population began to grow rapidly during the land boom of the late 1880s. In 1888 a new board of health was established by the mayor of San Diego after many complaints about the "filthy condition of the city" (see JANUARY 31).

JUNE 13, 1798

ON THIS DAY IN SAN DIEGO HISTORY the Mission San Luis Rey de Francia was founded in a fertile valley about five miles east of the present-day city of Oceanside, just off today's Highway 76. The mission was named for Louis IX, who was king of France between 1215 and 1270 and who was later made a saint for his crusades in Egypt and the Holy Lands. He was a supporter of the Franciscan order of the Catholic Church.

The mission was founded by the Franciscan padre Fermín Lasuén and was the 18th of the 21 California missions that were established between 1769 and 1823. The Mission San Diego de Alcalá was the first mission to be established in what is now the state of California, by Father Junípero Serra (see JULY 16). The Mission San Luis Rey was located about halfway between the San Diego Mission and the San Juan Capistrano Mission to the north in what is now Orange County.

The first adobe church at Mission San Luis Rey was built in 1802. The present church was begun in 1811 and dedicated in 1815. The mission was abandoned between 1865 and 1892 and rededicated in 1893. At its peak, Mission San Luis Rey was the largest and most populous Indian mission in America. The Spaniards gave the name "Luiseños" to the Indians associated with it. The Spaniards called the Indians of the San Diego Mission "Diegueños," but later these Indians reverted back to their original name of "Kumeyaay."

JUNE 14, 1881

ON THIS DAY IN SAN DIEGO HISTORY one of the earliest telephones in San Diego was installed at the new San Diego Gas Company offices at 10th and M (now Imperial) streets. The San Diego Telephone Company had just started up a week or two before with 13 telephone customers. San Diego had a population of 3,000 in 1881.

In those days, before electricity, the lighting was done with gas. The San Diego Gas Company—called by locals the "Gas Works"—had just been incorporated two months earlier, in April, with only 89 customers. Most people were used to their kerosene lanterns, and kerosene was inexpensive. Many people did not trust natural gas for heating or lighting since it was odorless, invisible, and could blow up.

The "Gas Works" produced gas from coal that was imported from Australia and England, since the San Diego area did not have any coal deposits to utilize. Later the San Diego Gas Company received coal from Vancouver Island in Canada.

Later, in 1877, when electricity became available to San Diego, the "Gas Works" became the San Diego Gas & Electric Light Company—precursor of today's SDG&E. People called it the "Gas and Light" then. Electricity was a lot slower reaching outlying areas of the San Diego area (see JANUARY 2).

In 1932 San Diego joined up with Southern California Gas Company's natural gas pipeline and closed down its "Gas Works." In 1963, as energy technologies became more sophisticated, SDG&E became a 20% owner of the San Onofre Nuclear Power Plant at San Clemente, which was the largest nuclear generating facility in the United States at the time.

JUNE 15, 1823

ON THIS DAY IN SAN DIEGO HISTORY the first land grant was made in what is now San Diego County. It was the 8,486-acre Los Peñasquitos Rancho. *Los peñasquitos* means "the little cliffs" in Spanish.

The grant was made to Captain Francisco María Ruiz, military commander at the presidio (Spanish for "fort") in San Diego, by Governor Luis Antonio Arguello, who was the first governor of Mexican California after Mexico won its independence from Spain in 1821.

Ruiz was born in Loreto, Baja California in about 1754. He enlisted in the Army at Loreto in 1780 and came to California shortly after that. He rose to the level of captain, and in 1806 he became *comandante* (Spanish for "commander") of the San Diego Presidio, a position he held for 21 years until his retirement in 1827. He is credited with building the first house and planting the first orchard down the hill from the presidio in Old Town in 1812.

Captain Ruiz never married and had no children of his own. He was godfather to three of Joaquin Carillo's children, and four years before he died he deeded his house and garden in Old Town to them. Two years before he died he transferred ownership of his Los Peñasquitos Rancho to Francisco María Alvarado, who had cared for him when he was ill in his later years (see MARCH 15). Captain Francisco María Ruiz died in 1839 at the age of 85.

JUNE 16, 1986

ON THIS DAY IN SAN DIEGO HISTORY a public meeting was called by the Center City Development Corporation (CCDC) to hear comments about a report by a University of San Diego history professor entitled "Research and Analysis of Buildings within the Marina Redevelopment Area to be Connected with Chinese History." The report had found very few buildings worth saving and gave very little support to the idea of a Chinese or Asian historic district.

Over 50 Chinese-Americans attended the meeting on this date in 1986 and expressed strong disagreement with the report. One comment was: "Los Angeles, San Francisco, Chicago, and New York all have a China Town, and we think here on lower Third Avenue is our China Town." Another was, "This area really does represent our roots in America."

Members of the San Diego Chinese community submitted a petition signed by 524 people requesting the city preserve and restore the buildings, including the Chinese Mission. The feeling was that the "Chinese people have contributed a lot to the growth of the West, the railroad, mining, and agriculture... [W]e hope that one day that history will be written. Meanwhile, it is imperative that we save these remaining structures in San Diego's Chinatown to testify to that history." Another observation was that: "These are the last remaining vestiges of Chinese culture, history, and architecture in downtown San Diego."

All of these efforts finally resulted in the San Diego City Council voting to create a Chinese/Asian Thematic Historic District. Twenty buildings associated with the Asian American community were designated to the local historic register, including the Chinese Mission, which was to be moved to the district. The mission, now located at 3rd and J streets, is the Chinese Historical Museum today.

See also MARCH 22 and AUGUST 18.

JUNE 17, 1869

ON THIS DAY IN SAN DIEGO HISTORY Ed Heuck wrote an article for the *San Diego Union* newspaper about the possibilities of finding gold in the mountains east of San Diego. In the article he said: "Persons owning property in the mountains should keep an eye open for the indications [of gold] and when opportunity offers apply the pick and shovel, and those who are not profitably engaged can do no better than to prospect the North and East of San Diego."

Heuck knew what he was talking about because—before the gold discoveries in the Julian area in 1870—he had put up the first quartz mill in San Diego County on the Rancho Rincón del Diablo near the present-day city of Escondido. He dug an inclined shaft to a depth of 140 feet. The quartz rock averaged $33 a ton. In two years the company took out $30,000 in gold. But the mine was forced to close down because of a lack of money and equipment.

Later, in 1870, as predicted by Heuck, gold was discovered in the mountains north and east of San Diego in the Julian area (see FEBRUARY 20 and NOVEMBER 27). Julian and Banner City were important towns during the 1870s because of the gold mines there. This was some 20 years after the big gold rush days of 1849 to 1855 in Northern California. You can visit an old gold mine today in Julian at the Eagle Mining Company.

Legends, which have grown over the years, tell of earlier findings of gold in San Diego County. The Indians were said to have given the padres gold dust in exchange for trinkets during the mission times in the 1700s and early 1800s. When the padres asked where the gold dust came from, the Indians said it came from far inland where they pounded a certain quartz mineral outcrop to extract the gold. The padres asked the Indians to show them the place, and it is said that the padres set up *arrastras* (crude stone mills for crushing gold out of rocks) and worked the area successfully for many years. There is also evidence of early gold mining activities by the Indians or the early padres in Escondido, and in the Black Mountain area east of Escondido and west of Mesa Grande.

JUNE 18, 1895

ON THIS DAY IN SAN DIEGO HISTORY the Nuevo post office was officially renamed Ramona. The town that we know today as Ramona had had the official post office name of Nuevo for its first 12 years. It was originally named Nuevo (Spanish for "New") because it was the new town that grew up west of Ballena, which was the first development in the Santa Maria Valley in the 1860s and 70s. All that remains of Ballena today are a few scattered houses, where the Golden Eagle Horse Ranch is now located on Highway 78 east of Ramona (see SEPTEMBER 5).

After the publication of Helen Hunt Jackson's novel *Ramona* in 1884, the name of the heroine in the book, Ramona, became very popular. Some of the town leaders in Nuevo tried to change the name of the town to Ramona, but there was already a town by that name in Los Angeles County. Then, in 1895, when the Ramona Post Office in Los Angeles County officially closed down, the name became available. The U.S. Post Office agreed to the name change on this date—June 18, 1895.

The town of Ramona eventually superceded Ballena as the major town in the backcountry of San Diego County. The Ballena Post Office closed down in 1902. The Witch Creek Post Office handled their mail until it closed down in 1938. Witch Creek, now reduced to a few old ranch houses along Highway 78, was located east of Ballena on the road to Santa Ysabel and Julian. In the early days, Witch Creek had a two-story hotel and also a general store, which was an important stagecoach stop on the trip between San Diego and Julian. The former general store can be seen today on Highway 78 between Ramona and Santa Ysabel as the attractively restored old wood-frame house and associated buildings—which have been painted green with white trim and red roofs.

Witch Creek got its name from a creek running through the area that the Indians named Haguochay, which means "Bewitched Water." An Indian legend tells of an Indian who drank water from the creek and dropped dead soon after. The Witch Creek Fire that caused so much damage in San Diego County in October 2007 was so named because it started in this area.

After 1938 Ramona handled the mail for all of the backcountry area. Today the Ramona Post Office handles rural delivery mail covering approximately 75 square miles in the backcountry of San Diego County.

JUNE 19, 1951

ON THIS DAY IN SAN DIEGO HISTORY Kellogg Park by the La Jolla Shores beach was dedicated. A large tract of land had been donated by Florence Scripps Kellogg, the widow of Frederick William Kellogg. She had donated the land in memory of her husband. The city of San Diego added some more land to her gift to complete the park.

Florence Scripps Kellogg was a niece of the beloved Ellen Browning Scripps, who made many generous donations to San Diego and especially to La Jolla (see OCTOBER 18). Florence Scripps' husband, Frederick William Kellogg, built and developed the La Jolla Beach & Tennis Club in La Jolla Shores. He bought the former La Jolla Beach & Yacht Club in 1935 (see JANUARY 29). Then he focused the club on tennis, built four tennis courts, and changed the name to La Jolla Beach & Tennis Club. Later, an Olympic-size swimming pool was added, as well as the 42-unit Beach Club Apartments, and eventually the Marine Room restaurant. When Kellogg died in 1940, his son William Scripps Kellogg took over management and development of the property.

The La Jolla Shores residential development began in 1926 when a giant auction was held to sell lots. Nearly 10,000 people turned out for the event (see APRIL 21). Even though as many as 120 lots were sold on auction day, it would be another ten years before any significant number of houses were built there, due to the San Diego land crash of 1927 and the national stock market crash of 1929. In 1929 there were only a few homes in La Jolla Shores. The earliest homes built were the "Seven Sisters"—seven homes built during the late 1920s in the Spanish style with red tile roofs, some of which still remain and are designated as historic sites.

Today the La Jolla Shores area, and especially Kellogg Park, is a popular place for people from all over San Diego who come to swim and sunbathe on the beach and picnic on the green grass of the park—which was dedicated on this date, June 19, 1951.

JUNE 20, 1918

ON THIS DAY IN SAN DIEGO HISTORY the Triangle Film Corporation sent a letter to the San Diego Board of Park Commissioners requesting to take a "moving picture of the pigeons in the Plaza at Balboa Park." The filming would include "several scenes of a man and a girl feeding the pigeons and one or two scenes at a table in an open air Cafe in Paris."

Ever since the international recognition that Balboa Park received during the Panama-California Exposition of 1915–16, it had become a favorite place for film companies to use for making their movies. Between 1915 and 1930 there were more than 50 inquiries into filming in Balboa and other San Diego parks.

The plaza at Balboa Park was an especially popular place for filming. The buildings there were originally built around a rectangular court or plaza that went from a gate at Laurel Street in the west to Park Avenue in the east. Two of the favorite places to film movies in the park in the early days were the Indian Village and the Painted Desert, which looked like the colored rock areas of Arizona.

One of the first movies to be filmed in Balboa Park was a Max Sennett comedy, *Fatty and Mable at the San Diego Exposition*, starring two popular comedians of the time, Roscoe "Fatty" Arbuckle and Mable Normand. It was filmed in 1915 during the Panama-California Exposition. Over 30 movies were filmed in in the park between 1915 and 2000, one of the most famous being the Orsen Wells' movie *Citizen Kane*.

In his article "San Diego Filmography" in the Spring 2002 issue of the *Journal of San Diego History*, Gregory L. Williams, curator of photographs at the San Diego Historical Society, lists a total of 752 movies, including TV movies, that were filmed in various locations in the San Diego area between 1898 and 2003. Coronado in particular was a favorite place for filming, where approximately 75 films were made between 1898 and 2000. One of the best known of these was *Some Like It Hot*, filmed at the Hotel del Coronado in 1959, starring Marilyn Monroe (see also MAY 28).

JUNE 21, 1877

ON THIS DAY IN SAN DIEGO HISTORY José Palomares, one of the Californio soldiers who fought for Mexico against the United States in the Mexican-American War, was reflecting back on the Battle of San Pasqual, which was fought in San Diego County on December 6, 1846. He wrote in his recollections:

> With our lances and swords we attacked the enemy forces, who could not make good use of neither their firearms nor of their swords… [W]e did not fire a single shot, the combat was more favorable to us with our sidearms [swords]. Quickly the battle became so bloody that we became intermingled one with the other and barely were able to distinguish one from the other by voice and by the dim light of dawn which began to break.

An Indian woman named Felicita, who was the daughter of Capitán Pedro José Panto, the head of the San Pasqual Indian Pueblo, also reported on the battle:

> The Americans did not shoot their guns many times: perhaps the rain had made the powder wet. They struck with their guns and used the sword, while the Mexicans used their long lances and their *riatas* [lariats or ropes used for lassoing]. The mules that the Americans rode were frightened and ran all through the willows by the river. After them rode the Mexicans on their swift horses, striking with the lance and *lassoing* with the riata; it was a very terrible time.

See DECEMBER 6 for more on the Battle of San Pasqual. See JANUARY 7 for more on Capitán Panto and his part in it.

JUNE 22, 1917

ON THIS DAY IN SAN DIEGO HISTORY a great "Whale Barbeque" was held at the La Jolla cove. This was during World War I, and an Army base called Camp Kearny was being constructed east of La Jolla on the mesa north of Mission Valley. Camp Kearny was later to become the Miramar Air Station, which is now operated by the Marine Corps.

Soldiers from Camp Kearny liked to visit La Jolla on their days off, so La Jolla often planned events for their entertainment. The soldiers were invited to the big Whale Barbeque on this date in 1917. The governor of Baja California was also present, and a 45-piece band was there for entertainment. Whale meat was obtained for the barbeque, and everyone said it was a great success. Somehow, though, no great demand for whale meat resulted from this event.

Six months later, on Christmas 1917, La Jolla entertained the troops from Camp Kearny again by putting on a play for them. The *La Jolla Journal* newspaper reported that:

> 25 big trucks from Camp Kearney came rumbling through the streets, each loaded with 50 fine, upstanding men hurrahing in true holiday style and cheering for La Jolla...the soldier boys filed into the Community House, singing lustily until the curtain rose on "Hyacinth Harvey," a delightful comedy which was put on especially for their benefit.

Another Army camp, Camp Callan, would later open up near La Jolla in 1941, during World War II, and those soldiers also flocked to La Jolla in large numbers on their days off (see NOVEMBER 6). Eventually a U.S.O. (United Service Organization) club was established in La Jolla to provide a recreation facility for the World War II soldiers (see JANUARY 15 and MARCH 8).

JUNE 23, 1891

ON THIS DAY IN SAN DIEGO HISTORY William E. Ritter married Dr. Mary Bennett, and they honeymooned in San Diego at the Hotel del Coronado. Dr. William Ritter would later become the first director of the Scripps Institution for Biological Research—now known as the Scripps Institution of Oceanography.

The story is told that, while on his honeymoon, the soon-to-be Dr. Ritter collected sea specimens for his doctoral thesis research. It seems that, while on a sailboat in San Diego Bay with his new bride, Mr. Ritter took the helm and, shortly thereafter, the boat capsized. They were rescued by the crew of a dredge working nearby. Mr. Ritter immediately began searching through the dredgings looking for interesting marine animals—even before his bride was hauled out of the water!

Dr. Mary Bennett Ritter was a physician and, while she and her husband were in San Diego on their honeymoon, they met up with two other physicians, Dr. Fred Baker and his wife, Dr. Charlotte Baker. Fred Baker was also a shell collector who was interested in marine biology. Baker later encouraged William Ritter to come to San Diego to start up his marine biological station and paved the way by convincing the San Diego Chamber of Commerce to set up the Marine Laboratory Committee for fund raising. Fred Baker also convinced Elisha Babcock, owner of the Hotel del Coronado, to offer the hotel's boathouse to William to use in the summers for his marine biological work.

For more information on the beginnings of the Scripps Institution of Oceanography, see MARCH 23.

JUNE 24, 1934

ON THIS DAY IN SAN DIEGO HISTORY the mystery of the exact location of the San Felipe Stage Station was cleared up when a *San Diego Union* newspaper article by William L. Wright reported on the findings of an investigative team who had searched the area for clues.

On County Highway S-2 about a mile northwest of Scissors Crossing—S-2's intersection with State Highway 78 in northeast San Diego County near Anza-Borrego Desert State Park—there stands a California Historical Landmarks monument. The San Felipe Stage Station was believed to have stood near this area, but it was torn down sometime between 1888 and 1892, and its exact location was not determined with certainty until the investigating party's 1934 site visit.

The team, which included representatives from the Automobile Club of Southern California, found an L-shaped rock foundation on a small hill next to a large cottonwood tree. There is a legend that the tree grew from a hitching post that was put into the ground near the stage station stables. The team also found dozens of handmade square nails in that same area, which is in keeping with old accounts of the stage station being a large wood-frame building. In an interview with Ed Mason, a long-time resident of nearby Mason Valley, Mason stated that the San Felipe Stage Station "was the only wooden station on the western length of the Butterfield [mail route]" and that the building "was built of bull pine, fir, and cedar, whipsawed almost at the summit of Volcan Mountain and hauled down by oxen."

Historical Landmark No. 793 states:

> San Felipe Valley and Stage Station. Here the southern trail of explorers, trappers, soldiers, and emigrants crossed ancient trade routes of Kamia [Kumeyaay], Cahuilla, Diegueño, and Luiseño Indians. On the flat, southwest across the creek, Warren F. Hall built and operated the San Felipe home station of the Butterfield Mail, which operated from 1858 to 1861. Later the station was used by Banning Stages and by the military during the Civil War.

See also DECEMBER 1.

JUNE 25, 1917

ON THIS DAY IN SAN DIEGO HISTORY the first bathing suit regulation was established in La Jolla. Ordinance 7056 made it illegal for anyone over the age of ten to appear on the street or any other public place in a bathing suit, except in the vicinity of La Jolla Cove, "unless there is worn over such bathing or swimming suit a coat, cloak, or other garment covering the entire person except for head, hands, and feet."

Violation could result in a fine of not more than $25 or imprisonment for not more than 25 days, or both!

Some 14 years later, in August 1931, the ordinance was rescinded. The newspaper wrote: "Henceforth, only good personal taste on the part of bathers will rule, unless lack of good taste becomes so marked that it becomes necessary to frame another ordinance."

Guidelines for what constitutes "good personal taste" have certainly relaxed over the years, as one can observe today when walking on the streets of La Jolla (and other beach cities) and observing the skimpy outfits people are wearing. The people of 1917 would probably get quite a shock if they came back today and saw what people are wearing now.

JUNE 26, 1927

On this day in San Diego history the following headline appeared in the *Coronado Journal*: "Local Architect Returns From a Visit to Spain." The local architect was William Templeton Johnson, who had won a competition to design three buildings to hold American exhibits in the 1929 Iberian-American Exposition in Seville. Johnson had competed against six other architects to design the buildings.

Johnson had built a local reputation in San Diego during the 1920s for designing such buildings as the La Jolla Library in 1921 (now the Athenaeum Music & Arts Library). He designed two buildings in Balboa Park—the Fine Arts Gallery in 1927 and the Museum of Natural History in 1932.

Johnson also designed two buildings in downtown San Diego: the San Diego Trust & Savings Bank building at 6th and Broadway in 1928, which is now the Marriott Courtyard Hotel, and the smaller building across Broadway—the Samuel I. Fox Building (also known as the Lion Clothing Company building) in 1929. This latter building now houses Western Dental and a few other miscellaneous businesses.

William Templeton Johnson was born in New York in 1877. He came to San Diego in 1912 at the age of 35 after studying architecture at Columbia University in New York and at the École des Beaux-Arts in Paris. One of the early buildings he designed in San Diego in 1912 was the Francis W. Parker School building at 4201 Randolph Street in Mission Hills. This school was founded by his wife, Clara Sturges Johnson, and was based on the educational philosophy of Colonel Francis W. Parker of Chicago. The Spanish Mission–style building still houses the Parker Elementary School.

One of Johnson's most beautiful and prominent designs for a building in San Diego is the Serra Museum, which was built in 1929 on historic Presidio Hill (see February 10 and May 8). He also participated in the design of the County Administration Building at 1600 Pacific Highway, along with several other architects, in 1936.

JUNE 27, 1542

ON THIS DAY IN SAN DIEGO HISTORY Juan Rodriguez Cabrillo sailed his two ships, the *San Salvadore* and the *Victoria*, from Navidad, near the present-day city of Manzanillo on the Pacific coast of Mexico. They were heading northward to search for a passage that was believed to exist connecting the Atlantic and Pacific Oceans. They never found the northwest passage, but they did find San Diego Bay.

Cabrillo had spent the previous four years building ships for Spain in Guatemala using wood from the Guatemalan forests, instruments and metal work from Spain, and native labor. He built a total of 13 ships, two of which were on this journey up the west coast of Mexico, across the Sea of Cortez, and northward up the Pacific coast of Baja California—which the Spaniards believed to be an island with a northwest passage at the northern end, which they called the Strait of Anian.

Six weeks later, in mid-September, Cabrillo and his ships spent five days at the port of Ensenada in Baja California before continuing northward. Then on September 28 they spotted Point Loma and entered what we know today as San Diego Bay—the first Europeans to come to the west coast of California (see SEPTEMBER 28).

Even though Cabrillo is credited with being the first European to enter San Diego Bay by boat, he may not have been the first European that the local Indians had encountered. In his interesting book *San Diego Legends* (published by Sunbelt Publications of San Diego), Jack Innis reports on the possibility that the Indians who greeted Cabrillo in 1542 had previously met up with Spaniards further inland. He speculates that they might have been exploring the southern Colorado River in the vicinity of Yuma as early as 1539 or 1540, and may have crossed over into what would later be San Diego County. One of these Spaniards could have been the well-known explorer Francisco Vasquez de Coronado. This could explain why it appeared to Cabrillo's party that the local Indians seemed to be somewhat familiar with the ways of European horsemen and soldiers.

JUNE 28, 1886

ON THIS DAY IN SAN DIEGO HISTORY a claim was made on a gold mine located on a steep hillside west of Banner and up the hill toward Julian. It was a small one named the Ruby Mine. Gold was first discovered in the Julian–Banner area some 16 years earlier in 1870 (see FEBRUARY 20 and NOVEMBER 27).

Six years later, in 1892, a five-stamp mill was built at the site of the mine. This saved the owners from hauling the ore down the mountain to Banner for another mill owner to process for them.

The Ruby Mine was one of the smaller mines in the Julian–Banner–Cuyamaca region—producing a total of less than $25,000 in gold. The overall gold production for the entire Julian–Banner–Cuyamaca district amounted to about $5 million. The most productive mine, by far, was the Stonewall Mine with a production of $2,000,000. The next most productive mines were:

Golden Chariot:	$700,000
Ready Relief:	$500,000
Helvetia:	$450,000
Owens:	$450,000
Blue Hill or **Gardiner:**	$200,000
North Hubbard:	$200,000
Ranchita:	$150,000

In addition, 15 mines produced between $25,000 and $50,000 each, and 16 mines, including the Ruby Mine, produced less than $25,000 each.

Compared to California's total of over $2.2 billion in gold at $20 an ounce, the $5 million produced by San Diego County's Julian–Banner–Cuyamaca district accounted for less than one-fourth of 1% of California's total gold production.

JUNE 29, 1936

ON THIS DAY IN SAN DIEGO HISTORY legislation passed by Congress made over 365,000 acres of federal land available to add to the Borego Palms Desert State Park. Two years later the name of the new expanded state park was changed to the Anza Desert State Park. This name had been suggested earlier by Guy L. Fleming, southern California state park district superintendent. Fleming was later instrumental in finding support for the Torrey Pines State Reserve, along the Pacific Ocean between La Jolla and Del Mar, where there is now a trail named for him (see MAY 7).

Fleming wrote a letter to Clinton G. Abbott, director of the San Diego Society of Natural History, explaining why he was recommending the new name for the park: "When the question of a name for this large Desert Park came up I proposed that it be called the Anza Desert State Park and that the area be dedicated as a monument to Captain Juan Bautista de Anza, who first explored and reported upon the region." Part of Anza's expeditions of 1774 and 1775 crossed over the desert areas that are now part of the park (see JANUARY 4 and OCTOBER 4).

We now know this largest state wilderness area in California as the Anza-Borrego Desert State Park (see JULY 6). According to Diana Lindsay in her book *Anza-Borrego A to Z*, the park:

> has received world acclaim for its unbroken Plio-Pleistocene fossil record...as a home for rare and endangered plants and animals, and for its designation as a United Nations Biosphere Reserve... It is a Natural National Landmark, so designated in the mid-1970s by Secretary of the Interior Rogers Morton.

JUNE 30, 1889

ON THIS DAY IN SAN DIEGO HISTORY the "First Annual Report of the San Diego County Hospital and Poor Farm" was prepared for the county board of supervisors for the year ending June 30, 1889. The report stated that the hospital had been established on July 1, 1872 and that "up to June 30, 1889 [had] accommodated 1,237 patients." That would be an average of nearly 73 patients per year. It should be noted that the population of San Diego County had and was growing substantially—from 4,951 in 1870 to 34,397 in 1890.

The San Diego County Hospital and Poor Farm was located on 140 acres in Mission Valley—about three and a half miles from the city of San Diego where today's Highway 163 heads south from Mission Valley toward Hillcrest. The hospital could accommodate 60 patients. On the farm there were four acres of orchards being cultivated with figs, apricots, peaches, and oranges. There was a four-acre vegetable garden. The farm had two windmills, chicken houses, and several outbuildings.

Some of the illnesses the people in the hospital were treated for at that time included abscess, apoplexy (stroke), arthritis, anemia, bronchitis, contusions (bruising), cardiac disease, cirrhosis (liver disease), conjunctivitis (inflammation of the eye surface), alcoholism, dysentery, malaria, phthisis (tuberculosis), and burns.

The hospital was later moved up the hill above Mission Valley, and the Poor Farm, later known as Edgemoor Farms, was moved to Santee. Mission Valley was later taken over by the Mountain Meadow Dairy Farm—quite a difference from the Mission Valley we know today that is filled with hotels, shopping centers, a giant football stadium, and multiple lanes of freeway.

JULY 1, 1769

ON THIS DAY IN SAN DIEGO HISTORY Father Junípero Serra and his overland party arrived at San Diego Harbor after traveling up the Baja California peninsula from Loreto, a distance of 900 miles that took 39 days. Awaiting their arrival were the two ships that had carried men and supplies from La Paz, Baja California, the *San Carlos* and the *San Antonio*. The men of the first overland expedition that had arrived six weeks earlier were also there. The purpose of these expeditions was Spain's attempt to start a mission and presidio (military fort) at San Diego and at Monterey.

Father Juan Crespí, the priest on the first overland expedition, wrote in his diary, "[T]he reverend father president [Father Serra] with the remainder of the expedition arrived between eleven and twelve in the forenoon on the first of July. Thank the Lord, all of them reached here well, without the slightest change or breach in their health."

Father Crespí had reason to be concerned about the health of the party, especially that of Father Serra. Serra, at the age of 55, had been suffering from poor health and an infected foot and leg at the start of the expedition. He had to be lifted up onto a mule to start the difficult 900-mile trip. No one at this time would have believed that he would live another 15 years after this grueling trip, to become a guiding force in the founding of Catholic missions in Alta California.

Father Serra wrote this in his diary after arriving in San Diego: "Thanks be to God, I arrived at this Port of San Diego. It is beautiful to behold and does not belie its reputation… [I]t was a day of great rejoicing and merriment for all…and for us a great source of happiness."

JULY 2, 1919

ON THIS DAY IN SAN DIEGO HISTORY efforts were being made to raise money for the restoration of the San Diego Mission. Headlines in an article in the *San Diego Union* newspaper stated: "Only $3,000 Needed to Finance First Step Toward Restoration of Mission: Citizens Urged to Aid Restoration."

Efforts had been made back in 1899 by the Land Marks Club and George W. Marston, an influential San Diego businessman, to save the deteriorating San Diego Mission, but not enough money was available to do anything but cap the crumbling walls and foundations to prevent further erosion and destruction (see OCTOBER 17). Then World War I (1914–18) interrupted any other attempts at restoration.

In 1919, after World War I was over, George Marston reorganized the local Land Marks Club Mission Restoration Committee. He was joined by Albert V. Mayrhofer, head of the Native Sons and Daughters of the Golden West. By 1929 money had been raised from various sources—including the Catholic church, the Nazareth House Orphanage (which was located right next to the old mission), and such local leaders as Ellen Browning Scripps, Colonel Ed Fletcher, and Marston himself

In 1929, the year of the stock market crash, one of the local San Diego banks containing $7,250 of the mission restoration money went out of business and the money was lost. The bishop of the Catholic Church came forth with a replacement of the $7,250 plus another $15,000 for the mission restoration cause. Finally, in 1930, the restoration of the mission began (see JULY 13).

JULY 3, 1872

ON THIS DAY IN SAN DIEGO HISTORY José Guadalupe Estudillo received a patent to the Janal Rancho. The Janal Rancho consisted of 4,436 acres and was located adjacent to the Otay Rancho. The name Janal is an Indian name that is believed to mean "Spongy Ground." It was a former Indian *rancheria* (Indian settlement).

The Janal Rancho was originally granted to José Guadalupe Estudillo's father, José Antonio Estudillo, in 1829 as a Mexican land grant. The adjoining rancho, the Otay Rancho, was also owned by the Estudillo family, a prominent San Diego family in the early days. The father, José Antonio Estudillo, was a former *alcalde* (mayor) of San Diego. His father, Captain José-Mara Estudillo, an army officer, built the Casa de Estudillo in Old Town in 1829, one of the original Old Town adobe houses, where several generations of the Estudillo family lived. It is now restored and is a museum that is open to the public to visit.

The grandson, José Guadalupe Estudillo, who received the Rancho Janal on this date in 1872, was also a respected citizen of San Diego. He served as San Diego County treasurer and also as California state treasurer.

The lands of the original Janal Rancho are located about seven miles east of the present-day town of Chula Vista. Part of the rancho lands are now covered by the Upper and Lower Otay reservoirs, which contribute to San Diego's water supply.

JULY 4, 1925

ON THIS DAY IN SAN DIEGO HISTORY the roller coaster known as the Giant Dipper opened at Belmont Park in Mission Beach. Back then the cost to ride the roller coaster was 15 cents per person.

The Giant Dipper has also been known as Earthquake and simply as the Belmont Park Roller Coaster, until the original name of the Giant Dipper was reinstated. It is one of only a very few wooden roller coasters in the country. There is also a wooden roller coaster in Santa Cruz, California.

Ownership of the Giant Dipper and of Belmont Park has changed many times over the years. Belmont Park was opened by the Spreckels Company in 1925 and then donated to the State Park Commission in 1934. In 1967 it was bought by Bill Evans, owner of the Bahia and Catamaran hotels. Evans planned to demolish the 47-year-old structure and build a hotel there. But there were many protests from people who wanted to preserve the roller coaster and the park. In 1976 the deteriorating park was closed down and suffered damage from vandalism—including fires in 1981 that further damaged the roller coaster, which by then had been listed on the National Register of Historic Places. In 1984 Evans donated the roller coaster to the Save the Coaster Committee.

Finally, in 1990, after much fundraising, the Giant Dipper was restored and reopened. The City of San Diego tried to buy it back, but it remains in private hands. Today, over 80 years after it first opened, people are still able to ride 2,600 exciting feet of track over 13 hills at 43 thrilling miles per hour on the Giant Dipper.

JULY 5, 1768

ON THIS DAY IN SAN DIEGO HISTORY José de Gálvez landed in southern Baja California after sailing up and across the Gulf of California from the west coast of Mexico. He had been appointed by the king of Spain, Carlos III, to be the visitador general (Spanish for "visitor general") to Mexico, a position empowered to create new reforms and programs in the Spanish-controlled Mexico.

Gálvez formulated the plan for Spain to establish missions and military settlements in Alta California, the first of which would be San Diego. Spain was worried about the Russians or the English making expeditions to claim areas there.

Gálvez's efforts led to the overland and sea expeditions from southern Baja California to San Diego in 1769 to establish the San Diego Mission and Presidio (military settlement) (see JANUARY 9). And he chose the people to lead the overland expeditions. In a letter to Captain Fernando De Rivera, Gálvez wrote:

> In accordance with my instructions, Governador Don Gaspar de Portolá will lead as chief in the important expedition... To prevent the failure of such an important enterprise, the governor needs a second in command to assist him in bringing about the success of the journey, one capable of substituting for him in any emergency that may occur. From the activity and zeal with which you serve His Majesty, and your practical knowledge of the Indian natives of the country, I have well-founded confidence that you will perform the duties of this commission to my satisfaction and that of the governor. I name you as his assistant and second in command.

So there would be two overland expeditions to San Diego—one led by Gaspar de Portolá and Father Junípero Serra and the other led by Captain Rivera and Father Juan Crespí (see JULY 1).

The rest is history. The Misión San Diego de Alcalá, the first Spanish mission in what is now the state of California, was officially founded on July 16, 1769 by the religious leader of the expedition, Father Junípero Serra (see JULY 16).

JULY 6, 1928

ON THIS DAY IN SAN DIEGO HISTORY the *Ramona Sentinel* newspaper reported about the desert area near Borrego Springs in northeastern San Diego County that was being considered for designation as a state park: "The proposed new park in Palm canyon has been bringing in a number of visitors the past week. Palm canyon would make an ideal winter park, with the beautiful wild flowers we have here in the winter, and no fogs—nothing but balmy old sunshine."

Five years later, in 1933, the Borego Palms Desert State Park was formed after receiving 185,000 acres of federal lands, according to Phil Brigandi in his book *Borrego Beginnings*. In 1936 another 365,000 acres of federal land was acquired to add to the park. In 1938 the name of the new expanded park was changed to Anza Desert State Park (see JUNE 29).

As more and more visitors came to the park, there was a need for more intense management. This resulted in the formation of two separate parks in 1953: the Anza Desert State Park in the south and the Borrego State Park in the north.

Four years later, in 1957, there was a need to recombine the two parks into one—the Anza-Borrego Desert State Park "in order to control hunting, destruction of Indian sites, vandalism, removal of plants and geologic specimens, and to prevent the misuse of motor vehicles, ground fires, and grazing," according to Diana Lindsay in her book *Anza-Borrego A to Z*.

Today the Anza-Borrego Desert State Park is the largest state wilderness area in California and the largest contiguous state park in the United States except for Alaska. It contains over 650,000 acres (over 1,000 square miles) and is designated as a National Natural Landmark. The park occupies over one-fifth (22%) of San Diego County.

The name of the park came from two sources: the Spanish explorer Juan Bautista de Anza, who led Spanish expeditions through the desert in 1774 and 1775 (see FEBRUARY 5 and OCTOBER 4); and *borrego*, the Spanish name for the yearling lamb of the endangered peninsular bighorn sheep that live in the park lands.

JULY 7, 1888

ON THIS DAY IN SAN DIEGO HISTORY the City & University Heights Railroad opened. It was also known as the Park Belt Motor Road and the University Heights Motor Road. It was a ten-mile railroad line that went from a terminal at 18th and A streets and traveled through City Park (now known as Balboa Park) by way of Switzer Canyon to what is now Marlborough Street. The train line then headed back to downtown via 5th Street.

The train line was opened up to entice buyers to real estate developments in the University Heights and Normal Heights areas. But the real estate bubble burst in the late 1880s, and the City & University Heights Railroad went bankrupt after one year and closed down. An economic depression followed in 1890. San Diego's population dropped from an estimated 40,000 in 1887 to 16,159 in 1890.

The University Heights and Normal Heights areas would not get going again until over ten years later, in the early 1900s. The San Diego State Normal School, forerunner of San Diego State University, started up in the Normal Heights area in 1897 (see MARCH 13). The train line, had it lasted, would have been important to the early development of those new areas of San Diego. In the early days, before the 1900s, the automobile had not been invented yet, so the only means of transportation were horse and buggy, stagecoach, train, and streetcar.

In 1890 a cable car line, the San Diego Cable Railway, also destined for failure, opened up. It went from downtown at 6th and C streets to Park and Adams Avenue. It lasted only a year before closing down, after great losses and the failure of the bank that was financing it (see JUNE 7).

Then John Spreckels, a successful businessman from San Francisco, arrived in San Diego in 1891. He rescued several businesses in San Diego, including buying the San Diego Streetcar Company that had started up in 1886 as San Diego's first public transit system with horse-drawn and mule-drawn streetcars that went from downtown San Diego to the bay. Spreckels also acquired the defunct City & University Heights Railroad, the Coronado Railroad, and the National City and Otay Railroad—expanding them and creating a successful electric public transportation system, the San Diego Electric Railway, that started in 1892 and lasted until the 1940s (see APRIL 23).

JULY 8, 1852

ON THIS DAY IN SAN DIEGO HISTORY the United States Senate rejected the Indian treaties that had been signed earlier that year, one of which was the Treaty of Temecula. Temecula was a part of San Diego County then, until 1893 when the northern portion of San Diego County was split off to form Riverside County.

Representatives of the Luiseño, Cahuilla, and Serrano Indian tribes had met with the United States Indian commissioner at the Pablo Apis Adobe in Temecula to sign the teaty. (For more on Pablo Apis, see SEPTEMBER 17). The treaty provided for a reservation to protect the Indians and their lands from takeover by Americans and Californios. The Indians were to cede all other lands to the government, and the government was to provide agricultural assistance to the Indians to provide food for their people.

A total of 18 treaties were signed between the U.S. Indian commissioners and the California Indian tribes, the 18th being at Santa Ysabel in northeast San Diego County. Unfortunately for the Indians, most of the Americans in California opposed the treaties because they threatened loss of their farming and/or mining lands. The California legislature recommended to the United States Senate that it not confirm the Indian treaties. And so the Indian treaties were rejected by the U.S. Senate on this date, July 8, 1852—another example of unfairness to the Indians on the part of the white people in those days.

Thirty years later, in 1882, Helen Hunt Jackson visited San Diego to research injustices to the Indians of southern California and to visit Indian sites. This was in preparation for writing her famous novel, *Ramona*, which exposed the unfair ways that Indians had been treated (see March 3).

JULY 9, 1857

ON THIS DAY IN SAN DIEGO HISTORY the San Antonio & San Diego Mail Line began. It was also called Birch's Overland Mail and the Jackass Mail. It got the latter name because instead of following the old Emigrant Trail to Warner's Ranch and then heading south to San Diego where stagecoaches could travel, they followed a more direct—and more rugged—route over the Cuyamaca Mountains. This necessitated using mules to carry the mail over the rugged mountain trails. This saved them many miles and lots of time compared to the other route through Warner's Ranch.

This same route was used previously by another Jackass Mail line started by Sam Warnock and his friend Joe Swycaffer to carry mail between Fort Yuma and San Diego between 1854 and 1856 (see FEBRUARY 9).

James E. Birch, founder of San Antonio & San Diego Mail Line, left his stagecoaches at Fort Yuma and proceeded with mules the rest of the way to San Diego. After crossing the Cuyamacas, he proceeded through Green Valley, Guatay, and Viejas, and then down Mission Valley to the San Diego Mission and to Old Town Plaza (see AUGUST 31).

The San Antonio & San Diego Mail Line lasted only three years. The Civil War during the early 1860s caused private mail service to the west to shut down. The Cuyamaca trails were not used again until after 1870, when gold was discovered in the Julian–Banner–Cuyamaca area. After that, the same route that was used by the old Jackass Mail was used again to bring in supplies and take out gold to and from the mines.

JULY 10, 1769

ON THIS DAY IN SAN DIEGO HISTORY a list of "Goods and Supplies Sent by Land to Alta California" was signed by José de Gálvez (see JULY 5). Two overland expeditions set out from the southern part of Baja California on their way to San Diego to start a Spanish mission and a presidio (military fort) (see JANUARY 9).

Here is the list of "Provisions, Cattle, Horses, and Mules for Officers and Troops" for the land expeditions to Alta California:

150 bushels of corn	6½ pounds of ground pepper
5 tons of white flour	500 pounds of beef tallow
1150 pounds of chocolate	354 pints of wine
4 cases of soap	144 pints of brandy
5½ tons of (dried) beef	600 pounds of sugar
140 pounds of cheese	300 cows and calves
7½ pounds of ham	262 horses and mules
4 barrels for water	2 female donkeys
6 bushels of pinole	105 fully equipped pack saddles
3½ bushels of garbanzos	
27 bushels of beans	24 sheepskin saddle pads
1,050 pounds of dried figs	13 woven rush saddle blankets
1,050 pounds of raisins	
30 bushels of wheat	11 loads of sacking material (for packing items on mules)
3 pounds each of clove, cinnamon, and pepper	53 horse blankets of sacking material

And, this was not all—there were additional extensive lists of "Armaments," "Utensils, Goods, and Replacement Materials," and "Holy Ornaments and Sacred Vessels" that were also brought along. The expeditions went through desolate desert and mountainous areas where there were no places to stop for supplies. They stopped to rest up at the few missions that had been established previously in Baja California by the Jesuits. But the lands around the missions were arid and sandy, and the missions could not grow enough crops to sustain themselves. So the overland expeditions to Alta California had to bring with them all of the supplies that they would need for the trip. The first land party took 51 days to get to San Diego and the second party took 39 days.

JULY 11, 1776

ON THIS DAY IN SAN DIEGO HISTORY Father Junípero Serra returned to San Diego from Monterey to arrange for the rebuilding of the San Diego Mission after it was burned down by the Indians the previous November (see NOVEMBER 5).

Father Serra was visiting the mission that he founded at Monterey in 1770, the second mission to be founded in Alta California. He returned to San Diego by boat when he learned of the damage to the San Diego Mission.

The San Diego Mission was rebuilt with the help of the Indians who were loyal to it and the sailors from the boat, who made adobe bricks, dug trenches, and gathered stone. Wood for the new mission was brought from Smith Mountain, 60 miles away. When a tree was cut down, the bark and branches were stripped off, a group of Indians lifted it from the ground, and a priest blessed it. The story goes that the logs were carried by relays of Indian converts (Indians who had been baptized into the Catholic faith) all the way to the site of the mission, and that the Indians never allowed the logs to touch the ground.

While the mission was being rebuilt, mission activities were conducted on Presidio Hill. The reconstruction down in Mission Valley was completed in December 1776, when the first Indian converts were baptized at the new mission.

JULY 12, 1912

ON THIS DAY IN SAN DIEGO HISTORY the 170-acre tract of land in the La Jolla Shores area that was occupied by the Marine Biological Association of San Diego was deeded over to the University of California, after which it was known as the Scripps Institution for Biological Research. Thirteen years later, in 1925, the name was changed to its present name, the Scripps Institution of Oceanography.

What would later become the Scripps Institution of Oceanography (SIO) started out in 1903 as a small laboratory for the Marine Biological Association of San Diego that was located in the boathouse of the Hotel del Coronado (see MARCH 23). After that, it moved to a small building that was built at the Cove in La Jolla in 1905 with the help of the Scripps family.

With further help from the Scripps family, the facility moved to its present location in La Jolla Shores in 1910. When the laboratory became a part of the University of California on this date in 1912, it meant that university courses could be taught and academic degrees could be awarded to students in marine biology—and later, after 1925—in all aspects of oceanography.

The first building at the new La Jolla Shores location was the two-story Scripps Biological Building, designed by the San Diego architect, Irving Gill (see AUGUST 29). The building still stands there today, having been designated as a San Diego Historic Site in 1977. When it was first built in 1910, the first floor was used as classrooms and research labs. Dr. William E. Ritter, a marine biologist and the first director of the Scripps Institution for Biological Research, lived on the second floor until a house could be built for him and his wife.

Between 1913 and 1916, 21 cottages were built to house the people who worked there. Some of those old cottages are still there, too—little wood-frame houses that continue to be used as offices and meeting-places. These inlcude the Martin Johnson House (named for a former professor of biological oceanography at SIO), where weddings and other social events are sometimes held, up on the hill above the campus, with its panoramic view of the La Jolla coastline.

JULY 13, 1930

ON THIS DAY IN SAN DIEGO HISTORY an article in the *San Diego Union* newspaper announced that the restoration of the run-down San Diego Mission—otherwise known as the Misión San Diego de Alcalá—would begin on July 16. This was exactly 161 years after the mission was first founded, when Father Junípero Serra in 1769 blessed its original location on Presidio Hill (see JULY 16). Efforts to restore the crumbling mission had been underway since 1899 (see JULY 2 and OCTOBER 17).

In order to restore the mission to its original state, special architects had to be hired, and old pictures and drawings had to be studied to determine what the original mission really looked like. Adobe bricks were used in the restoration using the same old methods that were used in the past—with local adobe clay mixed with water and cut straw. Hand-hewn wood from local oak or sycamore trees was used for the ceiling beams and rafters. The wood was then antiqued to look like the original old wood. Three former mission bells—and a fourth bell that was recast from the remains of several smaller bells—were re-hung in the *campanario* (Spanish for "bell tower") with rawhide-wrapped cables.

A little over one year later, in September 1931, nearly 400 people attended a historical pageant on the grounds of the restored mission, and a special high mass was held in the newly restored mission church, which was rededicated as a place of worship. The Native Sons and Daughters of the Golden West donated four flags which represented the different flags that have flown over the mission in the past—Spanish, Mexican, the bear flag of the California republic, and the flag of the United States.

The Misión San Diego de Alcalá is one of California's most important historic landmarks.

JULY 14, 1769

ON THIS DAY IN SAN DIEGO HISTORY Captain Gaspar de Portolá's exploration party stopped in a canyon to the north of San Diego Harbor on their way to establish a mission and presidio at Monterey. They had just arrived in San Diego two weeks before to establish a mission and presidio here. Father Junípero Serra remained in San Diego with a party of settlers and soldiers while Captain Portolá continued onward to Monterey with another group of soldiers and settlers.

One of the men on Portolá's expedition to Monterey, Miguel Constanso, wrote in his diary on this day: "We halted in a canyon to which we gave the name of San Diego and where there was an abundance of pasture."

The place they named San Diego Canyon was later named Rose Canyon after Louis Rose, San Diego's first Jewish settler who arrived in San Diego in 1850 and bought the land in 1854 (see MAY 30). Louis Rose had a tannery in Rose Canyon that produced over 4,500 skins a year from cows, sheep, goats, seals, and sea lions. The skins were shipped to San Francisco where they brought high prices.

Interstate 5 Freeway goes through Rose Canyon today—between Balboa Avenue (the turn-off to Pacific Beach) and Gilman Drive, just south of UCSD. This is the same route as the old Highway 101—Pacific Coast Highway—that was replaced by Interstate 5 in 1970.

JULY 15, 1991

ON THIS DAY IN SAN DIEGO HISTORY Dr. Roger Revelle died at the age of 82. Revelle was an oceanographer who was director of the Scripps Institution of Oceanography (SIO) from 1951 to 1964. Prior to that Revelle was a graduate student at SIO in the 1930s, receiving his Ph.D. degree in oceanography in 1936.

Revelle spent the war years during World War II in the Navy, where he participated in important naval research projects. In 1946 he was appointed as the Navy's chief oceanographer in Operation Crossroads, which tested the effects of atomic bombs on naval ships at Bikini Atoll in the Marshall Islands of the South Pacific Ocean. After the war, Revelle returned to Scripps.

During his years at Scripps as a student, as a research associate, and as director, he initiated and participated in many innovative programs, including leading oceanographic cruises to all parts of the world, which led to a greater understanding of the oceans. Under Revelle's leadership, SIO became well-known and respected worldwide. He was recognized as the nation's leading expert on global environmental issues and was appointed by President John F. Kennedy in 1961 as scientific advisor to the secretary of the interior.

In 1956 the regents of the University of California voted to build a university campus in the San Diego area, and Revelle was appointed to head the campus planning committee. He worked hard to promote the La Jolla location for the new university and to recruit distinguished faculty from all over the country. Although many people thought that Revelle deserved to he named chancellor of the new University of California at San Diego (UCSD), this did not happen. Herbert York, a physicist from UC Berkeley was appointed instead.

Roger Revelle left an important legacy of brilliance and innovative ideas to the Scripps Institution of Oceanography, UCSD, and to the world.

JULY 16, 1769

ON THIS DAY IN SAN DIEGO HISTORY San Diego was officially born. Father Junípero Serra and his fellow priests who had traveled from southern Baja California, Mexico to San Diego put up a wooden cross on Presidio Hill, blessed it, and officially dedicated the first mission in California. They also dedicated the first presidio (military settlement), which was set up to guard and protect the mission (see also JULY 1).

They built a chapel out of bushes and brush and soon after began constructing an adobe church. They named the mission Misión San Diego de Alcalá in honor of the Spanish saint for whom Vizcaíno had named the port back in 1602 (see NOVEMBER 12). The creation of the San Diego Mission on this day in 1769 was the first foothold of European civilization in California and became known as the "Plymouth Rock of the Pacific Coast."

Five years later, in 1774, because of poor soil and lack of water at the Presidio Hill site, the mission was moved six miles inland, where it is located today in Mission Valley.

Today the Junípero Serra Museum sits on top of Presidio Hill, thanks to the efforts of San Diego businessman George Marston (see JANUARY 12). There is a statue of Father Serra at Presidio Park located down the hill from the museum near the parking lot and the large brick cross. You have to look hard to find the statue of Father Serra—it is tucked away under the large pepper trees, at the site of the original presidio. You can reach it by a small path leading downhill from the parking lot.

The San Diego Mission and Presidio almost didn't make it. In March 1770, eight months after the mission was founded, it was almost abandoned. Supplies had become short, and the supply ship that was to come from Mexico did not arrive. Captain Portolá was ready to abandon the settlement and take his troops back to Mexico, but Father Serra asked him to wait a little longer. The supply ship arrived just in time to save the San Diego Mission from being abandoned (see MARCH 19).

JULY 17, 1929

ON THIS DAY IN SAN DIEGO HISTORY the *San Diego Union* newspaper reported on the day-long celebration of the day before, honoring the completion of the Junípero Serra Museum on Presidio Hill. The Serra Museum was built near the spot where, exactly 160 years before, Father Junípero Serra blessed a wooden cross and founded the first mission in Alta California, the Misión San Diego de Alcalá (see JULY 16).

Two thousand people turned out at 9:00 a.m. for the high mass celebrated outside the museum, followed by military bands from local marine and naval bases. The bands played for two hours, as more and more people came to view the museum and park.

Even though it was a hot day for San Diego, with temperatures in the 80s, an estimated total of 12,000 people arrived at the park by 2:30 p.m. for the official dedication ceremony.

At the ceremony a parade depicting historical events in San Diego was presented, starting with a portrayal of a Kumeyaay Indian village, followed by an enactment of the first contact between Indians and Spanish explorers, and ended with Father Serra raising the cross and blessing the land at Presidio Hill. Speeches were given by the governor of California, the Spanish ambassador to the United States, and other distinguished persons.

When George W. Marston got up to speak, he received a prolonged standing ovation. Marston was 79 years old on this date, and he was the one who had donated the Serra Museum and Presidio Park to the city of San Diego (see JANUARY 12).

In his speech Marston said, "In the arts of landscape and architecture the spirit of a city can be preserved for ages." He closed by entrusting the Serra Museum and Presidio Park to the citizens of San Diego "for safeguarding as a perpetual memorial to the Spanish people who brought civilization and the gospel to this Pacific shore."

JULY 18, 1834

ON THIS DAY IN SAN DIEGO HISTORY the San Felipe Rancho was granted to Luis Arenas, a Los Angeles merchant, by Mexican Governor José Figueroa. The rancho was located in northeast San Diego County in the San Felipe Valley northeast of present-day Julian and southwest of present-day Borrego Springs. It contained just under 10,000 acres and is bordered on the south by present-day State Highway 78.

In the past, several Indian settlements—called *rancherias*—were located here. Later, in 1846, when Governor Pío Pico approved Arenas' transfer of the rancho to Don Felipe de Castillo, it was with the provision that the Indians of the San Felipe Valley be treated fairly. Castillo was instructed to "observe a moral conduct and treatment towards the heathen Indians in the Valley of San Felipe and immediate neighborhood, to treat them with the requisite moderation and impart them good ideas and habits."

When Castillo died one year later and his son sold the property to Governor Pico's brother-in-law, Don Juan Forster, there was no provision for the Indians in the transfer. (For more on Don Juan Forster, see FEBRUARY 7, AUGUST 6, and DECEMBER 11). The Indians were often treated unfairly when it came to white people encroaching on their lands.

JULY 19, 1845

ON THIS DAY IN SAN DIEGO HISTORY the Guajome Rancho was granted to two Indians of the Mission San Luis Rey—Andrés and José Manuel—by the last Mexican governor of California, Pío Pico. The 2,200-acre Guajome Rancho was previously a part of the Mission San Luis Rey and was located west of the present-day Interstate 15 between today's towns of Vista and Bonsall.

The Indians did not hold onto the rancho but sold it to a prominent Los Angeles businessman and landowner, Abel Stearns, for $550. Stearns married Arcadia Bandini, daughter of Juan Bandini, a distinguished San Diego social and political leader. Later, when Arcadia's sister, Isadora Bandini, married Colonel Cave Johnson Couts in 1851, she was given the Guajome Rancho as a wedding gift (see APRIL 5).

This is another example of possible unfairness to the Indians about land grants—especially after California became a part of the United States following the Mexican-American War of 1846–48. The Indians were not as influential as the white people and were not able to deal as well with the legal negotiations required to obtain land grants. As a result, most of the land grants went to influential white people—even though the Indians were supposed to receive some of the former mission lands after the secularization of the missions and mission lands in 1834 (see SEPTEMBER 30).

Cave Couts, who lived on the Guajome Rancho after 1851, held many positions in San Diego's government over the years. He was a subagent for the San Luis Rey Indians and was said to show "a sympathetic and paternal attitude" toward the Indians. However, he was also a man with a violent temper who sometimes took the law into his own hands. Twice in 1855 he was charged by the San Diego grand jury with whipping two Indians with a rawhide whip. One of the Indians died from his injuries. Couts was later acquitted on a technicality—that one of the jurors was not an American citizen. Couts was also acquitted ten years later on a charge of shooting and killing a man in Old Town Plaza (see OCTOBER 9).

JULY 20, 1886

ON THIS DAY IN SAN DIEGO HISTORY Frank T. Botsford and his partner George W. Heald, who had purchased La Jolla Park a few months before, hired someone to drill for water—a necessity for developing the property into the residential lots he hoped to sell.

They drilled until they hit a granite ledge at 47 feet. Then Botsford bought another 20 acres east of La Jolla in Rose Canyon as another potential source for water. They finally found water there and put in a waterworks to supply the La Jolla Park subdivision.

The great La Jolla land auction to sell lots was held in 1887 (see APRIL 30), but water continued to be a problem. At first, large whiskey barrels were filled with water from the Rose Canyon well and carried up the hill to La Jolla by horses. Remember, there were no automobiles in the 1880s. At certain times water was not available at all for La Jolla.

Later, when water was piped to La Jolla, the pipes were so small that often the water pressure was too low to count on getting any water. An early visitor to La Jolla who ended up staying there, Walter Lieber (see APRIL 3), wrote this about La Jolla's water situation: "[W]ater only fed into the village by a two-inch pipe, and none in that pipe during the day, so we had to stay up at nights to get enough water for the next day's needs, gathered in tubs and buckets. There were at that time three bath tubs in the village, fed to cold water only."

The area had a history of water problems. A group of people in the early days thought La Jolla would be a good place for growing grapes. They imported grapevines from Italy and planted a vineyard in La Jolla, hoping to grow the grapes for wine. Unfortunately, the venture failed due primarily to the lack of available water.

JULY 21, 1905

ON THIS DAY IN SAN DIEGO HISTORY San Diego made national news because of the explosion of a ship in San Diego Harbor. The USS *Bennington*, a Navy gunboat, was anchored in the harbor when observers were shocked to hear a loud roaring noise.

A boiler had exploded on the ship below decks, killing 65 men and injuring 46. Military doctors were assisted by San Diego physicians in rescue operations. Open wagons were used to carry the large number of injured men to local hospitals.

Burials and funeral services were held at the military cemetery at Fort Rosecrans on Point Loma two days later. Hundreds of San Diegans attended the services, mourning the deaths of the sailors due to this unfortunate accident. A special monument was installed at Fort Rosecrans National Cemetery in their memory.

The *Bennington* was a steamship that burned coal to produce steam to power itself. It was scheduled to depart at noon, and the commander gave orders that morning for it to be steamed up. Then he left the ship and walked to town on Navy business. The crew began shoveling coal into the ship's furnaces. They shoveled for two hours, but the steam-pressure gauge registered zero, so they kept throwing on more coal. It turns out that a valve or air cock was incorrectly installed, preventing the steam from passing to the pressure gauge. The furnaces were building up steam even though the pressure gauge wasn't measuring it.

When the build-up of steam caused the *Bennington* to explode, the entire deck of the ship was lifted up. The bodies of many of the crew were thrown out into San Diego Bay, and many of those on board ship were severely burned. There were clouds of black smoke over the waterfront as the ship caught fire. The *Bennington* explosion is considered to be one of the deadliest peacetime disasters in the history of the U.S. Navy.

JULY 22, 1878

ON THIS DAY IN SAN DIEGO HISTORY the Cuca Rancho, located near Palomar Mountain, was granted to María Juana de Los Angeles by the United States Land Commission. She was previously granted this rancho by California governor Pío Pico in 1845 as a Mexican land grant when California was a part of Mexico. Ownership of ranchos in California had to be reapplied for through the U.S. Land Commission after the Mexican-American War of 1846–48. California became the 31st state of the United States in 1850.

The Cuca Rancho contained 2,174 acres and was later known as the Mendenhall Ranch—used primarily for raising cattle. At one point the Cuca Rancho was owned by a Luiseño Indian, Gregorio Trujillo, who married a descendent of the original owner of the rancho. The rancho is now contained within the 8,000 acre La Jolla Indian reservation that was established in 1892 for a band of the Luiseño Indians (Indians connected to the San Luis Rey Mission). *Cuca* is Spanish for a root used as a substitute for coffee.

The La Jolla Indian Reservation is not to be confused with the seaside community of La Jolla, even though they share the name. There is, in fact, some controversy over the origin of the name. Some people believe it came from the Spanish word *hoya*, meaning a hollow surrounded by hills. Some think it sounds like the Spanish word *olla*, which is a clay container for holding water. Others, especially those living in the beautiful coastal community of La Jolla, believe it comes from the Spanish word *joya*, meaning jewel. Some say that it could have come from an Indian word of unknown meaning that has been corrupted into some Spanish word that sounds something like the original Indian word—which has happened with many Indian words.

The La Jolla Indian Reservation is located on both sides of State Highway 76 south of Palomar Mountain and east of Pauma Valley.

JULY 23, 1875

ON THIS DAY IN SAN DIEGO HISTORY the *San Diego Union* newspaper published an account of the official report on the 1872 survey of former mission lands. The report included this information about San Clemente Canyon, which the Spanish called Cañada Clemente: "[A]bout one league from the Mission building is the Cañada Clemente...situated between the Mission and Las Peñasquitos; it was used as a vineyard, orchard, garden, etc.; it was so called after an Indian named Clemente who had charge of it." This is the valley that Highway 52 traverses today east of La Jolla toward Tierrasanta and Santee.

San is the Spanish word for "saint." Since there is no record of any Indian who had been sainted, it is suspected that someone along the way added San to the name assuming that Clemente Canyon was named after San Clemente, the town in Orange County, or San Clemente Island, offshore to the northwest of San Diego.

In the Catholic tradition, Saint Clemente was one of the early popes of Rome who was famous for achieving a miracle in finding water on an otherwise dry and barren island.

Today there is a wooded park that runs alongside of Highway 52, the San Clemente Canyon Park, used by hikers, bicyclists, and nature lovers. It is hard to imagine vineyards, orchards, and gardens there—as there were in the past.

JULY 24, 1943

ON THIS DAY IN SAN DIEGO HISTORY a full mounted review of the troops of the 28th Cavalry was held. The 28th Cavalry was a primarily African-American horseback unit that had trained at Camp Lockett, located 60 miles southeast of San Diego in Campo, near the U.S.-Mexico border.

Camp Lockett was built in 1941 and was the last cavalry base to be built in the United States. During World War II the army needed horseback soldiers to guard the Mexican border, the train bridges and tunnels of the San Diego & Arizona Eastern Railway, and to protect the reservoirs that supplied water to San Diego. The land in these areas was very rugged, and horses could go through areas that were not accessible to trucks and jeeps.

The *Los Angeles Times* newspaper had these headlines about the cavalry unit: "Mechanized Army Still Relies on Horses: Cavalry Squadron Will Be Brought to Full Strength for Patrol of Dams."

The *San Diego Tribune-Sun* wrote: "[E]astern San Diego county may well be a battle ground for a full scale invasion of the United States should the western hemisphere be violated via Mexico."

An unexpected task that the cavalry units had not trained for was putting out brush fires and forest fires. During September and October of 1943 there were four major fires that destroyed over 25,000 acres of the backcountry. The Indian Creek Fire on September 9 destroyed 4,100 acres. On September 22 there were two fires: the Potrero Fire burned 4,000 acres, and the Viejas Fire burned 1,000 acres. The Barrett–Cottonwood–Morena Fire in October burned for five days and destroyed 16,000 acres. Troops from Camp Lockett as well as marines from a small training base in Pine Valley were called on to help fight the fires.

In 1944 the 28th Cavalry unit from Camp Lockett ended up in North Africa, in the fighting in Algeria. Camp Lockett later became a military hospital, the Mitchell Convalescent Hospital. It closed down completely in 1946.

JULY 25, 1826

ON THIS DAY IN SAN DIEGO HISTORY José María Echeandia, Mexican governor of California, issued a decree to initiate the secularization of the California missions, which finally became effective in 1834 under Governor José Figueroa's administration. This was a process that would eventually change ownership of the mission lands from the church to the public.

Mexico had won its independence from Spain in 1821, and the Mexican government began the process of dividing up the mission lands in California into large land grants—called ranchos—each consisting of many thousands of acres. Even though a portion of the lands was supposed to go to the Indians, this did not always happen. More often than not, the ranchos were given to prominent citizens and people who had business or political connections.

There were a total of 30 ranchos in what is now San Diego County. Most of the ranchos were cattle ranches because the products from cattle—hides, meat, and tallow (tallow was used to make candles and soap)—were important items to trade when ships came to San Diego from the East Coast bringing manufactured products that the people in California needed—such as boots, shoes, and clothing.

After the secularization of the San Diego Mission, things changed drastically. At the peak of its prosperity, under the direction of the padres (Catholic priests), the San Diego Mission was wealthy in livestock (cattle, sheep, horses, etc.) and other improvements to the land by the work of the Indians who lived there. But after the secularization, the lack of religious authority and discipline brought disorder and decay.

The Indians drifted away, and many returned to their previous style of life. At the peak of the mission life there were thousands of Indians associated with the mission. Ten years after the secularization there were only 100 Indians left, and the once large herds of livestock had dwindled down to four cows, five calves, and one bull.

JULY 26, 1907

ON THIS DAY IN SAN DIEGO HISTORY the *San Diego Union* newspaper announced that work would begin in August on the construction of John D. Spreckels' personal residence in Coronado. The house would be constructed of reinforced concrete and would be "one of the finest homes in southern California." The Spreckels estate included a carriage house and garage, quarters for live-in help, and "the most extensive Italian garden in the west." This magnificent home was located across Orange Avenue from the Hotel Del Coronado (which was owned by Spreckels) on a bluff with panoramic views of Glorietta Bay.

The house was designed by Harrison Albright, a prominent southern California architect, who also designed the U.S. Grant Hotel, the *San Diego Union* building, the Coronado Public Library, and the Coronado Bank building.

John D. Spreckels was a wealthy San Francisco businessman in the shipping and import business who started investing in San Diego during the economic boom of the 1880s. He was also involved in the Spreckels sugar refining business, started by his father in Hawaii.

Spreckels' many investments in the San Diego area included the:

Hotel Del Coronado and a large part of Coronado Island.

San Diego–Coronado Ferry system.

San Diego Union newspaper (see OCTOBER 10).

San Diego Electric Railway (see APRIL 23 and JUNE 7).

First National Bank (formerly the Bank of San Diego, now known as Union Bank of California) (see JUNE 9).

San Diego & Arizona Railway ("The Impossible Railroad") (see SEPTEMBER 9).

Purchase of an eight-block area in downtown San Diego, including the construction of two office buildings and a million-dollar theater—the Spreckels Theater, still used today, on Broadway between 1st and 2nd streets.

Vice-Presidency of the Panama-California Exposition Company to help plan the exposition held in Balboa Park in 1915 to 1916 (see SEPTEMBER 3).

Donation of the Spreckels Organ Pavilion at Balboa Park.

Donation of money to help start the San Diego Zoo (see SEPTEMBER 27).

JULY 27, 1872

ON THIS DAY IN SAN DIEGO HISTORY a frantic race occurred down the mountain grade from Julian to San Diego between two rival stagecoach companies—Tweed's Pioneer Line and Stokes' Mail Stage.

Tweed's Pioneer Stage Line controlled the route between San Diego and Julian between 1870 and 1872. But in the summer of 1872, Adolph Stokes, who owned the Santa Maria Rancho (see MARCH 4) east of the present-day city of Ramona, went into competition with the Tweed Stage Line.

Tweed's stagecoaches charged six dollars for the 60-mile ride from San Diego to Julian and four dollars for the return trip from Julian. After the Stokes Mail Stage started service on the same route, fare wars began—and continued until passengers could ride from San Diego to Julian for free! Then the Stokes Mail Line offered to *pay one dollar* to each passenger who would ride with them. In response to that, the Tweed Stage Line offered passengers *one dollar each plus free drinks.*

The race between Julian and San Diego on this date in 1872 was a wild ride, with each stage being pulled by a team of four horses. One of the passengers reported on the race when the Stokes stage attempted to pass the Tweed stage:

> All was now excitement, drivers, horses, and passengers, all anxious to run… The wheels whizzed, the horses' feet clattering, drivers cracked their whips and lashed their panting, foaming coursers, clouds of dust filled the air and the excited passengers joined in the general din.

Two of the Stokes Mail Stage's horses were injured during the race. One horse stepped in a squirrel hole and broke his leg, but the stage continued on with the three remaining horses. Then another horse got overheated and gave out.

The race was won by the Stokes Mail Line—but only after getting fresh horses and then taking a short cut instead of the usual route through Old Town—surprising the Tweed Pioneer Line, who didn't know that the other stage had taken the short cut.

JULY 28, 1921

ON THIS DAY IN SAN DIEGO HISTORY the San Diego State Normal School, now known as San Diego State University, was granted college status by the California State Legislature. The school was renamed San Diego State Teachers College, and the curriculum was expanded from a two-year teacher-training preparatory school to a four-year liberal arts college.

When the school was first founded in 1897, it was located on 17 acres in the University Heights area near El Cajon Boulevard and Normal Street (see MARCH 13). By 1922 the school had outgrown its University Heights location, so a new location of 125 acres was found ten miles east of downtown San Diego near Alvarado Canyon, where San Diego State University is still located today (see OCTOBER 7).

In 1972 the College was elevated to University status and began offering graduate degrees that went beyond the four years of undergraduate schooling.

San Diego State University has had a total of five different names during its history:

San Diego State Normal School: 1897–1921.
San Diego State Teachers College: 1921–35.
San Diego State College: 1935–72.
California State University at San Diego: 1972–73.
San Diego State University: 1974–present.

JULY 29, 1846

ON THIS DAY IN SAN DIEGO HISTORY an American ship, the USS *Cyane*, sailed into San Diego Bay, captured a Mexican ship, and the next day raised the United States flag for the first time ever in Old Town Plaza.

This was during the Mexican-American War of 1846–48 when San Diego was a part of Mexico. The *Cyane* had occupied the port of Monterey, California's capital, since July 9, securing northern California for the Americans. The port of San Diego was well-known as one of the best ports in California after San Francisco, so Captain (later to become General) John Frémont was ordered to take the *Cyane* to San Diego with 160 men, including the scout Kit Carson, to secure the southern part of California for the United States.

According to the Americans, they got a friendly reception in San Diego, and no resistance was offered by the Californios (the residents of Mexican California). One week later, Frémont set out with 120 men to assist with the capture of Los Angeles.

But the Mexican-American War was far from over. In December 1846 the Americans under General Kearny were defeated by the Californios, led by General Andrés Pico, at the Battle of San Pasqual in north San Diego County (see DECEMBER 6).

The United States went on to win the war after winning the battle at Cahuenga Pass in January 1847—when the Californios, retreating from Los Angeles, surrendered to Frémont—and after the United States army captured Mexico City in September. The Mexican-American War officially ended in 1848 with the Treaty of Guadalupe Hidalgo (see FEBRUARY 2). After that, California, Arizona, New Mexico, and parts of Texas no longer belonged to Mexico but became part of the United States of America.

JULY 30, 1874

ON THIS DAY IN SAN DIEGO HISTORY Drury Bailey recorded a declaration of homestead for a 160-acre site that he named Julian City after his cousin, Mike Julian—who had served in the Civil War with him in Georgia where they lived before coming to California. Bailey's homestead is now the central part of today's mountain town of Julian.

Bailey donated part of his land for the first elementary school and high school in Julian. He also donated lots for a public hall and for a jail.

Previously, in 1870, he had discovered the first gold-bearing quartz ledge outside of Julian and later discovered an even richer gold mine at Banner, down the hill from Julian (see FEBRUARY 20).

Bailey is said to have explained that he named the town Julian because Mike Julian was "handsomer than himself." But Mike Julian had also shown leadership abilities, having been elected as recorder for the Julian Mining District, serving on the board of trustees for the Julian School District, and and serving as San Diego County assessor.

Today the mountain town of Julian is a popular place for San Diegans to go on the weekends to visit the interesting antique stores and museums, to take a tour of the Eagle Gold Mine, and to enjoy the famous Julian apple pies.

JULY 31, 1940

ON THIS DAY IN SAN DIEGO HISTORY the Borego Post Office was closed down—discontinued, as were a number of other smaller post offices in remote areas. After this the mail was delivered to the homesteaders in Borego from Julian via the Borego Star Postal Route.

The town that we know today as Borrego Springs was called "Borego" at first—a misspelling of *borrego*, the Spanish word for a lamb. Some people think the name referred to the desert bighorn sheep who used to water at the springs in the area. Others think that *borrego* refers to domestic sheep when sheepherders in the late 1800s watered their flocks at the springs.

At this time, in 1940, there were no paved roads in Borrego Valley and no electric lines or telephones. The little homesteader community of Borego was considered to be San Diego County's last frontier. The name Borego first appeared on county maps in 1883, when cattlemen started using the springs and established cattle camps there.

Homesteaders began to settle in Borrego Valley after 1910. In the mid-1920s, more and more homesteaders began to arrive. In 1922 the first road for automobiles was opened through Sentenac Canyon (today's Highway 78 from Julian to Brawley), making it easier to reach Borrego Valley. In 1928 Borego got its first post office, which lasted until this date in 1940 when it was closed down.

The modern community of Borrego Springs started up in 1949, and at that time the post office opened up again—the Borrego Springs Post Office bearing the same name as the new town.

AUGUST 1, 1947

ON THIS DAY IN SAN DIEGO HISTORY the town of Borrego Springs, located in the desert in northeast San Diego County, received telephone service for the first time. The service came through the El Centro telephone lines and required a 17-mile line from Ocotillo Wells.

At first there were only four phones in Borrego Springs. To make a call people had to first listen on the line and, if it was free, they had to crank the phone for an operator. With crank phones all you had to do was lift up the receiver to listen to any of your neighbors' conversations going on at the time. And your neighbors could also listen in on your conversations.

In 1952 there were a total of 19 phones in Borrego Springs. The old party lines were replaced with dial phones in July 1956, and by then there were over 100 phones in the Borrego Valley.

Today Borrego Springs is still a relatively small, quiet community of less than 3,000 people—in contrast to the typically populous, and consequently more crowded, areas of San Diego and southern California. Many people here are seasonal residents, with vacation homes that they occupy when the climate is not too hot. The surrounding Anza-Borrego Desert State Park attracts many visitors (see JUNE 29), and in years when there is enough rainfall, wildflowers bloom in the spring and large numbers of people visit here, often stressing the facilities in this small community.

See also JULY 31.

AUGUST 2, 1928

ON THIS DAY IN SAN DIEGO HISTORY La Jolla nearly became an aviation center. The Navy had a 1,500-foot-long practice landing strip on Mt. Soledad in the Muirlands located east of today's upper La Jolla Mesa Drive. The strip extended from the present-day Hartley Drive, across Buckingham Drive and La Jolla Rancho Road.

The landing strip was commissioned as an airport on this date in 1928. It served air travel between La Jolla and Agua Caliente, a fancy resort built at a hot springs location in Tijuana, Baja California—a popular place for San Diegans to visit during the 1920s because of the luxury hotel, gambling casino, race track, and legal alcoholic beverages—when there was a prohibition against alcohol in the United States. La Jolla residents at the time considered that La Jolla had entered the air age!

In those early days there were also gliders that were launched off Mount Soledad from where the cross is now located. The gliders were launched with a bungee cord that acted like a slingshot. They would land in the canyon that is now La Jolla Parkway (formerly Ardath Road).

In 1930 Anne Morrow Lindbergh, wife of the famous aviator, Charles Lindbergh, became the first woman in the United States to receive a first class glider license, after launching a sailplane from Mount Soledad (see FEBRUARY 29).

Today there is a popular gliderport, the Torrey Pines Gliderport, located on Torrey Pines Mesa above the ocean west of the University of California San Diego (UCSD) campus and near the Salk Institute for Biological Research. Recent plans for construction of a 14-story student housing project by UCSD and possible expansion of the Salk Institute have posed potential problems for the gliderport, which also had plans to expand its airfield landing space.

The gliderport was also in trouble because of a legal suit initiated by an environmental watchdog group claiming that the structures on the property, including a trailer, kitchen, bathroom, concession stand, and observation deck, were installed without coastal development permits. The Torrey Pines Gliderport is one of only five historically designated a National Soaring Landmark in the United States, having first been used as a gliderport in 1935. Hang gliding was suspended from Torrey Pines Mesa during World War II when the U.S. Army's Camp Callan occupied the property. Hang gliding resumed in 1947 after the camp was closed down.

AUGUST 3, 1969

ON THIS DAY IN SAN DIEGO HISTORY ceremonies were held for the opening of the San Diego-Coronado Bay Bridge. The impressive structure arching over the bay was designed by Robert Mosher of La Jolla. The California governor at the time, Ronald Reagan, was at the opening ceremonies.

Before the bridge was built, the only way to reach Coronado, aside from taking the long drive up the peninsula from Imperial Beach, was to take the Coronado Ferry, which took passengers and cars from the end of Pacific Coast Highway where the entrance to Seaport Village is located today.

In 1951 a study was conducted to determine the feasibility of building a tunnel under the bay between San Diego and Coronado. Even though the Navy approved the tunnel plan, it was never built.

The Navy required that the bridge be 200 feet above the water to allow for ship operations in the bay. The bridge took two and a half years to complete and cost $47.6 million. The Coronado Ferry Company went out of business after the bridge was built.

Today the San Diego Harbor Excursion Company provides ferry service to and from Coronado approximately every hour, departing from Harbor Drive at the Broadway Pier. The ferry takes passengers only, no automobiles.

AUGUST 4, 1898

ON THIS DAY IN SAN DIEGO HISTORY Bert Reed, the son of the mayor of San Diego, was badly injured when he attempted to dive into the ocean from the cliffs above the caves at La Jolla. His friends had advised him not the make the jump, but he did it anyway. He died from his injuries several months later.

Diving from above the caves at La Jolla had been made popular by "Professor" Horace Poole, who had made the dive successfully many times by diving from a springboard placed on top of the cliffs above the caves. He made one dive in a dramatic way in front of a large crowd of people on the Fourth of July, by coating his body with flammable oil and setting fire to it just before the dive. It is said that the San Diego, Pacific Beach & La Jolla Railway paid Poole $25 for each dive—since his dramatic dives were good publicity for getting people to travel to La Jolla on the train.

After the mayor's son died, the diving from that dangerous area of the La Jolla cliffs stopped. There is now a sign on the path above the caves that says "Dangerous Cliffs—No Diving."

Today you can walk on a narrow dirt path along the cliffs above the La Jolla Caves. The path starts at the Cave Shop and winds along the top of the cliffs to some wooden steps and a bridge over a small canyon to a paved road, Coast Walk, leading to Torrey Pines Road. It is a very scenic walk, with benches along the way to sit and take in the extensive vistas toward the north. There are also good views of the seals and sea lions on the rocks below. But, remember, no diving—it's too dangerous there!

AUGUST 5, 1856

ON THIS DAY IN SAN DIEGO HISTORY a frontier settler from Kentucky named Thomas Ryland Darnall wrote a letter to his family in Kentucky telling of the hot summer in San Diego:

> Usually, we have the most mild climate in the world, but for the last few days it has been intensely hot, and to alleviate the sultriness, I go bathing, almost every evening, in the ocean… We have the nicest beach in the world for bathing with just sufficient breakers to make it interesting and pleasant. It is very dangerous bathing in the bay on account of a kind of fish called, here, stingaree, which lays flat on the bottom, it takes its name from a sharp bony substance, resembling a needle, appended to its tail; and when tread upon or molested will strike with great force, its stroke is immediately followed by great pain, accompanied with swelling of the wounded part…

Darnall came to California during the gold rush of 1849. He was not successful at gold mining in northern California, so he came to San Diego in 1853 and opened up a store. He was chairman of the San Diego County Board of Supervisors at the age of 28 and also served as deputy sheriff.

He wrote this about life in the 1850s in San Diego in another letter to his family in Kentucky:

> There is but one american girl in the place unmarried who is grown, and she can neither read or write; scarcely any of the native Californians can read or write… The California girls are great for dancing; their principal dancing consists in waltz and polkas, in the execution of which they excel any girls I ever saw… As the women excel in dancing so the men excel in horsemanship, they are by far the most superior horsemen I ever saw, even the boys three or four and five years of age are expert…

AUGUST 6, 1866

ON THIS DAY IN SAN DIEGO HISTORY the ownership of the San Felipe Rancho was confirmed to Don Juan Forster. Forster had bought the ranch in 1847, but there was a mix-up in the title that wasn't settled until this date in 1866.

Don Juan Forster, formerly known as John Forster, was born in England in 1815. At the age of 16 he went to Guaymas, Mexico and then came to California two years later. He lived in Los Angeles, and in 1837 he married Isadora Pico, sister of Pío and Andrés Pico, both of whom were influential in California history (see AUGUST 22). Juan Forster also owned two other ranchos in San Diego County as well as lands in San Juan Capistrano in today's Orange County (see FEBRUARY 7 and DECEMBER 11).

The 9,972-acre San Felipe Rancho was located in the San Felipe Valley northeast of Julian near Scissors Crossing—today the intersection of Highway 78 and S-2. In times past, the San Felipe Valley was occupied by Indians, and the San Felipe Indian Village was located on the San Felipe Rancho, where the Butterfield Stage Station was later located.

There were conflicting reports by different explorers as to whether the area was occupied by Indians or not. This is because the Indians, the Kumeyaay, were seasonal in their use of the San Felipe Valley. They usually spent winters in the desert and summers in the mountains. These seasonal migrations led the white homesteaders to believe that the land was not occupied. When the Indians would reappear at their old village site, the ranchers considered them to be squatters on their homesteaded lands.

In 1901 a Supreme Court decision upholding the rights of the white homesteaders led to the final expulsion of the San Felipe Indians from their traditional land. Most of the remaining Indians moved to the Pala Indian Reservation or to the Santa Ysabel, Mesa Grande, or Los Coyotes reservations. Another case of injustice to the Native Americans who first occupied lands that the white settlers also wanted.

AUGUST 7, 1915

ON THIS DAY IN SAN DIEGO HISTORY three fires occurred in La Jolla, the most serious of which was the destruction of the home of Ellen Browning Scripps on Prospect Street in La Jolla. Miss Scripps' home—a large two-story building built of redwood in 1897—was named South Moulton Villa after the street on which she was born in London—South Moulton Street (see FEBRUARY 8 and OCTOBER 18).

The first fire broke out in the St. James by-the-Sea Episcopal Church across the street from Miss Scripps' house. The La Jolla Volunteer Fire Department put out the fire at the church before any serious damage was done. Less than an hour later, as Ellen Browning Scripps' sister, Virginia Scripps, was leaving her sister's home and walking down Prospect Street toward her guest house, Wisteria Cottage, she saw flames coming from the cottage. The tired firemen returned to Prospect Street to put out the cottage fire.

While the firemen were putting out the cottage fire, another fire erupted in Ellen Scripps' house. But when shifting their equipment to put out the fire in the larger house, the firemen discovered that the house was 550 feet from the nearest fire hydrant, and they had only 500 feet of hose. By the time the fire department from San Diego arrived to help, the house was nearly a complete loss.

Arson was suspected. Ellen's sister, Virginia Scripps was quoted as saying: "If only it had been an accident, it would have been much easier to bear. But my sister, whose life has been wrapped up in doing all she could to help mankind, cannot help but be stung by the thought of someone feeling malice toward her."

Four months after the fire, police found the culprit—a former gardener on the Scripps' grounds who had been dismissed almost a year previously. He was traced by an oil-soaked shirt found in the basement of Miss Scripps' house. He confessed to the crime when confronted with the evidence.

Ellen Scripps, at the age of 79, hired the architect Irving Gill (see APRIL 26) to design a new house made of concrete and stucco—fireproof and very modern for 1916—the building that now houses the Museum of Contemporary Art in La Jolla.

AUGUST 8, 1881

ON THIS DAY IN SAN DIEGO HISTORY the San Diego Board of Trustees set aside a little over eight acres at the south end of City Park (now known as Balboa Park) for an elementary school.

A lumberman named Joseph Russ donated wood to build the school, so the school, Russ School, was named for him. Russ School later became San Diego High School. San Diego High School is still at that same location, just south of Balboa Park at 1405 Park Boulevard at the corner of Russ Boulevard.

Later, another 100 acres was taken from City Park for an orphan's home and an industrial school. But the land was returned to the city when the new owner ran into trouble in the financial panic of 1893.

In these early days of the park that was later to become Balboa Park, the land was nearly barren, covered only with sagebrush and chaparral. Later, with the help of many civic leaders—including George Marston and the horticulturist Kate Sessions—many trees and other exotic plants from all over the world were planted there to make it the beautiful and lushly landscaped park that it is today (see DECEMBER 2).

The name of City Park was changed to Balboa Park shortly before the great World's Fair, the Panama-California Exposition, that was held at Balboa Park from 1915 through 1916 to honor the opening of the Panama Canal (see JANUARY 1 and SEPTEMBER 3). The Panama Canal was important to San Diego because it made a much shorter and easier trip for East Coast ships sailing to San Diego, which was the first port on the west coast of the United States after going through the canal.

Still later, in 1935, another large exposition was held at Balboa Park—the California Pacific International Exposition (see MAY 29).

AUGUST 9, 1985

ON THIS DAY IN SAN DIEGO HISTORY the giant, new outdoor shopping center Horton Plaza opened in downtown San Diego with 155 stores, including restaurants and movie theaters. On opening day an acrobat walked on a high wire 80 feet above the plaza of the new mall and, at the right time, he stopped in the center of the wire and lowered a pair of scissors for the ribbon-cutting ceremony.

The Horton Plaza concept began 11 years earlier, in 1974, when Ernest Hahn's company was chosen by the San Diego City Council and Mayor Pete Wilson to work on the development of the 11.5-acre site. The site covered 15 city blocks in downtown San Diego south of Broadway and across the street from the U.S. Grant Hotel. It extended westward from 4th Avenue for five blocks to Union Street and south another three blocks to G Street. This was an area of San Diego that had begun to go downhill and that needed to be revived in order for downtown San Diego to survive. Stores had begun to move to the suburbs, and the area was full of neglected buildings. Ernest Hahn's company also developed suburban malls in San Diego County including Fashion Valley, Parkway Plaza, University Towne Centre, and North County Fair.

According to Iris Engstrand in her book *San Diego: California's Cornerstone*, there was a bit of controversy over which buildings should be preserved in the area of the redevelopment. Historic landmarks such as the Spreckels Building and Balboa Theater were eventually retained, as was Horton Plaza Park with its famous columned fountain designed by architect Irving Gill in 1910 (see AUGUST 29).

The Center City Development Corporation (CCDC) was established by the San Diego City Council in 1975 to help plan the downtown redevelopment projects, the first of which was Horton Plaza. The $140 million structure was designed by architect Jon Jerde and has received many awards for its unusual architecture and unusual use of color. The *New York Times* called it "One of the most ambitious retail structures ever built in a single stroke in an American city...architecturally stunning."

Only in San Diego and southern California, with our mild, year-round climate, do we find the ideal setting for an outdoor, meandering structure like this for a shopping center. A multi-level parking structure was also built—a *must* for the success of the new shopping center in the middle of an already crowded downtown San Diego.

AUGUST 10, 1899

ON THIS DAY IN SAN DIEGO HISTORY the San Diego city council passed an ordinance to set aside 369 acres of pueblo lands, where rare Torrey pine trees were growing, as a public park. The ordinance stated: "That there is growing upon said lands certain rare and valuable trees known as *Pinus Torreyana*, it is the wish and desire of the City of San Diego to preserve these trees."

This was four years before the state of California opened the first state park to protect the coastal redwoods in northern California.

The Torrey pines are known from only two places in the world—the Torrey Pines Park above the ocean cliffs between La Jolla and Del Mar and also on Santa Rosa Island, one of the Channel Islands offshore from Santa Barbara—some 175 miles from the mainland grove of Torrey Pines in San Diego.

Even though the Indians were known to have come to the coast to gather pine nuts from the trees in this area, and even though the Spanish explorers who began charting the California coast in the sixteenth century used these pine-crested sea cliffs—called Punta de los Arboles ("Point of Trees")—as a navigational aid, the first scientific attempt to describe the trees did not come until the 1850s when Charles Christopher Parry, botanist of the U.S./Mexican Boundary Survey, came upon the grove. Parry recognized the pine trees as possibly a new species. He sent a sample to the renowned American botanist John Torrey, who verified that the pine trees were a species previously unknown to science. Parry named the new species *Pinus torreyana* in honor of his respected botanist colleague.

Later, between the years of 1908 and 1912, Ellen Browning Scripps contributed more acreage to the park by buying up pueblo lots from owners who were planning to develop the land, thereby saving some of the finest specimens of Torrey pine for inclusion in the park. Ellen Browning Scripps and her brother E. W. Scripps also provided a road to the park.

As early as 1916 and again in the 1940s, there were concerns about the safety of the Torrey pines in the park. Due to the efforts of Guy Fleming, former manager of the park, and many others, the Torrey Pines Association was formed in 1950 for the purpose of transferring Torrey Pines Park to the State of California Department of Parks and Recreation. This finally occurred in 1959 (see MAY 7). The park is now known as Torrey Pines State Reserve and now contains nearly 1,750 acres, consisting of beach, lagoon, cliffs, and uplands (see also APRIL 7).

AUGUST 11, 1845

On this day, in San Diego history—the Cuyamaca Rancho was granted to Augustín Olvera after he had filed a petition for it two months earlier (see JUNE 5). This rancho was located about 55 miles northeast of San Diego, where Cuyamaca State Park and Cuyamaca Lake are now located. The rancho contained over 33,000 acres. It extended from the present-day town of Descanso in the south to near Pine Hills in the north (just south of the mountain town of Julian). It was originally occupied by several Indian *rancherias* (small settlements).

Augustín Olvera petitioned for the Cuyamaca Rancho to governor Pío Pico, whose niece was Olvera's wife. A controversy developed later over the land grant because the grant made to Olvera did not give the exact size or boundaries of the grant. It was specified that the judge giving possession of the grant should require that it be measured and that maps be made. The files of the San Diego justice of the peace at that time state that "on account of heavy rains, roads to the mountains were impassable...and the tract will be measured as soon as weather permits." A crude map with no date was included in the files.

Later there was another dispute over the boundaries of the Cuyamaca Rancho after the discovery of gold in the areas near Julian 1870s (see NOVEMBER 14 and NOVEMBER 25).

This is another example of the confusion surrounding the fair administration of land grants in the Rancho Days, with respect to lands that previously belonged to the missions. Often the rights of the Indians to some of the lands were ignored in favor of the desires of prominent white citizens with political connections (see SEPTEMBER 30).

AUGUST 12, 1871

ON THIS DAY IN SAN DIEGO HISTORY the cornerstone was laid for the new courthouse that would be built in New Town San Diego. Just a few months before, the courthouse records had been moved from Old Town San Diego to a building in New Town, located at 6th and G streets in what is now the Gaslamp area of San Diego (see MARCH 31).

New Town San Diego was developed by Alonzo Horton (see OCTOBER 24). Horton had lived in San Francisco and came to San Diego in 1867. When he stepped off the boat in San Diego Harbor, he looked around and sized up the place as being the best location for building a city that he had ever seen.

When he saw Old Town, where the main part of San Diego was located at the time, he said he wouldn't give five dollars for the whole thing. So he proceeded to buy 960 acres of what is now downtown San Diego for $265—or 27½ cents an acre. He knew he was getting a good deal because good lots in San Francisco were selling for $10,000 or more each.

Horton knew he would have to spend effort and money to promote his new Horton's Addition in order to re-sell his lots for a profit. To help get things started, he gave lots to several churches to be built there, and he donated land to people who promised to build a house right away.

Alonzo Horton's venture was a great success and, one by one, businesses began to move from Old Town to New Town. After the courthouse records and the *San Diego Union* newspaper were moved to New Town, it was accepted as the future center of San Diego, and the construction of a new courthouse in New Town was begun on this date in 1871.

AUGUST 13, 1852

ON THIS DAY IN SAN DIEGO HISTORY a rowboat was stolen in San Diego Bay by a man in a red shirt. This would not be an unusual story except for the fact that a questionable trial was held a few days later, and the man in the red shirt was found guilty and sentenced to death by hanging. He was hanged on a hill south of Old Town, where the Whaley House is now located, just one month later on September 18, 1852.

The man in the red shirt was James "Yankee Jim" Robinson, who came to California from New Hampshire when he was in his late 20s during the California Gold Rush. In San Diego he was somewhat of a shady character who spent most of his time in the gambling houses around Old Town Plaza—but he was not known to have broken any laws until he was suspected of stealing the rowboat, along with two other accomplices. The thief was observed by one of the owners of the rowboat, who tried to shoot at him, but he was too far out of range, and he rowed off into the darkness in the stolen rowboat. The next day a search party found two "suspicious-looking" men at False Bay (now known as Mission Bay) whom they arrested. The man in the red shirt, "Yankee Jim," was brought in later that day.

The next day a citizens' committee obtained a "confession" from the men. According to the confession, the three men had come down to San Diego by horseback from Stockton, stealing and selling horses along the way. Upon arriving in San Diego, they sold the stolen horses and bought supplies for sailing off to Mexico in the stolen boat.

A jury trial was held just four days after the boat was stolen. Two of the jurors were the owners of the rowboat. An anonymous "reliable source" testified at the trial that James "Yankee Jim" Robinson was a dangerous robber who had robbed wagon trains and robbed and killed miners in California and Arizona. The trial was short, and the jury returned in 30 minutes with a verdict of guilty.

This is how a man was hanged for stealing a rowboat in San Diego Bay! You can visit James "Yankee Jim" Robinson's grave in the El Campo Santo Cemetery in Old Town, two blocks south of the Whaley House.

AUGUST 14, 1851

ON THIS DAY IN SAN DIEGO HISTORY hotels in San Diego at the time are described in the *San Diego Herald* newspaper. The article notes that the Exchange Hotel in Old Town is a place that rejects "rowdyism" and provides "quiet places of amusement, where all classes of liquors, and of the best qualities, can be found."

It was at the Exchange Hotel that the first meeting of the Masons in San Diego was held in June 1851. The property was sold to the Franklin family in July 1855, and the Exchange Hotel was torn down four months later to make room for the Franklin house. The Franklin house burned down in the Old Town fire of 1872. Today there is a plaque on the building at 2731 San Diego Avenue, marking the former location of the Exchange Hotel as a California registered landmark.

The article in the *San Diego Herald* on this date goes on to comment on a hotel in New Town—the Pantoja House:

> This house…has always been free from rowdys, riotous dissipation and unmannerly loafers, where the most fastidious can always find a cegar and glass of liquor to his taste, and enjoy it and a game of billiards with same security from molestation as if he were at a club house or a private dwelling.

It seems that it was important in 1851 for an acceptable hotel to have good liquor to enjoy in a quiet and "non-rowdy" atmosphere.

AUGUST 15, 1769

ON THIS DAY IN SAN DIEGO HISTORY the Kumeyaay Indians attacked the newly established mission and presidio in San Diego, which consisted of reed and sagebrush huts. The site had been dedicated only one month before by Father Junípero Serra on top of Presidio Hill when he blessed a wooden cross, thereby officially establishing the San Diego Mission and Presidio (see JULY 16).

The Indians killed Father Serra's servant José María Vegerano, who ran into Serra's hut with an arrow in his neck saying, "Father, absolve me, for the Indians have killed me." Then he collapsed and died at Father Serra's feet. The soldiers from the presidio drove the Indians away, killing five of them in the process.

There were nearly 20 Indian villages located within 30 miles of the location of the new San Diego Mission site when the Spaniards arrived. They called themselves Kumeyaay, but the Spanish missionaries referred to them as Diegueños because of their association with the San Diego Mission. According to Dolan H. Eargle Jr. in his book *The Earth Is Our Mother: A Guide to the Indians of California*, "The Kumeyaay people have a long history of fierce independence. Even when Spanish troops were rounding up natives for the coastal missions...many fled to these desolate hills to escape and evade. The same was true (later) of their avoidance of the U.S. Cavalry."

After the Indian attack, a protective stockade was built around the presidio and mission.

Six years later, in 1775, shortly after it had moved six miles inland (to what we now call Mission Valley), the mission was attacked by Indians who resented its location as too close to their *rancheria*, which they called Nipaguay (see NOVEMBER 5).

AUGUST 16, 1928

ON THIS DAY IN SAN DIEGO HISTORY San Diego's airport, Lindbergh Field, was dedicated. It was named for Charles Lindbergh, who was the first person to fly alone and nonstop across the Atlantic Ocean from the United States to Europe.

The same year that Lindbergh flew across the Atlantic (1927), San Diego Bay was dredged to make a turning basin for two of the Navy's large aircraft carriers, the USS *Lexington* and USS *Saratoga*. The dredged sand and mud was used to fill in the location for the new airport.

When Lindbergh returned to San Diego for a celebration of his historic flight (see SEPTEMBER 21) he spoke to the people of San Diego, promoting the idea of the new airport that was being considered. He said:

> I want to bring before you the necessity of keeping your city in the foreground of American aeronautics by constructing and equipping a good airport such as you are considering, and by backing the air development program of your city... There are very few cities that have this opportunity so close to them—so near to the business section as the proposed site here. I hope that you will continue to back a progressive airport in San Diego and keep this city on the airways of the United States... San Diego has always been in the foreground of western aeronautics and, I believe, it will always be in the foreground.

The new San Diego airport, Lindbergh Field, was indeed built on the location next to San Diego Bay created by dredged material, and was dedicated on this date, August 16, 1928.

Today you can see a large mural of Charles Lindbergh standing in his flight suit painted on the side of the commuter terminal as you approach the airport from downtown on Harbor Drive.

In recent years there has been disagreement as to whether San Diego should seek another location for its airport or find a way to expand Lindbergh Field to meet its future needs.

AUGUST 17, 1846

ON THIS DAY IN SAN DIEGO HISTORY the American military was occupying San Diego during the Mexican-American War—when San Diego and California were a part of Mexico. The Americans had been in San Diego for nearly three weeks, since sailing into San Diego Bay on the USS *Crane* (see JULY 29).

Commodore Robert Stockton, the U.S. Navy commander, ordered an election in San Diego to help obtain support from the Californios (the Mexican Californians). Miguel de Pedrorena, a Spanish merchant, was elected justice of the peace. On this date, August 17, 1846, the newly elected justice of the peace issued an order forbidding citizens and their servants from leaving the city. Pedrorena was pro-American, and he issued the order to help the Americans enforce their martial law requiring everyone in San Diego to be in their houses between 10 p.m. and sunrise.

In order to enforce his order and to frighten the local Californios into cooperating with the Americans, Pedrorena announced to the citizens of San Diego:

> [T]his territory is actually invaded by a party of fanatic adventurers called Mormons, who arrived by sea at San Francisco in order to form a large number of others who come by land well armed with the purpose of taking this country by force. We are threatened by another party of five hundred Indians called Piutes, who are already in this territory intent upon our complete destruction.

Pedrorena asked for volunteers and requested assistance from the rancheros, including donations of horses. The threat of the Mormons and Indians possibly invading San Diego helped to convince some of the local Californios that they needed to cooperate with the Americans for protection (see also JANUARY 27).

The Americans eventually won the Mexican-American War, and California (and San Diego) became a part of the United States (see FEBRUARY 2 and DECEMBER 6).

AUGUST 18, 1988

ON THIS DAY IN SAN DIEGO HISTORY the Chinese Mission was moved after much effort on the part of San Diego's Chinese community to save it from being destroyed (see APRIL 21).

The Chinese Mission was first established in the downtown area of San Diego in 1885 in a rented home. It changed locations several times before a permanent building was built in 1927 at 645 First Avenue between Market and G streets. The Chinese people worshipped in that building for 33 years, until 1960 when they sold it and built a new church at 1750 47th Street.

Later, in the 1980s, efforts were underway to revitalize San Diego's downtown and Gaslamp areas. The new owner of the old Chinese mission property proposed to demolish it and build high-rise housing on the site. But the Chinese community worked hard to save the old mission and to have it preserved as a historic building (see MARCH 22 and JUNE 16).

The Center City Development Corporation (CCDC) had studied the Chinese Mission Building prior to moving it and reported that it "had been structurally reinforced when it was constructed in 1927" and that "field testing of portions of the walls and inspection by several structural engineers confirmed that the building could he safely moved rather than dismantled."

After the move to a temporary location at 428 Third Avenue, the San Diego *Daily Transcript* reported: "Newsworthy about the move was how smooth it went. Not a brick came loose from the 1927-built structure."

The Chinese Mission Building was moved to its present location at 3rd and J streets and restored in 1995. It is now the Chinese Historical Museum and is well worth a visit. The old location occupied by the Chinese Mission for 33 years at 645 First Avenue is now the Ralph's Supermarket, with highrise buildings all around.

AUGUST 19, 1870

ON THIS DAY IN SAN DIEGO HISTORY the first telegraph line to San Diego was completed, and San Diego made its first telegraphic communication with the outside world.

The line was installed in the Otay Mesa area and extended eastward to Yuma, Arizona. If you have ever wondered where Telegraph Canyon Road got its name, it's for the canyon the telegraph line ran through. To construct the line, poles were delivered by wagon and then carried into the canyon. Remember, there were no gasoline cars or trucks in 1870—only horse-drawn wagons—and the railroad had not come to San Diego yet (see NOVEMBER 9).

The completion of the telegraph line to San Diego meant that San Diego could have instantaneous communication with many parts of the world. Before this, news spread very slowly. In the days before the telegraph, the raising of a flag on the old lighthouse on Point Loma was used to notify San Diegans of important events, such as the arrival of a ship in the harbor or the presence of a large school of whales.

The telegraph did not allow you to *talk* to anyone but used a code of dots and dashes tapped into the system to spell out words. It wasn't until 1882 that *telephone* service was available in San Diego, when the San Diego Telephone Company started up—with only 13 customers at first. Five years later, in 1887, there were 284 customers. By 1897, after completing a long-distance line from Santa Ana that connected San Diego to over 700 cities and towns in California, San Diego had nearly 3,200 telephone customers. Telephone lines did not reach the suburb of La Jolla until 1899 (see OCTOBER 11).

AUGUST 20, 1942

ON THIS DAY IN SAN DIEGO HISTORY the U.S. Army initiated a "dim-out" on the coastline of San Diego. This was during World War II, and there was a possibility that the coast might be attacked by the Japanese (see also DECEMBER 7).

With the street lights partially blacked out with paint and the top half of car headlights painted over, it was more difficult for enemy planes or submarines to determine the populated areas of the city at night. Also as part of the war defense efforts, San Diego closed off its harbor and installed underwater nets between Point Loma and North Island to prevent Japanese submarines from entering San Diego Bay. Near the end of the war, when it looked like the United States was winning, the Navy removed the nets. During the years the nets were in place, they made it difficult and time-consuming for U.S. ships to enter and leave the harbor.

Because of Consolidated Aircraft's importance and its location near the airport and the harbor, it was also in danger of an enemy air attack. If the Japanese could bomb the Consolidated Aircraft plant (later to become the Convair division of General Dynamics), it would stop the construction of military planes that the United States needed to win the war. To avoid this danger, the workers at Consolidated Aircraft attached acres of chicken wire over the buildings and across Pacific Coast Highway and covered the wire with chicken feathers to camouflage the activities going on there. They also used fake bushes and trees on top of the buildings, so planes couldn't tell from above that there was a factory there (see also OCTOBER 20).

In the coastal community of La Jolla, the Naval Anti-Aircraft Gunnery Training School was constructed in 1942. Guns were installed on concrete slabs on the bluffs in the Bird Rock area, west of La Jolla Boulevard at today's Calumet Park and extending southward for several blocks along Calumet Avenue. The gunnery school closed down in 1945, and the buildings were removed in 1952. Most of the remaining concrete slabs were pushed into the ocean below the cliffs. Today—in that upscale neighborhood of expensive homes built over the former gunnery site—you would have no idea of the past wartime activity that occurred there at what some people call "Gunnery Point."

AUGUST 21, 1849

ON THIS DAY IN SAN DIEGO HISTORY gold seekers traveling on the Gila Trail on their way to the gold rush area in northern California passed through Temecula, which was a popular place to camp. Temecula (which means "rising sun" in the Indian language) was an Indian settlement. Pablo Apis, an Indian leader, had built an adobe house there (see SEPTEMBER 17).

The Apis Adobe was located about three miles southeast of present-day downtown Temecula. Before the 1920s the Temecula Creek ran all year long. The padres from the San Luis Rey Mission dammed the creek and some springs to create a lake that they used for irrigation water. This water supply led to the establishment of the Temecula Indian village.

After Pablo Apis died in 1853, the Apis Adobe served as the Temecula station of the Overland Mail Company. The Gila Trail ran past the station on its way from the Yuma crossing of the Colorado River to Los Angeles, and was on the southern route from the eastern states and Mexico. In addition to the Gila Trail, the road has been called by many names including the Sonora Road, the Emigrant Trail, the Butterfield Stage Road, and the Overland Mail Road.

The Apis Adobe was also used as a store, where it was a social center of the Temecula community until 1872, when it was abandoned and became a pasture for over 100 years. In 1990 it was bulldozed away to make room for a housing development (see MARCH 7).

The Temecula Valley is in Riverside County now—just to the north of San Diego County. But it is still appropriate to talk about the Temecula Valley in San Diego's history because it was a part of San Diego County until 1893, when the northern portion of San Diego County was split off to form Riverside County. San Diego County was very large in the early days. It also included the present-day Imperial County, which was formed in 1907 from the eastern 4,089 square miles of San Diego County.

AUGUST 22, 1846

ON THIS DAY IN SAN DIEGO HISTORY Pío Pico, the last governor of Mexican California, ended his term. Pico had been governor for the past 18 months, and during that time he managed to convey many ranchos in San Diego County to San Diego families by way of land grants. After the end of the Mexican-American War of 1846–48, and after California became a state of the United States in 1850, owners of the ranchos had to refile with the U.S. Land Commission to reestablish land ownership under new guidelines.

Pico was born in San Gabriel, east of Los Angeles, in 1801. His father, José María Pico, a Spanish soldier, was of mixed ancestry—Spanish, Indian, and African. His grandfather came to California with the Anza Expedition—which traveled in 1775 from Mexico through the desert that is now part of San Diego County, on its way to Monterey and San Francisco to establish Spanish colonies there (see OCTOBER 4.)

Pío Pico grew up in San Diego and, after his father died in 1829, he operated a mercantile business in San Diego. He was known to be a gambler and a risk-taker. He played daring political games and ended up as the last governor of Mexican California between February 1845 and August 1846. While he was governor, he was notorious for recklessly giving land grants to his relatives and friends.

Pío Pico's younger brother, Andrés Pico, was also prominent in the history of California. He was born in San Diego in 1810 and became a general during the Mexican rule of California. During the Mexican-American War, General Andrés Pico was in charge of the Californio troops who fought against the United States Army in the Battle of San Pasqual (see DECEMBER 6). General Pico made the peace treaty with the Americans at Cahuenga, north of Los Angeles, at which time California became a territory of the United States. After the war, Andrés Pico became a loyal American citizen and helped to ease tensions between the Americans and the Californians. From 1860 to 1861 he was a California state senator.

AUGUST 23, 1940

ON THIS DAY IN SAN DIEGO HISTORY people in San Diego and southern California were reading the August issue of the *Desert Magazine* which contained an article written by Marshal South called "Desert Diary." It describes the South family's experiences living in isolation on top of Ghost Mountain in the Anza-Borrego desert of San Diego County (see also FEBRUARY 6).

Reflecting on summertime at his desert retreat, which he called Yaquitepec (from "Yaqui," a freedom-loving Sonoran Indian tribe, and *tepec*, the Aztec word for "hill"), South writes:

> HEAT!—and the distant phantoms of mirage. Desert summer is with us now and Yaquitepec shimmers in the heat of a midday glare that is thirstily metallic… It is hot these days. But not too hot. The human system is adaptive; it adjusts speedily to its environment. The desert dweller becomes used to his summer with its tingling strike of dry sunshine… There is a good deal of myth about the terrors of desert summer.
>
> Perhaps it is another indication of how far and how shamelessly we of Yaquitepec have slipped from the skirts of civilization in that we…like to bask on the rocks in summer. Sometimes the rocks are pretty hot and they have a damp appearance afterwards as though something had been frying on them. But as you lie there you do not think of these things. All you can feel is the tingle of life and of electricity striking healing rays through every bone of your body.

Marshal South continued to write articles for the *Desert Magazine* for eight years—from 1940 until his death in 1948. A book was published in 2005 by Sunbelt Publications in San Diego entitled *Marshal South and the Ghost Mountain Chronicles: An Experiment in Primitive Living*, which contains the complete collections of his writings from *Desert Magazine*. It was edited by Diana Lindsay and has an introduction by South's son and daughter-in-law, Rider South and Lucile South. The story of Marshal South and his experiment in primitive living in the desert of San Diego County is a very unusual and fascinating story.

AUGUST 24, 1937

ON THIS DAY IN SAN DIEGO HISTORY a Navy seaplane from North Island came in for a landing on the water of San Diego's South Bay at night. The plane hit a large obstruction, nosed over, and sank in eight feet of water. Six airmen were killed, and two more were injured. The plane had hit the remains of the old whaling vessel, the *Narwhal*.

The *Narwhal* was launched in 1883 and was involved in whaling in the Arctic Ocean. After serving for many years as the pride of San Francisco's whaling fleet, it was retired in 1908. It then served as a salmon packer for a time. In 1926 the *Narwhal*, which was a large sailing vessel that looked a lot like the *Star of India*, appeared in a movie about Moby Dick called *The Sea Beast*. Afterward, in February 1932, the ship was sold to Mexico to be used as a fishing barge and was anchored off Ensenada.

The *Narwhal* didn't stay there long. After it dragged its anchors and slammed into Ensenada's best pier, the ship was towed to San Diego. It was docked at the pier of the San Diego Marine Construction Company for a while, but scavengers began stripping things off the ship, including the brass rims from the portholes, the wheel, the doors, and even the galley cooking range. No one knew for sure who the owner of the *Narwhal* was.

Finally the ship was towed away and beached on the mudflats off National City, where a wrecker was supposed to tear it up and haul it away. But for some reason, that was never done. Over time, the ship was broken up into pieces by the wind and waves.

In October 1932 a newspaper reporter—Jerry MacMullen, who later became director of the San Diego Historical Society—wrote this poem reporting on the abandoned ship:

> A ship without a country,
> A mast without a sail.
> Then someone swiped the galley range,
> And that's the *Narwhal's* tale!

The final saga of the *Narwhal* occurred on this day in 1937, when the Navy seaplane crashed into the ship's hull in the dark of night.

AUGUST 25, 1800

ON THIS DAY IN SAN DIEGO HISTORY the first American ship entered San Diego Harbor to take on wood and water. It was the brig *Betsy*, and it had a crew of 18 men and was armed with ten guns.

At this time, San Diego and California belonged to Spain and did not become part of the United States until nearly 50 years later, after the end of the Mexican-American War of 1846–48. In those days, before the Panama Canal was built, ships from the east coast of the United States had to travel around the entire continent of South America to get to the Pacific coast of California.

Even though many Spanish ships had been to San Diego Harbor, the first ones being the ships of Juan Rodriguez Cabrillo in 1542 (see SEPTEMBER 28), the *Betsy* was the first American ship to visit San Diego. Word had spread about abundant sea otters on the Pacific coast of California and the high price that otter skins brought. This spurred on more trade by ships between the American east coast and the Spanish west coast.

Sea trade to and from the Pacific coast of California became much easier after the Panama Canal was built in 1914. The canal cut travel time considerably by eliminating the long route around the tip of South America. This was especially advantageous to San Diego, which was the first United States port that ships reached after passing through the canal. To honor its completion, San Diego held the Panama-California Exposition—a giant World Fair held in Balboa Park in 1915–16 (see JANUARY 1).

AUGUST 26, 1926

ON THIS DAY IN SAN DIEGO HISTORY an article called "The Vanished Cuyamaca" appeared in the August 26 issue of *Touring Topics*. The author, Margaret Romer, visited the ghost town of Cuyamaca in 1926 to search for remains of the Stonewall Gold Mine and Cuyamaca City. Cuyamaca City was located south of Julian on the south edge of Lake Cuyamaca in what is now Cuyamaca State Park.

On her visit to the ruins of Cuyamaca City, Romer found very little left of the town. She saw a long wooden building still standing that she identified as a "200-foot long boarding house." Only two other houses remained, one occupied by a caretaker, and a few deserted cabins. She described the rest of what she saw of the former bustling gold mining town of the 1880s and 1890s: "[T]he places where the buildings stood are as scars on the ground."

When she visited the location of the Stonewall Gold Mine, she found two large buildings made of corrugated metal painted red, with white window and door frames. She describes what she saw upon entering one of the buildings:

> [W]e see the huge mill of fifteen stamps and many troughs of different sizes to catch the gold as it was washed over them. In still another room we see the large yet finely adjusted scales on which the gold was weighed. Next we come to the room where the shafts go down into the darkness below. A chill creeps over us as we look down into the blackness. We feel the deadly silence. Then we call down and an unnatural voice answers us back. We shiver and move away from the hole.

What was left of the Stonewall Mine was totally gone two years later. The mine buildings and their contents were sold in 1928 to a Los Angeles salvage company for $500, and the mine shafts were filled in. Many people regret the loss of the historic remains of gold mining in the Cuyamaca area. For information on the value of the gold production of the mines in the Julian–Banner–Cuyamaca district, see JUNE 28.

AUGUST 27, 1869

ON THIS DAY IN SAN DIEGO HISTORY the United States superintendent of Indian affairs wrote a letter to the U.S. commissioner of Indian affairs in Washington, D.C. confirming the Indian leader Pedro José Panto's claim of his people's right to the pueblo lands of San Pascual. ("San Pascual" is the Spanish spelling, "San Pasqual" the Americanized version). San Pascual was located in the San Pasqual Valley in north San Diego County near where the Wild Animal Park is located today (see JANUARY 11).

In the letter to the commissioner of Indian affairs, it was explained that a paper written by Santiago Arguello, an influential political and military leader in San Diego and former commander of the San Diego Presidio, was not included in an earlier communication. Arguello had reinforced Panto's claim of the Indians' rights to the San Pasqual lands over those of the white squatters who had appeared on their lands. The letter states:

> I should have sent this paper [of Santiago Arguello] on with my report of San Pasqual...but in the hurry of business it was over-looked. I think the paper is important, as showing the government will take measures to have the valley reserved for the Indians, and have all the white settlers removed.

Unfortunately, the United States government did not come through for the rights of the Indians to their land in San Pasqual Valley. After the death of their leader, Pedro José Panto, the Indians of San Pasqual were forced off their land in 1878. The white squatters had prevailed (see APRIL 27).

Later, in 1883, Father Anthonio Ubach, a Catholic priest in San Diego wrote:

> San Pascual 17 years ago [1866] had a population of 300 souls with more than 600 acres of very good agricultural lands; it is now occu-pied by more than 20 squatters that with the rifle in hand scare away the Indians, not leaving one. Whisky and brutal force; nothing but the Cemetery and chapel left. The few Indians that were left, two years ago had to go away and live among rocky mountains like wild beasts; there are no lands in this vicinity for the Indian.

AUGUST 28, 1905

ON THIS DAY IN SAN DIEGO HISTORY the original La Jolla Cove Bath House burned down. The fire was caused by a defective gasoline lamp. Remember, electricity was not available in many places in those days, so they used gas lamps for lighting. Electric power didn't come to La Jolla until 1910 (see JANUARY 2).

At first it was feared that the new marine biology laboratory building that had just been built at La Jolla Cove would also be burned, but it escaped damage. The two-room building was donated by the Scripps family to the Marine Biological Association of San Diego—later to become the Scripps Institution of Oceanography (see MARCH 23 and JULY 12).

After the first Cove Bath House burned down, a new bath house was built in 1906 and was a much larger and more imposing building than the small and inadequate one before it. The new bath house had a swimming pool, a restaurant overlooking the cove, and an auditorium that was used for a time as a movie house (see JANUARY 22).

Initially, the new bath house was the pride and joy of La Jolla, but later it became a run-down, unsanitary eyesore. Contributing to the unsightliness were large-lettered and gaudy signs hanging on all sides of the building—as can be seen in old photographs. There were signs advertising not only the cafe and hot water baths, but also signs advertising spring water, a clothing company in San Diego, and the Ramona Tent Village.

The people of La Jolla began to complain about the bath house, and a group of citizens petitioned the park commission not to renew the lease. In September 1924 the park commission voted to have the 18-year-old second bath house torn down. In March 1925 the demolition was completed, and an uncluttered La Jolla Cove was returned to the residents of La Jolla.

AUGUST 29, 1910

ON THIS DAY IN SAN DIEGO HISTORY Irving Gill, a prominent San Diego architect of the time, organized the San Diego Architectural Association (see also APRIL 26).

In addition to numerous private residences, Gill designed many buildings in the San Diego area, such as:

St. James by-the-Sea Episcopal Church, 743 ProspectStreet, La Jolla, 1907.

Hotel Cabrillo (now part of the La Valencia Hotel), La Jolla, 1908.

Old Scripps Biological Building at the Scripps Institution of Oceanography, La Jolla, 1910.

First Church of Christ Scientist, 2nd & Laurel, San Diego, 1910.

The Bishops School, 7607 La Jolla Boulevard, La Jolla, 1910–16.

La Jolla Women's Club, 715 Silverado, La Jolla, 1912.

La Jolla Recreation Center, 615 Prospect Street, La Jolla, 1913.

Ellen Browning Scripps home (now the San Diego Museum of Contemporary Art), 700 Prospect, La Jolla, 1915–16.

First Church of Christ Scientist, 1123 8th, Coronado, 1928.

Fire and police station building, Oceanside, 1929.

Nevada Street Grammar School, Oceanside, 1931.

Blade-Tribune **newspaper building**, Oceanside, 1935.

Irving Gill also designed the columned fountain for the US Grant Hotel in 1910. The fountain is still located in downtown San Diego on Broadway across the street from the hotel—in front of Horton Plaza.

During the 1920s the more elaborate Spanish Colonial style of architecture became popular in California, as well as the Art Deco style. These were in contrast to and quite different from the simple lines of Irving Gill's style, which has been described as American Early Modernist.

Gill spent most of the 1920s in the Los Angeles area. He returned to the San Diego area in the late 1920s. Gill's Oceanside buildings were done during the last ten years of his life, during the great depression of the 1930s, when residential projects were not being built. Gill was living in Carlsbad then. He died in 1936—leaving his architectural mark on the San Diego area.

AUGUST 30, 1844

ON THIS DAY IN SAN DIEGO HISTORY Juan José Warner petitioned to receive a Mexican land grant in the San José Valley, located near the present-day Lake Henshaw in the northeastern part of San Diego County. The 44,000-acre rancho was granted to him a few months afterward (see NOVEMBER 28).

Later, the Warner Ranch would be an important stopping place and trading post along a well-known trail from the East known as the Southern Emigrant Trail—which was also the route of the Butterfield Stagecoach in the 1850s, with a stagecoach stop at Warner's Ranch (see SEPTEMBER 16).

Warner built a two-room adobe house on the rancho in 1845, and he was there on New Year's Day in 1847 to greet the first American wagon train from the East, when the Mormon Battalion stopped over on its way to San Diego to help out the Americans in the Mexican-American War (see JANUARY 27).

In those early days, the Southern Emigrant Trail coming from the east split into two directions at the Warner Ranch—with the northern route going to Los Angeles and then onto San Francisco. The left-hand turn, or southern route, went toward Santa Ysabel and on to San Diego. The Warner ranch house was located on the present-day Highway S-2 about a mile east of its junction with today's Highway 79. In 1851 the house was burned down in an Indian attack (see NOVEMBER 21). The house was rebuilt in 1857 by the Carillo family, who owned the ranch then.

Today the former Warner Ranch and former Carillo Ranch is owned by the Vista Irrigation District, which utilizes Lake Henshaw for part of its water needs. The Vista Irrigation District—with the help of San Diego County, state grants, and private donations—is in the process of renovating and restoring the Warner-Carillo Ranch House, which is registered as both a national and state historic landmark.

AUGUST 31, 1857

ON THIS DAY IN SAN DIEGO HISTORY the first stagecoach of the San Antonio & San Diego Mail Line reached San Diego from San Antonio, Texas—a distance of 1,476 miles. It took a total of 38 days with 34 days of actual travel. This was the first overland mail and passenger service to connect the eastern United States with the West Coast. It predated the more famous Butterfield Overland Mail & Stage Line, which didn't start until a year later and which bypassed San Diego on its way to Los Angeles and San Francisco (see SEPTEMBER 16).

When the stagecoach arrived in San Diego on this day in 1857, it was met with bells ringing and cheers from the crowd that had gathered in Old Town Plaza. Even the old cannon in Old Town Plaza was set off to boom the announcement of its arrival. The line was known as the Jackass Mail because pack mules had to be used for the part of the trip over the Cuyamaca Mountains east of San Diego (see JULY 9).

The fare for a person traveling from San Diego to San Antonio on the Jackass Mail line was $200. Each passenger was allowed 30 pounds of luggage, and extra baggage cost one dollar per pound. Each passenger was required to have a Sharps rifle, 100 cartridges, a Colt revolver with belt and holster, a knife and sheath, thick boots, a wool blanket, a rubber blanket, needles and thread, a sponge, a brush, a comb, and towels.

After the unexpected death in 1858 of James E. Birch, the owner of the San Antonio & San Diego Mail Line, the Jackass Mail continued to be operated by Birch's heirs, until 1861 when the Civil War caused disruption of the service.

SEPTEMBER 1, 1876

ON THIS DAY IN SAN DIEGO HISTORY the Rancho de la Misión San Diego de Alcalá was granted by the United States government to the heirs of Santiago Arguello. California had become the 31st state of the United States in 1850. This was the land that the San Diego Mission had occupied since 1774, when the mission was moved six miles inland from its first location on Presidio Hill because of poor soil and lack of water.

The San Diego Mission has had a stormy history. It belonged to the church for 65 years until the secularization of the missions in 1834 (see September 30).

The Rancho de la Misión San Diego de Alcalá originally consisted of nearly 59,000 acres and was the second largest rancho in San Diego County. Included in the area of the old rancho are the present districts of East San Diego, Normal Heights, Kensington, the San Diego State College district, La Mesa, Encanto, Lemon Grove, Clairemont, Linda Vista, and Allied Gardens.

The rancho had been granted to Arguello by Pío Pico, the Mexican Governor of California, in 1846, 12 years after the secularization of the mission lands. Arguello had been *comandante* (Spanish for "commander") of the presidio (military fort) and held many political and military positions in San Diego. He also helped the Americans in the war against Mexico in 1846, and some of the American soldiers were stationed at the dilapidated old mission for 12 years—from 1847 until 1859.

In 1862 President Abraham Lincoln returned ownership of 22 acres, occupied by the mission buildings and the graveyard, to the church (see MAY 23). The rest of the rancho lands were granted to the heirs of Santiago Arguello on this date in 1876. The lands were opened up for settlement in 1885. The buildings of the old mission were restored in the 1930s (see OCTOBER 17). Today, only these restored buildings, a few old olive trees in the orchard, and the ruins of the old dam in the river gorge two miles away are left as reminders of the San Diego Mission's past greatness.

SEPTEMBER 2, 1894

ON THIS DAY IN SAN DIEGO HISTORY Ramona's first high school opened in the upstairs loft of the Ramona Town Hall. It was essentially a one-room schoolhouse—but up in the loft under the rafters it could get very hot in September and October. So school was held downstairs in the main hall on hot days.

At that time the Santa Maria Valley had five elementary school districts which joined together to form the new high school district. Now the elementary school graduates in the Santa Maria Valley who wanted to continue their educations could go to high school locally instead of having to go farther away to another area for high school.

School hours for the new high school were 9 a.m. to noon and from 1 p.m. to 4 p.m. The first class at Ramona High School had fewer than 20 students, and the first high school graduation was held in 1897.

The Ramona Town Hall was new then—it was built the year before in 1893. Ramona's first library was also located in the town hall. The town hall was built with 16-inch thick adobe blocks, and the walls measured 22 inches thick after the pressed bricks were added to the front of the adobe. It was officially declared a historical site in 1973, and it was restored from its run-down condition. You can still see the Ramona Town Hall today, an imposing building standing on the north side of Main Street in downtown Ramona. It has been restored—yet again—after a fire partially destroyed it a few years ago.

SEPTEMBER 3, 1909

ON THIS DAY IN SAN DIEGO HISTORY the San Diego Chamber of Commerce formed a company called the Panama-California Exposition Company. This company was to plan for a large event in 1915 in San Diego to celebrate the completion of the construction of the Panama Canal. The Panama Canal joined the Atlantic and Pacific Oceans across a narrow part of the country of Panama in Central America. It allowed ships from Europe and from the east coast of America to get to the west coast of North America—and to California—much faster because they could avoid the long journey around the entire continent of South America.

The Panama-California Exposition of 1915 was like a large World Fair—and people came from all over the world to visit San Diego to see it. It was scheduled to last for one year, but it was so popular that it was kept open for another year. It was important for San Diego to celebrate the event of the completion of the canal because San Diego was the first United States port north of it on the Pacific coast where ships would stop.

The exposition was held at Balboa Park. Many of the ornate buildings there, including the Spreckels Organ Pavilion, the California Building that houses the Museum of Man, and the California Tower with the clock that chimes the time every 15 minutes, were built for the Panama-California Exposition. Some of the original buildings were designed as temporary buildings that were not intended to last past the exposition. The Old Varied Industries Building of 1915 lasted until the 1960s, when it was reconstructed and renamed the Casa del Prado in 1971 using recasts of the original building's ornate ornamentation.

The Panama-California Exposition called attention to San Diego and brought much new business to the city (see also JANUARY 1 and SEPTEMBER 12).

249

SEPTEMBER 4, 1946

ON THIS DAY IN SAN DIEGO HISTORY the world premiere of the movie *Gallant Journey* was held at the Spreckels Theater in downtown San Diego. Glenn Ford played the part of the early aviator John J. Montgomery in the film.

Montgomery, for whom Montgomery Field on Kearny Mesa is named, was born in 1858 in northern California. After graduating from college, where he obtained a bachelor's degree from Santa Clara College and a Master of Science degree in physics from St. Ignatius in San Francisco, he joined his family in the San Diego area at their Otay Valley ranch. There he built and flew the first fixed-wing, heavier-than-air aircraft in 1883 at the age of 25. This was 20 years before the Wright Brothers flight of their engine-driven plane, the *Kitty Hawk* in 1903.

John Montgomery and his brother, James, launched their "Gull Glider" to a height of 15 feet and flew it for 600 feet on Otay Mesa. It was called Gull Glider because its wings were shaped like a seagull's wings. John Montgomery described that first flight:

> I took this apparatus to the top of a hill facing a gentle wind. There was a little run and a jump and I found myself launched in the air... The first feeling in placing myself at the mercy of the wind was that of fear. Immediately after came a feeling of security when I realized the solid support given by the wing surface.

Montgomery later became foreman of the family ranch. He set up a workshop in the barn and continued to study, build, and test "aeroplanes," which was a word that he coined. At the age of 53, his doctor told him he should no longer fly. In spite of that advice, Montgomery flew one more time because he needed to test a new design of his latest aircraft. The plane stalled in the air and then crashed. He died before a doctor could get to him, on October 31, 1911.

In 1937 there was an airfield on Kearny Mesa called Gibbs Field. In 1947 the city of San Diego purchased the airport from William (Bill) Gibbs. In 1950, the field was renamed Montgomery Field, in honor of John J. Montgomery. Today it is an important airport for small, privately-owned aircraft.

There is a memorial to Montgomery in the form of a tall silver wing at the Montgomery-Walker Park in Otay Mesa. It is California Historical Landmark No. 711 honoring that first air flight made by Montgomery on Otay Mesa in 1883.

September 5, 1871

ON THIS DAY IN SAN DIEGO HISTORY one of the first rural school districts in San Diego County was established. It was the Ballena School District. Where is Ballena, you might ask?—and that is a very good question because it hardly exists anymore—even though during the 1860s and 1870s it was one of San Diego County's largest backcountry settlements. It was located between Ramona and Santa Ysabel on the road to Julian that is now Highway 78—near the present-day Golden Eagle Horse Ranch. Ramona, however, did not get started until over 20 years after Ballena was settled. Ballena means "Whale" in Spanish, and the town was so named because of a nearby mountain shaped like a whale.

In 1871 Ballena had about ten families living there. In those early horse-and-buggy days, wherever seven or more children who were five years old or older lived within walking distance of each other, an elementary school could be established under the County Rural School System. So Ballena formed a school district in 1871 that covered a large area—as far south as El Cajon, west to Poway (including the Santa Maria Valley where Ramona is now), and east to Julian. The district had 34 children between the ages of 5 and 15 years of age in 1871. A one-room school house was built, and it could be said that it was Ramona's first school because the present-day boundaries of the Ramona Unified School District cover the site of that original Ballena school.

Teaching conditions in the early one-room schoolhouses were far from perfect. A teacher told what it was like to teach in the 12-year-old Ballena classroom in 1883:

> The school was tiny, about 12 ft. by 16 ft., and I had 37 children there from 4-years-old to 18. It was a pretty old school even then. It was built from Julian lumber and it warped. You could put your arm through a good many places. There was no proper ceiling, just the rough boards. My desk was a carpenter's bench, and I had a stool to sit on. The benches for the children were not screwed down. They sometimes got knocked over, and all the books, ink, paper and everything would be spilled on the floor. Getting water for classroom use was another challenge. I had to send two children at a time over to the Swycaffer's place for water and they would get back with only about half a pail—not enough to go around.

Pay for the Ballena teacher in 1881 was $75 per month.

SEPTEMBER 6, 1859

ON THIS DAY IN SAN DIEGO HISTORY Dr. George McKinstry, who lived in Santa Isabel and Mesa Grande, was on his way back home on horseback after visiting in Old Town San Diego. The route he took followed the Indian trails up from San Pasqual—near where the San Diego Wild Animal Park is located today—and through Pamo Valley to Mesa Grande.

He had left Old Town late on September 5 and spent the night at Los Peñasquitos. On this date, September 6, 1859, he wrote in his diary: "9/6 left at daylight, stopped at San Pasqual, breakfast at Pancho's, left by 10am, arrived at Mesa [Grande] 4pm." So it took him two full days to get from Old Town San Diego to Mesa Grande, a trip taking about an hour and a half today by car.

Other times Dr. McKinstry took the St. Vincent Trail through the San Vicente and Barona valleys. That trail came through the El Cajon pass and crossed the San Diego River near Lakeside, following the route of the present-day Highway 67. Then it headed toward Foster's, located where the San Vicente Dam is today, and then turned east up the mountainside and into the Barona Valley and northward to Casner's, located on the Old Julian Road east of the present-day town of Ramona. The Old Julian Road continued through Ballena and Witch Creek to Santa Ysabel and Julian.

Later, after 1870 and the discovery of gold in the Julian area, stage-coaches and wagons carrying freight coming from San Diego to Santa Ysabel and Julian followed the "Government Highway." This road went up the Mission Valley Grade, up Murray Canyon, across Kearny Mesa, down a canyon into Poway Valley (spelled Paguay then) following what is today Pomerado Road, past the San Bernardo Rancho to Highland Valley overlooking San Pasqual Valley. Then the road continued across the Santa Maria Valley (where Ramona is located today) to Ballena, Witch Creek, and Santa Ysabel. This is the route of the present-day Highway 78. Those going to Julian continued eastward from Santa Ysabel up the mountain. At Santa Ysabel the road continued northward to Warner's, Oak Grove, and Temecula (today's Highway 79 North) and eventually to San Bernardino.

The early trails and "roads" were a far cry from the paved highways that we use today to get from San Diego to Santa Ysabel or Julian in much shorter travel times.

September 7, 1881

ON THIS DAY IN SAN DIEGO HISTORY the Santa Maria School District was formed in 1881 when Ramona's first schoolhouse was built just east of the present townsite of Ramona. It was built near a rock pile on the south side of the Julian Highway near Magnolia.

The town that we know today as Ramona was first called Nuevo (Spanish for "New"). Nuevo was the new town that started up in the Santa Maria Valley in 1883 when the Santa Maria Store and a post office were built on Main Street between 6th and 7th streets. The store later changed its name to the Pioneer Store, and it was run by the descendents of the original Verlaque family from France for 50 years—until 1933.

The Verlaques built a home next door to the store in 1886. The house is now the home of the Ramona Historical Society Museum. It was purchased by Mrs. Stanley Ranson in 1962 in order to preserve the rare old building. The Ranson family then donated the house to the Ramona Pioneer Historical Society to be used as a museum. You should go there sometime to see the exhibits of early life in the Santa Maria Valley.

In 1887 the Santa Maria Land & Water Company had subdivided over 3,000 acres in the Santa Maria Valley and proposed changing the name of the town from Nuevo to Ramona (see JUNE 18). Lots on Main Street 100 ft. wide were sold for $100. 80-foot-wide lots on other streets sold for $50. 5-, 10-, 20-, and 40-acre tracts were priced from $20 to $50 per acre. Terms: one-third cash, balance due at one and two years, with interest at 7%.

SEPTEMBER 8, 1900

ON THIS DAY IN SAN DIEGO HISTORY the San Diego County clerk informed county residents that in order to vote in the November 1900 national election, they must register by September 27.

The El Cajon township—it was not a city yet—had 74 male voters registered in time for the 1900 election. This was out of a total population of 563 people (334 males and 229 females). El Cajon's population in 1900 was only 2% of San Diego County's total population of 35,090. Only men could vote in the United States in those days. Women could not vote until 1920 when the 19th Amendment to the Constitution gave them the right to vote.

The 1900 election had a national presidential contest between the Democrat, William Jennings Bryan, and the Republican incumbent, President William McKinley.

El Cajon went Republican, with 55% (36 people) voting for President McKinley and 33% (22 people) voting for Bryan. San Diego County and the nation also went Republican, and President McKinley was reelected.

One of the local issues in the 1900 election was the anti-saloon ordinance, which El Cajon supported by 51% of the vote. Countywide, however, the anti-saloon legislation was defeated, with over 60% of San Diego city voters opposed to the ban on saloons.

The El Cajon community of 1900 was 98% white. Minorities in the 1900 census included ten Indians, two Chinese, and one Japanese. According to Victor W. Geraci in his article about El Cajon in the fall 1990 issue of the *Journal of San Diego History*:

> In the year 1900, the quiet township of El Cajon, California typified an agrarian, middle-class, politically conservative community, of northern European origins. It was as if a whole town from Nebraska or Illinois had moved to this agricultural suburb of San Diego.

El Cajon was incorporated as a city in 1912 with a population of approximately 700. By 1940 the population had doubled to over 1,400, and by 1950 there were 5,600. With a population in 2003 of nearly 100,000, it is now the fifth largest city in San Diego County—after San Diego, Chula Vista, Oceanside, and Escondido.

September 9, 1907

On this day in San Diego history the groundbreaking took place for the construction of the San Diego & Arizona Eastern Railway, spearheaded by an important San Diego businessman, John D. Spreckels, who owned the *San Diego Union* newspaper, the Hotel del Coronado, the San Diego Electric Railway (Trolley), and who later donated the Spreckels Organ Pavilion in Balboa Park. San Diego had been trying to get a railroad connection to the east for many years (see November 9).

The railroad would head south from San Diego to National City, through Baja California for 44 miles to avoid the rugged Laguna Mountains, then eastward through the Carrizo Gorge in the eastern mountains of San Diego County, and across the Imperial Valley desert to Yuma, Arizona. The railroad was not completed until 12 years later, in 1919, because of problems such as the Mexican Revolution of 1910, flooding of the Imperial Valley, World War I (1914–19), and the need for 21 tunnels to be built along the rail line.

The railroad was besieged with problems during the first few years, including avalanches, floods, and fires (see May 10). John Spreckels lost money on the railroad, and he sold it to the Southern Pacific Railway in 1933.

Passenger service continued on the railroad during the 1940s but ended in January 1951. During World War II, troop trains traveled on the railroad to and from the many military bases in San Diego. Freight trains continued to run until September 1976, when Hurricane Kathleen wiped out eight trestles and damaged tracks in 50 locations. By 1980 the railroad was restored, and freight trains were running again in 1982. But the next year brought heavy rains and flooding that resulted in lush vegetation—which later dried in the desert heat and caught fire, burning out two wooden trestles. So 1983 was the end of freight service on the San Diego & Arizona Eastern Railway—after 64 years of troublesome times for the "Impossible Railroad."

The railway donated the Carrizo Gorge to the Anza-Borrego Desert State Park except for a 300-foot right-of-way retained by the railroad. The Pacific Southwest Railroad Museum located at Campo is involved in education and preservation of railroad history. They offer train rides on weekends, some 12 to 16 miles up the mountains to Miller Creek. They also offer another one-day round-trip from Campo to Tecate, Mexico.

September 10, 1909

ON THIS DAY IN SAN DIEGO HISTORY the board of directors of the Panama-California Exposition elected Ulysses S. Grant Jr. to be president of the company that would plan San Diego's celebration of the completion of the Panama Canal in 1915 (see SEPTEMBER 3).

Ulysses S. Grant Jr. was the son of the former President of the United States (Ulysses S. Grant Sr.) and he was part owner of the US Grant Hotel in downtown San Diego, which was built three years before in 1906. It still stands today at the corner of 4th Avenue and Broadway, across the street from Horton Plaza. On this date also, John D. Spreckels, a successful San Diego businessman, was elected vice-president of the Panama-California Exposition Company. He and Grant and others began to plan the big event that would take place in Balboa Park in 1915 (see JANUARY 1).

It was at this time, in preparing for the 1915 exposition, that many of the ornate Spanish Colonial buildings were built in Balboa Park that we still admire today. This includes the California Building with its tiled dome that houses the Museum of Man, and the California Tower next to it that chimes the time every 15 minutes. The Spreckels Organ Pavilion was donated at this time by John D. Spreckels (see JULY 26). The Casa del Prado is a replica of the 1915 Varied Industries Building, also known as the Food and Beverage Building, that was demolished in the 1960s.

The Laurel Street Bridge over Cabrillo Canyon was built at this time, making a dramatic entrance to Balboa Park from the west. It was California's first multiple-arched cantilevered bridge. The bridge segments join at the midpoint of each arch with a one-inch space between segments to allow for expansion and contraction.

After the Panama-California Exposition, San Diego became well known throughout the country as a special place to visit.

September 11, 1888

On this day in san diego history the head of the California State Board of Health made an inspection of the San Diego County Hospital and Poor Farm that was located in Mission Valley.

The report stated that:

> [T]he hospital contained forty-five patients; twelve receiving alms [charity and financial aid]. We find the wards large, well-ventilated, comfortably furnished, and clean…but we must condemn the sanitary conditions of the outhouses and the want of cleanliness in the kitchen and dining room… [T]he officers in charge…promised that this matter would at once receive their attention and be remedied.

Most of the patients were men who were not able to work because of ill health or injuries. Most recovered and were later released but, of those who died, tuberculosis was the main cause of death—it being a disease for which there was no treatment in those days except rest and fresh air. San Diego and southern California were considered to be excellent places to recover from TB because of the mild climate.

Since 1880 the San Diego County Hospital and Poor Farm had been located on the south side of Mission Valley, where the 6th Street Extension (now Highway 163) came down the hill from what is now the Hillcrest area. The hospital remained there until 1904 when a new three-story hospital was built on the mesa above Mission Valley—next to where UCSD Medical Center is now located, at the north end of Front Street in the Hillcrest area.

The first county hospital was in what was formerly the old cobblestone jailhouse built in 1851 in Old Town. The cobblestones in that old jail were not set in cement, and the building was easily damaged by rain. The first prisoner was able to escape by digging out of the jailhouse with a pen knife. The first county hospital occupied the old jailhouse building until 1869, when it moved to a wood frame rental house on Twiggs Street in Old Town. For a time, the county would contract with the lowest bidder each year for space to house the sick and disabled.

Then in 1880 the location in Mission Valley was chosen. It was a 120-acre tract that the county bought for $1,500. It was formerly the José María Estudillo place and included a four-room adobe house with an attached kitchen. It was named the County Hospital and Poor Farm because there were gardens and orchards under cultivation there, and the needy patients, who were able to, could work there.

SEPTEMBER 12, 1913

ON THIS DAY IN SAN DIEGO HISTORY the cornerstone was laid for construction of the California Building and California Tower in Balboa Park in preparation for the Panama-California Exposition of 1915–16 (see JANUARY 1 and SEPTEMBER 3).

The California Building and Tower can still be seen today just past the west entrance (Laurel Street entrance) to Balboa Park. The tower contains a clock that chimes every 15 minutes that can be heard all over Balboa Park—including at the zoo. The California Building, with its domed roof next to the tower, houses the Museum of Man, which has interesting exhibits of human culture from all over the world. The California Building and Tower were modeled after an old 1762 church at a convent outside of Mexico City. They are decorated with tiles from the California China Products Company in National City (see APRIL 17).

When you go to Balboa Park be sure to look at all of the ornate carvings on the outside of the California Building, above the doors and so on. There are statues of many people who were important to the history of San Diego and California—such as the Spanish explorer Juan Rodriguez Cabrillo (the first European to discover San Diego Bay in 1542), the kings of Spain, and some Spanish priests—including Father Junípero Serra (who started the San Diego Mission and eight other missions in California). Also carved on the facade of the building is the Seal or Coat of Arms of the United States, the California State Seal, and the coats of arms from Spain and Mexico. All of these represent the past heritage of San Diego—which was influenced by Spain, Mexico, the United States, and the state of California.

SEPTEMBER 13, 1953

ON THIS DAY IN SAN DIEGO HISTORY Channel 10 broadcast its first TV program from a transmitting tower on top of Mount Soledad above La Jolla. It was San Diego's third TV Station. San Diego's first TV station (Channel 8, KFMB-TV) had started four years earlier in 1949 (see MAY 16). The second TV station in San Diego was Channel 6, XETV, which started in January 1953 with a transmitter on top of Mount San Antonio in Tijuana.

Channel 10 was known as KFSD-TV then because it grew out of the radio station KFSD, which had been operating since 1926. The KFSD call letters came from K- F(irst) S(an) D(iego). Channel 10 was affiliated with NBC from 1953 until 1977. It changed its call letters to KOGO-TV in 1961 and was bought by Time-Life Broadcasting in 1962, maintaining its affiliation with NBC. Later, in 1971, when it was bought by McGraw Hill Broadcasting, it changed its name to KGTV Channel 10, as it is known today. It changed its affiliation from NBC to the ABC network in 1977.

Both Channel 10, KFSD-TV, and Channel 8, KFMB-TV, were radio stations before TV was invented. It may be hard to believe, but TV has only been around for something over 60 years. Before that, people listened to the radio for news and entertainment. Ask your grandparents or your great-grandparents if they remember when there was no TV.

Back in 1950, there were only 25,000 TV sets in San Diego, which had a total population of over 600,000. Many families would watch the small nine-inch black-and-white TV (there was no color TV at first) in the windows of the local appliance stores. Today most homes have not just one but many TV sets—nearly one for each person. TV has come a long way in the last 60-plus years.

SEPTEMBER 14, 1730

ON THIS DAY IN SAN DIEGO HISTORY Father Junípero Serra, at the age of 18, decided to become a Franciscan monk. He was born Miquel Joseph Serra, but when he became a monk he chose the religious name of Junípero. (The original Junípero was a companion of St. Francis of Assisi, the man who started the Franciscan order of the Catholic Church).

Father Serra was born on the Spanish island of Mallorca (pronounced My-Yorka) in the Mediterranean Sea off the coast of Spain. He lived there until 1749 when, at the age of 35, he decided to become a missionary and went to the Spanish colony of Mexico.

Father Serra was especially important to the history of San Diego—as well as to the history of California. He founded the San Diego Mission in 1769, the first mission in Alta California (Upper California). Back then, Mexico (called New Spain then), Baja California (Lower California), and Alta California all belonged to Spain. Serra, a Franciscan priest, was asked by the King of Spain to leave Mexico City and to go to Baja California in 1767, when he was 54 years old, to take over the missions there. The missions had been started by the Jesuit order of the Catholic Church, who were no longer in favor with the king.

Then two years later in 1769, Spain decided to make an effort to create some missions in Alta California. The king wanted to convert the Indians to the Catholic faith; he also wanted to start farming and ranching there before countries like England or Russia tried to settle there. Three ships and two overland expeditions started out for San Diego from Baja California. Father Serra was chaplain and kept the diary for one of the overland expeditions (see JANUARY 9 and APRIL 29).

The Misión San Diego de Alcalá was founded on July 16, 1769, when Father Serra blessed a site on Presidio Hill as the first mission in Alta California. Father Serra went on to start 8 more of the 21 Alta California missions that were founded between 1769 and 1823. He died August 28, 1784 at the age of 79. He is buried at the beautiful Mission San Carlos Borromeo at Carmel, California.

September 15, 1940

ON THIS DAY IN SAN DIEGO HISTORY it was the last trip of the last car on the Electric Railway between San Diego and La Jolla. The Electric Railway—or Trolley—from San Diego to La Jolla was built 16 years before in 1924.

This trolley system is not to be confused with the *railroad trains* (the San Diego, Pacific Beach & La Jolla Railway) that ran between San Diego and La Jolla previously, from 1894 until 1917 (see APRIL 25). In 1919 they tore up the railroad tracks—maybe too soon because five years later they built the tracks for the electric trolley system. The trolley lasted 16 years, until this date in 1940 (see also APRIL 23)

There was a street in La Jolla named Electric Avenue because the tracks for the electric train ran down it. In the Bird Rock area, the name of the street was changed to La Jolla Hermosa sometime in the 1950s. The tracks on Electric Avenue were one block east of La Jolla Boulevard.

There was a fine trolley terminal building located at the corner of Fay and Prospect streets. The terminal was torn down in 1940. There was also a charming Mission-style trolley station in the La Jolla Hermosa area, the San Carlos Station, built in 1924—which now serves as a chapel for the La Jolla United Methodist Church. It is located at 6063 La Jolla Boulevard—just north of the Bird Rock area.

The new bus line between San Diego and La Jolla started the next day—right after the electric train took its last trip on this day in 1940.

SEPTEMBER 16, 1858

ON THIS DAY IN SAN DIEGO HISTORY John Butterfield opened up a stage-coach route between Tipton, Missouri—near St. Louis—and San Francisco, California. This was important for San Diego because the Butterfield Stage Line went through northeast San Diego County, following the route of the present-day County Highway S-2 (see OCTOBER 13).

You can follow the route the stagecoach took in your car today by taking Highway S-2 from Interstate 8 at Ocotillo through Carrizo Springs, Valle-cito—where there was a nice oasis in the desert for a stagecoach stop—up the San Felipe Valley—located several miles south of Borrego Springs—to Warner's Ranch—where there was another stagecoach stopping place. After Warner's Ranch, the stage route turned north, going past Warner Springs, Oak Grove, and then—via Aguanga, Temecula, and Chino—to Los Angeles.

The Butterfield Stage carried passengers and mail and took 25 days to go from Missouri to San Francisco—a total of 2,866 miles—at an average speed of just under 5 miles per hour. Even though it went through part of San Diego County, it bypassed the city of San Diego on its way northward to Los Angeles and San Francisco. However, San Diego did have the San Antonio & San Diego Mail Line that started up in 1857 and connected San Diego to the east. But this mail and passenger route had to use pack mules for the part of the route that crossed over the rugged Cuyamaca Mountains east of San Diego (see AUGUST 31).

The city of San Diego, however, depended primarily on ships for transportation and communication in the 1850s and 1860s, as there was no transcontinental railroad to southern California yet. Since the Panama Canal had not yet been built, ships from the East Coast had to make a long, long journey around the entire length of South America. Fortunately, San Diego has a good natural harbor and a protected bay for ships to come into.

September 17, 1849

ON THIS DAY IN SAN DIEGO HISTORY one of the gold seekers of the gold rush days was traveling through the Temecula Valley on his way to the northern California gold fields and wrote this in his diary:

> Near night we passed a poor-looking Rancho, and camped a short distance beyond, near a small Lake alive with Ducks and Geese. We visited the adobe House, and found it occupied by a Spanish Californian who was dressing a Beef. For 20¢ he gave us 9 pounds of good rump steak, which we devoured for Supper and Breakfast.

The "adobe house" is the Apis Adobe, which was the home of Pablo Apis, a prominent Luiseño Indian leader of the 1840s and 1850s. Luiseño is the name given by the Spanish to the Indians associated with the San Luis Rey Mission. It was not the name the Indians called themselves, until the Spanish came and named them that.

Pablo Apis was born around 1792 near Mission San Luis Rey. He had been educated at the mission, and he could read and write. After the secularization of the missions in 1834 (see SEPTEMBER 30) Apis was one of the Luiseño leaders who tried to save the mission lands for the church and away from the control of the Californios. In 1843 he was granted a half-league of land (about 2,200 acres) in the Temecula Valley as a reward for his service to the mission.

The "Spanish Californian" referred to in the diary entry above was none other than Pablo Apis, the Indian, himself. He usually disguised himself as a non-Indian in order to protect himself and his property from harm at the hands of the gold seekers coming into California on the Gila Trail, which went right past his adobe. Pablo Apis had learned Spanish at the mission, so it was easy for him to pass for a Spanish Californian when he was wearing rancher's clothes. Unfortunately, the white men coming from the East often had a mistaken view of Indians as being wild and dangerous savages, so Indians were often mistreated by the white men.

See also JANUARY 26 and MARCH 7.

SEPTEMBER 18, 1873

ON THIS DAY IN SAN DIEGO HISTORY the railroad industry collapsed in the financial panic of 1873, which put an end to the plans to bring the Texas & Pacific Railroad to San Diego. This day was called Black Friday.

San Diego had been trying to get a railroad from the East ever since the 1850s, when talk first began about a transcontinental railroad to the West Coast (see NOVEMBER 9). Finally, in 1871 it began to look possible when Congress passed a bill approving construction of the Texas & Pacific Railroad. It was planned that the railroad terminal on the West Coast would be at San Diego, and land was made available for the terminal to be built at the edge of San Diego Bay. But with the financial crash of 1873, all this came to a stop. Ten miles of graded road bed for the tracks were abandoned, and San Diego was left with many jobless and homeless railroad workers—and no railroad.

San Diego still had to depend on the long and cumbersome trips by ships for transportation and communication. In the 1800s there were no gasoline-powered vehicles to bring supplies or mail—and certainly no airplanes. There were only the railroads (which had not reached San Diego yet), ships, and horses and wagons—like the Butterfield Stagecoach, which bypassed the city of San Diego on its way to Los Angeles and San Francisco (see SEPTEMBER 16).

Previously the San Antonio & San Diego Mail Line carried mail and passengers between San Diego and Texas between 1857 and 1861, but it was discontinued because of the Civil War in 1861 (see AUGUST 31).

See also SEPTEMBER 9 and NOVEMBER 9.

September 19, 1914

ON THIS DAY IN SAN DIEGO HISTORY an attempted robbery occurred in the early hours of the morning at the La Jolla Post Office. At this time the post office was located on the west side of Girard Avenue just north of Silverado Street—near the present-day Warwick's bookstore.

According to the firsthand account of Nathan Rennels, a police officer at the time of the robbery who became the postmaster a few months later:

> I was awakened about two o'clock in the morning by the telephone operator, who told me that some one was in the post office. I thought it might be one of the town drunks awaiting an escort home, but from force of habit I buckled on my belt and revolver.
>
> I hurried from my father's house on Herschel down Silverado Street to Girard. The night was pitch black. Soon after I turned the corner I could see a man—he looked like a boy of 18—walking back and forth in front of the post office. He was evidently a look-out. I tried to hide behind a eucalyptus tree. I could see the light from a flash-light playing on the safe inside the building. Suddenly the boy must have spotted me, because he called "Look out! Look out!" Immediately two men joined him from inside the post office and began firing at me. Then they all began running toward Silverado Street. I returned the fire, emptying my revolver. I could hear the bullets in the tree above my head. My shots, too, went wild, and the men escaped.
>
> When the premises were searched, it was found that the safe had been drilled, and nitro-glycerine placed in the hole, which had been wired to the electric circuit. I hadn't been a minute too soon. Nothing was stolen. Federal and city investigations failed to discover the identity of the thieves.

SEPTEMBER 20, 1924

ON THIS DAY IN SAN DIEGO HISTORY street lights were installed on Prospect Street and on Girard Avenue in La Jolla for the first time. It probably seems amazing that before 1924 there were no street lights in La Jolla—since La Jolla had been settled some 40 years before, during the great land boom of the 1880s. We also need to remember that during those early times there were no electric lights yet. They used gas lamps for light before the electric light bulb was invented by Thomas Edison in 1879—and it took time for that technology to develop.

San Diego turned on its first street lights in 1881, but it took until 1924 to develop the power distribution lines to go to the remote, outly-ing area of La Jolla. What a difference electricity has made to La Jolla, San Diego, California, and to the rest of the world! The night scene—so rich with electric light today—looked mostly dark and dim with gaslight before electricity. And light was not the only thing—there were no air conditioners or fans before electricity either. People had to live in the hot weather without those luxuries—even though we often think of them as necessities now.

If you wonder why the San Diego area street lights are an orange hue instead of a brighter, whiter light, it is because the Mount Palomar Obser-vatory in northeast San Diego County requires darker surroundings in order to make the best use of its telescope to study the night skies (see OCTOBER 3 and NOVEMBER 18).

SEPTEMBER 21, 1927

ON THIS DAY IN SAN DIEGO HISTORY Charles Lindbergh returned to San Diego for a celebration—after being the first person in the world to fly a plane nonstop and alone across the Atlantic Ocean from the United States to Europe on May 21, 1927. Lindbergh had become a national—and a world—hero.

Lindbergh flew his plane, the *Spirit of St. Louis*, into San Diego for the celebration on this date in 1927. San Diego was a special place for Lindbergh since the *Spirit of St. Louis* had been built here under his supervision by Ryan Airline Company (see FEBRUARY 1). Although Lindbergh visited 67 other cities on his tour, to quote his own words, "our visit to San Diego did not follow the usual routine."

While flying into San Diego on this clear and sunny day, Lindbergh honored the Ryan plant by circling over it twice while flying the plane on its side. He then flew over North Island, where the military honored him with a gun salute. After that he made eight circles over the City Stadium, later known as Balboa Stadium, where a great crowd was waiting to welcome him. He buzzed over the stadium at only 100 feet elevation and dipped the plane's wings, to the thrill of the crowd.

Lindbergh then landed at Ryan Field—in an area called Dutch Flats, near the present-day San Diego Main Post Office on Midway Drive, where he was greeted by great crowds of people who had to be held back by over 650 Marines. Then he was driven in a flower-decorated car to the City Stadium for the big ceremony. There were over 60,000 people crammed into the stadium—it was the largest assembly of people in San Diego's history up until that time—10,000 more than for the President of the United States, Woodrow Wilson, when he visited San Diego in 1919 after the end of World War I.

While in San Diego, Lindbergh also held an honorary banquet for the employees of Ryan Airlines, where he thanked them for the work they had done on the construction of the *Spirit of St. Louis*.

When San Diego's new airport was finished in 1928, it was named for Charles Lindbergh (see AUGUST 16).

SEPTEMBER 22, 1880

ON THIS DAY IN SAN DIEGO HISTORY the first San Diego County Fair was held in National City. It was called the Horticultural Fair of 1880 and was initiated by the Kimball Brothers as a promotion to advertise their subdivision development of National City (see APRIL 1) and to show off the agricultural products of the area.

The *San Diego Union* newspaper reported on the fair:

> People were not prepared to witness such a scene as awaited them: fruits, vegetables, embroidery work, hair and fern work, shell work, and different types of paintings. Ball games at the foot of 7th Avenue. Some of the finest horses in the state have been brought here for display. No racing… Attendance for the second day was so great that long before noon, not a vehicle of any description, not a saddle horse could be had in town for love nor money.

The San Diego County Fair was held nearly every year afterwards, with a few exceptions, such as during parts of World War I and the early 1930s depression. It was held in various locations in the county: at the San Diego Armory Hall in 1885 and 1886, in Oceanside in 1888, in Escondido in 1889 and 1892, and in buildings in Balboa Park in 1916.

In 1904 the state of California organized the District Agricultural Association (DAA) to promote local agriculture, and from then on the 22nd District Agricultural Association sponsored the San Diego County Fair. In 1936 the association bought land in Del Mar—at the old Del Mar Golf Course in the San Dieguito River Valley—and the San Diego County Fair has been held there ever since. A $500,000 WPA (Works Progress Administration) grant from the federal government was obtained for construction of the first exhibit hall and auditorium, the stables for 600 horses, and the race track there. Also in 1936 the Del Mar Turf Club leased the race track from the agricultural association to operate horse racing events every year.

The first fair that was held at the Del Mar Fairgrounds in 1936 had various kinds of entertainment, including the U.S. Marine Band, the Naval Training Station Band, the Bonham Brothers Boys Band, a high wire act, an escape artist, daredevil motorcycle riders, and fireworks. Singer Bing Crosby entertained at the Fair in 1938—and in 1954, 1955, and 1956 Lawrence Welk entertained. The Navy Band Southwest has played at the fair every Fourth of July since 1993—more times than any other group.

September 23, 1963

ON THIS DAY IN SAN DIEGO HISTORY an article appeared in the Vista, California newspaper, the *Vista Press*, about a man they called "Mr. Water." His real name was Hans Doe, and the newspaper described him as "Southern California's most eminent authority on water problems."

The constant problem of supplying enough water to meet the needs of the people of San Diego has always been with us. With an average rainfall of less than ten inches per year, San Diego is actually a desert and not the tropical oasis it appears to be because of the water brought in from other areas (see DECEMBER 14).

As San Diego's population began to grow—40,000 people in 1910 and nearly 75,000 people in 1920—the city began to look elsewhere for a supply of water. The Metropolitan Water District was formed in 1928 by Los Angeles and other cities to handle the distribution of Colorado River water to southern California. Then a big political battle developed around the Metropolitan Water District, sometimes called the "Mighty Met." San Diego finally joined the Mighty Met in 1946, and the new aqueduct carrying Colorado River water to San Diego began to flow in 1947. Without it San Diego could not have met the needs of its 1948 population—over 430,000.

"Mr. Water," Hans Doe, was an engineer and part-time avocado rancher in Vista, and he held positions on various water agencies for 35 years—between 1951 and 1986 (see JANUARY 13). He was good at getting along with people and at settling conflicts. He helped the small, local guys and the large state agencies to get along and work with each other to solve the complicated problems of supplying and delivering California's lifeblood—water—to the communities of California and especially to San Diego County.

Today, with a city population of nearly one and a half million people and a county population of over three million, 90% of San Diego's water comes from two sources: the 444-mile California Aqueduct from Northern California and the 241-mile Colorado River Aqueduct. So when you turn on your water faucet, or shower, or sprinklers—remember that this precious water has been supplied to San Diego and other southern California areas only after great effort, energy, and expense. "Mr. Water" Hans Doe challenged all San Diegans to wake up each morning and thank the government and the water officials who made the delivery of water to San Diego possible. We also owe thanks to "Mr. Water" Hans Doe.

SEPTEMBER 24, 1883

ON THIS DAY IN SAN DIEGO HISTORY Amos Verlaque was appointed as Ramona's first postmaster. Except Ramona was called Nuevo then. Nuevo is Spanish for "New." The town was given that name because it was the new town that developed west of the original and larger settlement of Ballena in the Santa Maria Valley (see SEPTEMBER 5).

Some of the town leaders at the time, including Amos Verlaque and Milton Santee (the town of Santee was later named for him—see MARCH 4), tried to change the name of the town from Nuevo to Ramona, but a location in Los Angeles County already had the name. The name Ramona became very popular in California after the publication of Helen Hunt Jackson's novel *Ramona* in 1884 (see MARCH 3). Twelve years later, in 1895, the Ramona Post Office in Los Angeles County closed down. This made the name available for Nuevo in San Diego County, so the name was changed, and Ramona was officially recognized by the U.S. Post Office Department in June 1895.

Amos Verlaque also owned Ramona's first general store, which was built in 1883 on the north side of what is now Main Street between 6th and 7th streets. The Verlaque General Store also housed the post office. The building still stands today and is still used as a store. The Verlaque home, which was built next door to the store, is now the Ramona Historical Society Museum, also called the Guy B. Woodward Museum.

In 1887 Milton Santee, who was president of the Santa Maria Land & Water Company, began to develop the Santa Maria Valley, where Ramona is now located (see MARCH 4). Santee built the first hotel in Nuevo, the Ramona Hotel—later added onto and renamed the Kennelworth Inn. The 1887 San Diego County Directory listed only ten families in Nuevo, including two doctors, a stationkeeper, a blacksmith, a stockman (of livestock), a painter, a surveyor, a storekeeper (Verlaque), and a hotelkeeper (Santee). Nuevo was very slow to develop.

In the 1890s the town began to grow, and by 1900 there were over 115 families in Ramona. In 2000 the population of Ramona was 33,404, and by 2006 it had reached over 36,000.

SEPTEMBER 25, 1883

ON THIS DAY IN SAN DIEGO HISTORY one of the worst air disasters up until this time occurred in San Diego when two planes collided in the air above North Park and crashed to the ground, on this clear morning in 1978.

A Pacific Southwest Airline (PSA) Boeing 727 and a private Cessna 172 collided and fell to the ground just three miles northeast of Lindbergh Field. The wreckage of the 150,000-pound PSA jet was located at Dwight and Nile streets, just west of Interstate 805. The Cessna wreckage was located a few blocks north at 32nd and Polk.

PSA Flight 182 was on its daily morning flight from Sacramento to San Diego with a stopover in Los Angeles. The single-engine Cessna took off from Montgomery Field, seven miles northeast of Lindbergh Field, at 8:15 a.m.—at the same time the Flight 182 was on the ground in Los Angeles. After several practice approaches and simulated landings, the Cessna was leaving Lindbergh Field as the PSA 727 was approaching the area. The airport control tower told the Cessna to fly to the northeast and stay below 3,500 feet, which it did. Then, without informing the tower, the Cessna changed course, putting it on the same path as the approaching 727, which had been informed by the tower of the Cessna's location below 3,500 feet. The 727 spotted the Cessna at 9:00 a.m., then lost sight of it as the Cessna climbed to a higher altitude. The 727 continued its approach to Lindbergh Field assuming it had overtaken the Cessna.

When the Conflict Alert Warning System began to flash at the control tower, it was ignored because the PSA 727 had already notified the tower that it had the Cessna in sight. Less than one minute later, the two planes collided. It took only 17 seconds for the 727 to plunge to the ground, nose down, at a high rate of speed. With more than six tons of fuel on the 727, the explosion created a scorching fireball that one of the witnesses on the ground reported caused "apples and oranges to bake on the trees."

A total of 144 people were killed, including seven people on the ground and the two people in the Cessna. More than 20 homes were damaged or destroyed, as well as numerous automobiles, resulting in a four-alarm fire that required calling in off-duty fire fighters and other outside agencies to help fight the fires. PSA had been operating in San Diego since 1949 (see May 6).

SEPTEMBER 26, 1775

ON THIS DAY IN SAN DIEGO HISTORY Juan Bautista de Anza, a Spanish military officer, was in Mexico—known then as New Spain—traveling northward through what are now the Mexican states of Sinaloa and Sonora—gathering up people who wanted to join him on his expedition to colonize Monterey and San Francisco in Alta California.

The Anza Expedition would travel through the Anza-Borrego Desert area of what is now San Diego County, and they would camp out for several days in the cold weather of December, near the present-day town of Borrego Springs (see OCTOBER 4, DECEMBER 21, and DECEMBER 22).

This would be a trip of nearly 2,000 miles to a area that was even more primitive than the areas where they were coming from in Mexico—where they were barely scratching out a living. Some of the people that Anza gathered up for the trip were so poor that they had to be given money and clothes for the trip. Their incentive for joining the expedition was the promise of a good new land with fertile soil and plenty of water. It was a dry desert area where they came from in Mexico compared to the coastal region of San Francisco where they were headed to. They were motivated by the opportunity to make their lives better in this new land. But first, in order to get there, they had to travel through some very formidable desert and mountain territories.

Anza chose the autumn and winter months to make the trip, in order to avoid the extreme heat found in the desert during the summer. However, 1775 turned out to be an extremely cold year. The expedition encountered freezing weather in the desert and snow in the mountains during their trip through what is now southern California. Many of the cattle that were brought along on the trip froze to death (see DECEMBER 18 and DECEMBER 26).

SEPTEMBER 27, 1916

ON THIS DAY IN SAN DIEGO HISTORY Dr. Harry Wegeforth put an ad in the *San Diego Union* newspaper asking for interested parties to join together to form a zoological garden—which later became the San Diego Zoo.

A lot of animals were brought to the Panama-California Exposition during 1915–1916 (see SEPTEMBER 3), and it was uncertain during the last year of the exposition what would happen to them. So Dr. Wegeforth gathered a group of people together to plan for a zoological garden—or zoo. At first, for six years, some of the bears and other animals were kept in cages along Park Boulevard—until 1922 when the zoo moved to its present location in Balboa Park. Initially, it was difficult to attract interest and money to support the zoo. But eventually money was donated by many of San Diego's leaders, such as Ellen Browning Scripps, John D. Spreckels, and George W. Marston.

Dr. Wegeforth was in charge of the zoo for the next 25 years. It slowly grew from a small exhibit of wild animals to a fine institution, but its future was not secure until the 1930s when the city of San Diego took over its support. Now the San Diego Zoo is known worldwide as one of the most beautiful and well-run zoos in the world.

Dr. Wegeforth, a medical doctor, came to San Diego from Baltimore, Maryland in 1910. He had been chief surgeon at a Baltimore hospital for several years. In San Diego he operated a small hospital in Coronado for a short time. Later, in 1929, he built the San Diego Hospital—a small hospital specializing in bone surgery.

Before becoming a medical doctor, as a young boy, Wegeforth had been interested in animals. He caught crabs in Chesapeake Bay and collected snakes, frogs, and turtles in the nearby woods. It is said that his favorite animals were turtles.

When you visit the zoo and see the animal show in the Wegeforth Bowl, now you will know who the amphitheater was named for.

SEPTEMBER 28, 1542

ON THIS DAY IN SAN DIEGO HISTORY Juan Rodriguez Cabrillo and his crew, sailing on two Spanish ships, sailed into San Diego Bay, anchored off Point Loma near what is now Ballast Point, and went ashore, where they met some friendly Indians wearing animal skins for clothes. The Indians called their land Guacamal. Cabrillo named the "enclosed and very good port" San Miguel Archangel. The name was changed to San Diego de Alcalá 60 years later when the next Spanish explorer Sebastián Vizcaíno entered the bay (see NOVEMBER 10).

Cabrillo's visit to San Diego Bay marked the first time Europeans set foot on the west coast of what would later be the United States. But in 1542, the United States did not exist, and all the land was claimed by Cabrillo as a territory for Spain. Today, at the end of Point Loma, there is a museum and monument for Cabrillo—the Cabrillo National Monument.

There is a funny story concerning the celebration of the 350th anniversary of Cabrillo's landing in San Diego Bay, which was held on September 28, 1892. The festivities were held on the wharf at the foot of D Street. (Did you ever notice that there is no D Street in downtown San Diego between C and E streets? The old D Street is now known as Broadway.) On the day of the celebration, a man dressed in a velvet suit and a plumed hat was supposed to arrive at high tide in a ship that was supposed to look like Cabrillo's ship of 350 years before. But he missed the high tide, and his ship got stuck in the mud 300 feet from shore. The crowd of people ran to the wharf railing to get a better look, but the wooden structure gave way, and many important people, including the mayor of San Diego, fell into the mud.

The celebration went on anyway—featuring a parade up D Street with military marching bands, including a band from Mexico City. A group of Indians from San Luis Rey—the California mission located east of Oceanside—performed native dances. The celebration went on for three days and started a tradition of celebrating Cabrillo's discovery of San Diego Bay that is still held every September 28.

September 29, 1513

ON THIS DAY IN SAN DIEGO HISTORY Vasco Nuñez de Balboa discovered the Pacific Ocean and claimed the entire west coast of America for Spain.

San Diego's beautiful and famous Balboa Park was named in honor of this Spanish explorer. City planners made a wise decision early in San Diego's development. Led by Alonzo Horton (see OCTOBER 24), they set aside 1,400 acres in 1870 for a public park (see FEBRUARY 4).

The park was called City Park at first, but the name was changed to Balboa Park in 1910, as San Diego was preparing the park for the great Panama-California Exposition of 1915 to honor the opening of the Panama Canal. The canal would join the Atlantic and Pacific oceans through a narrow portion of Central America (see JANUARY 1 and SEPTEMBER 3).

Balboa Park was home for another great exposition and World's Fair in 1935, the California-Pacific International Exposition (see OCTOBER 30).

In 1967 a committee was formed to preserve the Spanish colonial architecture from the 1915 Panama-California Exposition in Balboa Park. When the old Varied Industries Building, also called the Food and Beverage Building, was torn down, the committee raised money to pass a bond to fund the authentic reconstruction of the building—including reproducing the ornate facade in every detail. It was completed in 1971 and renamed Casa del Prado.

The Reuben H. Fleet Space Theater and Science Center was added in 1973. In 1978 a fire broke out in the Electric Building where the Aerospace Museum was located, burning the building to the ground (see FEBRUARY 12). It was reconstructed and renamed Casa de Balboa. Another fire in 1978 destroyed the Old Globe Theater that was built for the 1935 exposition. It was rebuilt and reopened in 1982. The San Diego Automotive Museum opened in Balboa Park in 1986.

Balboa Park today is, indeed, a very important place for recreation, education, and beauty in San Diego.

SEPTEMBER 30, 1834

ON THIS DAY IN SAN DIEGO HISTORY a decree by Mexican Governor of California José Figueroa removed the San Diego Mission from church control and placed it under civilian control, with a portion of the land going to the Indians. This was part of a process known as the secularization of the missions. California was now under Mexican control since "New Spain" had won its war for independence from Spain in 1821 and formed the Republic of Mexico.

Even though some of the former mission land was to go to the Indians, the task of administering this fairly to the Indians—who were now removed from the strict mission discipline and protection of the church—was difficult to achieve. Many of the Indians—because of a lack of protection, training, and/or motivation—lost or gave up the lands assigned to them. Soon private ranchos took the place of mission farming and grazing lands. Some of the local residents who received grants of land for ranchos during the early Mexican period had been military men or prosperous merchants. All were well-connected politically. This was the beginning of the Rancho Days in California.

This secularization of the missions resulted in the eventual neglect, decay, and destruction of the mission churches and buildings. Over the years the San Diego Mission was allowed to decay into near ruins. It was finally restored in 1931 (see JULY 13 and OCTOBER 17).

OCTOBER 1, 1936

ON THIS DAY IN SAN DIEGO HISTORY a story appeared in the *San Diego Union* newspaper about a possible connection to the unsolved robbery of a Wells Fargo stagecoach some 60 years earlier.

Back in 1875 two robbers stopped the Wells Fargo stagecoach seven miles outside of Julian while it was slowly climbing a steep grade. Wells Fargo was a big bank in California at the time and also had a stagecoach line. Its stagecoaches often carried money from one bank to another, as well as carrying people on long trips. In those days there were no automobiles or good roads like we have today.

The robbers pointed a double-barreled shotgun at the driver and demanded the treasure box which contained $1,000. The robbers broke open the treasure box and took out the money. Then they ordered the driver to move on. When the driver got to Julian, he reported the holdup, and a posse was sent out to try to pick up the tracks of the robbers—but they were never found, in spite of a reward offered by Wells Fargo.

Sixty years later in the October 1, 1936 edition of the *San Diego Union*, an article told of a gaudily dressed man who was often seen in Julian about the time of the stagecoach robbery. He was a gambler known as "Slim Jim." He wore a high hat and a fancy coat. He didn't like to work but liked fancy jewelry. Slim had made friends with a Wells Fargo stage driver named Hicks who drove the stage to Santa Ysabel—seven miles down the western side of the mountain from Julian. Soon after the holdup by the two masked robbers, Hicks was fired by Wells Fargo.

Although he was out of work, Hicks bought a horse and buggy and, along with his friend Slim, visited Banner—a little town down the eastern side of the mountain from Julian—every day for a month (see NOVEMBER 27). For two men who didn't work, they spent a lot of money in saloons and amusement parlors in Julian and Banner. But no one was ever able to prove that they robbed the Wells Fargo stagecoach.

OCTOBER 2, 1944

ON THIS DAY IN SAN DIEGO HISTORY the Green Dragon Colony in La Jolla was sold to Jack and Alice Mosher. The Green Dragon Colony was a group of 12 cottages built by Anna Held between 1894 and 1902 in what is now the 1200 block of Prospect Street (see NOVEMBER 3).

Josephine Seaman had owned the cottages since 1926, and she had left them in their original state, using them for shops and tea rooms until the purchase by the Moshers on this date in 1944. The Moshers kept only four of the original cottages and incorporated the rest of them into larger buildings containing a nicely designed collection of shops. These four remaining cottages were designated as San Diego historic sites in May 1986. Previously the land where the cottages were located was designated a historic site in 1973.

Back in the early days when Anna Held was building her cottages, she planted some tiny sticks that were young eucalyptus trees at the suggestion of her friend Kate Sessions. Sessions was a horticulturist who was in charge of planting all of the interesting vegetation that we see today at Balboa Park (see MARCH 24). The eucalyptus trees grew large at the Green Dragon Colony and provided nice shade. Today there are only two or three of the giant 100-year-old trees left there.

In recent years a controversy emerged as to whether the remaining cottages could be destroyed to make room for remodeling and expansion of the Chart House restaurant at 1270 Prospect Street. La Jolla residents have always been very concerned about the preservation of historic buildings and sites in their charming seaside community. Unfortunately, even though many of the original small cottages have been incorporated into larger buildings, none of the Green Dragon Colony cottages that remain are in their original state. The building that was occupied by the Chart House with its spectacular ocean view and floor-to-ceiling windows, sat vacant for several years with a "For Lease" sign in front of the building because it was not allowed to destroy any of the remaining cottages for its expansion.

OCTOBER 3, 1947

ON THIS DAY IN SAN DIEGO HISTORY the California Institute of Technology in Pasadena, California (Cal Tech) issued a press release that had significance to San Diego County: "The most daring optical job ever attempted by man was finished today—polishing of the giant 200-inch telescope mirror for the Palomar Mountain Observatory."

No telescope in the world had ever been anywhere near that large. The 200-inch diameter—the distance across the center of the mirror—was nearly 17 feet—the same as three adults lying end-to-end. The largest telescope before this was the 100-inch (8-foot) diameter telescope at the Mt. Wilson Observatory east of Los Angeles—only half the size of the new Palomar mirror. But the background lights of the Los Angeles area had started to become a problem. The remoteness of Mt. Palomar would provide better viewing for the new "Giant Eye."

The glass for the 200-inch mirror was cast at the Corning Glass Works in New York, where 20 tons of molten glass was poured into a special mold. This was the largest glass casting ever made, the most expensive scientific instrument ever designed, the largest telescope in the world, designed to see farther into the sky than had ever been possible before.

It took nearly 20 years to finish this ambitious project—from 1928 until 1947. Scientists and technicians at Cal Tech would spend 13 years grinding and polishing the glass disk into the right shape and perfecting the control mechanisms that would move and focus the 200-inch mirror.

When it was decided in 1934 to locate the new telescope on Mt. Palomar in San Diego County, a work camp was built west of the observatory site to house the workers who would build the road up the mountain that the county had promised. The road was called the "Highway to the Stars." See NOVEMBER 18 for the dramatic transfer of the "Giant Eye" from Pasadena to Mt. Palomar.

OCTOBER 4, 1775

ON THIS DAY IN SAN DIEGO HISTORY Juan Bautista de Anza, a Spanish military officer, was trying to find a land route to transport settlers from Mexico to Alta California. Alta California was not very well settled yet. On this date Anza was at Magdalena in northern Mexico on his way to San Francisco and Monterey with 177 people, their baggage, and supplies carried by 140 mules. Anza would pick up 63 more people from what is now southern Arizona—at the Tubac Presidio (military fort) south of Tucson—bringing the total to 240. Some of them were soldiers and their families, who would settle the new presidio in San Francisco; the rest of the people would settle a nearby pueblo (Spanish for "town").

Part of the overland route of what would later be known as the Anza Trail involved going through what is now known as the Anza-Borrego Desert in northeastern San Diego County, camping for several days in what is now the Borrego Springs area (see DECEMBER 21, DECEMBER 22 and DECEMBER 26).

After leaving Arizona for California, the expedition had nearly 1,000 head of livestock (including 165 pack mules, 340 horses, a few burros, and over 300 head of beef cattle). Most of the animals would supply the new settlement, but 100 of the cattle would supply meat to eat during the trip.

They also carried the following supplies: six tons of flour, beans, corn-meal, sugar, and chocolate. There was another ton of cooking kettles, frying pans, and tools, plus another ton of extra clothing and blankets—not to mention saddles, bridles, horse-shoeing tools and nails, and tents. This trip was no small undertaking.

OCTOBER 5, 1930

ON THIS DAY IN SAN DIEGO HISTORY St. James by-the-Sea Episcopal Church in La Jolla was dedicated. The first building for this church was built in 1907, but it was replaced by the present building on this date in 1930. The land was originally donated in 1907 by Miss Virginia Scripps, half-sister of Miss Ellen Browning Scripps.

In 1906 Virginia Scripps donated her cottage on Prospect Street, Wisteria Cottage, so that the church could hold services there. She also donated the land for The Bishops School, a well-respected private school started by St. James by-the-Sea Church. When the railroad tracks were torn out in La Jolla on Prospect Street in 1919, leaving unpaved ruts in the newly paved street, "Miss Virginia" paid for having the ruts patched up between Fay and Cuvier streets. She was also known to deliver many food baskets to needy people.

Miss Virginia was also known for her eccentricities (see APRIL 28). It was reported that in church she would stand up in her pew while the collection plate was being passed in order to see what her friends and neighbors were contributing. In his book *La Jolla Year By Year*, Howard S.F. Randolph tells about the time—or times—when Miss Virginia "sat on the railroad track while some member of her family returned to the house for a forgotten article, and held the train, daring the engineer to start."

Another description of Miss Virginia is given by Theodore W. Fuller in his book *San Diego Originals*: "A typical day began with Miss Virginia making the rounds downtown wearing a pith helmet and putting litter into her wheel barrow. Pity the poor wretch who littered in her vicinity: she would run after the culprit, brandishing a stick."

Both Scripps sisters, along with their brother, E.W. Scripps, donated money and land for many projects in La Jolla. You have perhaps noticed the Scripps name on many places in the area—such as Scripps Institution of Oceanography, Scripps Memorial Hospital, Scripps Clinic, and Scripps Park.

OCTOBER 6, 1858

ON THIS DAY IN SAN DIEGO HISTORY the first Butterfield Stage stopped at Warner's Ranch in what is today northeastern San Diego County. You can still see the old ranch house that served as the stage stop on County Highway S-2 about one mile east of Highway 79—north of Lake Henshaw on the way to Borrego Springs. Today there is a California historical marker in front of the old ranch house.

The Butterfield Stage traveled from Tipton, Missouri (near St. Louis) to San Francisco on its 2,600-mile, 24-day trip, passing through part of the present-day northeastern San Diego County (see SEPTEMBER 16 and OCTOBER 13).

The 44,322-acre Warner Rancho was granted to Juan José Warner in 1844 (see AUGUST 30). General Kearny passed by the Warner Rancho in 1846 during the Mexican-American War a few days before the Battle of San Pasqual (see DECEMBER 6). The Mormon Battalion also passed by the Warner Rancho in 1847 on their way to San Diego to help out the United States army in the war (see JANUARY 27).

Before Juan José Warner owned the ranch, the area was visited as early as 1795 by the first white men to actually visit Warner Valley. A Catholic priest with a military escort from San Diego was looking for a site for a new mission to be located between the San Diego Mission and the San Juan Capistrano Mission. The priest named the valley Valle de San José, and they found ten large Indian *rancherias* (settlements) there. The priest, impressed with the size and fertility of the valley and the large Indian population there, recommended it as "a suitable place not only for a Mission, but for both a Presidio and a Mission." But that was not to be because a location east of Oceanside was selected as the site for the new mission, which would be named the Misión San Luis Rey de Francia.

OCTOBER 7, 1929

ON THIS DAY IN SAN DIEGO HISTORY an impressive ground-breaking ceremony was held at the new location of the San Diego State Teacher's College—now known as San Diego State University. Nearly 500 people attended the ceremony including students, faculty, and distinguished visitors such as the governor of California and prominent San Diego businessman George W. Marston (see OCTOBER 22), who was a former trustee of the college.

The college was originally called the State Normal School, "normal school" being the designation given to teacher training schools. It was started 32 years earlier in 1897 (see MARCH 13) and originally located on a 17-acre tract in the University Heights area near El Cajon Boulevard and Normal Street. But as the school grew, the campus became overcrowded. The land surrounding the campus had become too expensive for the school to expand, so a search was begun to find a new location suitable for building a large campus.

After a long search and after considering over ten different locations, the problem was finally solved when an investor from Los Angeles, Alphonso Bell, donated 125 acres to the college—from the 7,580 acres that he had bought ten miles northeast of downtown San Diego that he planned to develop into a new residential area. The acreage was located on a bare promontory overlooking the Alvarado Canyon/Adobe Falls area, which is near today's intersection of Interstate 8 and College Avenue.

Bell also donated an additional $50,000 to San Diego State College for landscaping the grounds. The future nicely-landscaped college would help Bell's residential development of the surrounding area. The college is still located there and has grown into a very large university (see also MAY 2).

OCTOBER 8, 1895

ON THIS DAY IN SAN DIEGO HISTORY the *Poway Progress* newspaper published a report on a possible railroad from San Diego to Poway and Ramona. The promoters of the San Diego, Pacific Beach & La Jolla Railway, which was just completed to La Jolla the year before, proposed running an extension of the railroad through the Poway Valley up to the Santa Maria Valley to Ramona and Ballena and possibly beyond. If you have never heard of Ballena, see the story for SEPTEMBER 5.

The railroad promoters agreed to put up $150,000 if the backcountry people would pledge another $150,000. They promised that the railroad would come as close as possible to the Poway Post Office but were vague about the route beyond Poway and the location of stations. In spite of vigorous efforts to raise the money from the land owners in the area, they were unable to raise enough money—so the project died.

There was already a railroad, however, from San Diego to Foster that was built in 1888 to 1890. Foster was located between El Cajon and Ramona on the present-day Highway 67 near Slaughterhouse Canyon Road. So even though the proposed railroad line to Poway and Ramona failed, the people in Ramona could still get to San Diego and back in one day. This required getting out at 5:00 a.m. to catch the stagecoach down Mussey Grade Road to Foster and then catching the train at Foster for the 25-mile train trip to San Diego. The round-trip fare in 1895 from Ramona to San Diego and back on stagecoach and train was four dollars.

The people in Julian paid six dollars round-trip, which involved a 34-mile stagecoach ride from Julian to Foster, where they got the train to San Diego. We need to remind ourselves that there were no automobiles in 1895, so the stagecoach and trains were very important to the people in the San Diego County backcountry.

OCTOBER 9, 1866

ON THIS DAY IN SAN DIEGO HISTORY a letter was published in the *San Francisco Bulletin* newspaper from a man who claimed that Cave J. Couts had shot "an unarmed man while walking in broad daylight across the San Diego Old Town Plaza."

Cave Couts and his wife Isadora Bandini owned the Guajome Rancho, located in northwest San Diego County between the present-day cities of Oceanside and Vista (see APRIL 5 and NOVEMBER 11).

The story goes that Cave Couts was in Old Town San Diego on business. When he looked out the door of the butcher shop (what they called the meat market then), he saw Juan Mendoza walking down the street. Juan Mendoza was a man who used to work for Couts on the Rancho Guajome and who had threatened to harm him in the past. Couts picked up a double-barreled shotgun and walked out on the street and shot Mendoza. Mendoza turned and ran. Then Couts fired the second shot, which killed Mendoza instantly.

To make a long story short, a trial was held and Cave Couts testified that he had "constantly received threatening messages from Mendoza," which he believed would be carried out. Certain witnesses testified that Mendoza was a dangerous man who had robbed and killed people in the past. Couts testified that even though he had avoided coming from Rancho Guajome into San Diego for fear of running into Mendoza, he had to make the trip into town for business reasons that day.

The jury voted "not guilty," and the people of San Diego were convinced that Cave J. Couts, an influential member of the community, had been treated fairly.

OCTOBER 10, 1868

ON THIS DAY IN SAN DIEGO HISTORY the first *San Diego Union* newspaper was published. The *Union* was not San Diego's first newspaper, however. Seventeen years earlier, the *San Diego Herald* started publishing a paper which came out once a week, but nine years later in 1860 it closed down and moved to San Bernardino.

In 1868, eight years after the *Herald* closed down in San Diego, the *San Diego Union* was started by Colonel William J. Gatewood, a lawyer from San Andreas, a gold town near Sacramento. Gatewood was publisher of the *San Andreas Register*. After visiting San Diego in early 1868, he became enthusiastic about the place. He moved his printing press from San Andreas to San Diego and started publishing the *San Diego Union* on this date in 1868.

Today you can visit the old *San Diego Union* building in Old Town on San Diego Avenue. The small wood-frame building that was constructed in 1850 has been authentically restored to what it was like in the 1860s—including the furniture and a Washington hand printing press of exactly the same type that printed the first edition of the *San Diego Union*.

Later, in 1890, the *San Diego Union* was purchased by an important San Diego businessman, John D. Spreckels. Spreckels owned the Hotel del Coronado and most of Coronado Island. He was also involved in planning the Panama-California Exposition of 1915 and was instrumental in getting the San Diego & Arizona Railroad to San Diego in 1911. (For more on John Spreckels, see JULY 26).

The *San Diego Union* experienced its greatest growth under Spreckels' ownership. In 1901 the *Union* took over the *San Diego Tribune*, which had started in 1895. By 1907, the combined papers built a new, six-story building in downtown San Diego. Still today, San Diego's main newspaper is the *San Diego Union-Tribune*, which has been publishing newspapers for over 130 years (see MARCH 20).

OCTOBER 11, 1899

ON THIS DAY IN SAN DIEGO HISTORY the first telephone was installed in La Jolla. The first phone went to Dr. Foster Post, and the second phone went to Mr. and Mrs. Anson P. Mills. Mr. Mills was a retired lawyer who had moved to La Jolla ten years before in 1889. He is well-known in La Jolla for writing a diary, giving interesting detailed information about life in the early days of La Jolla from 1895 until he died in 1933. His diaries are preserved in the archives of the La Jolla Historical Society.

Mrs. Mills, "Nellie," was a great leader in the La Jolla community. She helped to start many community projects such as the Women's Literary Club of La Jolla (which later became the La Jolla Women's Club), the Reading Room (which later became the La Jolla Library), the La Jolla Village Improvement Society, the Union Congregational Church, the La Jolla Red Cross, and the Women's Hospital Auxiliary. She also ran a successful real estate business from 1893 until 1924. She must have really needed that telephone to handle all of her business and community activities!

Telephones had already been in San Diego for eight years—since 1881 when the San Diego Telephone Company started out with 13 customers. San Diego had a population of 3,000 then.

Telephone lines took longer to reach some outlying areas. Ramona did not receive telephone service until 1904, when the telephone line was extended from San Diego through Lakeside to Ramona via Mussey Grade Road.

The mountain town of Julian, surprisingly, had telephones since the early 1890s. Robert Waterman, the owner of the Stonewall Gold Mine in Cuyamaca City, ten miles south of Julian (see JANUARY 8), brought in the first telephone line from San Diego to his mine in 1890. The town of Julian hooked up to it shortly afterwards.

Borrego Springs, the small desert town in northeastern San Diego County approximately 85 miles from San Diego, did not receive telephone service until 1947. Their service came from the El Centro line with a 17-mile phone line built from Ocotillo Wells. With a total population of less than 600 people, there were at first only four phones in Borrego. Five years later, in 1952, there were still only 18 phones there.

OCTOBER 12, 1879

ON THIS DAY IN SAN DIEGO HISTORY Rufus Morgan, a beekeeper who was in charge of the Glen Oak Apiary, or bee farm, in what is now the Rancho Bernardo area, wrote a letter to his wife in North Carolina describing life in the San Diego area in 1879.

Morgan had left North Carolina a few months before, traveled by train to San Francisco and then by boat to San Diego. He went into business with Ephraim Morse, a prosperous San Diego businessman, to run the Glen Oak Apiary for producing honey.

In his letter he wrote:

> October 12, 1879. Dear Mary—Am still feasting on venison—can kill one [deer] most any time now… They claim that we are sure of a wet winter from various signs, at any rate rain has commenced much earlier than usual—we've had two days… Winter has sett in & it feels cool and damp…at 60° to 75°—Went as low as 40° one night… There will be but little trouble to get help here. I saw yesterday a stout, intelligent indian girl, could do any thing, that would come for $8 per month…but she speaks only Spanish… Much love to all. Affectionately, Rufus Morgan

In a previous letter to his wife, Morgan described the area:

> The country looks very barren as all the hills are nearly devoid of timber, only covered with brush and shrubs… I visited many houses and all the people look poorly dressed, but I find its the style here—as I am sure all were well to-do & making money—but strange to say, never mind how poorly they might appear in dress, you would always discover that you were talking to what would pass with us for a gentleman & educated at that!… Mr. Morse's apiary [that] I have agreed to take…is 35 miles from town up a ravine in a very picturesque place… You must direct your letters to Bernardo, San Diego Co Cal… You will like [it] here I am sure—we will be in our glory as regards flowers and fruit—it really seems as if they grew by magic, they all look so luxuriant & thick!

Rufus Morgan's letters, written between January 1879 and April 1880, give interesting insights into the life and times of the San Diego area in those early days. Unfortunately, before his wife and new baby could join him in California, Morgan died unexpectedly in April 1880 at the age of 33 from eating poisonous mushrooms.

OCTOBER 13, 1858

ON THIS DAY IN SAN DIEGO HISTORY a passenger on the Butterfield Overland Mail Stagecoach wrote an article for the *New York Herald* newspaper about the first stagecoach trip from St. Louis, Missouri to San Francisco, California. His name was Waterman Ormsby, and he was the only passenger who traveled the entire way on that first 2,700-mile trip of the Butterfield Stagecoach.

Part of the route went through Northeast San Diego County along the route of today's Highway S-2—through Vallecito, Box Canyon, San Felipe, and Warner's Ranch (see SEPTEMBER 16).

Ormsby wrote about this portion of the trip:

> The average rate of speed on the whole route was a fraction under five miles per hour—Vallecito, or Little Valley, is a beautiful green spot—a perfect oasis in the desert...surrounded by rugged timberless hills, and the green bushes and grass and hard road are a most refreshing relief from the sandy sameness of the desert. There are a number of springs, some of them salt... The sand sparkles in the sun with large quantities of mica...often mistaken for gold dust...
>
> From Little Valley [Vallecito] the road leads, through a rough canyon, over a steep and stony hill into another valley, whose only characteristic is an abundance of grease weed [greasewood or creosote bush], which whether wet or dry is excellent fuel [for fires]. At the end of this valley, 28 miles from Vallecito, our road...proceeds through a very narrow pass—the most wonderful on the route [Box Canyon—there is a historical marker there now]... The channel appears to have been cut through the solid rocks... [A]mong these jagged peaks there are many varieties of curious weeds—cactus plants, Spanish dagger [*Yucca*], prickly pear, and maguey [*Agave* or century plant]—from which nutricious food and drink is obtained...
>
> In the valley of San Felipe we saw a number of prosperous Indian ranches, where they raise corn and melons and live much like white folks. Warner's ranche is a comfortable house, situated in the valley, in the midst of a beautiful meadow, and with its shingled roof looked more like civilization than anything I had seen for many days. There were hundreds of cattle grazing on the plain.

The Butterfield Stage route continued northward to Los Angeles and then inland up the California central valley to San Francisco. The entire trip from St. Louis to San Francisco took 24 days.

OCTOBER 14, 1960

ON THIS DAY IN SAN DIEGO HISTORY the Desert Lodge, which was the first hotel in the desert town of Borrego Springs, changed its name to La Casa Del Zorro after it was purchased by James Copley, owner of the Copley newspaper chain (see MARCH 20).

The Desert Lodge first opened in 1939 and centered around an adobe ranch house that was built in 1933. In 1940 four more guest rooms were added. Electric power lines did not reach the Borrego Valley until 1945, so the lodge had a generator to make electricity. Cows on the property provided milk.

During World War II, the Desert Lodge housed military officers and their families. In 1947 the DiGiorgio Fruit Company, who started Borrego Farms about this time, leased the entire Desert Lodge to house their employees until bunk houses could be built on their 1,000-acre ranch in the northern part of Borrego Valley (where DiGiorgio Road is located today). They grew early crops of grapes, which were harvested and sold before grapes were ready from other areas with less favorable climates. In June 1953 early grapes from Borrego sold for $12.50 per box in New York. By 1957 DiGiorgio had 2,500 acres producing grapes in Borrego. DiGiorgio closed down his grape vineyards in Borrego in 1966 as the farm workers unions became a threat to his business.

La Casa Del Zorro (Spanish for "House of the Fox" or "Fox's Den") began to thrive in 1960 under the Copley ownership. James Copley is quoted in the *Borrego Sun* newspaper as saying:

> The reputation of Borrego Springs, San Diego County's desert playground, as one of the nation's finest desert resorts, is being spread far and wide, and this reputation is bringing to Borrego and to San Diego County people from all parts of this country and Canada.

Copley held his annual newspaper conferences there, which were attended by people from all over the country.

La Casa Del Zorro expanded and became the largest and most prestigious hotel in the Borrego Valley. Portions of the original 1933 adobe ranch house are still there, incorporated into part of the lobby. In 2008 La Casa Del Zorro was sold to out-of-the-area investors who changed the name to Borrego Ranch Resort & Spa.

OCTOBER 15, 1910

ON THIS DAY IN SAN DIEGO HISTORY the US Grant Hotel was opened at the corner of 4th and D streets in downtown San Diego. (The name of D Street was later changed to Broadway, in 1914.) The new luxury hotel replaced the old Horton House Hotel, which had been a grand 100-room hotel built in 1870 by Alonzo Horton, the founder of New San Diego (present-day downtown San Diego) (see OCTOBER 24).

Ulysses S. Grant Jr., the son of the former general and former President of the United States, had bought the old Horton House Hotel in 1895 and made plans to replace it with a luxurious new hotel—the US Grant Hotel. When it was finished, the hotel featured a fancy fountain designed by the prominent local architect, Irving Gill (see APRIL 26 and AUGUST 29). The fountain was illuminated by electric lights with 15 color effects and contained portraits of three men who were important to San Diego history: Juan Rodriguez Cabrillo, Father Junípero Serra, and Alonzo Horton. The hotel cost more than $1 million to build—a lot of money for those times.

The Grant Grill, a popular restaurant in the US Grant Hotel since the 1940s, had a policy of serving "men only" for lunch. The restaurant allowed women after 3 p.m. This continued until 1969 when seven women entered the Grant Grill to have lunch and were turned away. The "men only" policy was finally changed after a $1 million law suit was filed in 1972 charging violation of the Federal Civil Rights Act. Later the hotel honored the seven women with plaques in the Grant Grill.

The US Grant Hotel is still a fine old San Diego hotel, having been completely remodeled and renovated from 1983 to 1985 at a cost of nearly $80 million. And Irving Gill's columned fountain is still there—across Broadway from the hotel—in front of the Horton Plaza Shopping Center (see AUGUST 9).

OCTOBER 16, 1852

ON THIS DAY IN SAN DIEGO HISTORY Andrés Ybarra filed a claim with the U.S. Land Commission for Las Encinitas Rancho. Ybarra had owned this rancho as a Mexican land grant since 1842—when California was a part of Mexico. But after the Mexican-American War of 1846–48, California became a part of the United States, and the old Mexican land grants had to be reapplied for with the United States government. Prior to receiving the Mexican land grant, Ybarra had owned a dram shop (the old name for a liquor bar) in Old Town.

The 4,431-acre Las Encinitas Rancho was located inland from the coast, several miles east of the present-day town of Encinitas and just north of the present-day community of Rancho Santa Fe. Encinitas means "Little Live Oaks" in Spanish.

A stage station was located on Las Encinitas Rancho for the Los Angeles–San Diego stagecoach. The ruins of the old stage station were located on the Encinitas–San Marcos road about three miles northeast of Encinitas. The most important development on this rancho was around Olivenhain (German for "Olive Grove"), which was a German agricultural colony established in 1885 in the southern part of the rancho. Today Olivenhain is a nice residential area with big homes on large plots of land.

OCTOBER 17, 1930

ON THIS DAY IN SAN DIEGO HISTORY the restoration of the San Diego Mission was underway. The restoration was begun earlier that year, on the 161st anniversary of its founding by Father Junípero Serra in 1769 (see JULY 16).

Before the restoration was started, the mission was in a very run-down condition. In fact, it was almost in ruins. Old pictures from the 1890s show the roof caved in and what was left of the adobe walls washed away.

Efforts had been made in the past to collect money to save the crumbling mission. Back in 1895 the Land Marks Club was formed in California for the purpose of helping to preserve the California missions. In 1899 the Land Marks Club offered to donate $500 to its San Diego chapter if the San Diego chapter would match it locally with another $500.

George W. Marston, an influential San Diego businessman (see OCTOBER 22), was president of the San Diego chapter of the Land Marks Club and, with his help, the club was able to come up with the other $500. The money would only pay for stabilizing the mission to prevent further decay and erosion. It was not nearly enough to rebuild it. It was like a Band-Aid until more money was available for more extensive preservation efforts. Specifically, the club was able only to reinforce the bases of the existing adobe walls with brick foundations and cap the walls with concrete or red tile to prevent further disintegration.

George Marston and John D. Spreckels (another important San Diego businessman—see JULY 26) tried over the years to raise more money for the restoration project, until 1917 when the United States entered World War I. After the end of the war, renewed efforts were made by Marston and others. Finally, in 1929 enough money had been collected, and the restoration of the mission started in 1930 (see JULY 13).

OCTOBER 18, 1836

ON THIS DAY IN SAN DIEGO HISTORY Ellen Browning Scripps was born in London. She came to the United States as a child and later settled in La Jolla in 1897 when she was 61 years old. Her house was on Prospect Street at Draper Street, where the San Diego Museum of Contemporary Art is now located. Before moving to La Jolla, she lived at the Scripps Ranch at Miramar with her half-brother, Edward Willis (E.W.) Scripps and her half-sister, Miss Virginia Scripps. The Scripps family made their money from the Scripps-Howard newspaper chain. They donated much of their wealth to community projects in San Diego—and especially in La Jolla.

If you live in San Diego or La Jolla, you surely must be familiar with the Scripps name: the Scripps Institution of Oceanography, Scripps Memorial Hospital, Scripps Clinic, and Scripps Hall at The Bishops School. Miss Ellen Scripps also donated money to many other projects that do not carry her name, such as the La Jolla Women's Club in 1914, the La Jolla Children's Playground and Recreation Center in 1915, the "new" La Jolla Library building in 1921, Torrey Pines Park and Lodge in 1923, and the Children's Pool in La Jolla (where the harbor seals live now) in 1931.

Miss Scripps loaned her brother E.W. Scripps part of the $5,000 that he paid in 1890 for his 400 acre Miramar Ranch—a bare mesa (Spanish for "table" or "flat land") located 16 miles north of San Diego. E.W. Scripps began to landscape and build roads on the ranch. He also added another 1,700 acres and planted the first of the eucalyptus trees that are flourishing there today. Today that land is no longer owned by the Scripps family but is a pleasant residential area called Scripps Ranch.

Miss Ellen Browning Scripps never married. She died in 1932 at the age of 95. Her generosity to the San Diego area, and especially to La Jolla, lives on beyond her 95 years (see JANUARY 30, MAY 3, MAY 24, MAY 31, and AUGUST 10).

OCTOBER 19, 1900

ON THIS DAY IN SAN DIEGO HISTORY Mr. Anson P. Mills (see OCTOBER 11) played golf for the first time on a new golf course in La Jolla. A few months later a group of La Jollans, including Mr. Mills, met at the La Jolla Reading Room and organized the La Jolla Golf Club.

According to Howard S.F. Randolph in his book *La Jolla Year by Year*, "This was the start of golf in La Jolla… The new golf course ran up Prospect Street from the corner of Cave Street, down Torrey Pines Road, then over toward the ocean, and back to the starting point [at Cave and Prospect streets]." That would be an area filled with houses, buildings, and a lot of heavy traffic today.

A summer visitor to La Jolla in the early days writes about the beginnings of that first golf course:

> [I]t was all very rough, dirt greens, etc. In those days we only used about four clubs. The balls were solid rubber and when they were damaged we soaked them in lye to take off the paint, then boiled them and pressed them in a mould, and after they had cooled we painted them and so had a new ball.

As the town grew it encroached on the golf course, so finally in 1927 the course was relocated to the present site of the La Jolla Country Club & Golf Course at the end of High Avenue up the northwestern slope of Mount Soledad. A club house was also built there in 1927.

Later, the Torrey Pines Golf Course was built north of La Jolla on the Torrey Pines Mesa above the coastal cliffs just south of the Torrey Pines State Reserve (see APRIL 7). In 1956 the city of San Diego held a special election to set aside 100 acres from the former Camp Callan military base for a public golf course. The remainder of the Camp Callan property (see JANUARY 15) was given to the state of California, and the University of California San Diego (UCSD) was built there in 1961.

The Torrey Pines Golf Course, noted for its sweeping views of the Pacific Ocean, has hosted many national golf tournaments over the years, including the Buick Invitational. In 2008 the US Open Golf Tournament, an event first held in 1895, was held at Torrey Pines Golf Course—the first time ever for it to be held at a public, municipal golf course.

OCTOBER 20, 1935

ON THIS DAY IN SAN DIEGO HISTORY 30,000 of San Diego's 170,000 residents turned out to welcome the Consolidated Aircraft Company to San Diego. The founder of the company and its president was Major Reuben H. Fleet. Now you know who the Reuben H. Fleet Science Center in Balboa Park is named for!

Consolidated Aircraft built airplanes and moved to San Diego from Buffalo, New York. They needed to have a good climate year-round for test-flying airplanes and ice-free waters for testing seaplanes. They started out in a 300- by 900-foot factory on Pacific Coast Highway bordering San Diego's Airport, Lindbergh Field. Within six years, by 1941, the company doubled its floor area 16.5 times.

During World War II, in the early 1940s, the company expanded to 13 divisions in ten states, employing a total of 101,000 people—45,000 in San Diego alone—and building over 33,000 military planes.

Consolidated Aircraft became the Convair division of General Dynamics in 1954. After the war Convair built planes for over 40 commercial airline companies. Convair then started building rockets for the space program. They built the Atlas Missile and the Centaur Booster. It was the Atlas-Centaur combination that sent Pioneer II on its mission to study the distant planets of Jupiter and Saturn.

Unfortunately, Convair closed down in San Diego several years ago, and that was a great loss for the city and the thousands of engineers, scientists, and other workers who were employed by them here. Subsequently, one of its old factory buildings on Pacific Coast Highway was torn down, and the area is now a parking lot. From the highway you can now see through the vacant area to the airport runway at Lindbergh Field.

October 21, 1972

ON THIS DAY IN SAN DIEGO HISTORY the National Marine Fisheries Service (NMFS) gave San Diego's tuna fishing industry a two-year relief from the recently enacted Marine Mammal Protection Act (MMPA). The MMPA was made into a law to try to prevent the deaths of dolphins and porpoises, which are often caught accidentally by gigantic nets called purse seiners used by the tuna boats. Dolphins and porpoises are air-breathing, fur-bearing mammals, in contrast to the gilled and scaled fish that they often swim with. When the dolphins and porpoises accidentally become tangled in the nets, they are trapped under the water and are unable to come to the surface to breathe, and many of them die that way.

San Diego was once home to the world's largest and most successful fleet of tuna-fishing ships. In 1980 there were a total of 180 tuna-fishing boats in the world. 130 of them were in the United States, and 110 were operating out of San Diego. Ten years later, in 1990, there were only 30 tuna boats in San Diego because of the problems the tuna fishermen had trying to obey the strict MMPA regulations.

To add to the fisherman's difficulties, in April 1990 three of the largest tuna packing companies in the U.S.—StarKist®, Bumble Bee®, and Chicken of the Sea®—decided to buy only "dolphin-safe" tuna. They were responding to environmental groups who were boycotting companies whose practices injured or killed dolphins in the process. Consequently, the companies stopped buying or canning tuna caught by San Diego boats.

By 1992 San Diego's tuna fleet had dropped from 30 to only 8 fishing boats. Most of the boats that left transferred their operations to countries where the fishing restrictions were not so strict—such as Guam or American Samoa in the South Pacific. While good for the dolphins, this was a great loss to San Diego—the loss of an industry that brought in a lot of money and that provided jobs for many people.

OCTOBER 22, 1850

ON THIS DAY IN SAN DIEGO HISTORY George W. Marston was born in Ft. Atkinson, Wisconsin. He would end up in San Diego and would play an important part in San Diego's history. Marston came to San Diego in 1870 at the age of 20. He had a job as the first clerk at the new, luxurious Horton House Hotel which opened that year in downtown San Diego. The hotel was owned by Alonzo Horton, an important San Diego businessman (see OCTOBER 24).

Marston later started the Marston's Department Store, which was located on Broadway in downtown San Diego—just down the street from the Horton House Hotel. Marston's survived the financial panic of 1893, when five of San Diego's eight banks went out of business. It went on to become San Diego's oldest and leading department store. It was bought out by the Broadway department stores in 1961. Later the Broadway was bought out by Macy's.

Marston's greatest gift to the city of San Diego was in establishing Presidio Park on the historic location where the first San Diego Mission was founded by Father Serra in 1769. Marston donated the land he had bought on Presidio Hill to the city of San Diego and hired an architect, William Templeton Johnson, to design a building appropriate to house the historical items that had been collected by the Pioneer Society and to honor Father Junípero Serra (see JANUARY 12). The city reluctantly accepted Marston's gift and agreed only to supply water for the park. Marston continued to pay other expenses for maintenance and improvements for ten years. The beautiful Mission Revival–style building that stands today on top of Presidio Hill is called the Serra Museum. It is operated by the San Diego Historical Society and is open for the public to visit.

The Marston House, the Marston family home that was built in 1905, is located next to the north end of Balboa Park at 7th Avenue and Upas Street. It was designed by Irving Gill (see APRIL 26). George Marston died in 1946 at the age of 95. His daughter, Mary G. Marston, lived in the house for 30 years after her father died until her death in 1976, at which time the Marston House was donated to the city of San Diego. It is now operated by the San Diego Historical Society and is open to visitors. The Marston House is a fine example of the Arts and Crafts style of architecture and furniture.

OCTOBER 23, 1849

ON THIS DAY IN SAN DIEGO HISTORY John Woodhouse Audubon, son of the famous naturalist and bird artist, John James Audubon, camped at Vallecito in what is today's northeastern San Diego County—on Highway S-2 near the Anza-Borrego Desert State Park. According to Diana Lindsay in her book *Anza-Borrego A to Z: People, Places and Things*, Audubon sketched a picture of the Indian village located there that was called Hawi or Haawii ("Water in Rock"). It was located near a spring. Agua Caliente (Spanish for "Hot Water") Regional Park with its hot mineral springs is located nearby in the Vallecito Valley. Audubon's 1849 drawing was the earliest depiction of what the Vallecito Indian village looked like.

Vallecito (Spanish for "Little Valley") was named by Lieutenant Pedro Fages when he first passed through the valley in 1772. Fages passed through the area again ten years later, in 1782, at which time he reported that some 500 Indians lived at the village.

These Vallecito Indians were a band of the Kumeyaay Indians, called Kwaaymii, whose numbers were decreasing. In 1862, eighty years after Fages' second visit, only 20 of them remained. By 1891 there was only one old man left at Vallecito. All the rest of his relatives had died off.

In the 1850s Vallecito became a stage stop for the Butterfield Stagecoach (see SEPTEMBER 16 and OCTOBER 13) and for the Jackass Mail line (see JULY 9). There is a California historical marker at the stage station that was originally built in 1852 and reconstructed in 1934. Today the Vallecito Stage Station is a San Diego county park with campsites available for a small fee.

There are stories that the Vallecito Stage Station may be haunted. The most intriguing of the ghost stories is about the "Lady in White." According to the story, a young lady was traveling on the stagecoach from the East in the 1850s, a mail-order bride intending to marry her fiancé who had "struck it rich in the California Gold Rush." Unfortunately, she became ill on her journey and died after leaving the stagecoach at its stop at Vallecito. She was buried there, dressed in the white wedding gown that was found in her luggage. Some people think they have seen a ghostly white figure near the stage station acting as if she were looking for the stagecoach.

OCTOBER 24, 1813

ON THIS DAY IN SAN DIEGO HISTORY Alonzo E. Horton—the founding father of modern-day San Diego—was born in Union, Connecticut. He came to California at the age of 38 during the gold rush days in 1851 and settled in San Francisco where he operated a furniture store. When he heard glorious reports about San Diego, its good climate, good harbor, a possible new railroad connection, and the availability of land for stores, homes, and factories, he decided to come here—arriving in 1867 at the age of 54.

Horton ended up buying 960 acres of land adjacent to San Diego Harbor (see MAY 11). He considered this to be a better location for a city than the Old Town area that was first settled as the "center" of San Diego. Alonzo Horton proceeded to develop his Horton's Addition by subdividing the land into buildable lots. He reinvested some of his profits from lot sales in the growing New Town area: $45,000 for a new wharf at the end of 5th Avenue and $150,000 for a fancy new 100-room Horton House Hotel, which he built in 1870 at the corner of Broadway and 4th Avenue. Today the US Grant Hotel is at that same location. Across the street from the hotel he set aside a half-block as a park so that hotel guests would have a place to sit outdoors in the sun. Today that is where the great shopping center Horton Plaza is located.

Alonzo Horton also helped to get some land set aside by the city for City Park, which was later to become Balboa Park. And Horton was president of San Diego's first bank, the Bank of San Diego, started in 1870. After several name changes over the years, the bank is now known as Union Bank of California (see JUNE 9).

One by one, businesses moved from Old Town to New Town. In 1871 the county records were moved from the Whaley House in Old Town, and then the *San Diego Union* newspaper moved to New Town, too (see MARCH 31). The final blow to Old Town came when it caught fire in 1872. Even though many families continued to live in the Old Town area, most of the important businesses had moved. The center of San Diego was now definitely New San Diego—mainly because of the efforts of Alonzo Horton. He died in 1909 at the age of 95, having made a great contribution to the development of San Diego.

OCTOBER 25, 1935

ON THIS DAY IN SAN DIEGO HISTORY Coronado's North Island was set aside for the Naval Air Station, which has become one of the largest naval air bases in the United States.

Actually, North Island is not an island. It is connected to Coronado and—by the Silver Strand peninsula—to the mainland at Imperial Beach. But in geologic past times, North Island was indeed an island. It was separate from Coronado, which was also an island. And in ancient times, nearby Point Loma was a third large island. Over the years, sediment deposited by the San Diego River and rearranged by ocean currents gradually filled in the spaces, connecting Point Loma to the mainland and North Island to Coronado. Then the currents and sediments formed the Silver Strand connecting Coronado to the mainland at Imperial Beach—thus forming the enclosed San Diego Bay which makes San Diego such a fine, protected port.

Now, forward to the twentieth century. In 1911 Glenn Curtiss, an early airplane pilot and pioneer in aeronautics, first used North Island as a private aviation school.

In 1912 William Kettner was elected to the U.S. Congress as a representative from San Diego. (Now you know where they got the name for Kettner Boulevard!) He was a member of the San Diego Aero Club, a local flying club, and had always been an active supporter of San Diego. He began to promote San Diego as an ideal location for the military. First, the U.S. Army Signal Corps Training School moved to the western part of North Island (see November 4), becoming known as Rockwell Field. Then in 1917 Kettner sponsored an act authorizing the United States to take permanent possession of North Island as an Army and Navy aviation school.

The military has been important to San Diego in many other ways, including Fort Rosecrans and the Marine base now known as the Marine Corps Recruit Depot or MCRD that were started in 1919. In 1932 the Navy completed its hospital in Balboa Park, and San Diego was named headquarters for the Eleventh Naval District. With all of this, the military was to become very important to San Diego's future growth and development (see MARCH 28).

OCTOBER 26, 1876

ON THIS DAY IN SAN DIEGO HISTORY title to the Jamul Rancho was granted to the Burton family (Maria A. Burton, Henry H. Burton, and Nellie Burton Pedrorena). Nellie Burton was the daughter of General H.S. Burton of the United States Army, and she married Miguel de Pedrorena, the son of a pioneer merchant in Old Town of the same name. The original owner of the Jamul Rancho, under a Mexican land grant, was Pío Pico, the last Mexican Governor of California before California became a part of the United States after the Mexican-American War of 1846–48.

The Jamul Rancho (Jamul means "Slimy Water" in the Diegueño or Kumeyaay Indian language) consisted of 8,900 acres located southeast of San Diego between the present-day towns of Jamul and Dulzura along State Highway 94. It was originally an Indian *rancheria* (settlement) before the land was granted to Pico in 1829. In 1837 the rancho was attacked by Indians. The *majordomo* (ranch manager) and three other people were killed. Two of the *majordomo's* daughters were captured by the Indians and were never recovered. His wife and a younger daughter were recovered from the Indians with the help of an Indian servant. Perhaps these were the Indians who originally lived on the land before it was taken away from them and given to the Mexican governor of California?

Somewhere along the way, John D. Spreckels, a prominent San Diego businessman, became owner of the Jamul Rancho. In 1915 the *San Diego Union* newspaper reported that Spreckels sold the rancho to Louis J. Wilde for $300,000. Wilde planned to make it a typical "wild west" ranch for the filming of western movies, but this venture was never realized. In 1960 the Jamul Rancho was known as the George R. Daley Ranch, and the old adobe house just north of Highway 94 served as the ranch headquarters.

The town of Jamul, located ten miles southeast of El Cajon, has had a post office since 1880. Jamul had a population of 5,920 in 2000. The Jamul Indian Reservation, consisting of six acres, was established in 1975.

OCTOBER 27, 1910

ON THIS DAY IN SAN DIEGO HISTORY the name of Balboa Park was chosen to replace the original name of City Park. Preparation was underway for the big World's Fair, the Panama-California Exposition that would occur at the park in 1915. The name City Park seemed too plain for the location of this great exposition that would celebrate the opening of the Panama Canal (see JANUARY 1, SEPTEMBER 3, and DECEMBER 31).

The 1,400 acres for the original park had been set aside in 1870 by the far-seeing early city fathers (see FEBRUARY 4). The new name for the park was in honor of Vasco Nuñez de Balboa, the Spanish explorer who discovered the Pacific Ocean and claimed the entire west coast of America for Spain in 1513.

Some of the lovely, ornate structures and buildings that we still admire so much today in Balboa Park were built at this time in preparation for the exposition—such as the California Building and Tower (see SEPTEMBER 12), the Spreckels Organ Pavilion, the Cabrillo Bridge (also called the Laurel Street Bridge), and the Western Gate (with its symbolic oceans connected by a canal at the top). The original Varied Industries Building was replicated, rebuilt, and renamed Casa Del Prado in 1971.

The Casa de Balboa was formerly the Electric Building, which burned down in 1978. It was replicated, rebuilt, and renamed in 1981. This is the building with the long, arched walkway where the Museum of San Diego History, the Museum of Photographic Arts, and the Model Railroad Museum are now located.

Today Balboa Park—with its interesting museums, lovely grounds, and attractive buildings—is a beloved asset to San Diego. It is enjoyed by tourists as well as residents of San Diego, who return time after time to enjoy its many attractions.

OCTOBER 28, 1901

ON THIS DAY IN SAN DIEGO HISTORY an article appeared in the *Los Angeles Times* newspaper exposing a "scandel" about the Point Loma Universal Brotherhood and Theosophical Society Homestead. The newspaper reported that a woman had "escaped" from the commune and that she had been locked up in a cell and forced to work in the fields "like a convict." The woman claimed that wives were separated from their husbands and children from their parents, that they were isolated, starved, and forbidden to speak.

Katherine Tingley, the founder and leader of the Point Loma religious community, immediately filed a lawsuit against the newspaper, stating that the story was "false, malicious, libelous, and untrue." At the trial the *Los Angeles Times* was unable to prove its claims, and Tingley won her case.

The Point Loma Universal Brotherhood and Theosophical Society Homestead was started in 1897 by Tingley and was popularly known as "Lomaland." It was the only successful Theosophical commune in the United States. Theosophy is a religious philosophy that is not based on traditional Christian principles but follows Buddhist or Brahman theories of ancient Eastern religions that originated in India and China. The Theosophical Society started in New York in 1875 and had three main aims: to form a universal brotherhood of humanity without distinction of race, creed, or color; to promote the study of Eastern literatures, religions, and sciences; and to investigate unexplained laws of nature and the psychic powers in man. The society attracted many well-known Americans, including Thomas A. Edison, inventor of the electric light bulb.

At Lomaland in San Diego, the society built many beautiful buildings: the Homestead, the Temple of Peace, and a school called the Raja Yoga Academy. There were as many as 500 adults and children living in the community after 1910. Katherine Tingley, the leader of the commune, died suddenly in a car accident in 1929. This unfortunate event plus the 1929 stock market crash threw the commune into financial trouble. It finally failed in 1941 when the property was foreclosed on by the bank. Today the Point Loma Nazarene University occupies the site, which is located next to Sunset Cliffs Park on Lomaland Drive (see also FEBRUARY 24).

OCTOBER 29, 1852

ON THIS DAY IN SAN DIEGO HISTORY José Domingo Yorba filed a claim for the Cañada de San Vicente Rancho (Spanish for "Glen" or "Valley of St. Vincent"), a 13,316 acre tract of land located in the San Vicente and Barona valleys—between the present-day towns of Ramona and Lakeside. The Yorba family also received other extensive land grants including the Santiago de Santa Ana Rancho in today's Orange County.

José Domingo Yorba was born in San Diego in 1795, making him 57 years old at the time of his claim to the rancho. He was the grandson of Antonio Yorba, one of the original Spanish Catalan volunteers for Don Pedro Fages' 1772 expedition in search of deserted soldiers from the San Diego Mission. The Fages expedition went from San Diego to San Francisco Bay via the Anza-Borrego Desert in today's northeastern San Diego County. Fages' expedition preceded the Anza Expeditions of 1774 and 1775 that went from Mexico to Monterey and San Francisco and traveled through the deserts of Imperial and San Diego counties (see OCTOBER 4). Captain Pedro Fages had been in charge of security to help Father Junípero Serra establish a mission in San Diego. Fages was on board the Spanish ship *San Carlos*, which arrived in San Diego in April 1769 (see APRIL 29).

Yorba sold the Cañada de San Vicente Rancho in 1869 to some San Francisco speculators who paid him "$8,000 in gold coin" for the land.

The Barona Valley in the southern part of the former rancho was named for Padre Joséf Barona, a friar at the San Diego and San Juan Capistrano missions. The Yorba family was especially fond of Padre Barona, and they changed the name of their rancho to include the valley that was named for him—giving it the name of Cañada de San Vicente y Mesa del Padre Barona Rancho. The Barona Valley is now the home of the Barona Indian Reservation (see JANUARY 25).

OCTOBER 30, 1935

ON THIS DAY IN SAN DIEGO HISTORY the California Pacific International Exposition that was being held in Balboa Park, dedicated this day to honor John D. Spreckels, a prominent San Diego businessman and philanthropist (see JULY 26). Spreckels had donated the Organ Pavilion at Balboa Park in 1914 for the Panama-California Exposition—the first big World Exposition to be held at Balboa Park in 1915–1916 (see JANUARY 1).

Several new buildings were built in Balboa Park for the California Pacific International Exposition (see MAY 29). The architect, Richard S. Requa, was the director of architecture for the 1935 exposition. He focused on providing examples of the different forms of architecture of the Spanish period in America, especially prehistoric and Native American architecture of the Southwest and Mexico. This new area designed by Requa was built in a location just to the southwest of the Spreckels Organ Pavilion. Requa was one of the architects who, in 1936, contributed to the design of the County Administration Building at 1600 Pacific Highway—along with Louis Gill (son of Irving Gill), Sam Hamill, and William Templeton Johnson (see JUNE 26).

Art Linkletter became program director for the California Pacific International Exposition in 1935. Linkletter, later to become a famous radio and TV personality, was a native San Diegan and graduated from San Diego State College in 1934. He went on to produce his popular radio and TV program "People Are Funny" from 1942 until 1961, after getting his start at the 1935 exposition in San Diego.

OCTOBER 31, 1941

ON THIS DAY IN SAN DIEGO HISTORY ground-breaking occurred for the Linda Vista Defense Housing Project, consisting of 1,450 acres on the southwestern portion of Kearny Mesa north of Mission Valley. Over 3,000 houses were built in a little over six months. By April 1942 all of the homes were rented to defense workers and military families. In May 1942 an additional 1,800 houses were started. It was the largest defense and low-income housing project in the world at the time. By 1943 there were nearly 16,000 people living there.

San Diego was an important location for the military and for defense plants such as Convair, which built military planes during World War II and which employed many thousands of people during the war effort (see OCTOBER 20). In 1940, 50,000 people arrived in San Diego, increasing the number of defense workers to 90,000. Before the Linda Vista Housing Project was built, aircraft workers camped in parking lots and makeshift trailer parks. Below Presidio Hill people were living in old, abandoned trolley cars that rented for $30 per month.

The Linda Vista area of Kearny Mesa was located over two miles from the nearest settled area in San Diego, so it was difficult at first to supply such city services as police protection, fire protection, ambulance service, trash collection, and public transportation. Transportation was especially difficult for the Linda Vista residents because the defense plants were far away—near San Diego Bay. Most workers drove their own cars to work, but in 1942, when gas and tire rationing began, many workers stopped driving and used public transportation. Since the old San Diego trolley system was being phased out, this put an extra burden on the existing transit system. The city ended up reestablishing part of the old trolley system using spare parts from all over the country.

The Linda Vista project, with 5,400 housing units, had water supplied to it by a single ten-inch water main, which later had to be replaced. At first there were no schools, shops, drug stores, or gas stations in the area. Later, in 1942, the Linda Vista Shopping Center was built. It was one of the first shopping malls in the San Diego area—and in the United States. The College Grove, Mission Valley, and Grossmont shopping centers were not built until the 1960s. The University of San Diego, the largest private university in San Diego, opened in 1949 and is an outstanding asset to the Linda Vista area.

NOVEMBER 1, 1902

ON THIS DAY IN SAN DIEGO HISTORY Professor Gustav Schultz hired two men to start digging a tunnel to the La Jolla Caves. The two men dug through the sandstone by hand, with one man digging in the tunnel with a shovel and filling a wheelbarrow that was hauled up to the surface by a rope. The other man at the top emptied the wheelbarrow and returned it down the shaft to fill again.

It took over five months to finish the tunnel, which was finally cut through in April 1903 down to the first cave. By July, Professor Schultz had visitors who paid to go down the tunnel to the Sunny Jim Cave, one of the Seven Sisters Caves that were located at the bottom of the cliffs. At first there were no steps down to the caves, and the tunnel had a low ceiling. People had to crawl on their hands and knees holding onto a rope that was anchored to the walls of the tunnel. Some 18 years later, in 1920, 133 steps and a wooden platform at the bottom of the tunnel would be added.

In September 1903 the *San Diego Union* newspaper reported that "Professor Schultz's tunnel is a success and is paying well."

Professor Gustav Schultz, born in Germany, was a civil engineer, geologist, artist, photographer, and he had a lot of other talents. He was raised in the Falkland Islands—in the Atlantic Ocean off the southern tip of South America—and had traveled all over the world looking for the right place to live. When he saw La Jolla, he decided it was the most beautiful place in the world, so he settled there.

Schultz bought the land above the La Jolla Caves in early 1902 from Anna Held, who was also from Germany and who had built the Green Dragon Colony cottages on the hill above La Jolla Cove (see NOVEMBER 3). Professor Schultz built a small studio cottage above the caves, which became the entrance to the tunnel.

Today, the Cave Store, in an old house above the caves, is still operating with new owners. According to Patricia Daly-Lipe and Barbara Dawson in their book *La Jolla: A Celebration of Its Past*, it is considered to be the oldest continuously-operated business in La Jolla, having evolved from the Cave Curio Store of over 100 years ago. You can still go to the Cave Store today and pay to go down the 133 steps to see the La Jolla Caves.

November 2, 1985

On this day in san diego history the restored Fox Theater / Symphony Hall reopened at 6th and B streets in downtown San Diego. It would be the new home of the San Diego Symphony Orchestra. The symphony purchased the Fox Theater in 1984, renovated it, and turned it into Symphony Hall. David Atherton had been hired as conductor in 1980. Atherton was from England where he had been conductor of the Royal Liverpool Philharmonic Orchestra. He had also conducted operas at the Royal Opera House for 12 years.

In spite of the symphony's financial problems during the early 1980s, Atherton continued to receive excellent reviews of his concerts. The March 1985 *San Diego Magazine* stated:

> Atherton and the SDSO have become synonymous; it is almost impossible…to conceive of one without the other… The product, the music, is all that matters in the end. Atherton's accomplishments with the orchestra have been the single most important of all the association's accomplishments in recent years.

But financial problems continued, and the symphony announced in February 1986 that it would file for bankruptcy. Its only asset was Symphony Hall, worth $6 million, but that didn't cover its debts totaling over $6.5 million. Fortunately, anonymous donors came through. KUSI-TV held a telethon in March 1986, and community support rallied with contributions. Large contributions came in from such San Diego philanthropists as the Copley newspaper family, the Judson Grosvenor family, and Dr. and Mrs. Roger Revelle. The bankruptcy had been avoided, thanks to the emergency fund raising, and David Atherton conducted Beethoven's 5th Symphony, as an expression of victory, in March 1986 in Symphony Hall.

But problems continued, as the musicians refused to accept the new terms regarding their pay. The 1986–87 season was cancelled. David Atherton resigned in 1987 with two years left in his contract after conflicts with the musicians over salary discrepancies and other issues. The San Diego Symphony returned in the fall of 1987 with guest conductors until the Israeli conductor, Yoav Talmi, was hired in 1989. He served as conductor until 1996 (see also February 28).

David Atherton has returned to the San Diego Symphony many times as guest conductor. He also founded the Mainly Mozart Festival in 1988, and he returns to San Diego each summer to direct that orchestra.

NOVEMBER 3, 1849

ON THIS DAY IN SAN DIEGO HISTORY Anna Held, who would later be important to the cultural and social life in La Jolla, was born in Germany. She came to America in 1869 at the age of 20. She ran a kindergarten in New York and then worked as governess for a family in Colorado. Then she went to London, where she was an actress on the stage. She was also an accomplished pianist. She returned to America in 1891, settled in San Diego, and worked as governess for the Ulysses S. Grant Jr. family, owners of the US Grant Hotel in downtown San Diego.

Held moved to La Jolla in 1894 and established the Green Dragon Colony, which was a group of cottages that she built, one by one, between 1894 and 1902. They were located on what is now the 1200 block of Prospect Street and extended down the hill to the ocean near the cove. She first built a fireplace on her lot from rocks she found on the property. The fireplace stood there alone for a while until she had a little cottage built around it with the help of the young architect, Irving Gill (see APRIL 26 and AUGUST 29). She named her fireplace cottage Green Dragon. The other cottages, eventually totaling 12, each had its own name. Collectively they became known as the Green Dragon Colony.

Anna Held invited many famous writers and artists of the day to visit her at her colony. In 1904, at the age of 54, she met Max Heinrich, a noted singer and musician. Their mutual love of music drew them together, and they were married the same year. Composers, artists, and writers continued to come and stay in the cottages to do their creative work in La Jolla—thanks to the hospitality of Anna Held Heinrich and Max Heinrich.

The Green Dragon Colony became the social and cultural center of La Jolla between the 1890s and the 1920s—when La Jolla was just beginning to grow. Anna Held Heinrich sold her Green Dragon cottage in 1912. Her husband died in 1916. Anna lived in a cottage on Torrey Pines Road in La Jolla for a while, then moved back to England shortly before she died in 1941 at the age of 93.

See also OCTOBER 2.

NOVEMBER 4, 1912

ON THIS DAY IN SAN DIEGO HISTORY the first army detachment of enlisted men arrived at Coronado's North Island to start a military aviation school which they named the Signal Corps Aviation School. It constituted the first military use—in a long tradition of military use—of the island.

North Island had been used as a private aviation school by Glenn Curtiss since 1911. Curtiss was an early pioneer in aeronautics. He established the first airplane manufacturing company in the U.S. in 1908—just five years after the Wright Brothers made their first air flight in their "flying machine." Curtiss used his "aerodrome" planes to participate in flying tournaments and aerial demonstrations.

In 1911 Curtiss perfected the first hydroplane, a plane which could take off and land in water. The Spanish Bight area near North Island was a perfect location for that operation. Curtiss leased North Island in 1911 from John Spreckels' Coronado Beach Company, which owned North Island and most of Coronado (see JULY 26). The Curtiss School of Aviation took over an old hay barn on the island and turned it into an airplane hangar.

Curtiss invited the Navy and then the Army to share the North Island flying facility. The Navy set up a camp called Camp Trouble on the northeastern corner of the island in January 1912, but the Navy operation was transferred to Annapolis, Maryland after only three months, so their camp on North Island was abandoned.

That same year, the Army was looking for a location for a permanent flying school. They rejected several other places: College Park, Maryland had bad weather in winter; Augusta, Georgia had too much rain and cold weather in winter; Phoenix, Arizona was too hot in summer. So San Diego's North Island was chosen by the Army, and they began arriving on this date in 1912. Later, after the U.S. became involved in World War I, the name of the Army Aviation School on North Island was changed to Rockwell Field, to honor Second Lieutenant Lewis C. Rockwell, a young Army pilot who had been killed in a plane crash at College Park, Maryland.

The Navy returned to North Island in 1918, occupying the north end of the island while the Army occupied the south part of the island. The Army's Rockwell Field stayed on at North Island until 1939 when it closed down, leaving North Island to the Naval Air Station, which is still there today, having occupied North Island for over 90 years.

NOVEMBER 5, 1775

ON THIS DAY IN SAN DIEGO HISTORY the San Diego Mission was burned down by Indians. The mission had been at its new location at Nipaguay, six miles inland from its old location on Presidio Hill, for only a little over a year. Nipaguay was the name of the Indian *rancheria* (settlement) there. Several hundred Indians attacked the mission at night, setting fire to the buildings and killing one of the two priests, Father Luis Jayme (pronounced "High-may"), and two other people.

A messenger went to the presidio (military fort) six miles away at Presidio Hill, and a military guard of soldiers was brought back to protect the mission in case of another attack, but the Indians did not attack again. The soldiers punished some of the Indians, and we are not sure how particular they were at getting the right ones. But the priests stopped the punishments and pleaded for mercy for the Indians. No other hostility was exhibited by the Indians in San Diego after the November 5 attack. The Indians were apparently unhappy about the mission's new location at Nipaguay and resented the Spanish intrusion on their lands.

Father Junípero Serra, who had founded the original San Diego Mission six years before, was visiting the Monterey Mission in Carmel at the time of the attack. When he heard the news, he returned to San Diego by boat and supervised the rebuilding of the mission (see JULY 11).

November 6, 1917

On this day in San Diego history a new military camp, Camp Kearny, increased in size to 24,000 soldiers. It was during World War I when the United States, England, France, and Russia were in a war with Germany. Built on the mesa 11.5 miles north of San Diego and just a few miles east of La Jolla, the camp was completed on September 1, and by November 6 there were 24,000 soldiers there.

On their days off, the soldiers liked to come to La Jolla, so the residents of La Jolla started to give parties and put on musical programs for them. But as the numbers of soldiers coming to La Jolla began to increase, the town became worried about how to control their youthful enthusiasm. A town meeting was held, and at the meeting Miss Lucile Jardeau suggested that La Jolla needed a policewoman. Everybody approved of the idea, but they wondered who would agree to do the job. Miss Jardeau herself agreed to take the job, and she became the first policewoman in southern California. She was very efficient at her job and was able to manage many of the problems that the regular police found difficult. She had the job for two years, until Camp Kearny was abandoned at the end of the war. The Miramar Marine Corps Air Station is now located at the site of the old Camp Kearny.

The thousands of servicemen who visited La Jolla from Camp Kearny during World War I ended up having a great effect on the future growth of the town. After the war ended, many of the young servicemen who had been impressed with the beauty of La Jolla returned in the 1920s with their young families to live there, creating a land boom and a period of big growth—similar to the previous land boom in the 1880s when the area was first settled (see March 16). During the 1920s boom, La Jolla was the beneficiary of new schools, a downtown commercial district, paved streets, and many other improvements.

NOVEMBER 7, 1941

ON THIS DAY IN SAN DIEGO HISTORY a well-known Impressionist artist, Maurice Braun, died in San Diego at the age of 64. Braun was especially noted for his landscape paintings of scenes in the San Diego and southern California areas.

"Certainly Braun was San Diego's most famous artist during the first third of the twentieth century. He familiarized a generation, in the East and in the West, with the Southern California landscape," says Martin E. Petersen in his article "An Overview of San Diego Artists" in the Summer 2001 issue of the *Journal of San Diego History*.

Braun, who was born in Hungary in 1877, came to America as a child with his parents, who settled in New York City in 1881. While in New York, Braun studied at the National Academy of Design. He moved to San Diego in 1909 at the age of 32. He opened his San Diego Art Academy in 1910 in the former Fisher Opera House on B Street in downtown San Diego. (For another story about the Fisher Opera House, see MAY 17.) Braun was co-founder of the San Diego Art Guild in 1915 and co-founded Contemporary Artists in San Diego in 1929.

Braun became interested in the beliefs of the Theosophy movement when he lived in New York, and he was influenced to move to San Diego by Katherine Tingley, leader of a Theosophy School on Point Loma known locally as "Lomaland" (see FEBRUARY 24). Braun later moved his home to Point Loma and set up his art studio there, where he often held open house for his paintings and for the flowers in his garden.

Braun loved nature and the out-of-doors. He has been described as a Plein Air artist, meaning that he painted the outdoor scenery. According to Braun's children, Charlotte Braun White and Ernest Boyer Braun:

> [H]e wanted to get acquainted with the San Diego countryside and understand how to portray it in form and color... [His] strategy for getting a strong understanding of the content of the landscape he wanted to paint was the careful sketching of the details of the landscape—grasses, rocks, trees, the nature of washes in hillsides, and the form and color of receding hills and mountains.

Braun's paintings are mostly privately owned, but some have been donated to the San Diego Historical Society.

NOVEMBER 8, 1852

ON THIS DAY IN SAN DIEGO HISTORY Joshua Bean died under mysterious circumstances. Bean was the former *alcalde* (Spanish for "mayor") of the pueblo of San Diego and then became mayor again after San Diego no longer belonged to Mexico. He was also the brother of the notorious and unscrupulous Judge Roy Bean, who lived in Texas and practiced his own brand of the law.

Joshua Bean was a little controversial himself. He was involved in some shady behaviors and questionable land deals. He stopped attending city council meetings and then resigned as mayor in 1851 after the city council refused to accept the salary increase that he had proposed for himself.

Bean then left San Diego and moved to San Gabriel—east of Los Angeles. One night he was riding alone on his way home from a social event when two men stopped him. While one man held the reins of Bean's horse, the other man dragged him off his horse, then stabbed him and shot him. The identity of the murderers remains a mystery.

Originally from Kentucky, Bean joined the U.S. Army in 1840. He came West to fight in the Mexican-American War of 1846–48 and became an Army general—which was probably the reason why he became mayor of San Diego, since military officers were often picked to govern cities in California during those times.

Bean presided over the trial that convicted the Indian leader Antonio Garra of participating in the raid on Warner's Ranch and sentenced him to die before a firing squad (see NOVEMBER 21). Bean also headed the military tribunal that convicted Garra's son and had him executed for his participation in the attack.

So Joshua Bean had made a few enemies during his controversial life, any one of whom could have been motivated to participate in his murder.

NOVEMBER 9, 1885

ON THIS DAY IN SAN DIEGO HISTORY the California Southern Railroad connected San Diego to the AT&SF (Acheson, Topeka & Santa Fe) Railroad at Barstow—in the desert northeast of Los Angeles. This was important to San Diego because it finally gave the city a train connection to the eastern United States.

San Diego had been hoping for a direct connection to the East ever since the 1850s when talk first began about a transcontinental railroad to the Pacific coast. The first railroad to the Pacific coast was built by the Union Pacific and the Central Pacific in 1869, but it bypassed San Diego completely and went on a northern route to San Francisco.

Six years later San Diego's hopes for a direct southern route to the East by the Texas & Pacific Railroad were dashed by the financial collapse of the railroads in 1873 (see SEPTEMBER 18).

In 1876 the Southern Pacific Railroad built a connection between Los Angeles and San Francisco, giving Los Angeles access to the transcontinental railroad to and from the East. But San Diego was left out from this connection. Then the Santa Fe Railroad came from the East to Los Angeles, bypassing San Diego yet again.

San Diego finally had a connection to the railroad from the East when the California Southern Railroad finished its tracks. Construction began at National City in 1881, continued through San Diego, Encinitas, Fallbrook, Temecula, and San Bernardino, and then over Cajon Pass east of San Bernardino, joining up with the Santa Fe Railroad Transcontinental Line at Barstow on this day in 1885.

Later, in 1919, San Diego got a more direct railroad line to the East when the San Diego & Arizona Eastern Railway was built (see SEPTEMBER 9).

NOVEMBER 10, 1602

ON THIS DAY IN SAN DIEGO HISTORY Sebastián Vizcaíno, a Spanish trader and explorer, entered San Diego Bay with three ships, 200 men, and two priests. They had sailed from Acapulco, Mexico. Even though the harbor had been named San Miguel by Juan Rodriguez Cabrillo when he discovered it 60 years before in 1542 (see SEPTEMBER 28), Vizcaíno chose to give it the name San Diego de Alcalá in honor of a Spanish saint from the University of Alcalá near Madrid, Spain, whose feast day they were celebrating on this day. If it were not for Vizcaíno's renaming, we would be living in San Miguel now instead of San Diego.

When Vizcaíno's party went ashore, they saw about 100 Indians with bows and arrows on a nearby hill. The Spanish party gave them gifts and assured them that they came as friends and meant no harm to them.

Father Antonio de la Ascensión, a member of Vizcaíno's party who went ashore, recorded these notes about his findings: "In the sand on the beach there is a great quantity of yellow pyrites, all full of holes, a sure sign that in the neighboring mountains and adjacent to the port there are gold mines; for the water, when it rains, brings it down from the mountains."

Gold was discovered much later in San Diego County, in 1870, in the mountains near Julian and Banner and in the Cuyamaca Mountains (see FEBRUARY 20 and NOVEMBER 27). By 1913 there were as many as 73 recorded mining claims in the Julian area, and many of the mines continued to produce gold from the 1870s until the 1940s.

The Vizcaíno party spent ten days at San Diego and then sailed northward to Catalina Island and then to another port on the California coast which they named Monterey.

NOVEMBER 11, 1821

ON THIS DAY IN SAN DIEGO HISTORY Cave Johnson Couts was born in Tennessee. He later attended West Point and became a U.S. army officer in 1843. He came to San Diego in 1849 to act as a military escort for the Mexican-American Boundary Commission that was to decide the location of the border between Mexico and the United States after the Mexican-American War of 1846–48. Before the war, California was part of Mexico. After the war, California became a state in the United States.

While in San Diego, Couts, the handsome young military officer, met Isadora Bandini, daughter of Juan Bandini, a well-known land owner prominent in the social and political affairs of San Diego and California. Couts and Isadora Bandini were married in 1851, and among the wedding gifts to the bride was the Rancho Guajome—a 2,219-acre tract of land located between the present-day cities of Oceanside and Vista (see APRIL 5). Guajome comes from an Indian word meaning "frog pond." The Guajome Regional Park is located there today—off North Santa Fe Avenue.

Cave Couts served as a judge in San Diego for two years after his marriage. After that, he and Isadora moved to Rancho Guajome, and he started building the 7,000 square foot, 28-room Guajome Ranch House, which has been preserved in the Guajome Regional Park. It is described by the U.S. National Park Service as "the finest existing example in the United States of the traditional Spanish-Mexican one-story adobe hacienda [Spanish for "ranch house"]." It was designated as a National Historic Landmark in 1970. Cave Couts and Isadora had a total of ten children, eight of whom were born at the Guajome Ranch.

Couts was a successful cattle rancher on the Guajome Ranch for several years, until 1862 when flooding rains struck the area and drowned many of the cattle. This was followed by two years of drought. Couts survived this financial setback by selling off some of his land and by adding sheep, orange groves, avocados, and vineyards to his ranching activities. He developed a cleverly engineered irrigation system by converting Rancho Guajome's "frog pond" into a network of basins and streams.

Cave Couts died suddenly at the age of 53. His wife, Isadora, lived on at the ranch and managed it with the help of her son, Cave Couts Jr., until her death 23 years later in 1897.

NOVEMBER 12, 1973

ON THIS DAY IN SAN DIEGO HISTORY a housewife in Mira Mesa reported that she saw a UFO crash when she was on her way home from a night class. The *San Diego Evening Tribune* newspaper quotes her as saying, "I saw it for about five seconds before it fell to earth and disintegrated." She described the wreckage as a "beautiful flashing green with streamers..."

This was not the only UFO sighting during this time. The newspaper reported three other sightings in November 1973. On November 13 an 18-year-old college student, while walking near her dormitory with a friend, saw a UFO shaped like a bullet "with white lights on the side and red lights in the middle" that made a humming sound.

On November 14, a retired Navy captain saw a UFO fall into the ocean north of Coronado. He said, "It was 10 or 15 degrees above the horizon, a sparkling blue-white ball of flame with a tail approximately 100 times its length."

Then on November 15, a Clairemont man saw a UFO outside his window, moving slowly from east to west. He said, "It was shaped like an oil drum and had a cross of bright white lights."

According to Jack Innis in his book *San Diego Legends*, there was yet another UFO sighting in Lemon Grove on November 16:

> [T]wo 11-year old boys were walking through a back yard on Crane Street when they claim to have encountered a dark disc-shaped object about 20 feet in diameter. It was topped with a silver dome and was perched on three legs. When one of the boys tapped the craft, it levitated about 5 feet off the ground and began flashing green and red lights. The boys ran off.

Innis describes several other UFO sightings in other years—including one of the earliest sightings, in 1952, by George Adamski in the Anza-Borrego Desert when he was approached by a space alien. According to Innis:

> Witnesses sketched the alien as they watched him converse with Adamski. The space visitor was rendered as a male, about 5 feet tall... Adamski claimed that the alien radiated "a feeling of infinite understanding and kindness with supreme humility." During the next few years Adamski met with his alien friends on numerous occasions and wrote three books on his experiences before his death in 1965.

Some people think that so-called UFO sightings are secret military maneuvers that the military refuses to explain—but who knows?

NOVEMBER 13, 1886

ON THIS DAY IN SAN DIEGO HISTORY a great land auction began in Coronado. Elisha Babcock, a railroad man from Evansville, Indiana and Hampton L. Story, a piano manufacturer from Chicago, had bought the entire Coronado peninsula, consisting of 4,185 acres, in 1885 for a price of $110,000. They immediately began clearing off and burning the brush and laying out the lots for the big auction.

They named their investment the Coronado Beach Company—named for the nearby Mexican offshore islands, Los Coronados. Coronado means "Crown" in Spanish. Babcock and Story also built a wharf and started the Coronado Ferry Company.

They began an advertising campaign in most of the country's major cities. They promised free water for one year and 120 local ferry and railway tickets to people who would buy a lot and spend $1,000 improving it.

Over 6,000 people turned out for the first auction—on this date in 1886—squeezing onto ferry boats to get to Coronado. There were refreshment booths, bands playing, and tents erected so people could sit down in the shade. A San Diego attorney topped the bidding at $1,600 for the first lot sold. Before the end of the day, he is said to have turned down an offer of $2,000 more than he paid for it. The land auctions continued for several more weeks earning a total of $2.2 million for the developers—enough to begin construction of the grandest hotel of its day four months later in March of 1887—the Hotel Del Coronado (see FEBRUARY 14).

NOVEMBER 14, 1874

ON THIS DAY IN SAN DIEGO HISTORY the official land description of the Cuyamaca Rancho was finally drawn up—after a long controversy over its boundaries. This was important to the settlers in Julian because gold had been discovered in the area (see FEBRUARY 20 and NOVEMBER 27).

The new owners of the Cuyamaca Rancho, who were from Los Angeles and San Francisco, believed that the original land grant extended northward to include the gold-producing territory. They expected the gold miners to pay them a royalty on the gold that was mined there.

The miners and most of the people of San Diego opposed this demand for royalties. Public meetings were held in Julian and San Diego, and money was collected for surveys and legal defense. The demands of the "land grabbers" were violently criticized by the newspapers and in local churches.

The decision was made on this date in 1874 in Washington, D.C. at the office of the U.S. Land Commissioner to accept the original crudely-drawn *diseño* (Spanish for "design" or "map") that went with the original land grant to the first owner, Augustin Olvera, and not the map that the new owners had drawn up showing different boundaries (see AUGUST 11). This meant that the new owners of the Cuyamaca Rancho were not due any royalties from the gold that was mined in the area because the gold mines were not located within the boundaries of the rancho.

One month later, on December 19, 1874, this decision was finalized when President Ulysses S. Grant signed the official land grant to the Cuyamaca Rancho, excluding Julian and most of the gold mines—much to the relief of the gold miners and the residents of Julian.

NOVEMBER 15, 1885

ON THIS DAY IN SAN DIEGO HISTORY the first train left from the depot at the end of D Street (now known as Broadway) in downtown San Diego. The California Southern Railroad finally connected San Diego to the Santa Fe Transcontinental Railroad and to the eastern United States.

This meant that passengers could now get to the East Coast from San Diego in one week and that agricultural products from the San Diego area—such as honey, oranges, lemons, fish, salt, butter, and wool—could be shipped to new markets in the eastern United States.

Six days later, on November 21, the first transcontinental train from the East arrived in San Diego. After this a great land boom began. People from the East could now easily reach San Diego. They spread the word of the beauty and good climate. Land speculators began buying up land, having it surveyed and divided into lots, and rushing to put them up for sale. Some people didn't even bother to go out to look at the property they were buying. They would just rush to the real estate office, look at a map, and buy the lot sight-unseen. San Diego's population zoomed—going from a sleepy little town of 2,600 in 1880 to 40,000 only seven years later in 1887.

In the city, the prices of lots went sky high. One day a lot might be $5,000—the next day it would be $10,000—and the next week it would sell for $40,000. The land boom also extended to the suburbs of San Diego and the surrounding areas such as University Heights, La Mesa, El Cajon, Escondido, Ocean Beach, Carlsbad, Oceanside, La Jolla, and Coronado.

San Diego had been trying to get a railroad connection to the East for many years but was bypassed again and again for many reasons (see NOVEMBER 9).

Finally, San Diego had a railroad line that connected to the Santa Fe Transcontinental Railroad in Barstow, in the desert east of Los Angeles, and the first train departed from San Diego to the East on this day in 1885—a very important day for San Diego.

November 16, 1774

ON THIS DAY IN SAN DIEGO HISTORY Juan Bautista de Anza, a Spanish military officer, arrived in Mexico City after finding a land route from Mexico to the central California coast. Anza had tested out this land route across the desert and through the mountains of southern California, part of which went through the eastern part of what is now San Diego County. This was in preparation for a larger expedition that was to take a group of settlers to Monterey and San Francisco. It had taken him four months to go to Monterey and back again to Tubac (a Spanish frontier fort in what is now southern Arizona). He was accompanied by 21 soldiers, two personal servants, two priests, and an Indian guide.

On this day—November 16, 1774—in Mexico City, Anza was recommending to the Spanish viceroy of Mexico (a viceroy is the ruler of a region representing the king of Spain) that a second expedition to Monterey, this time with settlers, would be possible—and that he would be able to lead it. Anza recommended that the colonizing expedition should leave in October of the next year, 1775, so that they would be traveling through the desert in the winter when it would not be so hot and there would be more water available. They would find out later that this would be one of the coldest winters ever, and they would run into freezing weather and snow in the desert and nearby mountains (see DECEMBER 16 and DECEMBER 18).

This story is important to San Diego because the Anza Expedition went through what would later be called the Anza-Borrego Desert in northeast San Diego County. They camped for several days near the present-day town of Borrego Springs (see DECEMBER 21, DECEMBER 22, and DECEMBER 26). Anza and the priest on the expedition, Father Pedro Font, wrote in their diaries about their observations of the area and of the native people they encountered there.

This route would later become an important road from the East to the West Coast in the 1800s that would be used by the San Antonio & San Diego Mail Line (see AUGUST 31), the Butterfield Overland Mail Route (see SEPTEMBER 16), and the Southern Emigrant Trail.

NOVEMBER 17, 1919

ON THIS DAY IN SAN DIEGO HISTORY the railroad tracks of the San Diego, Pacific Beach & La Jolla Railway were removed. The railroad had been serving La Jolla for the previous 25 years—since 1894. An article from the *San Diego Union* newspaper on this date stated: "Six thousand tons of steel, part of the equipment of the disbanded La Jolla railway, will be loaded aboard the steamer, *Colorado Springs*, for shipment to Japan."

Gasoline cars had become more popular for transportation. The paved road from San Diego to La Jolla was completed in 1920, making it even easier for automobiles to get to and from La Jolla.

The railroad that was previously known as the San Diego, Old Town & Pacific Beach Railway had been extended to La Jolla in 1894 (see APRIL 25). This was seven years after the great land auction to sell lots in the new La Jolla Park subdivision (see APRIL 30). After the railroad was extended to La Jolla it became known as the San Diego, Pacific Beach & La Jolla Railway—or sometimes as the Abalone Express. La Jolla in those days was a popular place for people to come to on weekends to picnic and enjoy the beach—just as people like to do today.

Prospect Street in La Jolla had to be paved after the railroad was discontinued because the tracks that were torn out had left unpaved ruts in the center of the street. Five years later, in 1924, new tracks were built for the new electric trolley system that would serve La Jolla for 16 years—until 1940, when the trolley was abandoned in favor of the more flexible buses that did not require tracks to run on (see SEPTEMBER 15).

NOVEMBER 18, 1947

ON THIS DAY IN SAN DIEGO HISTORY a meteorologist at the California Institute of Technology (Cal Tech) in Pasadena, California predicted two days of good weather between Pasadena and Mount Palomar in San Diego County, starting on November 18. This was important because they were getting ready to move the "Giant Eye"—a 200-inch telescope mirror that was to be installed at the Mount Palomar Observatory. Many years and much energy and effort had been put into this project (see OCTOBER 3).

After final phone calls to check the weather along the route, the big 16-wheel diesel tractor trailer carrying the "Giant Eye" started up at 3:15 a.m. on this Sunday morning. Ten highway patrolmen on motorcycles accompanied the truck to pave the way. People lined the roads along the route to see the "Giant Eye" go by. Some people took their hats off as a gesture of honor, knowing that they would have something to tell their children and grandchildren about.

By the end of the first day of travel, the giant load had reached Escondido—a distance of 126 miles. They had averaged a speed of only 11 miles per hour. In spite of the predictions of good weather, the skies had turned misty in the early afternoon, and later on a steady, cold rain had started. On the second day the visibility was very poor. The workmen on the truck said they could see only 50 feet ahead. For the climb up Mt. Palomar, the lead tractor was followed by two other tractors pushing the load from behind.

The "Highway To the Stars" had been designed and built for this load so that the crated 200-inch mirror would just clear each turn up the mountain. One of the men stood on top of the load as it went up the mountain, shouting directions to the men who were walking alongside and ahead of the trucks to mark the edges of the road. The cold rain turned into sleet, ice, and snow. The visibility was so bad that the second and third tractors could not see the exhaust smoke from the first tractor but listened to the sounds of the engine of the first tractor in order to know when to shift their gears.

In spite of all the unexpected weather difficulties, the priceless 200-inch telescope mirror was finally delivered safely to the waiting telescope in the dome of the Mt. Palomar Observatory.

NOVEMBER 19, 1775

ON THIS DAY IN SAN DIEGO HISTORY the second baby on the Anza Expedition was born. The baby was a boy, and he was named Diego Pasqual Gutierrez. He was baptized by the priest on the expedition, Padre Font. The expedition was camped on the Gila River (pronounced Heela) in what is now Arizona on their way to California to establish a colony and presidio (military fort) at Monterey and San Francisco (see OCTOBER 4). They stayed there for two days while the new mother and baby rested.

The expedition, led by Juan Bautista de Anza, would later cross the Colorado River into what is now California at Yuma, travel through the Colorado Desert, and then camp for several days in northeastern San Diego County near what is now the town of Borrego Springs (see DECEMBER 21, DECEMBER 22, and DECEMBER 26).

The Anza Party would travel 1,200 miles from the last loading-up place in Arizona and would take more than five months to get to Monterey. Anza himself and some of the settlers from southern Mexico that he rounded up for the trip would travel almost 2,000 miles and were on the trail for nearly a year.

Three bands of people traveled one day apart so that everyone could drink at the slow-filling desert water holes. The *vaqueros* (Spanish for "cowboys") brought the cattle in another separate group. They traveled on trails—not well-established roads. There were no wagons on this trip because the trails were too narrow and rugged for wagons. Everything was carried by pack animals and had to be loaded and unloaded each day. It was a brave and hardy bunch of people who volunteered for this trip. The motivation was to find a better life and free land in the new settlements to the north.

NOVEMBER 20, 1602

ON THIS DAY IN SAN DIEGO HISTORY the Spanish explorer Sebastián Vizcaíno and his ships and men sailed away from San Diego after spending ten days in the area. They had anchored in San Diego Bay and went ashore for several days to look around. They met up with some Indians who took them to the Indian *rancherias* (small settlements), where the women were dressed in animal skins and cooking food in homemade pots.

From the hill at the top of Point Loma, the priest on the expedition, Father Antonio de La Ascensión, discovered "another good port"—what we know today as Mission Bay. He noted that the land was fertile, that there was a great variety of fish, and that gold pyrites were abundant along the beach, indicating that there might be gold mines inland in the hills and mountains. This later proved to be true when gold was discovered in 1870 near the mountain area where Julian is located today (see FEBRUARY 20 and NOVEMBER 27).

It would be another 167 years after Vizcaíno's visit before Father Junípero Serra would arrive in San Diego to start the San Diego Mission in 1769 (see JANUARY 9).

Sebastián Vizcaíno gave San Diego its name, as well as naming many other places along the Pacific coast—including Monterey Bay, named for the Spanish viceroy of Mexico.

See also NOVEMBER 10.

NOVEMBER 21, 1851

ON THIS DAY IN SAN DIEGO HISTORY an Indian attack occurred at the Warner Ranch. The Warner Ranch was originally known as San José del Valle Rancho (Spanish for "St. Joseph of the Valley") and Valle de San José Rancho (Spanish for "Valley of St. Joseph")—two of the ranchos that were in the northeastern part of San Diego County near the present-day Warner Springs. The San José del Valle Rancho was also known as Aqua Caliente (Spanish for "Hot Water")—named for the hot springs located there.

The Warner Ranch got its name from a man from Connecticut named Jonathan Trumbull Warner, who, after becoming a Mexican citizen, called himself "Juan José" Warner (see DECEMBER 5). He was granted ownership of the ranchos by the Mexican California governor in 1844 (see AUGUST 30).

After the secularization of the missions (the changing of ownership from church land to public land) in 1834, even though many of the Indians in San Diego County were supposed to have received some of the land, most of the good land was owned by the white people. After Juan José Warner took possession of the rancho, he kept some of the Indians to work for him, paying them three dollars per month and often using a whip to keep them "motivated" to work.

When the sheriff and tax collector tried to force the Indians who owned cattle to pay taxes on their herds, one of the Indian leaders, Antonio Garra, who had been educated at the Mission San Luis Rey, thought the taxes were unfair. He organized a war party of Indians to attack the ranch in the early morning hours on this day in 1851. At first Warner was able to hold off the Indians, killing four of the attacking party. But the Indians killed four people at Aqua Caliente and also one of Warner's servants.

Warner was running out of ammunition, so he escaped from the rancho. The Indians then proceeded to burn his ranch buildings and drive off his cattle. Many of the Indians were later captured, found guilty by military tribunal, and executed—including the leader, Antonio Garra (see DECEMBER 23).

NOVEMBER 22, 1899

ON THIS DAY IN SAN DIEGO HISTORY work began in La Jolla Cove on the construction of a large glass-bottom boat. It was built just behind the original Cove Bath House and took nearly eight months to build.

The boat was built by two Scandinavian fishermen and boat builders—an uncle and a nephew named Thorson and Larson. They named their boat the *Viking*. The *Viking* was launched at the cove and it took large fishing parties out to see the sights on the ocean bottom in La Jolla Bay.

The glass-bottom boat was a great success for Thorson and Larson, and it sailed in the waters around La Jolla for six years. Shortly after the Scandinavians sold the *Viking* to another owner, it was wrecked in a storm in 1906 on the rocky beach near the La Jolla Caves.

The rocky coastline of La Jolla in the vicinity of the cove is an interesting area rich with marine life. The Marine Biological Association of San Diego—later to become the Scripps Institution of Oceanography—had a marine biological laboratory at La Jolla Cove between 1905 and 1910, the "Little Green Lab" (see MARCH 23). This was an excellent location for collecting a variety of marine specimens to study in those early days.

Today you can see many snorkelers and scuba divers swimming off the cove to observe the interesting underwater life there—the same that was viewed from the glass-bottom boat over 100 years ago, long before scuba gear was invented.

NOVEMBER 23, 1987

ON THIS DAY IN SAN DIEGO HISTORY an earthquake with a strength of 6.2 on the Richter scale occurred in the Fish Creek Mountains in the Anza-Borrego Desert State Park, near Borrego Springs and Ocotillo Wells in northeast San Diego County. The next morning an even stronger earthquake occurred with a strength of 6.6. This was southern California's strongest earthquake in six years.

The earthquakes were felt throughout the Colorado Desert and Baja California. Ninety-four people were injured, and the earthquakes contributed to two deaths. Windows were broken and walls were cracked, but no serious damage was done in the Borrego Valley. Fortunately, this was not a heavily populated area.

In the Anza-Borrego Desert State Park, there were cave-ins and rock falls in some of the canyons—especially at Split Mountain and Arroyo Seco del Diablo (which means "Dry Wash of the Devil" in Spanish—sounds like an unfriendly place!). Boulders and landslides also covered sections of the pavement on Montezuma Grade (San Diego County Highway S-22) and Yaqui Pass (Highway S-3)—two of the main roads coming into Borrego Springs.

There are many small faults in the area of the Anza-Borrego Desert which are part of the San Jacinto Fault Zone. Geologists tell us that the zone is one of the most seismically active areas in all of North America—with over 20 large earthquakes measuring greater than 6.0 since 1899 and over 11,000 measurable quakes per year (see also APRIL 9).

The large San Andreas Fault, which runs almost the entire length of California, including through San Francisco and the Los Angeles area, passes more than 100 miles east of San Diego—on the eastern side of the Salton Sea in Imperial County. Even so, the San Diego area could be affected by an especially large earthquake in the southern portion of the fault. The great earthquake of 1906 which caused so much damage in San Francisco measured 8.3 and was caused by movement along the San Andreas Fault.

November 24, 1713

ON THIS DAY IN SAN DIEGO HISTORY Father Junípero Serra was born at Petra de Mallorca—on the Spanish island of Mallorca (pronounced My-Yorka) in the Mediterranean Sea off the coast of Spain. He was born Miquel Joseph Serra, but he chose the religious name of Junípero at the age of 18 when he decided to become a Franciscan monk (see SEPTEMBER 14). The Franciscan order of the Catholic Church was named after St. Francis of Assisi, who lived in the little town of Assisi, Italy in the thirteenth century.

Father Serra would be important to San Diego 56 years later, in 1769, when he started the San Diego Mission halfway around the world from where he was born (see JULY 1 and JULY 16). The Misión San Diego de Alcalá was the first of a total of 21 missions that were founded by the Franciscans in California between 1769 and 1823. Father Serra was responsible for starting 9 of the 21 California missions before he died in 1784.

There are two statues of Father Serra at the San Diego Mission—one in front next to a cross in the middle of a circular drive leading to the mission, and the other in the inner garden near the Indian burial grounds. There is also a statue of him on Presidio Hill, where he founded the original Misión San Diego de Alcalá before it was moved to its present location six miles inland in Mission Valley.

There is a plaque from the citizens of Petra de Mallorca, Spain that is displayed on the wall of the portico at the San Diego Mission. The plaque was given to the San Diego Mission in 1969, on the bicentennial of the founding of the San Diego Mission as a "link between Petra de Mallorca and San Diego."

NOVEMBER 25, 1872

ON THIS DAY IN SAN DIEGO HISTORY the controversy over the boundaries of the Cuyamaca Rancho started all over again with the reopening of the case by the four new owners of the rancho. They had bought the Cuyamaca Rancho three years before from the original owner, Augustín Olvera. This was the same Olvera for whom Olvera Street in Los Angeles was named (see JUNE 5 and AUGUST 11).

The new owners were trying to claim that their rancho included Julian and the newly discovered gold mines around Julian. Their first claim had lasted for a whole year before the court ruled in favor of the miners that the Cuyamaca Rancho did not extend as far as Julian and the gold mines.

Sixteen months after that decision, the case was reopened by the rancho owners on this date, November 25, 1872. One of the new owners had a history of questionable land dealings in San Francisco and had also tried to claim ownership of some San Diego pueblo land by simply going there and putting a fence around it, so the people in Julian figured that they were just out to grab the valuable gold mines.

The case was finally settled—again—in favor of the Julian miners. But it took nearly two years for the final land description of the rancho to be drawn up and filed (see NOVEMBER 14). In an odd twist to the story, one gold mine was legally within the boundary of the rancho—the Stonewall Jackson Mine (named for the Confederate general in the Civil War) which turned out to be the richest gold mine in the area (see JUNE 28). In order to clear the title on the Stonewall Mine, the mine owners "purchased" the mine and its equipment from the owners of the Cuyamaca Rancho in 1874 for $6,000.

Leland Fetzer's book *A Good Camp: Gold Mines of Julian and the Cuyamacas*, published by Sunbelt Publications, relates the interesting and complex details of the Stonewall Mine and the other gold mines in the Julian–Banner–Cuyamaca area.

NOVEMBER 26, 1915

ON THIS DAY IN SAN DIEGO HISTORY an official of the Cuyamaca Water Company (CWC) made a complaint to the Railroad Commission about water customers who were playing a game with the CWC by claiming to own land that qualified for the lower irrigation rate rather than the higher domestic rate. The Railroad Commission, created in 1879 to control unjust rates and services, had been given authority by the Public Utilities Act of 1911 to regulate, in addition to railroad companies, private companies delivering telephone or telegraph services, oil, heat, power, and water.

The dual rate structure allowed growers who owned tracts of land over one-half acre to be charged a lower water rate than what individual homeowners with smaller plots of land were charged. It turned out that many of the CWC customers owned land only slightly over one-half acre and were claiming to be involved in agriculture that qualified for the lower irrigation rate.

After the complaint by the Cuyamaca Water Company, the railroad commission investigated the situation and did away with the dual rate structure in 1917. It was replaced with a flat rate of four dollars for the first 2,000 cubic feet of water used each month. After that an irrigation rate of 2.5 cents per 100 cubic feet was charged.

The Cuyamaca Water Company was owned jointly by Ed Fletcher and James Murray, who purchased the San Diego Flume Company in 1910 and changed the name to the Cuyamaca Water Company. Water was brought into the San Diego area from Lake Cuyamaca, some 35 miles away, by the flume that was built in 1888 (see FEBRUARY 22).

Ed Fletcher had owned several businesses in San Diego before becoming a real estate developer. In 1908 he developed Mt. Helix and Grossmont with his partner, William Gross. He also laid out the subdivision of Del Mar for the South Coast Land Company. In addition, Fletcher laid out Pine Hills in the Julian area and built the Pine Hills Lodge in 1910.

Ed Fletcher was involved in raising funds for many San Diego civic projects including preserving the buildings in Balboa Park after the Panama-California Exposition, the creation of the Naval Training Center, and the building of the YMCA. He was a state senator for 12 years, from 1935 to 1947, and he drafted the law creating the San Diego County Water Authority that brought in water from the Colorado River. Fletcher Parkway is named for him.

November 27, 1870

On this day in San Diego history a group of over 80 gold miners in the Banner area—down the mountain east of Julian—joined together to form the Banner Mining District.

Gold was first discovered in the Banner area just two months before by a man named Louis B. Redmond, who stumbled onto a rich gold-bearing quartz rock ledge while he was picking berries in San Felipe Canyon. Gold had already been discovered near Julian City earlier in 1870, starting a gold rush to the Julian area (see February 20).

Redmond marked the location of his claim by putting a small flag, or banner, on a pile of rocks. The town of Banner City, which soon grew up in the canyon nearby, got its name from Redmond's flag. At one point Banner City had a population of 600 to 1,000 and had at least 40 buildings, including three stores, one hotel, boarding houses, and several saloons.

Shortly after the Banner Mining District was formed, a wagon road was surveyed and laid out between Julian City and Banner City—a seven-mile stretch down the mountainside. During the 1870s the Banner Grade Road was considered to be the most dangerous road in San Diego County. But before it was built, the route down the mountain was so steep that mining equipment, machinery, and other supplies had to be tied to a sled that was lowered over 1,000 feet down by ropes. To keep the load from going too fast, a tree was tied behind the sled as a brake.

Banner Creek runs down Banner Canyon, and heavy rainstorms caused the creek to overflow and flood the town in 1873 to 1874 and again in 1926, wiping out the town each time. The town was not rebuilt after the last flood devastation.

What is left of Banner today—the Banner Store and a few homes scattered nearby—is located on Highway 78 east of Julian on the way to the desert towns of Ocotillo Wells and Borrego Springs. No evidence remains of the once-flourishing town.

November 28, 1844

On this day in San Diego history Juan José Warner was granted the land of the San José Del Valle and Valle de San José ranchos, later known as the Warner Ranch.

See December 5 for more information on Juan José Warner—previously known as Jonathan Trumbull Warner before becoming a Mexican citizen and changing his name. California was a part of Mexico before 1848, and then it became part of the United States after the Mexican-American War of 1846–48.

The rancho contained over 44,000 acres. The area covered by the rancho had been occupied by Indian tribes before the white men came to claim the land. This was an area that connected three different Indian groups. The Cupeños, who occupied the lands of the old rancho, were a mixture of Cahuillas who lived to the north and east, and the Diegueños (also called Kumeyaay) who lived to the south. Also to the west was another group of Indians, the Luiseños, connected to the San Luis Rey Mission. The Indians used the hot springs there, called Agua Caliente (Spanish for "Hot Water"), to bathe in, to wash their clothes in, and to leach their acorns which they used for food.

The old Agua Caliente of the Indians is now Warner Springs, a health and vacation resort. The southwestern end of the old rancho is now covered by Lake Henshaw which was created in 1922 by building a dam across the San Luis Rey River. You can see the lake at the junction of Highways 79 and 76—between Santa Ysabel and Warner Springs. Today there is a beautiful view of Lake Henshaw and the surrounding mountains from the Santa Ysabel Indian Casino that was built on the hills above the lake on the eastern side of Highway 79. The land of the old Warner Ranch is now owned by the Vista Irrigation District and leased by a cattleman. Large herds of cattle graze there now—just like in past times.

See November 21 for more information on the Warner Ranch and about the Indian attack that occurred on that day.

NOVEMBER 29, 1898

ON THIS DAY IN SAN DIEGO HISTORY an item in the *San Diego Union* newspaper stated:

> Rancho Santa Margarita y Las Flores, which was sold two months ago by the heirs of John Forster, to Richard O'Neill for a consideration of $250,000, has just been recorded in this county as sold by O'Neill to James Flood of San Francisco for the amount of $450,000.

This was a pretty good profit after only two months of ownership. The Rancho Santa Margarita y Las Flores, containing 133,441 acres, was the largest rancho in San Diego County. The rancho was originally granted to the Pico brothers, Pío and Andrés, in 1841 as a Mexican land grant. The Pico brothers transferred ownership of the rancho to their brother-in-law, Juan Forster, in 1864 (see FEBRUARY 7 and APRIL 24).

The U.S. Marine Base at Camp Pendleton is now located on the former ranch lands. The United States government bought 132,000 acres of the old rancho in 1942 at a cost of $4 million to create the largest Marine training base in the world. To give you an idea of the size of what was once the Rancho Santa Margarita y Las Flores, Camp Pendleton now includes three mountain ranges, five lakes, three rivers, 425 miles of fences, 250 miles of roads, and many granite and flagstone quarries.

NOVEMBER 30, 1775

ON THIS DAY IN SAN DIEGO HISTORY the Anza Expedition crossed the Colorado River into what is now California. They were on their way to start a Spanish colony in San Francisco. But first they had to cross the desert in what is now Imperial County and eastern San Diego County, where they would camp for several days near the present-day town of Borrego Springs (see DECEMBER 21, DECEMBER 22, and DECEMBER 26).

The November 30 entry in Juan Bautista de Anza's diary tells of crossing the Colorado River:

> At 7 o'clock in the morning we began our march along the bottom lands up the Colorado…then we unloaded in order to take over all the provisions and equipment in half loads. This having been done, we began to cross the first branch of the river on the largest and strongest horses, leading by the bridles those on which the women and children were riding; and as a precaution, in case anyone should fall, I stationed in front ten men on the downstream side… After this the second branch of the river was crossed…all the families, the baggage, and most of the provisions got over to this bank of the river.

Exactly 221 years later, on this same date in 1996, the Juan Bautista de Anza Relay Race ended at the presidio in San Francisco, having started in Hermosillo, Sonora, Mexico. Sponsored by the Heritage Trails Fund, the relay included horseback riders, bicyclists, hikers, and runners who, in six-mile relays, repeated the 1,468-mile route that had been traveled by the Anza Expedition in 1775. However, the pioneers and soldiers on the Anza Expedition did not have the luxury of doing their trip in 6-mile relays. Each person in 1775 had to persevere for the entire 1,468 miles.

Some historians claim that Juan Bautista de Anza's expedition was the third most important event in California history—after the discovery of California by Juan Cabrillo in 1542 (see SEPTEMBER 28) and the establishment of the first mission and presidio in California by Father Junípero Serra and Gaspar de Portolá in 1769 in San Diego (see JULY 16).

DECEMBER 1, 1846

ON THIS DAY IN SAN DIEGO HISTORY General Stephen Kearny's Army of the West camped at San Felipe in San Diego County. This was during the Mexican-American War of 1846–48. After the war, which was won by the United States, California no longer belonged to Mexico but became a part of the United States.

General Kearny was marching overland from Santa Fe, New Mexico to California with 110 men to reinforce the American troops at San Diego. He was being led along the trail by Kit Carson, a well-known hunter, trapper, and western scout who knew all the western trails. They were using an old trail from the east across the desert that was used over the years by many explorers and traders. It has been called by many names: Sonora Road, Colorado Road, Southern Emigrant Trail, and the Butterfield Stage Route. The trail went through San Diego County roughly along the route that County Highway S-2 follows today—from Ocotillo in the desert on today's Interstate 8 to the present-day Highway 79. It then continued northward past Warner Springs and Temecula to Los Angeles (see also SEPTEMBER 16).

San Felipe, where Kearny and his troops camped on this day in 1846, is located in the San Felipe Valley—north of Julian and southwest of Borrego Springs (see JULY 18). Today County Highway S-2 travels up San Felipe Valley on the way toward Warner's Ranch, another stopping place along the old trail. Kearny and his troops would also stop at Warner's Ranch two days later where they would rest up from their 1,000-mile overland journey.

Five days later Kearny and his troops fought the Californios in an unexpected encounter in the San Pasqual Valley at the Battle of San Pasqual (see DECEMBER 6).

DECEMBER 2, 1887

ON THIS DAY IN SAN DIEGO HISTORY the San Diego city trustees set aside 100 acres from the 1,400-acre City Park for an orphan's home and an industrial school. They also set aside five acres for a home for poor and homeless women. Previously, they had set aside eight acres from the City Park acreage for an elementary school that later became San Diego High School (see AUGUST 8).

The 1,400-acres of City Park was set aside 17 years before, in 1870, by some far-sighted San Diego leaders (see FEBRUARY 4). The name of the park was later changed to Balboa Park (see OCTOBER 27).

Originally the land was covered with a scraggly growth of sagebrush and chaparral—nothing like the lush and beautiful trees and plants that are there today. Early on, many San Diego leaders, including George Marston, asked the city trustees for permission to plant some eucalyptus trees at their own expense—a generous and far-sighted thing for them to do (see OCTOBER 22 for more information on George W. Marston).

Later, the Ladies Annex of the San Diego Chamber of Commerce raised $514 for planting trees and bushes on 14 acres on the west side of the park. Kate Sessions, a horticulturist (plant specialist) and a graduate of the University of California at Berkeley, supervised the planting of nearly 700 trees and shrubs. She also landscaped the Hotel Del Coronado when it first opened in 1888. Later, she leased 30 acres of the park for a plant nursery in exchange for planting 100 trees per year in the park and giving the city another 300. Called the "Mother of Balboa Park," she introduced trees from many faraway places—such as cork oak from Spain, camphor from Asia, and rubber from the tropics. She also cultivated seeds from Baja California and South America. There is a park named for her in La Jolla—Kate Sessions Park. For more information on Sessions, see MARCH 24.

DECEMBER 3, 1846

ON THIS DAY IN SAN DIEGO HISTORY Edward Stokes, an English seaman who had settled in San Diego, was visiting General Kearny's U.S. Army camp at Warner's Ranch during the Mexican-American War. He volunteered to carry a message from General Kearny to Fort Stockton, the American fort in San Diego, requesting extra troops.

Edward Stokes owned the Santa Ysabel Rancho along with his father-in-law, José Joaquin Ortega (see MAY 14). They also owned the Santa Maria Rancho, near the present-day town of Ramona (see MARCH 4). Stokes made arrangements for General Kearny and his American troops to camp at his two ranchos on their way to San Diego.

The 17,700-acre Santa Ysabel Rancho was located 52 miles northeast of San Diego, in the valley below the present-day mountain town of Julian. It belonged to the San Diego Mission before the secularization of the missions in 1834 (see SEPTEMBER 30). The chapel of the Santa Ysabel Mission, which was an *asistencia* or sub-mission of the San Diego Mission, is located there with its cemetery (see MAY 14). Spanish padres had visited the Santa Ysabel Valley in 1795 and again in 1821. They were impressed with the large number of Indians who lived there and noted that they were especially intelligent.

After the secularization of the missions, the Santa Ysabel Rancho was granted to Ortega and Stokes as a Mexican land grant in 1844—in spite of the large Indian population living there. Four years before, in 1840, the Indians had complained to the land commissioner that Ortega had taken their land. The Santa Ysabel Valley has many streams and springs, and it had some of the best grazing land for cattle of any of the ranchos. In his response to the complaint, the land commissioner wrote to the governor: "Ortega had been administrator of the San Diego Mission and thus he utilized his information of the best pieces of land—whether the Indians fare well or badly."

It was not until 1875 that part of the land was set aside as the Santa Ysabel Indian Reservation to provide land for the local Indians, who now operate the Santa Ysabel Casino—built high on a hill overlooking Lake Henshaw.

The Santa Ysabel Rancho was sold in the 1880s to farmers from Sonoma County in northern California who brought cattle and dairy farming to the area. The land is still used mainly for cattle raising.

DECEMBER 4, 1875

ON THIS DAY IN SAN DIEGO HISTORY there was a shootout at the Gaskill Brothers General Store in Campo between the Gaskill brothers and six Mexican bandits. Fortunately, the Gaskill brothers had been tipped off, so they were prepared when the bandits arrived. They had hidden loaded pistols and shotguns in their store and in other buildings on their property.

Lumen and Silas Gaskill arrived in Campo in 1868 and built a mill, a blacksmith shop, a small hotel, and a store on their 900-acre ranch. They successfully raised cattle, sheep, and hogs. They also kept beehives and produced honey.

Campo, located 60 miles southeast of San Diego and only a little over one mile from the Mexican border, was located on the wagon and stage route from Yuma. Settlers began to arrive there in the 1860s and by 1869 there were 400 people in the Campo Valley. Many Texans settled at Campo, and at one time it was known as "New Texas" or "Little Texas." The early Kumeyaay Indians who lived in the area called it Milquatay (Kumeyaay for "Large Meadow"). Campo is the Spanish word for "Field."

Jack Innis in his book *San Diego Legends* gives a play-by-play account of what happened in the gunfight that occured on this day in 1875. Lumen Gaskill was shot in the store by one of the bandits. He lay on the floor, wounded and bleeding, when he saw one of the bandits aiming a gun at his brother, Silas. Lumen shot the bandit from his position on the ground, thereby saving his brother's life. After the dust settled, four bandits were dead, and the other two rode out of town. The Gaskill brothers recovered from their wounds.

According to Jack Innis, "Few San Diegans are aware that a shootout in East County exceeded in intensity—and in fact predated—the legendary gunfight at the O.K. Corral."

The Gaskill Brothers Store was a wood-frame building in 1875. It was rebuilt as a large two-story stone structure in 1885 and more recently has housed the Mountain Empire Historical Society Museum. Campo also has the historic Campo Railroad Depot and Pacific Southwest Railway Museum.

DECEMBER 5, 1831

ON THIS DAY IN SAN DIEGO HISTORY Jonathan Trumbull Warner arrived in California at the age of 24. He would later become a Mexican citizen and the owner of the Warner Rancho in northeastern San Diego County in the area where Lake Henshaw is located today (see AUGUST 30 and NOVEMBER 28).

Warner was born on the East Coast in Connecticut. In his early 20s he went to St. Louis, Missouri looking for a better climate for his health. He then moved on to New Mexico and later joined a trapping party sent out to the West Coast. After settling in Los Angeles, he became a Catholic and a naturalized citizen of Mexico and changed his name to Juan José Warner. The Indians called him "Juan Largo" (Spanish for "Long John") because of his 6'3" height. Later, after the United States took over California from Mexico in 1848, he was known as John J. Warner.

In 1837, at the age of 30, he married Anita Gale, the adopted daughter of the Pico family. Pío Pico was the last Mexican governor of California, and his brother, Andrés Pico, was the Californio general who fought against the Americans in the Battle of San Pasqual in 1846 (see DECEMBER 6).

Warner returned to the East in 1839, and for two years he gave several lectures on the "Far West," describing the need for a Pacific railroad and promoting the idea of the United States acquiring California. Warner returned to California in 1841. After receiving the land grant in 1844 for the San José del Valle Rancho—later known as the Warner Ranch—he and his family moved there.

After the Indian attack on the Warner Ranch in 1851 (see NOVEMBER 21) when the ranch buildings were burned down, Warner and his family moved to Los Angeles. He later became a California state senator, and he stood up for the Indians and their rights.

DECEMBER 6, 1846

ON THIS DAY IN SAN DIEGO HISTORY the Battle of San Pasqual was fought in the San Pasqual Valley of San Diego County—near where the present-day Wild Animal Park is located. General Kearny, head of 110 United States troops, fought against General Andrés Pico (brother of the Mexican California governor, Pío Pico), leader of 200 Californio soldiers. California was part of Mexico then, and the Mexican Californians called themselves "Californios."

Instead of waiting for reinforcements from San Diego, which had been sent for by messenger, General Kearny made a rushed and unorganized attack on the Californios. His troops suffered 13 injuries and 18 deaths in the ensuing battle, while the Californios escaped unharmed. To avoid further losses, Kearny's troops retreated to a nearby hill to camp, but they were surrounded by the Californios. With nowhere to go, Kearny and his men were forced to burn their baggage and to cook and eat their mules for food. The hill they camped on is now known as Mule Hill.

Five days later, on December 11, two hundred U.S. Marines and sailors from Fort Stockton in San Diego finally arrived and escorted Kearny's troops back to San Diego. Pico's Californios withdrew, but they were defeated one month later, on January 13, 1847 at Cahuenga Pass near Los Angeles, when U.S. General John Frémont arrived with his troops from northern California.

Most of the battles of the Mexican-American War were fought in Texas and Mexico. Only two major battles took place in California—the one at San Pasqual in San Diego County and the other at San Pedro in Los Angeles County. It is said that the Californios fought well and were excellent horseback riders. The problem was that Mexico did not have enough troops to fight in California, so the United States won the war—and California became a part of the United States. California, and San Diego especially, still carry a strong influence and heritage from their Spanish and Mexican past.

You can visit the little museum in San Pasqual Battlefield State Historic Park to see a video about the battle. It is located on State Highway 78 about a mile east of the entrance to the Wild Animal Park.

DECEMBER 7, 1941

ON THIS DAY IN SAN DIEGO HISTORY Japan made a sneak bombing attack on the United States Naval Station and ships at Pearl Harbor, Hawaii, resulting in the United States' decision to enter World War II. This would have an especially important effect on San Diego, with American participation in the war lasting from 1941 until 1945.

Some people say that the United States and the West Coast were so unprepared for the attack that if the Japanese planes had continued on toward the California coast, they could have bombed San Diego, Los Angeles, or San Francisco without much trouble. Thank goodness that did not happen, but San Diego was, nevertheless, in an important location on the Pacific coast.

San Diego has had many military bases ever since World War I (1914–19), starting with Camp Kearny and the Army and Navy defense stations at Fort Rosecrans and Coronado's North Island. In 1921 the Naval Air Station came to San Diego. The military presence continued to grow during World War II, and the citizens of San Diego joined together in a united effort to win the war, postponing many city improvements which had been planned before the war began.

Immediately after the war began, Major Reuben H. Fleet, head of San Diego's Consolidated Aircraft Corporation (later to become the Convair Division of General Dynamics) sent a message to President Franklin Roosevelt telling him that Consolidated Aircraft was "on the job and at your command" to build military aircraft. The company went on to build a total of 33,000 planes for the war effort. (For more on Consolidated Aircraft, see OCTOBER 20.)

For more of the effects of World War II on San Diego, see AUGUST 20.

DECEMBER 8, 1812

ON THIS DAY IN SAN DIEGO HISTORY an earthquake damaged the San Diego Mission. The fourth church to stand on the site was under construction when the earthquake struck—after having been destroyed by a previous quake in 1803! Father Fernando Martín and Father José Sanchez decided that flared wings should be added to the front of the church for support against future earthquakes rolling north-to-south.

The year 1812 in California was known as "El Año de los Temblores" (Spanish for "The Year of the Earthquakes"). Seven other missions in southern California, in addition to the San Diego Mission, suffered earthquake damage in 1812.

The San Diego Mission was started in 1769 by Father Junípero Serra. Initially, the mission was located at Presidio Hill, but in 1774 it was moved six miles inland to its present location in Mission Valley (see JULY 16). In 1775, it was burned down by Indians and had to be rebuilt (see NOVEMBER 5).

Later, after the secularization of the missions in 1834 (see SEPTEMBER 30), the mission lands were turned into public lands and ranchos. This was the beginning of the neglect and ultimate decline of the mission buildings.

After the Mexican-American War of 1846–48, U.S. Cavalry soldiers occupied the mission until 1862. They built a second floor inside and kept their horses on the ground level. The 5-bell campanile collapsed. The mission buildings were falling into further disrepair.

After the Army departed, the condition of the unoccupied mission went from bad to worse. By 1892 half the church had caved in, and the roof tiles were gone, having been taken for use on roofs in Old Town.

In 1900 the mission ruins were capped over with concrete as a temporary measure to prevent further erosion of the adobe walls. In 1930 enough money was finally raised to start a proper restoration, giving us the beautiful mission we have today (see JULY 13 and OCTOBER 17).

DECEMBER 9, 1927

ON THIS DAY IN SAN DIEGO HISTORY the architect Frank W. Stevenson signed the preliminary plans and blueprints for construction of the new Colonial Apartment Hotel at Prospect and Jenner streets in La Jolla. The old Colonial Apartment Hotel, a wood-frame structure that had been on the site since 1911, was designed by Richard Requa, who later became the architectural director for the California Pacific International Exposition of 1935 (see OCTOBER 30). The old building was moved down the hill to the rear of the lot, where it still stands today, and the new four-story concrete hotel that was built in the front opened on June 28, 1928.

The owner of the property, George Bane, chose to build a new hotel out of concrete that "would rival anything in the West." It was the first fireproof hotel to be built west of the Mississippi—with the first fire sprinkler system, with reinforced cement stairways, and with fire doors on each floor. There had been many arson fires in La Jolla in 1915, including the home of Ellen Browning Scripps, and that had many La Jollans concerned (see AUGUST 7). So Bane, like Miss Scripps, chose to rebuild with a concrete, fireproof structure.

During World War II, the Colonial Hotel was used by many of the top brass from the nearby Camp Callan army base, and during the 1950s, Hollywood celebrities who were performing in the La Jolla Playhouse stayed there. But in the 1960s the hotel did not fare so well. In 1976 it was sold to new owners for $1 million.

After four years and $3 million spent on restoration, the hotel reopened in 1980 with 75 rooms, designed "like an elegant European hotel," according to the hotel brochure. Now known as the Grande Colonial, it was named as one of the Historic Hotels of America by the National Trust for Historic Preservation.

The architect, Frank. W. Stevenson, designed many other buildings in the San Diego area including the Bush Egyptian Theater on Park Boulevard, the C Street Theater at 4th and C streets, the California Savings & Commercial Bank at 5th and B streets, the Coronado Apartment Hotel on Orange Avenue, the Coronado Community Hospital, the Coronado Methodist Episcopal Church, the National City Methodist Episcopal Church, the Ocean Beach Elementary School, the Saint Agnes Catholic Church, and the Y.M.C.A. building on Broadway in downtown San Diego.

DECEMBER 10, 1928

ON THIS DAY IN SAN DIEGO HISTORY a bank robbery was attempted in La Jolla. Because the San Diego police had been informed that there would be bank robberies at four San Diego banks that day, two policemen were stationed near the La Jolla banks.

The La Jolla National Bank of San Diego—which later became the Security Trust & Savings Bank and is now the Citibank—was located at the corner of Wall and Herschel streets. At 12:30 p.m. there were only four people in the bank, including the vice-president and cashier of the bank, Mr. Deane Plaister.

About this time a young man with a gun entered and ordered a customer to one side. The vice-president, Mr. Plaister, said to the robber, "You can't pull that here" and reached for his own revolver. The robber fired, and Plaister returned fire. A total of 11 or 12 shots were fired. The other people in the bank dodged the shots by hiding behind partitions and furniture. Plaister was wounded in the head by a bullet that grazed his forehead, and his hands and face were cut by flying glass.

When he robber's gun was empty, he ran away down Wall Street. The two policemen heard the gunshots and rushed up in time to fire several shots at the escaping man, who was then running down the alley behind the Granada Theater between Herschel and Girard streets. He managed to reach his car and drove down the alley to Silverado Street with the policemen following and firing their guns. They caught up to the car on Ivanhoe Avenue and found him slumped over the wheel, unconscious.

The injured robber was taken to the hospital, where he regained consciousness long enough to say that his name was Leander J. Schmelz, a former Marine, and that he was working alone on the bank robbery with no accomplices. He died on the operating table. The bank vice-president had only minor injuries, and he was highly complimented for his courageous action.

DECEMBER 11, 1845

ON THIS DAY IN SAN DIEGO HISTORY Pío Pico, the Mexican governor of California, granted the Rancho de la Nación to John Forster. Forster just happened to be married to Pico's sister!

John Forster, who also owned several other large ranchos in San Diego County (see FEBRUARY 7), was born in England and moved to Guaymas, Mexico in 1831 at the age of 16. Two years later he came to Mexican California where he became known as "Don Juan" Forster.

His Rancho de la Nación (Spanish for "National Ranch"), consisted of 26,600 acres, including the present-day National City, Chula Vista, and the area inland to Sweetwater Lake. Because of modern development, and with the exception of the pueblo lands granted to the city of San Diego, the rancho lands have become some of the most valuable of the original San Diego County land grants.

In the early days, when California and Mexico belonged to Spain, the Rancho de la Nación was known as Rancho del Rey (Spanish for "King's Ranch" or "Royal Ranch") and was controlled by the San Diego Presidio as a grazing ground for its horses and cattle.

Don Juan Forster kept the Rancho de la Nación for only nine years, selling it in 1854. Later, in 1868, when the Kimball brothers from New Hampshire arrived in San Diego via San Francisco, they realized the potential of this rancho land on the southern part of San Diego Bay and bought it for $30,000. They then began to survey a site for a new town to the south of San Diego that they called National City (see APRIL 1).

The Kimball Brothers were also involved in convincing the Santa Fe Railroad to extend its railroad line southward to San Diego and to National City. They offered the railroad 10,000 acres of land, and the railroad promised to build a railroad station and shops in National City (see NOVEMBER 9).

DECEMBER 12, 1872

ON THIS DAY IN SAN DIEGO HISTORY ownership of the Agua Hedionda Rancho passed to the heirs of Captain Juan María Marrón, who had died 19 years before in 1853. Marrón was a sea captain who had lived in San Diego since 1821. He and his family were important in the political life of San Diego in the early days when California was a part of Mexico. These early days in California—from the 1830s until the 1860s—were known as the Rancho Days (see APRIL 20 and JULY 25).

The 13,000-acre Agua Hedionda Rancho, located along the Pacific coast near the present-day city of Carlsbad, was granted to Marrón in 1842. Hedionda means "Stinking Water" in Spanish—a reference to the smell emanating from the area's sulfer-rich mineral springs.

Many years later, the movie actor Leo Carillo bought the rancho and remodeled the old ranch house into a charming hacienda. He was the grandson of Don Pedro Carillo, who had owned the Coronado and North Island land grants—originally known as the Peninsula de San Diego Rancho (see JUNE 11).

San Diego Gas & Electric Company later built an electric generating plant on Agua Hedionda Lagoon, but the company chose not to use the stinking water name for their plant, calling it instead the Encina Plant—after the Spanish name for "Oak Tree"—even though there were no oak trees in the area.

The present-day Carlsbad State Beach Park is located on the ocean-frontage of the former Agua Hedionda Rancho.

DECEMBER 13, 1928

ON THIS DAY IN SAN DIEGO HISTORY George W. Marston started the San Diego Historical Society as a non-profit cultural and educational institution. (For more information on Marston, see OCTOBER 22.)

The San Diego Historical Society operates a museum in Balboa Park, where there are many interesting displays of old-time San Diego. The society also restored and operates the Serra Museum in Presidio Park, the Villa Montezuma at 20th and K streets, and the Marston House at the north end of Balboa Park at 7th Avenue and Upas Street. All of these fascinating historical places are open to the public.

The Marston House was one of the most famous designs of the architects Irving Gill and William Hebbard. In 1904, Gill wrote a description of his plans for the Marston House:

> Work will be commenced early in August on a handsome new residence for George W. Marston, which is to be erected on his lately acquired property...at the northwest corner of the city park. It will be of the low, rambling order, and in general style will be old English.
>
> The house will be situated on the hill at the head of Park canyon, and will face to the south, overlooking the park. The front entrance will be towards Seventh street, but the broad elevation will be to the south. The first story will be of red brick. And the principal feature will be the broad, open terrace on the south, and the porches or loggia extending out from the house at either corner. The second story will overhang the first by eighteen inches, and will be of plaster and exposed timbers.
>
> There will he sixteen rooms in the house, and in general they will conform to the old English idea of architecture, including large fire places, low ceilings, and window and hearth seats.

For more information on Irving Gill, see APRIL 26.

DECEMBER 14, 1928

ON THIS DAY IN SAN DIEGO HISTORY the Swing-Johnson Bill passed as law in the United States Senate. This would allow San Diego to receive 100 million gallons of water a day from the Colorado River. San Diego planned to build a pipeline through the mountains to carry the water to the city.

The bill was named after two California legislators—Congressman Phil Swing who helped to get the law passed in the U.S. House of Representatives, and Senator Hiram Johnson who got the bill passed in the U.S. Senate.

As far back as 1773, when the San Diego Mission padres unsuccessfully tried to grow their crops on the land at the original mission site on Presidio Hill, getting enough water was a problem. The mission moved six miles inland in 1774 to its present location in Mission Valley, closer to the San Diego River. New crops were planted and irrigated by ditches running from the river. Then the padres built their famous dam, reservoir, and aqueduct—the first artificial irrigation system in the western United States. The dam and reservoir can still be seen at the Mission Trails Park located off Mission Gorge Road west of Santee.

San Diego has always had an off-and-on water problem because of its mainly desert climate, which alternates between droughts and floods. As the population began to grow, supplying enough water became difficult. Private companies developed the mountain reservoirs and sold water to the city. Six major dams and reservoirs were constructed in the 10-year period between 1887 and 1897—including the Sweetwater Dam built in 1888, the Cuyamaca Dam in 1889, Morena Dam in 1895, Upper and Lower Otay Dams in 1897. Later even more dams were built, such as Lake Murray Dam in 1917–18, Barrett Dam on Cottonwood Creek completed in 1923, El Capitan Dam in 1932–35, and Lake San Vicente Dam in 1941–43.

Today there is not enough local water from rain and the local reservoirs to meet the city's needs. Only 10% of San Diego's water comes from within the county. The other 90% comes from outside the county by way of aqueducts—the 444-mile California Aqueduct from northern California and the 241-mile Colorado River Aqueduct from Lake Mead, which was dammed up by the Boulder Dam Project, now called Hoover Dam after President Herbert Hoover.

DECEMBER 15, 1926

ON THIS DAY IN SAN DIEGO HISTORY the La Valencia Hotel opened on Prospect Street in La Jolla. It was built as an apartment hotel. The original name was going to be Los Apartementos del Sevilla, but the name was changed to La Valencia Hotel before the opening. It was built in two parts. The first part opened on this date in 1926. The second addition opened two years later.

The first phase of the hotel had 21 apartments, 12 single rooms, a tea room, and a banquet room. It was described as "beautifully furnished throughout...overlooking the ocean with a wonderful view and...one of the most attractive places in La Jolla."

The La Valencia Hotel became popular with movie stars and other important people. There are still autographed photographs of old-time movie stars from the 1920s and 1930s hanging today on the wall near the stairway in the hotel.

The hotel became so popular that it was not large enough to accommodate all the people who wanted to stay there. So two years after the first part opened, an addition was built that increased the number of rooms to 125 and also added a large lobby and living room, roof gardens, and the tower where the lovely Sky Room restaurant is now located.

The hotel was known locally as "The First Lady of La Jolla." It is still a lovely and popular place for out-of-town visitors to stay and for locals to dine in its three restaurants—the Mediterranean Room, the Whaling Bar, and the Sky Room. Many married couples who spent their honeymoon at the La Valencia in years past return to spend their anniversaries there. You can spot the hotel at 1132 Prospect Street by its pink stucco Mediterranean style and its tall pink tower.

In 1987 the La Valencia Hotel was named as a historic site by the San Diego Historical Site Board.

December 16, 1775

On this day in san diego history the Anza Expedition, on its way to settle colonies at Monterey and San Francisco, stopped for four days at San Sebastián Marsh because of a desert snow storm and freezing weather. San Sebastián is located between the Salton Sea and the present town of Ocotillo Wells near the Anza-Borrego Desert. Juan Bautista de Anza wrote in his diary on this date:

> This morning 4 of our cattle died from injuries and cold because of severe freezing weather. At 11 o'clock my men informed me that when they were looking for some saddle animals which had disappeared from sight, they found that they were being driven off by 4 of the heathen [this is what the Spaniards called the non-Christian Indians] who had come to see us. I therefore ordered the sergeant and 4 soldiers to go and follow them… At 7 o'clock the sergeant returned with the report that he found the horses in 2 different villages, where not a single man was to be seen.

When the Anza party first arrived at San Sebastián a few days before, Father Pedro Font—for whom Font's Point is named in the Anza-Borrego Desert State Park—wrote the following in his diary:

> Here live a few mountain Indians…who, I should judge from what I saw, must be about 20 or 30 souls. They are very miserable, hungry, weak, emaciated, and of degenerate bodies. They came out to see us when we arrived, although when they saw the soldier who went ahead of us as a guide, they started to run; but they stopped when they saw that the soldier was calling them. With the cold which is experienced here, it is a surprising thing to see these Indians naked, and so hardy that in the morning the first thing they do is to go and bathe at the spring, as we have seen.
>
> They use bows and arrows, although the arrows are few and inferior. They have another weapon, which is made of hard wood, thin, about 3 inches wide, and shaped like a crescent or sickle. With this stick they hunt hares and rabbits, throwing it in a certain way and breaking the animals' legs. They are accustomed to hunt them also with nets which they have made of a thread very well spun and so soft that it appears like hemp. They regularly live on the beans of the mesquite tree and the tule which grows around the spring, for which reason their teeth are very black and rotten.

DECEMBER 17, 1957

ON THIS DAY IN SAN DIEGO HISTORY the Atlas Intercontinental Ballistic Missile was launched at Cape Canaveral, Florida. The missile was built in San Diego by the Convair division of General Dynamics Corporation and was the world's first intercontinental ballistic missile.

Convair was an important company in San Diego that provided jobs for many people. It had been in San Diego since 1935 and was originally known as Consolidated Aircraft Company (see OCTOBER 20).

Later, Convair's Atlas missile would be used by the National Aeronautics and Space Administration (NASA) to launch rockets into space and to the moon.

Convair also developed the Centaur booster, first used in 1963. In 1973 the Atlas-Centaur combination launched the space probe *Pioneer II* on an expedition to the faraway planets of Jupiter and Saturn.

Convair had a plant in Kearny Mesa as well as the large plant on Pacific Coast Highway at the eastern end of Lindbergh Field. The Kearny Mesa plant had engineering and laboratory testing facilities. It also manufactured three versions of the cruise missile that were important to the U.S. defense program.

In addition to the thousands of military planes that were built at Convair in San Diego during World War II, they also built commercial jets after the war ended, including the widebodied DC-10.

General Dynamics also had an electronics division located at their Convair division in San Diego, where they developed and manufactured electronic systems for military purposes—including test equipment for the F-16 fighter jets.

Convair, which created so many jobs for San Diegans and contributed so significantly to airline and missile technology for over 60 years, was deactivated by General Dynamics in 1996, and the old San Diego plants were closed down.

DECEMBER 18, 1775

ON THIS DAY IN SAN DIEGO HISTORY the Anza Expedition, led by Juan Bautista de Anza, a Spanish military officer, entered the Borrego Valley in northeast San Diego County on their way from Mexico to establish a colony in San Francisco. They had been following the San Felipe Wash (a dry creek bed), and they camped near Borrego Mountain, just southeast of the present-day town of Borrego Springs. They were fighting the cold weather.

On this day Anza wrote in his diary:

> Notwithstanding the care which we have tried to observe with the cattle, it has not been possible to keep down the mortality both from the cold and from injuries. This morning 2 of them were found dead and 5 others it is thought will not be able to go forward from this place. We have made use of them as has been possible, making of them jerked beef and salting it well, but even so it is unpalatable because of its scent, color, and taste.
>
> All the sierras [Spanish for "mountains"] which we have seen today in all directions have appeared covered with snow except those along the line of our route. Today's march has been made with some comfort, because the weather has been quiet and the sun shining, this last being a blessing which we have not enjoyed for the last 6 days. After nightfall the cattle arrived at our camp, having been made to march since 10 o'clock this morning, in order that they might make some stops, but this precaution has not been sufficient to prevent the loss of 5 of them from weariness and injuries.

The year of 1775 turned out to be an extra-cold winter in the deserts and mountains of southern California. Whereas Anza had chosen the winter months for the expedition to avoid the killing summer heat of the desert, he ended up having unexpected problems with the extreme cold.

The expedition then camped at San Gregorio in the Borrego Sink—a low spot in the Borrego Valley. This was one of the springs from which Borrego Springs got its name. Today there is a historical marker at San Gregorio marking the spot where it is believed the Anza party camped (see also OCTOBER 4 and DECEMBER 21).

DECEMBER 19, 1922

ON THIS DAY IN SAN DIEGO HISTORY the search was called off for a missing military plane, and the military search planes were ordered to return to their bases. The missing army plane had flown out of Rockwell Field on Coronado's North Island on a three-hour flight to Tucson on December 7, but it never arrived.

Two men were on board the twin-seat U.S. Army Air Service DeHaviland DH4B biplane: the 26-year old pilot, First Lieutenant Charles F. Webber, and 55-year-old Colonel Francis C. Marshall, a World War I veteran and assistant chief of cavalry on an inspection tour of cavalry posts.

An intensive search for the missing plane was started on December 8—at first by air, with planes following the route the lost plane presumably took. Then intensive ground searches began. They searched wide areas in California and Arizona. By December 12 there were 40 military planes, two civilian planes, and 100 pilots and observers flying along the 1,500-mile U.S.-Mexico border between San Diego and El Paso, Texas looking for the missing plane. It soon became the largest combined military air and ground peacetime search in United States history. Then on this date, December 19, 1922, 12 days after the disappearance of the plane, the men were presumed to be dead. The *San Diego Union* reported that the military had called off the air search. Only the ground search would continue.

On May 4, 1923, some five months after the plane went missing, a local rancher and a companion were horseback riding along Japacha Ridge in the Cuyamaca Mountains north of Descanso and west of Highway 79 in what is now Rancho Cuyamaca State Park. They spotted a large engine lying on its side and a lot of twisted metal around it. Next to the wreckage they saw two piles of charred bones. The tops of two nearby trees had been broken off, indicating that the plane had hit the trees and crashed. A military inquiry later determined that it would have been impossible to see the wreckage from the air because it was located under a canopy of branches.

On May 23, 1923 a large group of men from Rockwell Field returned to the crash site to install a bronze memorial plaque imbedded in concrete covering the plane's engine. It read: "In Memory of Colonel F.C. Marshall and First Lieutenant C.L. Webber Who Fell at This Spot December 7, 1922."

DECEMBER 20, 1881

ON THIS DAY IN SAN DIEGO HISTORY writer Helen Hunt Jackson arrived in Los Angeles to begin a tour of southern California to gather information before writing her famous novel *Ramona*—a story about the mistreatment of the Indians. She visited San Diego as well as Riverside, San Bernardino, and many small southern California mission Indian villages.

Jackson wrote a letter to Ephraim W. Morse, who was a prominent San Diego businessman and civic leader, asking for some historical information she needed before writing *Ramona*. Here is what she wrote in her letter:

> Dear Mr. Morse,
> I am going to ask some help from you… I want an accurate account of two things that have happened in San Diego County: 1) the ejection of the Temecula Indians from their homes in Temecula, and 2) the taking of a lot of sheep from some of the Pala or San Luis Rey Indians by Major Couts.

Major Cave Johnson Couts owned the Rancho Guajome—located between the present-day cities of Oceanside and Vista, four miles east of the Mission San Luis Rey—and had a history of mistreating Indians (see JULY 19).

Her letter continues:

> I think the legal records of both cases are in San Diego… I am going to write an Indian novel, the scene laid in So. California. I would rather you did not speak of this, as I shall keep it a secret, until the book is done, from all except my more intimate literary friends. I hope that I can write a story which will do something to influence public sentiment on the Indian question.
> Yours always cordially—Helen Jackson

After *Ramona* was published in 1884, efforts were made to establish permanent reservations for the Indians of southern California, including those in San Diego County—to try to make up for the lands that had been taken away from them.

Every year in early May the Ramona Pageant is staged in an outdoor setting in Hemet in Riverside County. It is a dramatic reenactment of Helen Hunt Jackson's Ramona story about the southern California Indians during the 1870s (see also MARCH 3).

DECEMBER 21, 1775

ON THIS DAY IN SAN DIEGO HISTORY the Anza Expedition was in Coyote Canyon just to the north of the present-day desert town of Borrego Springs in northeastern San Diego County. They were on their way from Mexico to establish a Spanish colony in San Francisco (see OCTOBER 4) and would be traveling up Coyote Canyon for seven days (see DECEMBER 22 and DECEMBER 26).

There is a story that is told in the Borrego Springs area that Juan Bautista de Anza wasn't sure which canyon to take northward to get out of the Borrego Valley. The story goes that he and Father Font saw an outcropping of white rock against the brown color of Coyote Mountain that looked like the form of an angel pointing its arm in the direction of Coyote Canyon. So, on the basis of that good omen, Anza decided to take that route. As good as the story may sound, there is no evidence from Anza's diary that he had any problem knowing which way to leave the Borrego Valley. He had scouted the trip the year before, in 1774, and he had Indian guides who knew the best trails. Today in Borrego Springs you can see "Anza's Angel" in white on the brown Coyote Mountain—pointing its "arm" toward Coyote Canyon.

Anza wrote in his diary after entering Coyote Canyon:

> On arriving at this place, which we called El Vado ["Water Crossing" in Spanish], we saw 5 of the heathen [what the Spaniards called the non-Christian Indians] living here, but as soon as they caught sight of us they began to flee, leaving behind the vessels [bowls] in which they were gathering seeds. In order that they might not be afraid I sent one soldier after them to bring them to the camp so that I might give them presents. Having overtaken them he had them come a little nearer, but when they saw our men closer up, they again fled. Seeing this I gave orders that they should not be pursued, lest they might consider it an act of violence. Their vessels, a bow, and 3 of their blankets of jack rabbit skin, which they had left behind, were gathered up and placed where they could find them.

It is obvious from Anza's diary that he was being very careful to be friendly with the Indians and not to frighten them.

December 22, 1775

ON THIS DAY IN SAN DIEGO HISTORY the Anza Expedition was camping in Coyote Canyon—just north of the present-day town of Borrego Springs. The expedition was led by Juan Bautista de Anza, a Spanish military officer, and they were traveling from Mexico on their way to San Francisco to establish a Spanish colony and military post there (see OCTOBER 4).

Father Pedro Font, the chaplain of the expedition, wrote in his diary on this day:

> The day continued very cloudy, although not very cold. After noon 3 very timid, lean and dirty mountain Indians came, perhaps drawn by hunger and need. They were given something to eat. A short time after this some other Indians permitted themselves to be seen at the tents of the camp, for perhaps they had now begun to lose their fear, seeing that we did them no harm. In my opinion these are among the most unhappy people in the world. Their habitation is among the arid and bleak rocks of these sierras [mountains]. The clothing of the men is nothing at all, and the women wear some tattered capes made of mescal [agave cactus] fiber. Their weapons are a bow and a few bad arrows. Their food consists of tasteless roots, grass seeds, and scrubby mescal, of all of which there is very little. They are so savage, wild, and dirty, disheveled, ugly, small, and timid, that only because they have the human form is it possible to believe that they belong to mankind.

Harsh words about these Indians who were living in a harsh land. However, they had learned how to live with the land. When the desert was hot in the summer, they migrated to the cooler mountain areas. When it was cold in the mountains in winter they returned to the desert. But this winter of 1775 was an especially cold one—even in the desert. The Indians were amazing in their ability to scratch out a living and survive at all in such a hostile environment. The Spaniards, who obviously did not understand the Indian way of life, were just passing through—carrying their food and supplies with them. They did not have to survive the harsh environment wihout all the accouterments of civilization. They were on their way to settle a more pleasant land, near the ocean at Monterey and San Francisco where the climate and living conditions would not be so extreme.

DECEMBER 23, 1851

ON THIS DAY IN SAN DIEGO HISTORY the Battle of Coyote Canyon was fought at the Indian *rancheria* (settlement) of Wiliya in a remote area of Coyote Canyon about 20 miles north of the present-day town of Borrego Springs.

U.S. Army Major Samuel Heintzelman and his troops were chasing about 40 of the Indians who had attacked and burned the buildings at the Warner Ranch and also killed four white men at the Cupeño Indian village of Kupa (or Cupa), now called Warner Springs. The Indians were part of a band of rebels led by Chief Antonio Garra (see NOVEMBER 21).

One of Garra's main followers was Chief Chapuli of Wiliya, a Cahuilla Indian village in Coyote Canyon. Chief Chapuli had led the attack on Warner's Ranch. Major Heintzelman marched about 50 soldiers from Warner's Ranch down the San Felipe Valley (today's Highway S-2) to the desert and then up Coyote Canyon. He reached the Indian village on this date in 1851, and a battle began.

The Indians shot arrows, threw spears, and fired rifles from behind big boulders. The soldiers recognized Chapuli, the chief, and concentrated their gunfire on him. When Chapuli fell from gunshot wounds, the rest of the Indians retreated up the mountains. Seven other Indians were also killed. Major Heintzelman then ordered for the deserted Indian village to be burned.

As the soldiers were following the retreating Indians, suddenly an Indian woman carrying a child stepped out from the Indian group. She walked without fear down the slope, around the boulders, and up to the line of soldiers. The woman told Major Heintzelman that she would order the Indians to surrender if he would stop shooting and have a peace conference with them. He agreed, and this was the dramatic end of the Battle of Coyote Canyon.

The soldiers called the Indian woman the "Madonna of the Mountains." She was the widow of Bill Marshall, an American sailor who had left his ship in San Diego and later operated the trading post at Warner's Ranch. He married the Cupeño Indian woman, and the baby she was carrying was their son. Her husband had died only ten days before as a result of the raid on Warner's Ranch.

After the Battle of Coyote Canyon and after the execution of the Indians who had been involved in the Garra Raid, most of the Indians moved away from their Coyote Canyon villages never to return.

December 24, 1861

ON THIS DAY IN SAN DIEGO HISTORY it started to rain, and the rain continued for four weeks. It blocked up the road from San Diego to Los Angeles, so no overland mail could get to San Diego for three weeks. The only mail arriving in San Diego was that which came by boat. Large trees were washed out by the roots in the little valleys that were usually dry. Some houses in Old Town were destroyed or washed away, as well as many yards and gardens. Old adobe buildings and walls were washed down to small piles of sand and dirt. The banks of the San Diego River, where the roads led out of Old Town to the beaches, were eroded out, leaving 10-foot-high cliffs.

Augustus S. Ensworth, who was renting the Whaley House in Old Town, wrote about the rainstorm to the owner of the house, Thomas Whaley, who was living in San Francisco at the time:

> The house leaked awfully and the whole wall, against which the south-east storm beat, became so thoroughly saturated and wetted that the water stood in large drops on the inside of it, and trickled down in little rills. I would have never believed, had I not seen it, that it was possible to so wet through a lime and morter wall... There is not a door in the whole house that will close or come anywhere near it... But this weather, while injuring some, will help others. The rancheroes are much pleased at the grass. The weeds in the [Old Town] Plaza are two feet and anywhere about in the neighborhood of your house, it is good grazing.

The Whaley House, one of the oldest brick structures in southern California, is now a historical museum located at the corner of San Diego Avenue and Harney Street in Old Town (see also MARCH 31).

This is not the only story about heavy rainfall in San Diego—see JANUARY 5.

DECEMBER 25, 1875

ON THIS DAY IN SAN DIEGO HISTORY Nellie Burton and Miguel de Pedrorena Jr. were married at the Horton House Hotel in New Town San Diego. Nellie Burton was the daughter of General H.S. Burton of the United States Army. Miguel de Pedrorena Jr. was born in Old Town San Diego, where his father was a well-respected merchant and importer who had one of the early stores in Old Town.

Nellie and Miguel de Pedrorena owned the Jamul Rancho and lived there between 1876 and 1882 (see OCTOBER 26).

María Antonia Estudillo—mother of Miguel de Pedrorena and daughter of José Antonio Estudillo, *alcalde* (Spanish for "mayor") of San Diego—had received a grant to the El Cajon Rancho in 1845. This was the third largest rancho in San Diego County and contained 48,800 acres. El Cajon means "The Box" in Spanish, referring here to a narrow pass between two hills. The El Cajon Rancho included what is now El Cajon, Mt. Helix, Grossmont, Santee, Lakeside, and Flynn Springs.

Before the secularization of the missions (see SEPTEMBER 30), the El Cajon Rancho was part of the original San Diego Mission lands and was one of the mission's most important grazing grounds. After his parents died, Miguel de Pedrorena Jr. and his three sisters became owners of the El Cajon Rancho in 1876 (see JANUARY 16).

The old adobe house La Casa de Estudillo is still located in Old Town and is open for visitors to see. The Pedrorena house in Old Town, known as the Altamirano-Pedrorena House, is still standing today on San Diego Avenue and is now an Old Town Historic Park shop. It is next door to the building where the *San Diego Union* newspaper was first published in 1868 (see OCTOBER 10).

DECEMBER 26, 1775

ON THIS DAY IN SAN DIEGO HISTORY the Anza Expedition, led by Juan Bautista de Anza, a Spanish military officer, was in Upper Coyote Canyon at San Carlos Pass—where they experienced an earthquake! San Carlos Pass is located north of the present-day desert town of Borrego Springs in northeastern San Diego County and south of the town of Anza in southern Riverside County.

Originating in Mexico, the expedition was still 400 miles from its destination of San Francisco and Monterey where they planned to establish a Spanish colony and military fort. The expedition included 240 people and nearly 1,000 head of livestock, including 165 pack mules, 340 horses, a few burros, and 300 beef cattle.

Two days earlier, on Christmas Eve, the expedition had celebrated the birth of the third baby born on the trip, Salvador Ignacio Linares. Today, there is a monument at this spot noting his birth—one of the first non-Indian children born in California. Salvador Canyon, a small canyon that connects with Coyote Canyon, was named in honor of him. The next day, the expedition celebrated Christmas in the canyon as best they could.

Father Pedro Font, the chaplain on the expedition, wrote in his diary on December 26:

> A little before we entered the narrow part of the canyon a fine sleet began to fall, and lasted until after we halted… This place has a spring of water and a small arroyo [small valley] nearby, with plentiful and good grass… In this flat we found an abandoned Indian village, and from the signs it was evident that as soon as they sensed our coming they left their huts and fled, judging from their fresh tracks. Being so savage and wild, when they saw the cattle which went ahead, who knows what they thought they were. And so we were not able to see a single Indian. It must have been about 5 in the afternoon when we felt a tremor of very short duration that appeared to be an earthquake, accompanied by a short, sharp rumbling. After a short time it was repeated very indistinctly.

Earthquakes have continued to occur in this area, which is part of the San Jacinto fault zone (see APRIL 3 and NOVEMBER 23).

DECEMBER 27, 1875

ON THIS DAY IN SAN DIEGO HISTORY 52,000 acres of land were granted to the Indians of San Diego County in an executive order by President of the United States Ulysses S. Grant. This was a victory for the Luiseño Indians of the San Luis Rey Valley who were trying to hold onto their traditional lands by resisting the government's efforts to force them onto reservations at San Pasqual and Pala.

The leader of the Luiseño Indians, Manuel Olegario, took a strong stand by advising his people to stay on their ancestral *rancherias* (Indian settlements). The white settlers in the San Luis Rey Valley resented Olegario's resistance. There was fear that a war would break out between the Indians and the white settlers. The *San Diego Union* newspaper reported, "The danger is imminent, a conflict may occur at any moment between the desperate Indians under the control of Olegario."

Olegario was feared and respected by the whites. The U.S. government Indian agent John G. Ames described Olegario in one of his reports to Congress: "He is intelligent, above average, peacefully disposed towards whites, capable of controlling his Indians…and is at the same time an enthusiastic defender of his people and disposed to take advanced grounds on questions of their rights."

In November 1875 Olegario traveled to Washington, D.C. to meet with President Grant. Grant promised relief and protection for Olegario's people. This was followed by the granting of 52,000 acres of land to the Indians on this date, December 27, 1875.

But problems between the whites and the Luiseño Indians continued. In 1877, Olegario with 50 Indians forced white ranchers from Indian land near Pala. The white settlers wanted to have Olegario arrested. The newspapers reported in July 1877, "A collision is likely to happen at any moment." Then Olegario was found dead in his own bed, having died in his sleep. The Indians suspected he had been poisoned. The justice of the peace and the county coroner examined the body and found no trace of poison. They claimed Olegario's death was due to a ruptured blood vessel. Still, the Luiseño Indians continued to question the cause of their leader's sudden death.

The Diegueño (Kumeyaay) Indians in the San Pasqual Valley had similar problems with encroachment of their lands by white settlers (see AUGUST 27).

DECEMBER 28, 1930

ON THIS DAY IN SAN DIEGO HISTORY Lloyd Kelsey, a resident of Borrego Springs and a member of the Borrego Springs Chamber of Commerce, wrote an article in the *San Diego Union* newspaper describing the beauty of Borrego Palm Canyon and making a case for establishing a state park in the desert area of northeastern San Diego County. He wrote:

> Snugly tucked away in a rugged rocky fastness of the San Ysidro mountains lies Palm canyon, which despite its virtual isolation has been an irresistible lure to hundreds of San Diegans seeking new fields to explore... Trickling its way amid these marvelous specimens [of palm trees]...is a mountain stream, clear and icy, to lose itself in the valley sands below. The canyon, inviting further exploration, we went up and up, more palms greeting us at every turn. A thousand there must be there... These trees, in their almost perfect natural setting, should be preserved for all posterity and the people of San Diego county should take some steps to insure their permanent care by their inclusion in some park site.

The palm found there—the California fan palm, *Washingtonia filifera*—is the only variety native to California and to San Diego County. All of the other palm trees that we see in San Diego, including the date palm, have been brought in from elsewhere. The fan-shaped leaves at the top of the California fan palm become like a skirt of dead leaves hanging down over the trunk unless an effort is made to trim them off. For this reason the tree is sometimes called the "petticoat palm."

In 1932, California accepted the first parcel of land that would in 1933 become the Borego Palms Desert State Park, containing 185,000 acres of federal land. In 1936 another 365,000 acres of federal land was acquired to add to the park, and the name was changed to Anza Desert State Park (see JUNE 29).

Today the park, now known as the Anza-Borrego Desert State Park, contains over 650,000 acres—over 1,000 square miles. More acreage is being added to the park when possible by the Anza-Borrego Foundation, which raises funds to buy land that is for sale adjacent to the park.

DECEMBER 29, 1848

ON THIS DAY IN SAN DIEGO HISTORY Cave Couts, a United States Army officer, stopped off at Warner's Ranch in northeastern San Diego County south of Warner Springs. He was traveling with the Army after the end of the Mexican-American War of 1846–48.

In his diary, Couts described the owner of the ranch, Jonathan Trumbull Warner, also known as Juan José Warner, as a "white man, famed for his ability in telling lies, but not surpassed even in this by his notoriety as a rascal." According to historian Diana Lindsay in her book *Anza-Borrego A to Z*, during and after the Mexican-American War, Warner's loyalty to the United States was questioned, and he was often at odds with authorities.

Warner had come to California from Connecticut in 1831 (see DECEMBER 5). He became a Mexican citizen of the then-Mexican California, learned to speak Spanish, and changed his name to Juan José Warner. During the Mexican-American War, he tried to remain neutral, but he was arrested by the Americans in San Diego. Consequently, was not at the ranch when General Kearny stopped there with his American troops just prior to his unexpected encounter with the Californios at the Battle of San Pasqual (see DECEMBER 6).

Warner was later released, and he returned to his ranch in time to greet the Mormon Battalion on New Year's Day 1847. The battalion wass on its way to San Diego to help the Americans in the war (see JANUARY 29). It was the first American wagon train to stop at Warner's Ranch.

In spite of Cave Couts description of him and the distrust of him by the American authorities after the Mexican-American War, Warner went on to become a California state senator from 1851 to 1852. He was also a county supervisor from 1853 to 1855. Later, in 1860, he was a representative in the California State Assembly. Warner ended up poor and blind, dying in 1895 at the age of 88.

DECEMBER 30, 1936

ON THIS DAY IN SAN DIEGO HISTORY the San Diego Building and Loan Bank became a federal bank association and changed its name to San Diego Federal Savings and Loan Association.

The bank had started 41 years before, back in 1885 during the San Diego land boom of the 1880s. After World War II, which ended in 1945, there was another big land and building boom as many military men and their families—who had discovered San Diego while stationed here during the war—returned here to live. This building boom continued through the 1950s and 1960s, and San Diego Federal was an important bank for making loans to people building or buying homes.

The bank continued to grow, and in 1969 it had 23 branches across San Diego County. In 1974 it moved into a new 24-story headquarters in downtown San Diego, and by 1980 it had 70 branches statewide and more than 300,000 customers. From a hometown San Diego bank, it had grown to one of the country's largest and most successful banks.

During the 1980s San Diego Federal became Great American Bank. You could tell its branch buildings by the Spanish Style architecture and the blue tile roofs. Then in 1991 a large well-known bank with headquarters in San Francisco, Wells Fargo Bank, bought out Great American. Many San Diegans were disappointed to see their own hometown bank taken over by the great Wells Fargo Bank.

December 31, 1916

ON THIS DAY IN SAN DIEGO HISTORY the Panama-California Exposition closed down. The exposition, which was something like a World's Fair, had opened on January 1, 1915. Scheduled for only one year, it was so successful it continued for a second year (see JANUARY 1).

The exposition was held in Balboa Park and was put on to celebrate the opening of the Panama Canal—the opening of which meant that ships coming from the eastern part of the United States or from Europe had a shorter trip to California. Instead of going around the entire continent of South America, they could now take a shortcut through the narrow part of Panama in Central America, saving many weeks of travel time. San Diego was the first seaport in the United States that ships would reach after going through the canal.

At the closing ceremonies in Balboa Park—at midnight on December 31, New Years Eve—a lady sang "Auld Lang Syne" at the Spreckels Organ Pavilion, and a fireworks display followed that spelled out "World Peace, 1917." World War I was being fought in Europe, and the United States was about to enter—so everyone was hoping for peace.

Most of the beautiful buildings that we see today in Balboa Park were built for the Panama-California Exposition of 1915–16 (see SEPTEMBER 12).

REFERENCES

Abbott, Patrick. 1999. *The Rise and Fall of San Diego: 150 Million Years of History Recorded in Sedimentary Rocks*. Sunbelt Publications, San Diego.

Amero, Richard W. 1990. The Making of the Panama-California Exposition 1909–1915. *Journal of San Diego History*, vol .36, no. 1, 1–47.

Brackett, R.W. 1960. *The History of San Diego County Ranchos*. Union Title Insurance Co., San Diego.

Brigandi, Phil. 2001. *Borrego Beginnings: Early Days in the Borrego Valley 1910–1960*. Anza-Borrego Natural History Assoc., Borrego Springs, CA.

California State Parks, Office of Historic Preservation. 1996. *California Historical Landmarks*. California State Parks, Sacramento, CA.

Crawford, Richard W. 1995. *Stranger Than Fiction: Vignettes of San Diego History*. San Diego Historical Society, San Diego, CA.

Crosby, Harry W. 2003. *Gateway to Alta California: the Expedition to San Diego, 1769*. Sunbelt Publications, San Diego.

Daly-Lipe, Patricia and Barbara Dawson. 2002. *La Jolla: A Celebration of Its Past*. Sunbelt Publications, San Diego.

Davidson, Ed and Eddy Orcutt. 1939. *The Country of Joyous Aspect: A Short History of San Diego*. San Diego Trust & Savings Bank, San Diego, CA.

Eargle, Dolan H., Jr. 1986. *The Earth Is Our Mother: A Guide to the Indians of California, Their Locales and Historic Sites*. Trees Co. Press, San Francisco.

Engstrand, Iris H.W. 1980. *San Diego: California's Cornerstone*. Continental Heritage Press, Tulsa, Oklahoma.

———. 2005. *San Diego: California's Cornerstone*. First paperback edition. Sunbelt Publications, San Diego.

Evarts, Bill. 1994. *Torrey Pines: Landscape and Legacy*. Torrey Pines Assoc., La Jolla, CA.

Fetzer, Leland. 2002. *A Good Camp: Gold Mines of Julian and the Cuyamacas*. Sunbelt Publications, San Diego.

———. 2005. *San Diego County Place Names, A to Z*. Sunbelt Publications, San Diego,

Fuller, Theodore W. 1987. *San Diego Originals: Profiles of the Movers and Shakers of California's First Community*. Calif. Profiles Publications, Pleasant Hill, CA.

Garate, Don. 1994. *Juan Bautista de Anza: National Historic Trail*. Southwest Parks & Monuments Assoc., Tucson, AZ.

Geraci, Victor W. 1990. El Cajon, California 1900. *Journal of San Diego History*, vol. 36, no. 4, 221–233.

Goldzband, Melvin G. 2007. *San Diego Symphony from Overture to Encore*. San Diego Symphony Orchestra Association.

Gunn, Douglas. 1887. *Picturesque San Diego*. Knight and Leonard Co., Chicago.

Innis, Jack Scheffler. 2004. *San Diego Legends: The Events, People, and Places That Made History*. Sunbelt Publications, San Diego.

Kooperman, Evelyn. 1989. *San Diego Trivia*. Silver Gate Publications, San Diego.

Krell, Dorothy & Paul C. Johnson, Eds. 1997. *The California Missions: A Pictorial History*. Sunset Books, Inc., Menlo Park, CA.

La Jolla Historical Society. 1987. *Inside La Jolla, 1887–1987*. La Jolla Historical Society, La Jolla, CA.

Leftwich, James A. 1984. *La Jolla Life*. La Jolla Press, La Jolla, CA.

LeMenager, Charles R. 1990. *Ramona and Roundabout: A History of San Diego County's Little Known Back Country*. Eagle Peak Publ. Co., Ramona, CA.

————. 1992. *Julian City and Cuyamaca Country*. Eagle Peak Publ. Co., Ramona, CA.

Lindsay, Diana. 1973. *Our Historic Desert*. San Diego Union-Tribune Publishing Co.

————. 2001. *Anza-Borrego A to Z: People Places and Things*. Sunbelt Publications, San Diego.

————. Ed. 2005. *Marshal South and the Ghost Mountain Chronicles: An Experiment in Primitive Living*. Sunbelt Publications, San Diego.

Madyun, Gail and Larry Malone. *Black Pioneers in San Diego, 1880–1920*. San Diego Historical Society, San Diego, CA.

McKeever, Michael. 1985. *A Short History of San Diego*. Lexicos, San Francisco.

Mills, James R. 1985. *San Diego: Where California Began*. San Diego Historical Society, San Diego, CA.

Petersen, Martin E. 2001. An Overview of San Diego Artists. *Journal of San Diego History*, vol. 47, no. 3, 137–149.

Pourade, Richard F. 1971. *Anza Conquers the Desert*. Copley Books, Union-Tribune Publishing Co., San Diego, CA.

Price, James. 1988. *The Railroad Stations of San Diego County: Then and Now*. Price & Sieber, San Diego.

Pryde, Philip R. 2004. *San Diego: An Introduction to the Region*. Fourth Edition. Sunbelt Publications, San Diego.

Randolph, Howard S.F. 1975. *La Jolla Year by Year*. The Library Association of La Jolla, La Jolla, CA.

Remeika, Paul and Lowell Lindsay. 1992. *Geology of Anza-Borrego*. Sunbelt Publications, San Diego.

Ribbel, Arthur. 1990. *Yesterday in San Diego*. Rancho Press, San Diego.

Schaelchlin, Patricia A. 1988. *La Jolla: the Story of a Community, 1887–1987*. The Friends of the La Jolla Library, La Jolla, CA.

Scripps Institution of Oceanography. 2003. Scripps Centennial Issue; Celebrating 100 Years of Exploration and Discovery. *Explorations*, vol. 10, no. 1, Univ. of California, San Diego, La Jolla, CA.

Starr, Kevin. 1990. *Material Dreams: Southern California Through the 1920s*. Oxford University Press, New York.

Stein, Lou. 1988. *San Diego County Place Names*. Rand Editions/Tofua Press, Leucadia, CA.

Sunset Editors. 1997. *The California Missions*. Sunset Books, Menlo Park, CA.

Sutro, Dirk. 2002. *San Diego Architecture*. San Diego Architectural Foundation, San Diego, CA.

Weber, Msgr. Francis J. 1988. *The Life and Times of Fray Junípero Serra*. EZ Nature Books, San Luis Obispo, CA.

Williams, Gregory L. 2002. San Diego Filmography. *Journal of San Diego History*, vol. 48, no. 2, 149–174.

INDEX

Díaz, Padre Juan Marcelo, 38
Diegeño Indians, 9, 74, 92, 167, 178, 335
Discrimination (racial), 140
District Agricultural Association, 268
Doe, Hans ("Mr. Water"), 15, 269
Dutch Flats, 90, 267

E

Eagle Mining Company (Julian), 171
Earthquakes, 102, 150, 330, 345, 363
Echeandia, José María (governor), 209
Edgemoor Farms, 184
Edward, Prince of Wales, 101
El Cajon, 254
El Cajon Mountain, 110
El Cajon Rancho, 18, 22, 362
El Cajon Valley, 18, 97
El Campo Santo Cemetery (Old Town), 228
El Capitan Dam and Reservoir, 351
El Rincón del Diablo Rancho, 49
Electric Building (Balboa Park), 45
Electric power, 4
Electric Railway, 116, 148, 261
Emigrant Trail, 28, 193, 236, 245, 338
Encina Electric Plant, 349
Encinitas Rancho, 292
Ensworth, Augustus (Old Town resident), 150, 361
Escarcar, Pedro José Panto (Indian leader). *See* Panto, Pedro José
Escondido, 49, 171
Estudillo, Captain José María (early Old Town resident), 187
Estudillo family, 22, 187, 362
Estudillo, José Antonio (rancher, mayor), 22, 187, 362

Estudillo, José Guadalupe (rancher), 187
Estudillo, Magdalena (ranch owner), 22
Estudillo, María Antonia (ranch owner), 362
Evans, Bill (businessman), 188
Exchange Hotel (Old Town), 229

F

Fages, Don Pedro (Spanish army officer), 299, 305
Figuer, Father, 92
Figueroa, José (governor), 111, 202, 209
Financial Panic of 1873, 264
Fine Arts Gallery (Balboa Park), 180
Fires, 208
First National Bank, 163
Fish Creek Mountains, 330
Fisher, John C. (theater owner), 140
Fisher Opera House, 140
Fitch, Henry (early city attorney), 158
Fitzallen, Captain Charles (ship captain, rancher), 104
Fleet, Major Reuben H. (airplane manufacturer), 296, 344
Fleet Science Center (Balboa Park), 275
Fleming, Guy (park superintendent), 130, 183, 225
Fletcher, Colonel Ed (army officer, businessman), 186, 333
Flinn Springs, 18
Flood, James (landowner), 336
Floods, 7, 30, 50, 73, 361
Flume, 55
Font, Father Pedro, 326, 353, 359, 363
Font's Point, 102
Ford Bowl (Balboa Park), 152

Lindbergh, Anne Morrow (author), 62

Lindbergh, Charles (aviator), 62, 231, 267

Lindbergh Field Airport, 231, 267, 271

Lindsay, Diana (author, historian), 183, 238, 366

Linkletter, Art (TV personality), 306

"Little Green Lab" (La Jolla), 85, 329

Lomaland, 57, 304, 314

Lopez, Juan (ranch owner), 27

Lorenzana, Doña Apolinaria (ranch owner), 104

Los Peñasquitos, 252

Los Peñasquitos Rancho, 77, 106, 169

Los Vallecitos de San Marcos Rancho, 63

Luiseño, Indians, 142, 167, 178, 192, 206, 263, 335, 364

Lumpkins, William (architect), 21

M

Mahoney, B. Franklin (aviator, businessman), 34

Mainly Mozart Festival, 309

Manuel, Andrés (landowner), 203

Manuel, José (landowner), 203

Marcelli, Nino (musician, symphony conductor), 61

Marina Redevelopment Project (Old Town), 170

Marine Biological Association of San Diego, 85, 196, 243, 329

Marine Corps Recruit Depot (MCRD), 90, 301

Marine Room (restaurant, La Jolla), 31

Marrón, Captain Juan María (city councilman), 158, 349

Marshall, Bill (American sailor, businessman), 360

Marston, George (businessman), 14, 36, 43, 79, 87, 131, 186, 201, 273, 293, **298**, 339, 350

Marston House, 119, 298, 350

Marston's Department Store, 298

Martín, Father Fernando, 345

Mason, Ed, 178

Mason Valley, 178

Masonic Lodge, 44

Mayoral election of 1905 (Mayor Sehon), 97

Mayrhofer, Albert V. (businessman), 186

McClain family (Jacumba homesteaders), 164

McCorkle, Archibald (Burlingame resident), 72

McCoy, James (politician, rancher), 149

McFadden & Buxton Company, 72

McFadden, Joseph (Burlingame developer), 72

McKinstry, George (Santa Ysabel), 252

McKnight, John H. (mineralogist), 110

Mendenhall Ranch, 206

Mendoza, Juan (ranch worker), 285

Mercereau Bridge & Construction Company, 147

Mesa Grande, 252

Mesa Grande Indian Reservation, 25

Metropolitan Transit System (MTS), 116, 148

Metropolitan Water District, 15, 269

Mexican-American War of 1846-48, 9, 29, 35, 106, 108, 146, 175, 213, 232, 237, 318, 338, 340, 343

Meyers, Andrew Jackson (Oceanside developer), 135

San Diego Telephone Company, 168
San Diego Transit, 116
San Diego Tribune (newspaper), 82, 286
San Diego Trolley System, 148
San Diego Trust & Savings Bank (building), 180
San Diego Union (newspaper), **82**, 93, 97, 255, 286, 300
San Diego Water Company, 166
San Diego Yacht Club, 89
San Diego Zoo, 273
San Dieguito Indian Pueblo, 111
San Dieguito Rancho, 111
San Felipe, 338
San Felipe Indian Village, 221
San Felipe Rancho, 202, 221
San Felipe Stage Station, 178
San Felipe Valley, 178, 202, 221, 262, 289, 338
San Gregorio Springs, 74, 355
San Jacinto Fault Zone, 102, 330
San José (Spanish ship), 11, 122
San José de Valle Rancho, 23, 328, 335
San Luis Rey Mission, 98, 263, 282
San Luis Rey Valley, 364
San Marcos, 63
San Miguel Archangel (original name of San Diego), 274, 317
San Miguel Mountain, 104
San Onofre Nuclear Power Plant, 168
San Pascual. *See* San Pasqual
San Pasqual, 242, 252
San Pasqual (concrete ship), 157
San Pasqual Indian Pueblo, 9, 13, 120, 175, 242
San Pasqual Indian Reservation, 25
San Pasqual Valley, 13, 120, 242, 343
San Salvadore (Spanish ship), 181
San Sebastián Marsh, 353
San Vicente Dam, 27, 50, 252, 351

San Vicente Valley, 27, 67, 252, 305
Santa Fe Railroad, 94, 111, 316, 322, 348
Santa Fe Railroad Depot, 110
Santa Margarita y Las Flores Rancho, 40, 117, 336
Santa Maria Land & Water Company, 66, 253, 270
Santa Maria Rancho, 66, 340, 341
Santa Maria School District (Ramona), 253
Santa Maria Store (Ramona), 253
Santa Maria Valley, 92, 172, 253
Santa Rosa Mountains, 155
Santa Ysabel, 192, 252, 277
Santa Ysabel Indian Reservation, 25
Santa Ysabel Mission, 137
Santa Ysabel Rancho, 66, 137, 340
Santee, 18, 66
Santee, Milton (businessman), 66, 270
Saratoga, USS (ship), 231
Schultz, Gustav (La Jolla), 308
Scissors Crossing, 178, 221
Scripps Biological Building, 196
Scripps Clinic, 294
Scripps, E.W. (businessman), 85, 97, 281, **294**
Scripps, Ellen Browning (philanthropist), 32, 41, 85, 100, 121, 126, 130, 147, 154, 173, 222, 225, 273, 281, **294**
Scripps Institution for Biological Research, 88, 147, 177, 196
Scripps Institution of Oceanography, 85, 88, 147, 177, **196**, 199
Scripps Institution of Oceanography Pier, 147
Scripps Memorial Hospital, 126
Scripps Park (La Jolla), 96
Scripps Ranch, 294
Scripps, Virginia (philanthropist), 121, 222, 281